Thirty Dollars and a Cut Eye

J Russell Peltz

BennieBriscoe—Philadelphia, PA
ISBN: 978-1-7375696-1-9
Title: *Thirty Dollars and a Cut Eye*
Author: J Russell Peltz
Digital distribution | 2021
Hardcover | 2021

Front cover: Referee John Fitzpatrick moves in to count over Wendell Newton, who has been knocked out by Leotis Martin in the seventh round of their 1969 heavyweight main event at the Blue Horizon. (From the Philadelphia Inquirer @ The Philadelphia Inquirer)

Back cover: J Russell Peltz hanging posters in North Philadelphia in March, 1971. (Mary Anne Seymour photo)

Published in the United States by New Book Authors Publishing

Dedication

For every man who ever strapped on the cup.

Table of Contents

Foreword

It was early October in 1969 when the phone rang in my barebones apartment. It was J Russell Peltz. We'd never spoken to each other before, but I knew what it was about.

I had attended his debut promotion, at the Blue Horizon, a week or so prior. It was everything a first-time promoter could have hoped for—a record-setting crowd, a charged atmosphere and fun fights. Everybody went home early and happy after Bennie Briscoe brutalized Tito Marshall in the main event. Tito didn't last a round.

Caught up in the excitement of having a new promoter in town, I wrote Russell a letter, suggesting matches he should make in the future. He was calling to inform me that the matches I'd recommended were between boxers in different weight classes. In other words, I didn't know what the hell I was talking about.

Even now, 50 years later, I still hear from him every time I get a fact wrong in a story or make a grammatical error. The worst part is that he's always right.

The phone call was the start of an enduring friendship. There is far more to the story than I can tell here. This is just snapshot, an effort to give some idea of what happened to two young men who met by happenstance and traveled different but parallel paths.

Boxing brought us together, but we soon discovered we shared other common interests, and it wasn't long before we began to socialize beyond the boxing scene. Believe it or not, Russell soon became an enthusiastic regular at wild parties my first wife and I threw.

We also hung out at the bar at the Society Hill Hotel, 3rd and Chestnut Streets, where the drinks were cheap and the entertainment free and bizarre. The main attraction was broken-down country singer Ray Hatcher, billed as the *Human Jukebox*.

I had never been to a boxing gym until I started making the rounds with Russell. He had business to do and I was his sidekick, thrilled to suddenly have entree to the inner workings of boxing. It was the best education a struggling boxing writer could have.

We would invariably end up watching Briscoe train, first under the tutelage of Quenzell McCall at the 23rd PAL, and later with Georgie Benton at Joe Frazier's Gym. Everybody has a favorite fighter and Bennie was ours. Russell promoted and guided him for most of the second half of his career, including three world title shots. I was the star-struck hippie who tagged along for the ride.

Experiencing the Briscoe era up close was magical, gut-wrenching at times, but magical nonetheless. Despite his menacing appearance and uncompromising fighting style, Bennie was a friendly guy who never let success go to his head. He liked to tease Russell, pretending to be drunk, staggering down the street toward the gym, where the "Boy Promoter" was nervously awaiting his arrival. It was Runyonesque scoundrel Ben $$$ Greene who gave Russell the nickname, which stuck to him like flypaper, even after his hair turned gray.

It's the little things from that period I treasure the most, stuff you can't find in a record book, such as the time in 1972 when Russell turned up at my door at sunrise, looking like he'd just walked away from a train wreck. Bennie had lost a decision to Luis Vinales the night before in Scranton that was supposed to be a tune-up. Russell couldn't sleep and needed a friend with whom to commiserate. The tables were turned when I broke up with my first wife, and Russell let me sleep on his couch for a few months.

Bummers were counterbalanced by joyful occasions. I remember attending Bennie's victory party at a subterranean nightclub called *The Cave*, a few hours after he'd stopped Art Hernandez at the Spectrum. Years later, Tony Thornton (*The Punching Postman*) had a Christmas party at his house, where the good times rolled late into the night.

In the early 1970s I worked for Russell as a ticket seller at the Philadelphia Arena, manning the same cockroach-infested box office where I'd formerly purchased tickets. My pay was a fast-food lunch and a few bucks. I couldn't have been happier, but it didn't last long.

It was during this time that Russell was hired to be Director of Boxing at the Spectrum, one of the biggest breaks of his career. He took advantage of it, building one of the most successful boxing programs in the country.

With my box office gig gone, Russell suggested I become a manager so I bought pieces of Jerome Artis, Alfonso Hayman, Wade Hinnant, Leroy Jefferson and Fred Jenkins. It was fun for a while and I made a little money, but I wasn't cut out for the job. It just wasn't me. I sold Hayman's contract, Jenkins quit and became a trainer, and I released the others.

By then I was *The Ring*'s Philadelphia and Atlantic City correspondent, a position Russell helped me obtain. It was the beginning of my decades-long association with the venerable publication that didn't end until 2011.

Peltz' time at the Spectrum, from December 1972 to March 1980, is considered the last golden age of Philadelphia boxing, and I had a ringside seat. Hanging out at the gyms with Russell allowed me to build relationships with many local boxers and out-of-town fighters, many of whom are now enshrined in the International Boxing Hall of Fame.

For a year or so when I wasn't working for *The Ring*, I did public relations for Peltz Boxing Promotions at the Blue Horizon and Harrah's Marina in Atlantic City. I quickly discovered that on fight night Russell is in a world of his own, so focused on doing his job, it is like he is in a trance. It is best to leave him alone.

When I published *Boxing Babylon* in 1990, Russell showed fight films at the book-launch party at Dirty Franks, Philly's beloved dive bar. Later, after I became editor-in-chief of *The Ring* a second time, Russell quipped that I was "the only editor to regain the title."

We drifted apart socially for a few years. Work and our family consumed us. These days, however, we meet on a semi-regular basis when he's in town. There's usually an abundance of laughter, but not always. I'll never forget one dinner we shared in early 2011. Bennie had died in December 2010, and as we sat across the table from each other that night, trying to hold back the tears, we talked about old times. It was then, more than ever, that I realized how close we are and how special the time we've shared has been.

We're in our 70s now with plaques on the wall in Canastota, still working and trying to keep doing what we love as long as we can. On this, Russell's 50th anniversary as a promoter, the most important thing I have to say is thank you.

Nigel Collins

Introduction

I saw Vito Antuofermo in a six-round fight in the summer of 1972, outdoors at the Singer Bowl in Flushing, Queens. He stopped a kid named Jerry Caballero in four rounds. It was Caballero's second loss on his way to a career record of 0-9. It was Antuofermo's seventh victory in eight pro bouts—one draw—but he looked so devoid of skills I wondered why any promoter would waste money on him. Seven years later, Antuofermo won the middleweight championship of the world.

In the years following that summer night, I turned down a piece of Marvin Hagler, terminated Buster Douglas from our promotional agreement and made no effort to re-sign Antonio Tarver to another. Despite these massive faux pas, I made it to the International Boxing Hall of Fame in 2004. When I told these stories during my speech at the Saturday night banquet in Canastota, New York, I added that, while in college in 1965, I had walked out of a fight card before the main event…featuring Sugar Ray Robinson. Emcee Bert Sugar got up and called for a recount of the vote that got me in.

When I was a kid, playing softball or basketball or football on my block, I'd see Dad coming home from his plumbing company around 6 pm. He'd get out of his car and lug his thick, wide briefcase—with all those blueprints in it—into the house where he'd invariably study them at night. I remember thinking, "Wouldn't it be great if when I grew up I could keep playing outside and never have to go to work." In some ways, that's what happened to me.

Dad passed away at the age of 69 in 1983, eight years after Mom died at 59. At the time, Dad was the oldest living member of the Peltz family, to be surpassed by an uncle, who was 80 when he died in 2003. My sister died at 67 in 2009 so, at 74, I'm the only one left from my immediate family. My first-born son died at 38 in 2017, and while I take shots at the alphabet groups, I can never forget that the IBF's Daryl Peoples and Lindsey Tucker came from North Jersey to his funeral.

Other boxing friends attended. Jimmy Burchfield drove down from Rhode Island. So did Teddy and Elaine Atlas from Staten Island. Richard Schwartz and Harold Lederman were there from New York. I remember everyone who came—and everyone who didn't.

I had been threatening to write this book for years, but never found the time until Covid-19 came along. Timing is everything—as you'll read in these pages—because the pandemic arrived six months after my 50th anniversary in the sometimes wonderful, sometimes wretched world of professional boxing.

Some fighters will be upset for not making it into these pages. There simply was not enough room for tough-as-nails junior middleweight Darren Maciunski, of Toms River, New Jersey, whose eight-round split-decision loss to West Philly's Billy Mastrangelo in 1994 was a Blue Horizon classic. We almost had a co-feature minutes later in the dressing rooms between ex-pro "Tough" Tony Suero, who trained Mastrangelo, and Hall-of-Fame middleweight champion Joey Giardello, who was with Maciunski.

There was North Philly lightweight Mike Brown, who lost a few more than he won in the 1980s. Brown was trained by grouchy old Leonard Pate, who had been blind since the Korean War but gave instructions while listening to the sound of leather on heavy bags and sparring partners. Brown and Pate often went fishing for eels in the Schuylkill River, then steamed and grilled them for dinner.

How could I forget Burnell Scott, of Camden, New Jersey, who boxed as Nikita "The Cheetah" Tarhocker. He wore leopard print trunks and a turban. Nikita was a fun guy and claimed he came from Nigerian royalty. He was knocked out 23 times in 17 different cities, including once in 1974 by Youngblood Williams after they rode together in the back seat of my car to their fight in Allentown, Pennsylvania. None of Nikita's eight wives made that trip.

Brian McGinley, the Fishtown welterweight, was a Blue Horizon regular. He boxed there 12 times in the 1980s. He fought Miguel Montero three times, Bill Robinson three times and Kenny Brown twice. He never complained about rematches.

I have tried to show what purses paid during my 50 years would be worth today—adjusted only for purchasing power based on inflation. Realistically, it's probably closer to the theory that money doubles every 10 years. The internet says that the $40,000 purse Bennie Briscoe got to fight Marvin Hagler in 1978 is worth $168,000 in 2021. But it also says that the $15 ringside ticket is worth $63 today and we know that same ticket would go for a minimum of $300 in 2021.

There was scant network TV when I began and cable didn't enter the picture until 1980. We made—or lost—money by selling tickets. When TV came along, it paid what a fight was worth, not like today when ESPN and DAZN are overpaying, perhaps to control the market. If Sergiy Derevyanchenko got five million from a streaming service (DAZN) for challenging Gennadiy Golovkin for a piece of the middleweight title in 2019, imagine what Bennie Briscoe would get. Asset management and financial planning companies like Waddell & Reed were not interested in pouring 500 million dollars into boxing.

The internet often is the *misinformation highway* and I want to set the record straight as to what actually went on in boxing in the Philadelphia area since the late 1960s. I'm tired of reading tweets or Facebook posts or Instagram accounts from people who were not around and have no idea what went on, but write like they do. I saved every contract I ever signed, most profit-and-loss statements, photos, souvenir programs, posters, and videos. You name it—I saved it.

I don't recognize TKOs—technical knockouts. A fighter wins or loses by decision, disqualification or knockout. He is knocked out of time. That's the way Nat Fleischer saw it and why would I argue with a boxing historian who founded, published and edited *The Ring* magazine, once known as "The Bible of Boxing." Did you ever read or hear someone say that so-and-so has a record of 25-2 with 11 K0s and 10 TKOs? Of course not! He has a record of 25-2 with 21 K0s.

Philly's Herman Taylor is the man I consider the greatest promoter ever. Taylor began in 1912 and ran his last card in 1975. Nearly every heavyweight champion from Jack Dempsey to George Foreman boxed for him. More undisputed world champions in Canastota fought for him than for any other promoter, yet he never wrote a book about his life. So maybe I'm demonstrating *chutzpah* by writing this one, but then Taylor never had a journalism background.

When I told boxing columnist Bernard Fernandez that writing about my half century in the sport was so overwhelming I was ready to throw in the proverbial towel, he told me I'd regret it on my death bed. What a thought!

Chapter One

Mister Molotov, Have a Cocktail

Molotov Cocktail Madness

Bob Cline, Nationwide Insurance Co. investigator, looks over damage the firebombs caused to office of boxing promoter J. Russell Peltz at 25th and Brown streets

Firebomb knockout

Boxing promoter's North Phila. office torched

By **Don Russell**

Daily News Staff Writer

In this file photo taken in his office, Peltz is shown holding one of the pieces from his private collection of boxing memorabilia

See **FIREBOMB** Page 12

The phone rang around 1:30 am. Technically, it was June 25, 1999. My wife, Linda, and I were in the suite we'd been comped at the Foxwoods Casino in Mashantucket, Connecticut. I was there as consultant/matchmaker for ESPN2's Friday Night Fights. We had made the five-hour drive from Philly in time for the TV interviews of the main-event fighters, Vinny Pazienza and Esteban Cervantes, and the weigh-in for all the boxers.

We had been in the suite 10 minutes after a send-off party in the VIP Lounge for Anthony Giordano, the show's director. Rob Beiner, the producer, Brian Zwolinski, associate producer, and the announcers, Bob Papa and Teddy Atlas, had been with us.

Calling me was Maureen Sacks, my office manager and vice president. She lived on the second floor of my four-story brownstone four blocks from the Philadelphia Art Museum, where Rocky ran up the steps. "Somebody firebombed the building!" she cried into the phone. "The fire department's here."

Maureen and her boyfriend, Joe Mellek, had been asleep. The air conditioning compressor on the deck outside their second-floor bedroom had drowned out the alarm that went off when the bomb crashed through the front-office window.

According to the *Philadelphia Inquirer,* a neighbor, Mike Clancy, "had watched the firebombing from a bay window across the street and had his brother dial 911. Three Black men in a yellow pickup truck (had pulled up). Two got out and walked unhurried to the sidewalk and each threw a firebomb. The first one bounced off a window and shattered on the curb near a car. The second one fell inside but didn't ignite so the two went back to the truck for more. Next time they succeeded. The office burst into flames. The yellow pickup pulled away just minutes before fire trucks and police appeared."

"It looked like something out of a movie," Clancy told Don Russell, of the *Philadelphia Daily News*. He and other neighbors pounded on the door downstairs, woke up Maureen and Joe and told them to get out.

If you stay in any business long enough, you make enemies as well as friends. I was three months short of 30 years in boxing. One of my cards had been picketed by a disgruntled manager, one by a rival promoter. I had been punched in the jaw in Joe Frazier's gym, and threatened with murder by one of the fighters I had under contract. Things like this were not supposed to happen to nice boys from nice suburbs, like Bala Cynwyd on Philadelphia's Main Line.

Linda and I got back to Philadelphia around 6 am. A trip that had started as part-work, part-vacation, had come tumbling down. "It was the first time out-of-town I didn't have to worry about the kids," Linda said. Our sons were 20 and 18.

By the time we arrived, the fire department had extinguished the blaze. Mark Kondrath, our handyman, had driven in from Delaware and was sweeping up debris. After he got the electricity working, we surveyed the damage. Maureen's eight-windowed, corner office was a wreck. She and Joe were okay physically, but Maureen still looked shaken.

The building had been a museum of Philadelphia's boxing history. Two three-sheet posters (81x41 inches) were destroyed, one from the 1941 Joe Louis-Arturo Godoy heavyweight championship fight at Yankee Stadium, one from my favorite movie, *Body and Soul*, starring John Garfield and Lilli Palmer.

Eight paintings–oil and water color—of *The Ring* magazine covers from the 1930s, '40s and '50s, were burnt beyond recognition. A life-size color photo of 1980s middleweight Frank "The Animal" Fletcher and a 22x28-inch poster from the 1952 welterweight title fight between Kid Gavilan and Gil Turner were gone. All were originals; none could be replaced.

Jerome Artis, an ex-pro lightweight, popped in, looking to grab burnt posters to sell. Maureen threw him out.

The first person to call with condolences was Lou DiBella, senior vice president of programming at HBO Sports. Five years later, when I was voted into the International Boxing Hall of Fame, DiBella, by then a promoter himself, was the first to offer congratulations. I don't forget those things.

WIP All-Sports Radio called, too, but I wouldn't talk to them. "WIP Some-Sports Radio," I called them. They never talked boxing. So why should I?

Who did it? Was it a pissed-off fighter? The threat to kill me had come earlier that year from a fighter when I wouldn't let him box on another promoter's card, a threat he repeated to the police. Did a promoter think I was screwing him out of dates on ESPN?

The police and FBI investigated, but came up empty. Insurance covered the damage and repairs and put Maureen and Joe up at the Franklin Plaza in Center City until the second floor was livable. The smoke smell was gone within a week and the water damage was repaired. Kondrath got the office together. I received the value of the posters, photos and art, but I would have returned the money in a heartbeat to have them back.

Long-time trainer and cut man Leon Tabbs suggested it was time for me to get out of the business, but two weeks later I was in Hyannis, Massachusetts, for an ESPN2 card.

A 1995 armed robbery had been more harrowing. Two characters, figuring there was cash in the office the day of a fight, came by asking about tickets for that night's Blue Horizon card. They acted strange enough for Maureen to hit the silent alarm button under her desk. But before the police arrived, they had me face down on the floor, a gun to my head, handcuffed to my niece Cynthia Weiss, who handled press seating for us on fight night. They were unable to pull a cat's-eye ring my father had given me off my finger. They took off with $750 in cash and the unsold tickets, but missed $30,000 in my briefcase.

I called Linda in a matter-of-fact tone to tell her we had just been robbed at gunpoint. "Funny," she said. It took me a few seconds to convince her I wasn't joking. She couldn't understand how I could remain so calm even though she always accuses me of being emotionally constipated.

The police drove me and Cynthia around the neighborhood, hoping we could spot suspects. After the fight that night, Maureen and I looked at hundreds of mug shots at the police station, but the only arrest made was of a man selling the stolen tickets outside the Blue. He was not one of the robbers, but he had a long rap sheet and he knew the system inside out. The FBI got involved but came up empty. After two or three court hearings with the man who had the tickets, I gave up.

I had fallen in love with the *sport* of boxing when I was 12. No one ever explained to me the *business* of boxing. Maybe Mom was right when she told Dad to stop taking me to fights when I was a teenager. But I don't think so.

We had a better security system installed, put a buzzer on the front door, added thicker windows, stopped cashing checks for fighters, and moved on.

Chapter Two

A Brief History

I became friends with my boyhood idol, Harold Johnson. (Peltz collection)

From the end of the 19th century until just past the mid-point of the 20th, only three professional sports mattered in this country—baseball, boxing and horse racing. Philadelphia, New York, Los Angeles, San Francisco, Chicago, Detroit and Boston were major boxing hubs. In the first decade of the 20th century, there were 2,541 boxing shows in Philadelphia; the second decade, 2,479; the third, 1,525.

World champions in every division from flyweight (Midget Wolgast) to light-heavyweight (Philadelphia Jack O'Brien) grew up in—or moved to—Philly. Hall-of-Famers Harry Lewis, Battling

Levinsky, Lew Tendler, Benny Bass, Tommy Loughran, Bob Montgomery, Harold Johnson and Joey Giardello lived here.

Fight clubs dotted the city, from the Olympia at Broad and Bainbridge and the National AC at 11th and Catharine in South Philly, to the Arena at 46th and Market and Convention Hall at 34th and Spruce in West Philly, to the Met at Broad and Poplar and—for the bigger ones—Phillies Ball Park (Baker Bowl) at Broad and Huntingdon, and Shibe Park at 21st and Lehigh in North Philly.

Philadelphia never had its own heavyweight champion in boxing's glory days, but Hall-of-Fame promoter Herman Taylor staged two of the division's most notable title fights—Jack Dempsey vs. Gene Tunney, which drew 120,727 fans in 1926, and Rocky Marciano vs. Jersey Joe Walcott in 1952, which Taylor called "the greatest heavyweight fight I ever looked at." Both were on September 23 in the same South Philadelphia venue, known as Sesquicentennial Stadium in 1926, Municipal Stadium in 1952.

Things began to change in 1958, when the nationally televised NFL *sudden death* overtime championship game between the Baltimore Colts and New York Giants jump-started pro football's popularity. The NBA became a major attraction in the 1980s with the duels between the Larry Bird-led Boston Celtics and the Magic Johnson-led Los Angeles Lakers. The NHL's expansion from six to 12 teams in 1967, which placed the Flyers in Philadelphia, added to the competition for the public's attention and dollars.

In the 1940s, there had been 849 fight cards in Philadelphia. That number fell to 447 in the 50s, and never again reached half that. The rise of television and boxing's compatibility with it, compared to other sports—the action was confined to a ring rather than a ball field—brought the sport into households, but forced many small clubs to close as fans stayed home to watch. Congressional probes into boxing for mob influence also hurt.

Boxing had appealed to the downtrodden—the Irish, the Jews and the Italians. But after 1945, World War II, veterans (mostly White) took advantage of the G.I. Bill and enrolled in college. Others used the G.I. Bill for technical job training. Better job opportunities became available to White fighters and they gradually left the sport, taking some of the White audience—who were moving from the cities to the suburbs—with them. Black and Hispanic fighters began to dominate the sport in the 1950s.

The death of Benny "Kid" Paret in 1962, following his nationally televised knockout by Emile Griffith, brought cries for boxing's abolition and contributed to the end of weekly network bouts in 1964.

That same year, however, the young, charismatic Cassius Clay had followed an Olympic gold medal (1960) with the world heavyweight championship, upsetting big, bad Sonny Liston in Miami Beach. Clay, who then became Muhammad Ali, almost single-handedly kept boxing alive in mainstream America. That Ali's primary foe, following his return to the ring in 1970 after being stripped of his title for refusing induction into the Army three years earlier, was Philadelphia's Smokin' Joe Frazier, helped fan what flames still burned in Philly.

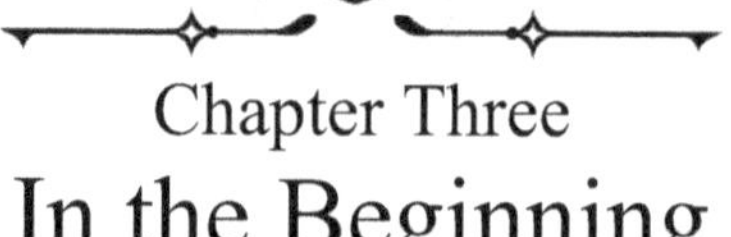

Chapter Three

In the Beginning

With Temple basketball alum Guy Rodgers in 1966. (Mike Feldman photo)

When she was 11 in 2018, one of my granddaughters, Nuni (born Chaya Menucha Peltz), asked, "Pop Pop, why would anyone pay money to see two men hit each other?" How do you answer with any trace of intelligence? You don't and I didn't.

Boxing has been my mistress since I was 12. I was one of the lucky kids who fell in love with something that turned into my life's work. When someone asks me why I love boxing, I can't explain it. Perhaps it was a vicarious thrill since I never was the toughest kid in the neighborhood and my neighborhood, Bala Cynwyd, on Philadelphia's Main Line, was not exactly a hotbed for the Sweet Science. Or maybe it was because Dad watched and Dad was my hero. At least until I discovered Harold Johnson.

I was part of Philadelphia's last golden age of boxing. There were no cruiserweights, super middles, super bantams or mini flys. The only alphabets that counted were studied in the classroom or floating in your cereal. The Top 10 was not the Top 15 or Top 20, and it meant something to be a contender in *The Ring* magazine, not that *it* was any citadel of honesty. People who went to football, basketball or baseball games cared about boxing, and each of the three major Philadelphia dailies—*Inquirer, Bulletin, Daily News*—had its own boxing writer.

I was born December 9, 1946, in Wynnefield, a predominantly middle-class Jewish neighborhood, seven miles from Center City. My dad, Bernard Peltz, was in plumbing, heating and air-conditioning. He was 5-foot-9, overweight, and had a dry sense of humor. When his high school English teacher assigned students to write about a baseball game, Dad handed in, "No game, rain!" He failed, but Bernie Peltz was the talk of the teachers' lunchroom.

Mollie Hanick was a housewife. She was a 5-foot-4 American version of the French-born actress Claudette Colbert. Mom had a Black Belt in shopping and always was the best-dressed, prettiest woman at weddings, Bar Mitzvahs, any social gatherings. Saturday night was her night.

Bernie Peltz and Mollie Hanick dated in the 1930s, though her parents did not want their daughter marrying "the plumber's son." When a traveling salesman promised her the world, Mollie married him. In less than a year, she threatened to run away. So her mother, Lena, and younger sister, Belle, drove to Virginia and brought her home.

The marriage was annulled and Mollie married Bernie on September 10, 1939. Years later, when her parents were struggling in the window display business, Mom asked Dad to help out. He did, but he told Mom to remind them that the money came from "the plumber's son."

My sister, Bootsie (Beverly), four years older, was the creative one in the family, an artist, and my confidante when I was sneaking out to the fights. She and I went to Mann Elementary. Beginning when I was 4 and Bootsie was 8, we were shipped to overnight camp each summer for eight weeks. I went to four different camps over 11 years. Bootsie went to three over seven. In my late 20s, I asked Dad why he had sent us away when we were so young. In that sing-song Jewish voice, he said, *"You think you were so easy?"*

Dad moved the family to Bala Cynwyd in 1954. Our new house was less than two miles from our old one, but it was a new world: city to suburbs, concrete to grass, wallball to soccer.

Other than baseball, sports did not interest me until the summer of 1959 when I saw Gene Fullmer's televised fight against Carmen Basilio for the world middleweight title, which the National Boxing Association (NBA) had stripped from Sugar Ray Robinson. Robinson still was champion by New York, Massachusetts and Europe, but the rest of the country recognized Fullmer after he stopped Basilio in the 14th round.

I began watching *Wednesday Night Fights*—usually from Chicago with Jack Drees behind the microphone—and *Friday Night Fights*—usually from Madison Square Garden with Don Dunphy. When he didn't join me, Dad would ask, "Which ham-and-eggers are you watching tonight?" I knew what he meant, but it took me years to learn the literal definition. A ham-and-egger was a veteran who fought often enough so he could afford breakfast the next day.

That December, I bought Nat Fleischer's *A Pictorial History of Boxing*. Today it would be called a coffee-table book, then a picture book. I devoured it and thought I knew everything there was to know about boxing. I bought my first copy of *The Ring* two months later, and, deciding to become light-heavyweight champion, took boxing lessons after Hebrew school Saturday afternoons at the Elks Club downtown. I still have the copper-plated medal I received for a draw in the season-ending tournament. But I realized if I couldn't knock out Greg Ghen—two years younger—I would never win the world title.

Dad took me to my first live fight as a 14th birthday present on December 6, 1960. I wore a tie and jacket because that's how men dressed for the fights. I thought I was the coolest kid on my block. When we walked into Convention Hall and I saw the empty ring with the cigarette and cigar smoke hanging over it, I knew I would make boxing a big part of my life. Going to the fights was what grownups did and maybe I was in a hurry to be one.

Local lightweight Len Matthews lost to Doug Vaillant, of Cuba, in the main event, but I was hooked. I never had been around so many Black and Hispanic people. Other than two men who worked for Dad, the only Black people I had known cleaned our house. The first Black students I met were at Lower Merion High School. Nineteen of 459 were in my graduating class in 1964.

My friends idolized Phillies pitcher Robin Roberts or Eagles wide receiver Tommy McDonald. I fawned over Johnson, a light-heavyweight from Manayunk. Dad and I sat first row at the Arena when Johnson knocked out crosstown rival Von Clay in the second round to defend the NBA version of the title he had won two months earlier. I cut my hair like Johnson, as close to shaven-headed as possible. My head looked like a dirty tennis ball. Friends would say, "There goes Peltz with his Harold Johnson."

Mom was no boxing fan. She didn't want me associating with "that element" and she didn't want Dad taking me to the fights. So one Saturday in the spring of 1962, I said I was going to a party, put on a sport jacket and pork pie hat and walked two blocks to the Bala Cynwyd Shopping Center, where I took the bus to 54th and City Line Avenue. I transferred to another bus which took me to 52nd and Market Streets, in the heart of the West Philadelphia business and entertainment district.

It was warm so I walked six blocks down Market to the Arena. You could hear the roar of the EL overhead. Locals sat on doorsteps. One man said I looked like Frank Sinatra with my sport jacket and hat. I was the first person inside and an usher said, "That's a pretty expensive ticket ($10) for someone your age."

I was so nervous I broke the ballpoint pen I scored the fight with in my program, but Johnson gained universal recognition as champion with a 15-round decision over Doug Jones, of New York. Thirty years later I purchased from Johnson the robe he wore and the championship belt *The Ring* awarded him.

A 1961 doubleheader at the Palestra on the University of Pennsylvania campus hooked me on college basketball. Going there was like entering college basketball heaven. It was built in 1927 and still is considered the game's *Cathedral.* Every night seemed a sellout, 9,269 people surrounding the court. Every game seemed to come down to a last-second shot. The spirit of the Big Five (St. Joseph's, La Salle, Villanova, Penn and Temple) was surreal with the streamers and the rollout banners and the mascots exhorting the crowd.

You'd walk out at the end of the evening high and bursting inside. You couldn't wait to tell someone what you had witnessed, and what better way to tell someone, I thought, than to write about it. That's when I decided, in ninth grade, to study journalism and become a sportswriter for a big city newspaper.

I became assistant sports editor of my high school paper, the *Merionite,* and co-sports editor of the yearbook, the *Enchiridion.* I covered our football and basketball games for the suburban weekly, *Main Line Times*. You cannot imagine the thrill of seeing your byline in a real newspaper for the first time. I landed a job with the Scholastic Score Service and was paid $15 every time I called in the results of a football game for it to send to the *Inquirer* and *Bulletin.*

But I still had to beg my way into journalism class, which was restricted to seniors. To qualify, you needed a B average in English. That was not happening. I hated books unless they were about boxing. "Call me Ismael," the first three words, is all I can tell you about *Moby Dick,* except for what I learned from the Gregory Peck movie. I couldn't concentrate even on CliffsNotes.

I spent 11th grade begging, whining, pleading and pestering my English teacher, Agnes Raycroft, to recommend me. It would have been humiliating for this future sportswriter to have been excluded from the only journalism class at his high school. Ms. Raycroft came through, but the journalism teacher, Margaret Hay, was determined to show me I didn't belong. Her class was half English, half Journalism, and I wavered between a B and C.

When she assigned us to write about a sports event, my friend, Matthew Naythons, offered me five dollars to write his story. I got a B, but when Mrs. Hay passed out the graded papers, Matthew, with the only A, did a victory dance any touchdown-scoring NFL player would envy.

I spent the night before the SATs trying to find a channel televising the Harold Johnson-Henry Hank fight from North

Philadelphia's Blue Horizon. It was blacked out locally, so I tuned the TV to a non-Philly channel, trying to locate an out-of-town feed. Every time I did, the screen filled with a zillion dots. I put my ear next to the speaker and listened to the somewhat scratchy voice of Don Dunphy describing the action.

My lack of sleep could explain Northwestern, NYU, Wisconsin and Syracuse rejecting me. So I chose Temple. Sometimes you win by losing, and Temple was one of the best things to ever happen to me. I got a terrific journalism education, became sports editor, makeup editor and city editor of the *Temple News.* And I stayed close to the local boxing scene.

Ray Didinger, a journalism classmate who became a lifelong friend, followed me as *Temple News* sports editor. One day we sat around the *Temple News* sports office and Ray talked about wanting to sit in the press box at Shea Stadium and write about Joe Namath. I was dreaming about promoting fights. Eventually, we both made it to the Hall of Fame in our respective sports, but I'm getting a little ahead of the game.

My junior year, the *Bulletin* hired me on its Saturday sports desk. I took high school scores over the phone, did short write-ups, edited wire service stories and wrote headlines. The next summer, I worked full time, doing the same thing on the "Lobster Shift," midnight to 8 am. It was a dream job for a college kid.

Jackie Wilson, the sports editor, was a calm chain-smoking father figure. Then in his late 40s, Wilson perfectly represented the Bulletin's don't-rock-the-boat style. Temple's athletic department had told him I could not be trusted because I had criticized the caliber of opposition Temple scheduled. But he had seen my work and liked it. He did tell me, however, that what I could do with a hatchet, columnist Sandy Grady could do with a scalpel.

One morning in August, 1967, Wilson came in early. "Russell, you're going back for your senior year," he said. "Concentrate on school and you can work here Saturday nights. We'll bring you back full time when you graduate." I felt like someone had shot ice water through me. I had an almost tearful look when I said, "Mr. Wilson, if you keep me on, I will work for nothing." I loved having a full-time job on a newspaper while in college and I *would* have worked for nothing. Wilson smiled and said, "We'll keep you on full time *and* pay you."

During my senior year, I again worked the "Lobster Shift," went to school from 9am to 1pm, went home, slept, and went back to the *Bulletin*. That job, I believe, won me the award as the *Outstanding Male Graduate in Journalism, Temple University, 1968.*

My goal was to become the *Bulletin* boxing writer. Jack Fried, who'd held that post since 1928, and I did not get along. I corrected mistakes in his stories and he saw me as a threat. Fried used the old hunt-and-peck style on his manual typewriter, pounding the keys with both forefingers as if he was trying to hurt them. You almost expected to see smoke.

As late as 1969, Fried still referred to Muhammad Ali in print as Cassius Clay. Once I changed it to Muhammad Ali and he stormed downstairs to the composing room and ordered the Linotype operator to change it back in the later editions. This was five years after Clay had announced his preferred name. At Ali-Frazier I, Fried scored it 13-2 in rounds for Frazier. Official scores for Frazier were 8-6-1, 9-6 and 11-4.

During my two years at the *Bulletin*, I covered a high school basketball game and wrote features about college athletes in non-major sports. I wrote about one of Harold Johnson's post-championship fights, and welterweight Gypsy Joe Harris' slide into obscurity. I covered amateur cards and one pro card when Fried was on vacation.

After graduating Temple, I went into the Army Reserves. I did Basic Training at Fort Bragg, North Carolina, and, when my six months were up, I went back to the *Bulletin.* Fried got an extension on his retirement and I thought, "Do I want to wait for this man to die?"

A newspaper "morgue" contains files of every story and every photo ever published, and the *Bulletin,* then the country's oldest continuous afternoon newspaper, had a huge one. Editing stories from midnight until 8 am left me time to visit. Some nights I came early and studied the files. My subject was the Blue Horizon, the small fight club at 1314 North Broad Street. I listed the date of every card from 1961 to 1963, the last time it had hosted professional boxing on a regular basis. I noted the night of the week, the main event, and the gross and net receipts.

If I couldn't write about boxing, maybe I could promote fights others could write about. I had saved $5,000. I had been paid as an editor at the *Temple News*, maybe $30 a month, plus extra money for pasting stories down and laying them out in the composing room. I'd lived at home and netted about $125 a week at the *Bulletin*.

The woman I would marry in August, 1969, Pat McKeown, worked full time at the *Inquirer*, writing feature stories. One night she asked, "What makes you think you can do this?" I told her if worst came to worst, it would take six months for me to lose the $5,000 and one day we'd have a scrapbook to show our kids about the time their daddy was a boxing promoter.

Mom wanted Dad to talk me out of it. He had tried earlier when I wanted to be a sportswriter. He knew they did not make a lot of money. I had no interest in his business since my mechanical skills consisted of turning on and off a light switch. I had worked for him for two summers as a plumber's helper, and the less said about that, the better. He tried to convince me to get a "real job" and promote boxing on the side, but making a living never entered my mind. I wanted to do something I would enjoy.

In the summer of 1969, I told Jackie Wilson that I was leaving to promote boxing. He offered to keep me on payroll one night a week for $30, in case my new venture failed. I accepted and we agreed I would work full time during the Christmas holidays.

Some *Bulletin* staffers scoffed. Veteran sportswriter George Kiseda asked me, "Why'd you get married and decide to become a boxing promoter at the same time?" I said, "I like fights!"

One night I came across an interoffice memo. It was signed, *Russell B. Back.*

Chapter Four

Opening Night

Timing is everything and 1969 was perfect for a boxing revival in Philadelphia. From 1960 through 1963, there had been 123 local fight cards, but from 1964 through 1969, there had been 63. The big ones were at the Arena, Convention Hall and the Spectrum, which opened in 1967 in South Philadelphia. There were five cards at the 2,500-seat Philadelphia Athletic Club in 1965 and a final one in 1966. Small clubs like the Cambria in Kensington and the Alhambra in South Philadelphia were gone by 1963—the former converted into a warehouse, the latter a parking lot. The Blue Horizon in North Philadelphia hosted bingo, weddings, church services and cabarets.

Joe Frazier was aggressive with his left hook and knockout hungry, but his early career fights here had been against less-than-stellar opponents and he never caught on with local fans. He didn't hang out on street corners and he was married with kids and that made him anything but your typical Philly fighter.

Madison Square Garden, the boxing mecca, especially for heavyweights, was where Frazier had knocked out Buster Mathis to win a piece of the world heavyweight title in 1968. When he outpointed Argentina's Oscar Bonavena in his second title defense later that year at the Spectrum, promoter Lou Lucchese lost money, his own and that of his "backers," which included Cloverlay, Inc., Frazier's management company.

Lucchese was a toy salesman and Justice of the Peace in Reading, Pennsylvania, 50 miles away. "I guess we're in the toy business now," said Joe Hand, an ex-cop and Cloverlay executive.

Official attendance figures and gate receipts never were released, but fewer than 6,000 people paid about $115,000—enough, after taxes, to cover only Frazier's purse. Frazier would unify the title in 1970 beating Jimmy Ellis, and defeat Muhammad Ali in the *Fight of the Century* in 1971, but he would never again box in Philadelphia.

Lucchese got to keep his toy business. Cloverlay also returned the rare coin collection he had put up as collateral. "Taking a man's business would not have been a good look for us," Hand said.

From January through August, 1969, there were five cards in Philadelphia, all at the Arena. One was promoted by Herman Taylor on May 1 as part of his 82nd birthday celebration. It featured middleweight contenders George Benton, of North Philadelphia, and Juarez DeLima, a Brazilian living in New York. Benton, who had turned pro in 1949 when he was 16, won a 10-round split decision in front of 2,526 customers.

Lucchese's first three cards would not have filled the 7,000-seat Arena once, but he did well May 19 when 3,431 paid to see junior middleweight Bennie Briscoe knock out crosstown rival Percy Manning in their "rubber match." There were no fights in June, July or August and a terrible thing happens when you don't promote—nothing.

The Blue Horizon was the only place I could afford. I went to see the owner, Jimmy Toppi, Jr., in the spring of 1969. His father, Jimmy Toppi, Sr., had been Taylor's main rival in the 1940s, promoting fights at the 5,000-seat Metropolitan Opera House on North Broad Street, half a mile south.

Broad Street runs 13 miles from the Naval Yard in South Philadelphia through North Philadelphia, Cheltenham Township and West Oak Lane. Along the way it makes a brief trip around City Hall, where it switches from South Broad to North. The Blue Horizon was in the heart of North Philadelphia, accessible by car, bus or subway.

North Philadelphia was once an industrial center and home to middle- and upper-class White families. But with an influx of Blacks migrating from the South in the 1950s and 1960s, Whites had fled, especially after the 1964 riots on Columbia Avenue. North Philly became home to 400,000 of the city's 600,000 Black residents, many living close to the poverty line. By the late 1960s, most of the city's best fighters lived there.

The Blue Horizon was built in 1865 as a residence for wealthy businessmen. In 1915, it was converted to a Moose Lodge and used for meetings and cabarets. Toppi, Sr., bought it in 1960 for $80,000 and changed its name from Moose Hall to Toppi's Auditorium.

Inspired by the 1944 re-release of the song *Beyond the Blue Horizon*, from the movie *Follow the Boys*, Toppi, Jr., renamed the building in 1961. It was perfect for boxing with a balcony around three sides of the ring, close enough to the action that fans in the North and South sections could jump into it. It sat 1,346.

The building had hosted two professional boxing cards in 1938. That was it until 1961 when Steve Tomassi promoted one with Benton in the main event. Marty Kramer, who'd been in boxing for 20 years, mostly as a manager, took over six nights later and staged cards on Thursday nights with small subsidies ($250 to $350 per show) from Madison Square Garden to develop talent.

Kramer lasted two years and 30 fight cards. He had the exclusive right to lose money at 1314 North Broad. Air conditioning was non-existent so summer fights were out. There had neen no boxing there since 1966.

I spent many spring and summer afternoons in Toppi's office. He wanted to help, though he later told the *Daily News,* "He (Peltz) was 22 and looked to me like 17. I thought the kid was wacko and would never get a license." But Toppi helped me get started. So did Pat Duffy and Tom Cushman.

Pat Duffy, a graduate of Roman Catholic High School, worked in the research lab at Gulf Oil during the Depression, eventually becoming lab foreman. He had been involved with amateur boxing since 1936 when he opened a gym in South Philadelphia. Duffy brought Sugar Ray Robinson to Philadelphia in 1940 for his last amateur fight—he turned pro seven days later in New York—and later managed the USA boxing teams in the 1960 (Cassius Clay) and 1968 (George Foreman) Olympics.

I met Duffy when I covered amateur fights for the *Bulletin,* most of them at the John C. Hennelly Boys Club, a second-floor walkup over a beer distributor on Clearfield Street in the Kensington section of the city. Boxers trained there and the gym could be converted into a 400-seat amateur fight club. It later became known as the Front Street Gym and was used in the Rocky spinoff movie, *Creed.*

Duffy had a pipeline to professional boxing through Pinny Schafer, the boisterous boss of Bartenders Union Local 115. When Pinny got excited, his voice was so loud ships could navigate by it. He had managed fighters since the 1950s, but none had made it big. His current stable was better with heavyweight contender Leotis Martin, of North Philadelphia, and featherweight Sammy Goss, of Trenton, New Jersey. Schafer also had a minority interest in Briscoe.

Duffy offered me Briscoe for a $1,000 guarantee against 25 percent of the net gate (ticket sales, less city and state tax and commission officials), whichever was more. He put me in touch with the manager of Rodolfo "Tito" Marshall, a Panamanian living in New York. Marshall had beaten Briscoe four years earlier. It didn't matter that Marshall was 4-7-5 since and 0-5-1 in his last six fights. It was a chance for Briscoe to gain revenge and fans knew Marshall fought solid opposition. Marshall got $600 against 15 percent of the net. I set the date for September 30, a Tuesday night.

I met Cushman in December, 1966, in Oklahoma City. He had come from the *Denver Post* the previous month to work for the *Philadelphia Daily News* and he was there to cover Temple's basketball team in the All-College Classic, one of the big Christmas tournaments. He was an ex-Marine who had studied journalism at the University of Missouri. I was in Oklahoma City as a "stringer" for the *Bulletin.* Cushman would become the finest boxing writer of his generation and our friendship lasted until his death in 2017.

Cushman and I ate with the team and sat next to each other courtside. He was 32, I was 20. In Philadelphia, we would run into each other at fights after he was assigned the boxing *beat*. He loved the idea of a college graduate diving into the swamp of professional boxing. That was fortunate because I had trouble getting coverage from my own paper, the *Bulletin*, due to my frosty relationship with Jack Fried.

Gene Courtney, who covered boxing for the *Inquirer*, was, like Fried, a veteran writer. Promoters historically "took care" of the press. Cushman said if he ever found out I was doing that, it would end our relationship. I reminded him I was a journalism student in college and such thoughts were foreign to me. The headline on Courtney's story the day of the fight: "Is Peltz Ready To Get Skinned?"

Bob Wright covered boxing for the *Camden Courier-Post.* Harvey Pollack, writing as K.O. Battle, provided publicity in neighborhood weeklies. Pollack worked for the Philadelphia Warriors and, later, the 76ers. He was the person who wrote "100" on a piece of paper and handed it to Wilt Chamberlain the night Wilt scored 100 points in 1962 in Hershey, Pennsylvania. The simple black-and-white photo became iconic.

I paid four-round fighters $50, six-round fighters $75. All 746 reserved ringside floor seats were $5. General admission in the 600-seat balcony was $3. Dad bought 90 ringside tickets and mailed them—with mimeographed copies of newspaper stories about me—to friends and business associates.

People viewed boxing promoters as short, fat men who wore fedoras, smoked cigars, talked out of both sides of their mouth and paid their bills in the dark. Few could grasp the idea of a 22-year-old promoter, especially one with a college degree. Most of the fighters were older than I was. The managers and trainers were boxing lifers. I was walking into gyms in hardscrabble neighborhoods and dealing with athletes I had paid to see or had watched on television. I loved every minute.

I had written a story in the *Bulletin* about a local amateur, Bobby "Boogaloo" Watts, who trained alongside Harold Johnson in the basement gym of the Annunciation Church at 12th and Diamond Streets, next to Temple's concrete campus.

Watts was born in Sumter, South Carolina, the same town that had produced our Hall-of-Fame lightweight champion Bob Montgomery. He lost to Armando Muniz, of Los Angeles, in the 147-pound finals of the 1968 U.S. Olympic Trials, but he was 3-0 as a pro. He was 19 and agreed to make his local debut in a six-round bout against Ron Nesby, from the same New York gym as Marshall.

I spent evenings at the gyms, mostly in North Philadelphia, mostly Champs Gym, then on Ridge Avenue, around the corner from the 23rd PAL, on Columbia Avenue. Champs was on the second floor of a former residential property, directly over the aptly named Roach's Café. Quenzell McCall ran the gym, which once had been someone's living room, dining room and bedroom.

One evening, Sam Solomon, a one-time catcher in local Negro League baseball, asked me to watch his 17-year-old, 152-pounder, Eugene Hart, spar a few rounds. Solomon nicknamed him "Cyclone" and he would turn pro on my first card.

I added two four-round bouts, one featuring heavyweight Jerry Judge. Judge had lost his only pro fight, but I billed him as "Kensington Heavyweight Champion." He would go on to beat Chuck Wepner, lose to Larry Holmes and take part in the 1975 Toronto fiasco as one of five men to box George Foreman the same day in circus-like exhibition fights. Judge trained at Champs Gym as did George Hill, who wanted to turn pro and agreed to fight him. Fighters did not complain then about fighting someone who trained in the same gym.

Posters were important. They were known as "half sheets," 22x28 thin cardboard. I drove around the city Sunday mornings, stapling them on abandoned buildings and light poles. I once got stopped by a cop after I ran a red light on Columbia Avenue. When I opened the car trunk to get my license from my briefcase, he saw the posters. "Are you the young guy who's promoting the fights at the Blue Horizon?" he asked. When I said I was, he wished me luck and let me go.

Toppi closed his office at 2 pm on weekdays, so I would park in front of the Blue Horizon. If someone rang the bell or knocked on the door, I would call them over and sell him tickets out of my trunk. I was determined to sell them all. But I never forgot promoter Marty Kramer's credo: "The only thing I wish on my worst enemy is that he becomes a small-club boxing promoter."

The night before the fight, my wife, Pat, popped a bottle of champagne and hung *Good Luck* paper cutouts around our one-bedroom apartment in the West Mount Airy section of Philadelphia. "I thought we had better celebrate while we could still afford it," she told Sandy Grady, of the *Bulletin.* Her mother had bigger fears. "What about the Mafia?" she asked. "Won't there be sub-machine guns?"

Fighters weighed in at noon the day of the fight at the boxing commission offices at Broad and Spring Garden Streets. I drove to the North Philly train station and picked up Marshall, Nesby and their trainers. Contracts often were not signed until the weigh-in in the days before fax machines and email. If you mailed a contract and did not include a self-addressed stamped return envelope, you rarely got them back.

The first fight was 8pm. When the men I'd hired to sell tickets didn't show up, Mom, Dad and I sold them. After we sold out, we sold raffle tickets from a roll for standing room until the police shut us down.

The *Daily News, Inquirer* and *Bulletin* were there, along with the Associated Press. Cushman wrote it best:

"Oscar Coor won last night and so did Gene 'Cyclone' Hart. Jerry 'Whew' Judge, puffing like an overworked retriever, finally dispatched George 'Puff' Hill with a thunderbolt right hand in the fourth round. And Bobby 'Boogaloo' Watts out-danced Ron Nesby in six. Bennie Briscoe capped it, of course, with an instant kayo of unwilling Tito Marshall. A little too instant, maybe.

"Never mind, the big winner was J Russell Peltz, the mustachioed, 22-year-old first-run promoter who had them hanging out the exits of the salty Blue Horizon. Peltz, a mod-mod Mike Todd (without the capital, or Liz) promised he would restore club fighting to Philadelphia, and maybe he will.

"For openers, Peltz had a record 1,606 customers jammed into the compact auditorium on N. Broad St. And he had to lock the doors…not to keep them in…but to turn away 300 more customers. Read it and weep, Lou."

The Blue Horizon's previous largest crowd had been the 1,554 who saw George Benton knock out Clarence Alford in three rounds six years before. Our ticket sales were $6,010, also a house record. Briscoe's percentage came to $1,314.58, Marshall's $788.75. My profit was $1,438.83 ($10,320 in 2021 dollars), more than I made in three months at the *Bulletin*. I spent most of the evening in the box office, never having thought about filming my fights. I saw maybe five minutes of action.

Classmates from Temple congratulated me. I answered questions from the press. Customers recognized me from newspaper photos and wished me luck. The *Temple News* was there.

I am sure Dad was proud of me though he never said a word. Dad was from the old school where men had to show a tough exterior. I wonder what he and Mom said about their son on the ride home that night, the one who had fallen in love with boxing at 12.

Chapter Five

Thirty Dollars and a Cut Eye

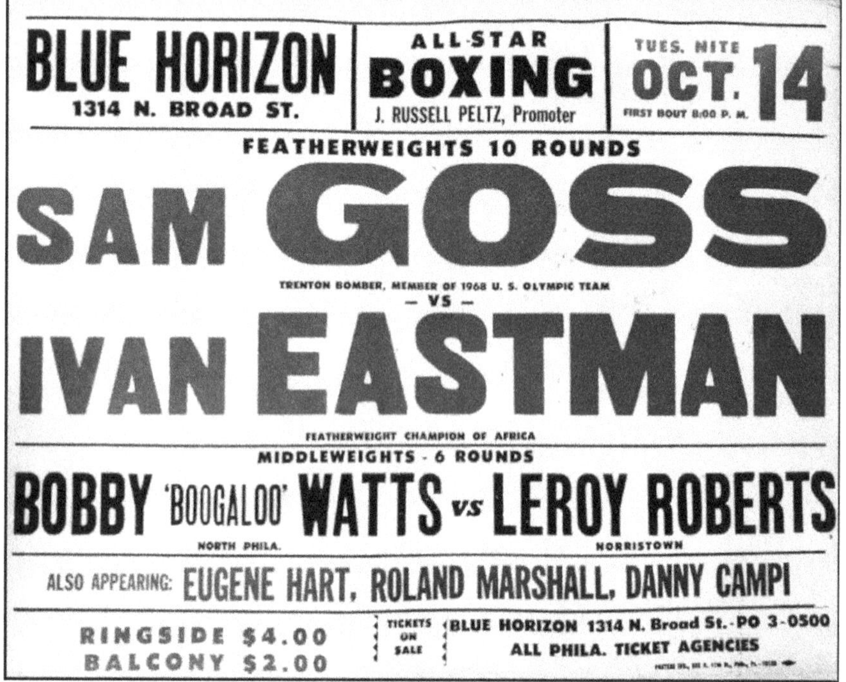

It was my second promotion, October 14, 1969, at the Blue Horizon. Featherweight Sammy Goss, of Trenton, had stopped Ivelaw Eastman, of New York, in seven rounds in the main event. The crowd was 919, the gate $2,476, the profit $133.78. Tickets were $4 and $2. Fans were filing out and fighters were waiting to get paid.

One of the fighters was junior middleweight John "Wildcat" Saunders, a part-time hair dresser, known more for his sartorial splendor, as *Daily News* boxing columnist Tom Cushman once wrote, than for his boxing ability.

Two weeks earlier, Saunders had been introduced in the ring prior to the main event on my first card. He had worn a three-piece suit with a long tailcoat, a bow tie, top hat and he sported a fancy walking cane. Not too shabby for a guy winless in four pro fights.

Two days after that, trainer Nick Belfiore called. Saunders was willing to fight fellow-Philadelphian Roland Marshall. I stopped by Belfiore's one-room Juniper Street Gym in South Philadelphia to close the deal. We were the only people there. Sanders, still dressed to the nines, said $50 for a four-round fight was insulting. I shrugged and walked down the gym stairs. When I got to the door, Belfiore called me back so Saunders could sign.

The fight between Saunders and Marshall was entertaining but brief. Marshall ripped a nasty cut over Saunders' left eye, getting the K0 31 seconds into round two.

Now, an hour later, Saunders wore the same three-piece suit, minus the top hat and cane. His shirt collar was open and his face showed beads of sweat. There was a bandage above his cut eye. We deducted $10 for his license, $8 for medical insurance, $1.50 for city wage tax.

Saunders stared at the pay sheet with the $30.50 net figure at the bottom. He didn't move an inch or say a word for 30 seconds. Finally, he signed the pay sheet, picked up the cash, shook his head and said with more than a trace of disgust: "Thirty dollars and a cut eye." Then he turned and left the building.

Chapter Six
The Fox

Pop Bates (left), me and Joe Gramby in the 1980s. (Peltz collection)

George Benton boxed from 1949 to 1970, winning 61 of 74 fights with one draw. He beat three future world champions—Freddie Little, Joey Giardello, Jimmy Ellis—but never got a title shot because his manager, Herman Diamond, refused to give up a piece of his contract for the opportunity. When I was in high school and college, I had seen Benton fight several times in person and on television. He was one of my early favorites and had become known as the Mayor of North Philadelphia.

As the fans were leaving the Blue Horizon after Benton's first-round knockout of David Beckles on January 13, 1970, I was speaking with Joe Gramby, who had managed Benton for two years. Gramby wanted another fight. I agreed to March 25.

Gramby, known as "The Fox," was one of the sharpest boxing people I ever knew. He was born in 1912 in Norfolk, Virginia, and his family moved to Philadelphia when he was 10. He boxed at Central High School and, in the late 1920s and early '30s—before Federal ID cards—had a handful of amateur and pro fights under the name "Ginger Graham." He boxed on the "chicken-bone circuit," where Black fighters, mostly from the South, went from town to town fighting under different names.

Daily News boxing writer Jack McKinney once wrote that Gramby "had a certain charm and he commanded respect from everybody. He had charisma before the term was coined." To a young college grad, Gramby was intimidating. He was 57 and always wore a suit and tie. I was 23 and wore jeans and Mickey Mouse T-shirts. He was more cultured than most boxing people. I often ran into him at theatres in Center City.

Gramby had managed lightweight champion Bob Montgomery in the 1940s and welterweight contender Charley Scott in the 1950s and '60s. Later he would manage Richie Kates, Randall "Tex" Cobb and Tony Thornton. In the 1940s, Gramby and Montgomery broke the all-White color barrier for sportswriters. They told promoter Herman Taylor they would refuse to box until Black writers were permitted into the ringside press section.

As a gym regular in North Philadelphia, Gramby worked with Taylor and Lou Lucchese, who never came to the gyms. He would suggest matches, make deals with managers and contact out-of-town agents for their boxers. He knew everyone and everyone knew him, and he advised Yank Durham during Joe Frazier's career. Then I came along and went to the gyms myself. What's the point of being a boxing promoter, I thought, if you don't make your own matches?

The promoter takes care of the business side—signing the main event, renting the venue, handling the publicity and marketing, selling the tickets, arranging for travel. The matchmaker controls the undercard, making fights which are competitive and fun to watch. Puncher vs. puncher is always a good matchup as is puncher vs. boxer. You try to steer clear of boxer vs. boxer. Many boxers are counter-punchers who wait for the other guy to punch before punching back. If both guys are waiting, no one is punching. Who wants to watch that?

A few days after agreeing to March 25, I reviewed the numbers. I had paid Benton $1,000, Beckles $600. The $3,665 gross gate left me with a profit of $234.58, which was good, but paying $1,600 for the main event equaled what I'd paid for Bennie Briscoe vs. Tito Marshall and Leotis Martin vs. Wendell Newton and I had done better with them.

Did I want to risk $1,600 for another Benton fight, plus travel, hotel and meals for the opponent? I had been paying half that for most main events. I was afraid to tell Gramby I had changed my mind. Another card was coming up January 27 so I worked on it. January turned into February and Benton was not in the gym. I had two cards in February and I was busy.

By mid-February, I still had not seen Benton. Was he sick? Injured? Did Gramby take another fight for him? Could I worm my way out of this? Four weeks before March 25, I was at the top of the stairs at Champs Gym when Benton came walking up with the raggedy pale yellow suitcase he always carried.

"Oh, George!" I whined, my face contorted like someone had punched me in the gut. "What are you doing here?"

"I thought I was fighting for you next month."

"I hadn't seen you so I started making other plans."

There was a pay phone at the entrance to the gym. Benton put in a coin and called Gramby. I couldn't hear what he said but he handed me the phone.

"Hey, promoter, George tells me we may not be fighting for you." Gramby rarely called me Russell—it was "promoter" or "impresario" or "entrepreneur."

"Well, Joe, we never signed a contract."

"What's the matter, isn't your word any good?"

I felt two feet tall.

"Forget what I said, Joe. The fight is on."

Benton decisioned Eddie "Red Top" Owens, of Pittsfield, Massachusetts, in 10 rounds. Attendance was 1,027, gate receipts $3,779. I lost $93.66, but I had done the right thing. Benton went to New York nine days later and lost a rematch to Juarez DeLima.

A month later, Lamont A. "Chinaman" Bonham shot Benton with a .32-caliber pistol because Benton's younger brother, Henry, had punched Bonham for assaulting their sister inside a bar at 18th and Susquehanna. The bullet went in Benton's left side and lodged in his back. It could not be removed. Benton was listed in critical condition at Temple Hospital. He recovered, but never boxed again and soon was tending bar at the *Tic Tac Toe* at 11th and Venango.

Fast forward 12 years. Dan Duva, head of Main Events, a Totowa, New Jersey-based promotional company, had linked half a dozen cable television systems to televise monthly boxing cards, most of them from Atlantic City. The opener was April 19 at Resorts International and Duva wanted a *name* in the main event. He asked me if heavyweight contender Tex Cobb was available.

I was involved because I had delivered PRISM, Philadelphia's regional premium cable channel. Cobb was coming off a win over Colombian heavyweight Bernardo Mercado. His only losses in 21 fights were by split decision to former champ Ken Norton and by majority decision to future champ Michael Dokes. He also had K0d hard-hitting contender Earnie Shavers.

Cobb was managed by Gramby, now a good friend. I picked Gramby up at his house in the Fairmount section of Philadelphia on a cold Sunday morning in February and we drove to the Famous Deli in Queen Village. At breakfast, we signed contracts for Cobb to get $20,000 against 30 percent of the net receipts for a 10-round fight with Jeff Shelburg, of Salt Lake City, Utah. I took Gramby back and drove 20 minutes to my home in Wynnewood, where I had moved in 1977 with my second wife. When I got inside, Linda told me Gramby had called.

I am a pessimist and the eternal pessimist is never disappointed. I called Gramby.

"What's up, Joe?" I asked.

"Guess who just called me?" he said.

"Who?"

"Don King."

I went silent. This was not good news.

"What do you think he offered me?"

"I have no idea." I was sliding down the kitchen wall.

"He offered me half a million dollars for Cobb to fight Larry Holmes."

By now I was on the floor in a fetal position. We needed Cobb for our opener, but you can't ask a fighter to turn down a world championship fight for that kind of money?

"What do you think I told him?" Gramby asked.

"I have no idea, Joe."

"I told him I had a commitment to you and even though the contracts were not filed I was not going to break my word."

"What did King say?"

"You don't wanna know."

The lesson I had learned in 1970 came full circle. Cobb knocked out Shelburg in seven rounds. His purse was $24,000. Seven months later, he got his shot at Holmes and his $500,000. "Larry never beat me," Cobb insists to this day. "He just won the first 15 rounds."

Chapter Seven

That First Season

That first season seemed like a celebration. (Mike Feldman photo)

The blue Edwardian suit I wore that first night gave the writers a chance to dub me the "Mod Boy Promoter." Often I would show up in bell bottoms with a white belt two inches wide. I had an Afro I rarely cut, and wore "granny glasses." I looked like I belonged at Electric Factory concerts, not the Blue Horizon.

From September 30, 1969, through May 18, 1970, I promoted 15 cards, working out of our one-bedroom apartment at the Mayfair House, nine miles from the Blue Horizon. We had a television, a mattress and a Siamese cat named Ophelia. No secretary, no answering service. There were no pre-fight medical requirements—all you needed was a heartbeat—and the gyms were packed with fighters.

There were 80 fights on those 15 cards; 53 ended in knockouts, 27 in the first round. Of the 23 fighters who made pro debuts, three became legitimate Top 10 contenders: middleweights Cyclone Hart and Willie "The Worm" Monroe, and heavyweight Jimmy Young. Boogaloo Watts would join them. Four fighters already were ranked: Bennie Briscoe, Leotis Martin, George Benton, and Joe Shaw. Sammy Goss became an attraction—later a contender—winning five main events and reviving interest on the East Coast in the lighter weight classes.

Goss came from a boxing family. His dad, Jesse, Sr., had 69 pro fights from 1924 to 1935 and later worked with Ike Williams, Trenton's Hall-of-Fame lightweight champion. Three of Goss' brothers were amateur boxers. At 15, when Sammy wanted to follow in their footsteps, his dad sent him to the Trenton PAL. He won five New Jersey Golden Gloves titles, the National AAU flyweight title in 1965 and the National AAU bantamweight title in 1968. He represented the USA in the Olympic Games in Mexico City, but lost in the opening round. By the time Goss boxed for me in 1969, he was 8-1, but eight of his fights had been outside Philadelphia.

Watts won three times on my first four cards. He was managed by Frank Hamilton and Tim Tyler, both in their 20s. I was paying Watts $75 for the six-round semifinals and his managers were hustling tickets. After Watts got to 6-0, Hamilton and Tyler wanted more money, but I could not afford it. People think the promoter always makes money, but few have a clue as to what goes into promoting. When Watts decided to move to the West Coast, I had made $2,192.37 from my first five cards, but $1,438.83 had come opening night, leaving me with an average profit of $189.64 per show for the next four.

I wanted Watts to be the first young boxer I would help to build from the ground up. Losing him hurt, but I could not pay him what his team wanted, even after Hart's manager, Sam Solomon, offered to let Cyclone fight six-round fights for four-round money to help out. Young, also managed by Hamilton and Tyler, went 2-0 on my first five cards, then joined Watts on the West Coast. Watts went 2-2 and Young 1-1 before coming home a year later.

Hart boxed on 10 of those 15 shows, winning every time by knockout inside four rounds. His most impressive was over Vernon Mason, of Baltimore, occurring a second or two *after* the bell ended round two. Jack Fried wrote that, in his 40 years of covering fights, he never had seen a fighter get knocked out after the bell and the result upheld.

Monroe, originally from Alabama, went to high school in Crestview, Florida, then in Rochester, New York, where he began boxing as an amateur. He made it to the 1969 National Golden Gloves semifinals before a fever forced him out of his semfinal fight. He then moved to Philly to work with Yank Durham, Joe Frazier's trainer.

He went 6-0 that first season, all by knockout, four in one round. One of Monroe's victims was 34-year-old Ted Hamilton, whom I'd billed as the middleweight champion of West Virginia even though he'd lost 10 of his 11 fights. Years later I learned that Hamilton had been knocked out four days prior in Ohio. *Boxrec.com* did not exist then and fighters' records were easy to hide.

Alva Theodore Hamilton was a gawky country kid who came to the weigh-in that morning carrying a pair of high school gym shorts. When he said they were his boxing trunks, I told him to hide them before the commissioner saw. I asked Monroe to "carry" Hamilton for a couple of rounds. The fight lasted 48 seconds. I wonder how long it would have lasted had I not asked. Monroe hit him so hard that Hamilton broke a bone in his right ankle and spent the night in the hospital. By the time he retired in 1981, his record was 1-31. He had been knocked out 26 times.

George Benton headlined twice. It was an honor to have promoted his last two fights in Philadelphia. He had been one of my boyhood heroes. I saw him spar Hart at Champs Gym when both were getting ready for my January 13 card. Hart tried to blow Benton out of there with a *blitzkrieg* of left hooks and right hands.

Benton stayed in the pocket, slightly bent at the waist, his right glove by his chin, his left across his waist. He was in the eye of a hurricane, or, in this case, a cyclone. He moved his left shoulder to avoid right hands from Hart and his right shoulder to guard against left hooks. He slipped punches, rolled with some and took the rest on his arms, elbows and gloves. By the third round, after Hart had expended so much energy he could hardly lift his arms, Benton took over. I looked at Joe Gramby, who was managing Benton. He smiled and whispered, "Sometimes you have to teach these kids a lesson."

The first time Benton boxed for me, as I said, was against David Beckles, of Trinidad. Beckles was living in New York and he was late to the noon weigh-in. Benton was accustomed to opponents ducking him. He sat by the front door of the boxing commission offices on the 11th floor, staring at the eight elevators in the hallway, praying Beckles would arrive.

I had no way of contacting Beckles' manager, Robert Robbins, who worked as a pimp in New York City and managed fighters on the side, or maybe it was the other way around. By the time he and Beckles arrived at 1 pm, Benton had smoked half a pack of cigarettes, putting each one out by stomping it on the floor. After the four prelims had lasted less than eight rounds, I went to Benton's dressing room and asked him to "carry" Beckles for a few rounds. He nodded just as Monroe did and knocked Beckles out in less than three minutes.

Despite all the knockouts, the fans kept coming. They were aware of the punching power of youngsters like Hart and Monroe and they knew what we were trying to develop. We drew a total of 14,964 customers for the 15 cards and total receipts were $53,157. My first season profit was $4,648.68 ($31,340.49 in 2021 dollars). Not quite what I made at the *Bulletin*, but I was having more fun.

On my third card, local heavyweight contender Leotis Martin was to fight Wendell Newton, of The Bahamas, in the main event, but that morning I lost two prelims.

Humberto Trottman, a Panamanian middleweight from New York, never arrived to fight Dennis Heffernan, and Richie Kates, of Millville, New Jersey, weighed in at 172 pounds for his fight with Monroe, who was 157. Pennsylvania rules allowed a maximum difference of 10 pounds between fighters, except heavyweights. I was left with two four-round fights and the 10-round main event. A sanctioned card required a minimum of four fights and 28 rounds. The four-round boxers agreed to go six, leaving me one fight and six rounds short.

I had been in business two months and had few contacts. I spent the day calling everywhere—New York, Baltimore, Pittsburgh,

Boston, Washington, DC. No luck! Pat Duffy offered me Goss in a three-round exhibition with headgear, not exactly a show-saver. At the Blue Horizon that evening I was standing with Solomon—who also managed Heffernan—in the box office area. He went into the lobby, put his arm around a 30-something-year-old Black man and brought him back.

"This is Clarence Preston and he's agreed to fight Dennis tonight," Solomon said. I didn't know Clarence Preston from *Sergeant Preston of the Yukon*, a popular TV series in the late 1950s. Preston filled out the license application and went upstairs to get ready. He weighed 162 on the only scale the Blue Horizon had, ironically, a meat scale. I did not know that he had boxed as a pro in the early 1960s, winning two of seven fights, the last one in 1966 when he'd weighed 185 pounds. I also didn't know he was a heroin addict.

When I went into the dressing rooms, Preston was wrapping his own hands, which should have tipped me off that he knew something about boxing.

"How much am I getting?" he asked.

"We pay $75 for six-round fights," I said.

"I'm not fighting for $75."

"What do you want?"

"$200."

"Okay, we have a deal." Did I have a choice?

Jimmy Young, the heavyweight who, one day, would nearly beat Muhammad Ali and who did end George Foreman's first career, knocked out Jimmy "Rag Man" Jones, of Norfolk, Virginia, in 1:02 of the first round. Local welterweights Jose Rodriguez and Roy Ingram went six rounds with Rodriguez getting the decision. Heffernan versus Preston was next.

Not knowing if Preston could even spell fight, I stood off to the side, praying I would not insult the fans and embarrass myself. When the bell rang, Preston came out holding his hands in a stance which showed he might know what he was doing. A minute later, a short Heffernan left jab dropped Preston to his knees in mid-ring.

I slowly made my way to the rear, under the protection of the balcony, in case fans started to throw objects into the ring. Preston got up, and Heffernan threw a punch which was half hook, half uppercut. The punch started in Miami Beach and ended in Boston.

Preston collapsed like an accordion. To this day, I don't believe the punch landed. I was standing next to Jack Puggy (born Salvatore Riccuiti), who had been a manager and matchmaker since the 1920s.

"Jack, can you believe that crap?" I asked.

"Russell, that was the best left hook I ever saw," he said.

The fans loved it. In the main event, Martin had his right eye closed by Newton's steady punching, but rallied to score a one-punch knockout in the seventh round to keep alive his fight six weeks later against Sonny Liston in Las Vegas. Unfortunately, after knocking out Liston, Martin suffered a detached retina in his right eye and never boxed again. Did he first suffer the injury against Newton?

There were nights when the intermission before the main event lasted longer than the entire card. One time the four prelims lasted five rounds and I hid in Jimmy Toppi's office.

Nelson Cuevas, already retired for three years and working as a trainer, boxed for me under the name of Manny Valdez, whom I advertised as middleweight champion of Ecuador. Joe Shaw, who was from New York like Cuevas, had upset Briscoe the previous November. He toyed with Cuevas/Valdez for two rounds. Tom Cushman called me over and asked when the farce was going to end. I went to Shaw's corner and yelled at trainer Rollie Hackmer to get it over with.

In the *Daily News* the next day, Cushman wrote that the fight was "like watching your wife play bridge with Charles Goren." Cuevas returned to the Blue Horizon on the final show that season, this time as a corner man. I told him to wear sunglasses so no one would recognize him, but Cushman did. He pointed that out in the newspaper, and I learned that first season: "Trust no one and don't try to fool anyone."

I spent most evenings at Champs, where "Bow-Legged" Charlie Brown trained lightweight Eddie "Flash" Tomlin. Charlie was 5-foot-1 and wore pants two sizes too big. He reminded me of a plastic toy cowboy whose legs were as wide as an inverted U so they could snap onto the back of a plastic toy horse. Brown, noticing all the young talent being developed, constantly reminded me that "if you crush the grapes, make sure you drink the wine." I should have paid more attention.

There were preliminary fights you never forget. Lightweights Ricky Thomas, of Brick Town, New Jersey, and Giles Williams (Baby Charles), of West Philly, met twice in four-round brawls, two weeks apart. Thomas won the first, Williams the second. Pudgy heavyweight George Hill, of Champs Gym, was dropped twice in the first round by the 23rd PAL's Donald Branch, who paraded around the ring, yelled to the crowd and raised his arms in victory. Then Hill got up and stopped the muscular Branch in round two.

After the May 18 finale—Hart and Monroe respectively blasting out Sonny Floyd, of Trenton, and Alberto Millan, of New York—even Fried wrote something nice:

"Rookie boxing impresario J Russell Peltz called it a season—his first and perhaps his last—after staging a riotously exciting show at the Blue Horizon last night, his 15th production since last Sept. 30th. After undefeated Eugene 'Cyclone' Hart topped off the evening with a spectacular 52-second knockout in the seventh bout, Peltz treated boxing commission officials and friends to champagne in paper cups and said he is undecided about coming back for another shot at the tough and frustrating business next fall. Whether he does or doesn't return, he already has left a mark on the fight game in Philadelphia. Besides keeping it alive and lively through the fall, winter and early spring, providing 'work' opportunities for several dozen youngsters, he developed two remarkably able prospects."

Fried named Goss and Hart as rising stars. I would have added Monroe.

The skinny teenager from the suburbs was in Candy Land, dealing with fighters he had idolized as a kid. Hell, I *was* a kid. I wonder if I took the time to enjoy it as much then as I do looking back now. The old cliche that "youth is wasted on the young" is so true.

Chapter Eight

Game Changer

Pencil drawing of Bennie Briscoe by Tom Palmore.

After I closed shop for the season on May 18, 1970, Lou Lucchese promoted June 15 at the Arena. The only other card that summer was Herman Taylor's when 1968 Olympic heavyweight champion George Foreman knocked out shopworn Roger Russell, of South Philadelphia, in one round on July 20 at the Spectrum. It was out of character for Taylor to make such a fight. Foreman was 20-0, 17 K0s, as a pro. Russell, a former National AAU champion and once a hot prospect with a 1967 win over Leotis Martin and a 1968 draw with Zora Folley, had lost six in a row, two by knockout. Eight years after losing to Foreman in one round, he retired with 17 defeats in his last 18 fights. Taylor's card drew 4,721 fans. Local rivals Sammy Goss and Augie Pantellas, on a collision course, helped the gate, winning in separate 10-round bouts.

The biggest local fight of early 1970 had been the 10-round rematch between Bennie Briscoe and Joe Shaw at the Arena. Shaw had outpointed Briscoe the previous November at the Spectrum, knocking him out of a possible junior middleweight title fight with Freddie Little. The return bout was set for March 16.

A three-time Middle Atlantic AAU champion, Briscoe had turned pro in 1962 with Yank Durham as trainer and Pinny Schafer as manager. This was two years before Joe Frazier won Olympic gold, and Durham was just another trainer toiling in the North Philly gyms, schooling Briscoe and Martin. Later he would manage welterweight Gypsy Joe Harris.

Briscoe was with Durham until December 6, 1965, when he lost a 10-round decision to Stanley "Kitten" Hayward at the Arena. Briscoe was passive early in the fight and by the time he poured on the pressure, Hayward's lead was insurmountable. But afterward, Hayward hallucinated in his dressing room and spent the night in Presbyterian Hospital.

Schafer was not happy with Durham's strategy and replaced him with Quenzell McCall—who had been in Hayward's corner—as trainer for Briscoe and Martin. Briscoe went 6-3-2 in his next 11 fights, while matched tough. His opponents included Hall-of-Famers Carlos Monzon in his home country, Argentina, George Benton and Luis Rodriguez (twice). He also was disqualified in Paris when he had the nerve to hit Frenchman Yolande Leveque in the stomach.

With Briscoe's career treading water in 1968, Schafer sold his managerial interest to Jimmy Iselin, whose dad, Phil, was president of, and a major shareholder in, the New York Jets pro football team. Iselin had formed Peers Management, Inc., which included Buster Mathis on its roster. With big money behind him, it was thought Iselin could take Briscoe to another level. Joe Fariello, who worked with Mathis, became Briscoe's trainer.

Managers wielded absolute control in those days. Contracts were bought and sold. You could call it a form of slavery, but fighters signed with managers because they believed the managers knew how to guide their careers. Pennsylvania limited contracts between fighters and managers to three years, but one clause read: "Fighter must faithfully fulfill any contract entered into on his behalf by the manager." So if a manager and promoter agreed to an opponent and financial terms and signed a contract, the fighter had to honor it even if the fighter had not signed himself.

Many fighter-manager contracts were 50-50. The fighter was guaranteed half of each purse and the manager paid all the expenses (trainer, corner men, sparring, equipment, gym dues) out of *his* half. Fighters had day jobs. Briscoe worked for the city in sanitation. Lightweight Flash Tomlin worked for the company which printed fight posters. Another lightweight, C.L. Lewis, worked in a clothing store owned by his manager. Joe Frazier was the only local fighter I can recall who supported himself solely from boxing.

Years later I asked manager Joe Gramby if he had 50 percent of heavyweight Tex Cobb. "No," Gramby replied, "Tex Cobb has 50 percent of me." It was a line Gramby stole from the legendary Jack Kearns, who managed Hall-of-Fame champions Jack Dempsey, Mickey Walker, Joey Maxim and Archie Moore. Shrewd managers were as valuable as good fighters, sometimes more so.

Briscoe was born in 1943 in Augusta, Georgia, but came to Philadelphia in 1957. He hung out on North Philly street corners with pimps and other hustlers, but never got into trouble. Briscoe worked for the city, first in rat control, then on a garbage truck. He rarely missed a day. I once asked him if he used poison to kill the rats. "Are you kidding?" he said. "We club those suckers to death with a baseball bat." He and his wife, Rita, lived in North Philadelphia with their four kids.

When his contract was sold to Peers, Briscoe took it in stride. "I have no complaints about Mr. Schafer, he always treated me good," Briscoe told *Daily News* boxing writer Tom Cushman. "But because of money and other reasons, we never could get the right fight. Sometimes it seemed like we never could get any at all. Mr. Iselin, though, said he would move me. He said he would get me fights, and that's all I ask."

Fariello had replaced Cus D'Amato as head trainer at Peers after Mathis complained that D'Amato did not treat him like a man. Like D'Amato, Fariello employed a punch-by-the-numbers system. Their Catskill Mountains training camp featured a mattress wrapped around an oversized heavy bag. The mattress was called a "Willie" because it was first used in 1965 by Jose Torres when he was training to challenge Willie Pastrano for the world light-heavyweight title. The mattress had a head and body crudely drawn on it with numbers at different points. Each punch Fariello wanted thrown also had a number, and when he called out numbers, the fighter was to throw that punch at that spot—either on that mattress or on an opponent in the ring.

"I had seen it before," Briscoe told Cushman. "I helped train Mathis for the Joe Frazier fight and I watched him work on it. Fariello would yell out a bunch of numbers, like 9-4-6-3, and Buster was supposed to hit those four spots on the mattress. It was all right for him, I guess, because Buster was a boxer. But I couldn't believe they'd want *me* to punch that thing. I thought Peers bought my contract because they liked what they saw when I worked with Mathis. First thing I knew they had me punching at the doo-dad, trying to make me box. I tried, but I am what I am."

Bouie Fisher, who later trained Bernard Hopkins, was a close friend of Briscoe, as was Bouie's brother, Willie. Neither Fisher brother was happy with Peers, even though Briscoe won eight out of 11 fights with Fariello. Iselin wanted me to promote the rematch with Shaw, but I blew the deal when I said, "I hope I can handle this." I had been in business six months and the 7,000-seat Arena would be more work than the Blue Horizon. So Iselin gave the fight to Lucchese.

Briscoe was not going back to the Catskills. He was a city guy and he wanted Quenzell to train him. Fariello had trained, or would train, world champions Torres, Floyd Patterson, Mark Breland, Junior

Jones and Tom "Boom Boom" Johnson. He was a good trainer, but not for Briscoe.

After contracts were signed, Willie Fisher went to Briscoe's house and dialed Fariello. He told Briscoe to listen on another phone. Willie asked Fariello about strategy, but Fariello said it was difficult to teach Briscoe anything. He said all you can do is wind him up and send him out. When Briscoe heard that, he was more determined than ever to train at home.

Briscoe told Iselin he was going back to McCall. When Iselin threatened to cancel the fight, Briscoe appealed to the Athletic Commission. He wanted to know if the fight could be canceled if he went with a new trainer. Assured by commission secretary Bob Patterson that the contract was valid, the fight went on with McCall in the corner. In a brutal war, Briscoe forced Shaw to quit on his stool after six rounds in front of 4,967 fans.

I was in Briscoe's dressing room afterward. He was on his back on a rubbing table and in pain. It had been a grueling, bloody contest. Shaw's stick-and-move strategy worked early, but Briscoe's body work slowed him down by the fifth round. It was toe-to-toe from there and Briscoe made the 18-foot ring seem like a phone booth. Shaw couldn't handle the pressure. He never fought again. Iselin collected Briscoe's purse—for the last time.

Four months later, I was outside *Sherry's Tickets* on 15th Street above Walnut. Jack Puggy was there to check on sales for Herman Taylor's upcoming Foreman-Russell card. It was a hot July day and Puggy had his sport jacket draped over one arm. He was 5-foot-7, wore a hat and a scowl, and puffed away on a cigar. Puggy had managed and trained fighters his entire working life. The best may have been world-rated heavyweight Willie Reddish in the 1930s and 1940s. Reddish had boxed at the Blue Horizon in 1938 when it was known as Moose Hall.

"I've been offered Bennie Briscoe's contract," Puggy said, "but at my age (68) what do I need another fighter for."

"How much do they want?" I asked.

"Twenty-five hundred," he said.

My brain went into overdrive. I stayed a few minutes, said goodbye, drove to my apartment and called my brother-in-law, Arnold Weiss, a CPA with his own accounting firm, and paymaster at each Blue Horizon fight.

“Bennie Briscoe’s contract is for sale!” I said. “The price is $2,500. Why don’t you manage him and I’ll promote him.”

There were three talented young middleweights in Philly—Cyclone Hart, Boogaloo Watts, Willie Monroe—each of whom would have to fight Briscoe to see who was top dog in the city. Whoever controlled Briscoe would control those fights. Whoever controlled those fights would control boxing in Philadelphia.

“Can I turn a profit or at least make my money back?” Arnold asked.

“Absolutely,” I said. “Bennie is only 27.”

Arnold agreed. I telephoned Iselin in New York to confirm that the contract was still for sale. He said that Briscoe owed them $800, making the total $3,300.

“Not a problem,” I said. Briscoe’s largest purse at this point had been $3,600.

The first time I recall seeing Briscoe was in the 1962 Middle Atlantic AAU championships at Convention Hall. His style did not turn me on. He plodded forward, punching to the body like a machine, trying to beak ribs. But I was 15 years old so what did I know. Briscoe had dropped out of Simon Gratz High School in 10th grade and turned pro that year.

I had watched him on undercards, fighting like the “Baby Bull” the writers called him, more than a few of his punches landing low. His fights were workman-like and he was lost in the shadows of a pair of flashier local favorites the same size, Hayward and Gypsy Joe. I saw Briscoe as a villain. When Percy Manning handed him his first loss in 1965, I was the happiest guy in the Philadelphia Athletic Club, staring at the second hand on my watch, praying that Manning would last the 10 rounds and win with his punch-and-clinch strategy.

By the time he split with Peers, however, Briscoe was the last man standing. Gypsy Joe, blind in one eye, lost his license late in 1968. Hayward, a man-about-town fighting in Europe, enjoyed the sights of Paris and Rome more than he liked the inside of a gym.

After the phone call to Iselin, Arnold and I had breakfast with Briscoe and Quenzell at Linton’s on North Broad Street near Temple. Quenzell was the key. Even though I was at Champs Gym nearly every weeknight and weekend afternoon, Briscoe and I did little more than nod. I was not the most outgoing guy, often the only

White face in the gym, but Briscoe believed in Quenzell and Quenzell believed in me.

Quenzell asked for one third of the management contract but when Arnold told him he would have to put up one third of the money, he accepted a standard trainer's fee of 10 percent. That started his icy relationship with Arnold, whom he considered a "front" for me.

Though we got along, Quenzell often acted like he was the smartest person in the room. He'd held the lease on Champs Gym for over 20 years and he and his wife, Thelma, owned a small seafood store in North Philadelphia. He also was special assistant to then-Congressman, future mayor Bill Green, and he taught electronics at the Opportunities Industrialization Center (OIC). He spoke fluent Spanish and passable French which came in handy when we traveled abroad.

Quenzell came to the gym every night wearing a tie and jacket. He removed the jacket, always one size too big, and trained fighters in his white shirt and tie. He had been a decent amateur fighter and won four of seven pro fights as a featherweight within 13 months in the early 1940s. He had trained Percy Bassett, a hard-hitting, world-class featherweight who turned pro in 1947 but retired, at 25, in 1955, with a record of 65-12-1, 42 K0s, and a detached retina.

Bassett had been managed by Mike Sokoloff, also known as Mike Bananas because he owned a fruit and vegetable stand in South Philadelphia. Bassett never got a shot at Sandy Saddler's title because Sokoloff and Quenzell refused to give a "piece" to mob guys Frankie Carbo and Blinky Palermo, who controlled Saddler through manager Charley Johnston.

Quenzell later had teenage lightweight sensation Len Matthews, who left when he turned 21 because he didn't like the strict training and living regimen. He'd also trained Leotis Martin when Martin knocked out Sonny Liston the previous December in Las Vegas and had reveled in that glory for six days until Martin underwent surgery for *his* detached retina. One month later, Martin, a wonderful but introverted man with a terrible speech impediment, retired, becoming the second fighter Quenzell had guided to within breathing distance of a world championship, and lost to the same injury.

I took the train to New York City with Arnold's check. I met Iselin at The Palm restaurant. He was 27, I was 23. We sat at a booth and I was nervous. When he ordered a string bean and onion salad, I did, too. Repulsive as it sounds, it was good. After the usual niceties, I handed him Arnold's check and he gave me the release of contract. My heart was pounding.

Iselin went into the kitchen to call Fariello, happy to have closed the deal. I was much happier. I controlled a world-class fighter who would spearhead my business. And for the first time, Briscoe would be the Number One guy in his own stable. He had played second fiddle to Gypsy Joe Harris and Joe Frazier and Buster Mathis. Now he was the main man and would be treated as such. He just didn't know it yet.

"It's essentially an investment," Arnold told Cushman when the story broke, "but I'm also a fan. I got to know and like a lot of the fight people last winter. I think Bennie is an excellent fighter, but I also think he is a sensitive man. He's disappointed. He's been in the game for years and has nothing to show for it. I've promised him that when he's through with me he'll have some money, and a name that may be a marketable commodity. I have no pre-conceived plan but I am a businessman. I have learned that if you take care of your business, sooner or later you'll realize a dividend. Let's just say that Quenzell will handle the training without interference and I will handle the financial end."

Briscoe had doubts. "I guess I'm a bad luck fighter," he told Cushman. "Everyone talks about me getting a title shot, and I always wind up sitting and watching (Nino) Benvenuti fighting somebody like (Tom) Bethea. I'll tell you, there have been days when I get in the mood to quit. I hope this works out."

Neither Bennie nor I had any idea what lay ahead but we couldn't wait to get started. My business no longer was a one-trick pony. I had the Blue Horizon, but with a major addition. I knew how the Yankees must have felt when they purchased Babe Ruth's contract from the Red Sox in 1920. Bennie Briscoe was about to lead us into the last golden age of boxing in Philadelphia.

Chapter Nine
Sophomore Season

TONIGHT'S BOXING PROGRAM

25 ¢

"BAD NEWS" NELSON

When we say the Blue Horizon "swings" back into action... we mean it..!!!

Tonight's card is featuring a showdown between two hard punching left hookers, Lloyd "Bad News" Nelson and Perry "Li'l" Abner. This 8 rounder should be a humdinger down to the wire and thrust a 160 pounder into the Monroe & Hart situation as "Philly's most promising middle prospects."

Backing up the main go is the co-feature. Veteran C. L. Lewis plays host to New Yorker "Smooth" Gary Bailey in a fast 8 between two knowledgeable welterweights.

Lots of prelims round out J. Russell Peltz's 3rd show of his 1970-71 season. A pair of six rounders are on tap.....

N.Y. Golden Gloves champ, "Baby" Harold Weston tangles with Bobby Zeiggler of Philly (147 pounders) and William Watson meets royalty in "Price" Nikita Tarhocker of Nigeria and countless other exotic hamlets (147 pounders).

Two more bouts of four round duration are scheduled.... Arthur Kettles of Asbury Park faces Robert Williams (147 pounders) and "Irish" Joe Johnson from Atlantic City draws Clarence Mann of Germantown. Both 140 pounders are making their pro debuts.

A well-rounded card with lots of fresh young talent on display as usual... PLUS.... your last chance to enter J.R.P.'s "Blue Horizon Quiz" (win 2 ringside seats to the next Horizon show free.!!!)

As we say down here.......
BOMBS AWAY..!!!!

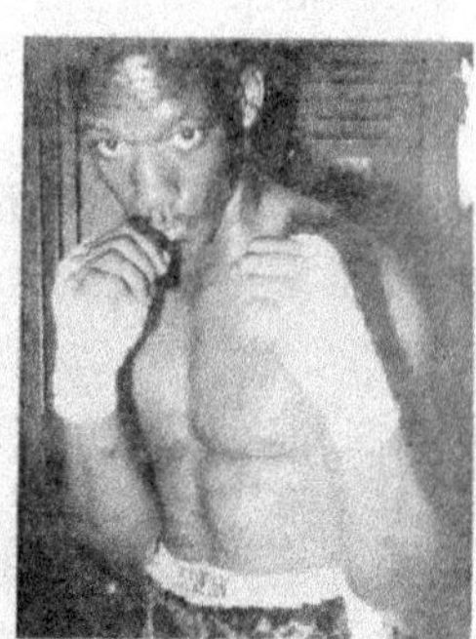

PERRY "LI'L" ABNER

C. L. LEWIS

"SMOOTH" GARY BAILEY

The number of boxing cards in Philadelphia increased from 11 in 1968 to 13 in 1969. It ballooned to 25 in 1970, the most since 1963 when there were 24. Jimmy Riggio, proprietor of the Passyunk Gym in South Philadelphia, had promoted at local venues since 1952, his biggest fight being the 1964 middleweight championship between Joey Giardello and Hurricane Carter at Convention Hall. But after his terrific lightweight match between Frankie Narvaez, of North York, and Roger Evans, of South Philly, drew a skimpy crowd into the Arena, he walked away, leaving the city to me, Lou Lucchese and Herman Taylor.

I reopened the Blue Horizon in September with middleweights Cyclone Hart and Leroy "Hurricane" Roberts, of Norristown, in the eight-round main event. Hart had fought twice since my last card in May, once in Delaware, once at the Arena. He was 12-0, 12 K0s. Roberts was a veteran (16-10, 5 K0s) who once had been on the fringes of the Top 10 welterweights.

Referee Frank Cappuccino had problems with the trash-talking Roberts, but a left hook from Hart in the third round shut Roberts up. In the fourth, another hook sent him flying—one leg suspended in mid-air—on his way to the canvas. He got up but Cappuccino stopped it at 2:59.

"He (Cappuccino) told him (Roberts) to quit biting me on the ear," Hart told Tom Cushman, of the *Daily News*. "What he did was kiss me. Now, don't ask me why. He was a pretty rough fighter, dirty enough. It was a good experience for me because I learned a few things. He hollered when I hit him with that left hook to the body in the fourth. He didn't try to kiss me after that."

The fans were back, buying 973 tickets at $3, $4 and $5. The gross receipts were $3,543 and my profit $205.64. I was now paying $100 for six rounds, $60 for four. Decisions outnumbered knockouts for just the second time and only one fight ended in the first round when Leroy Hunter, lured out of a North Philadelphia taproom the day of the fight, got stopped by Jose Rivera, of New York. Hunter boxed four more times in the next 28 months and never heard the bell for round two. I have no idea how old he was or if he ever saw the inside of a gym, but he was one of those soldiers who kept the cards alive and never got visibly hurt.

Rivera had slept in his manager's car until it was time to fight. This was not uncommon but I had a room for him. Out-of-town preliminary fighters often spent the day in movie theatres before I came along. I put them in hotels and fed them.

For the first time, one of my fights was filmed and it was by a New Yorker named Abe Fox, a New York bus driver.

I'd met Abe early in 1969 outside the Felt Forum, the 4,800-seat auxiliary arena at Madison Square Garden. I was working at the *Bulletin* and going by train to New York where I'd met him and other boxing junkies: Malcolm "Flash" Gordon; Johnny Bos; Don Majeski, and Jack Obermayer. Majeski, 16, was the youngest; Obermayer, 24, the oldest. Flash was 5-foot-5 with long, frizzy hair, often tied in a ponytail. He was founder, publisher and editor of *Flash Gordon's Tonight's Boxing Program & Newsletter*, a 25-cent 10-to-12-page underground newsletter produced on a mimeograph he had bought with his Bar Mitzvah money.

Flash ragged on everyone in the boxing establishment, from World Boxing Council (WBC) president Jose Sulaiman to Garden matchmaker Teddy Brenner to promoter Don King (aka Dung King). He'd post odds on his *Upcoming Fights* schedule and if he did not know the names of the so-called B-side prelim opponents, he would list them as Willie Standup, Izzy Human and Kenny Last.

Flash's artwork, a mélange of sketches and cartoons, was brilliant and he previewed not only the main event but also each undercard fighter with photos, some of which he took himself. The program included write-ups from Bos, Majeski, Obermayer and Bruce Trampler, a newcomer from Ohio University. It was so good some people bought it outside the Garden and never went in.

"Flash would generously let Bos and me sell his programs until we had enough money to buy a ticket and go inside and watch the fights," Trampler said.

One night in the summer of 1972, before an outdoor fight at the Singer Bowl in Flushing, Queens, Flash was arrested for selling without a license. After the police took him away in a paddy wagon—which added to his legend—a bunch of us crowded around the one guy who had bought a program prior to the arrest. That's how valuable his programs were.

Flash was first to expose Don King's United States Boxing Championships which ABC televised in 1977. King claimed he was featuring the best American fighters in different weight classes. *The Ring* magazine ratings allegedly added credibility but Flash revealed they were rigged, and bogus fights were added to records of King-picked fighters. Many solid pros, like Marvin Hagler, were not invited, while others had to turn over part of their contracts to King-favored managers.

Alex Wallau, then head of on-air promotion and later president of ABC, worked with Flash on the stories and notified Jim Spence, the No. 2 guy at ABC. The press picked up on it. ABC dropped out after a few telecasts and the tournament folded. One editor lost his job at *The Ring*. Thieves, disguised as booking agents, who had been making a score on the tournament, called Flash a "sewer mongrel" and "beatnik pothead with body odor" and threatened him physically. One had attacked him in Atlantic City.

Flash sold programs at my fights from 1969 to 1980. Abe Fox occasionally came and his Hart-Roberts video is the oldest in my collection.

In the early 1980s, Flash disappeared. He became a recluse and rarely left his apartment in Queens. He passed away in 2015 at the age of 65. Fox had passed from cancer sometime in the late 1970s or early 1980s. Bos, who became one of boxing's most influential matchmakers and booking agents, died in 2013 of congestive heart failure and pneumonia. Obermayer was 72 when liver cancer took him in 2016. He had seen 3,514 fight cards in 49 states and over 400 cities.

Two weeks after Hart-Roberts, Bennie Briscoe boxed Red Top Owens. Owens had 78 fights from 1964 to 1982. Though he finished barely above .500, he was a "tough out" for any middleweight or light-heavyweight of that era.

Owens was managed by Vito Tallarita, who twice had fought Willie Pep in the amateurs and was a matchmaker in New England during the 1960s, '70s and '80s. He accepted the $600 purse, but told me Owens could not make the 162 pounds he had made against George Benton in March. I told him to do his best.

At the weigh-in, Owens was 172. Briscoe was late but I knew the no-more-than-10-pounds rule and that when Briscoe was right, he was 158. This was the first time I controlled his career and I might have to cancel. Briscoe showed up and told me he had to piss. I begged him not to. I needed every ounce of liquid in his body, but he insisted. I followed him to the bathroom, stood next to the urinal and pleaded. But he pissed and got on the scale.

"One hundred sixty-three pounds, Bennie Briscoe," called out Sam Skversky, deputy commissioner. The fight was on. Briscoe never complained about the weight. He did not ask for extra money. He got examined and went home. This mindset was light years from 21st century boxing, where one or two pounds can cost the overweight fighter part of his bankroll and his first-born son.

Quenzell McCall, Briscoe's trainer, was not at the weigh-in, but that night at the Blue Horizon, I said, "I'm sorry, Quen, there was nothing I could do." He stuck his forefinger in my chest and said, "We're gonna knock him into your fuckin' lap." In the next day's press, McCall laid into the boxing commission for not fining Owens for being overweight, but that night only winning mattered.

The three prelims lasted less than six rounds but Briscoe and Owens saved the night. The head-snapping jab Briscoe had been inhibited from using when he was with Peers Management repeatedly nailed Owens, opening a cut over his right eye. Briscoe floored Owens in the sixth with a jab-left hook combination and it was over at 1:22. The crowd of 1,156 contributed a gross gate of $4,334. My profit was $459.16 ($3,200 in 2021 dollars). The top ticket still was $5.

The biggest fight of late 1970 in Philadelphia was between Sammy Goss and Augie Pantellas, of Broomall, a suburb 26 miles from Center City. Goss had boxed for me five times the first season and I wanted the fight.

Augustus Socrates Pantellas was the most popular White fighter in the area since Joey Giardello. He'd turned pro in 1967, the year Giardello retired. He had wrestled at Upper Darby High School at 103 pounds, making it to the semifinals of the state tournament in 1962, his senior year. He joined the Air Force at their Lackland Base in Texas, but was discharged six weeks after boot camp.

"Air Force is mostly schooling," Pantellas said. "If I was in the Army or Marines there's no way I would've got out, but I hated the schooling and just wouldn't do it. I kept complaining and one day I faked falling over as a captain was walking by. They sent me to several doctors and one thing led to another and I got a 1Y disability."

Pantellas told his friend, Jerry DeCaprio, that he wanted to box and DeCaprio introduced him to Marty Feldman, an ex-pro middleweight, to train him. Feldman took Pantellas to the basement of the Roman Bar at 39th and Sansom to teach the basics, then to the Passyunk Gym. With no amateur experience, Pantellas won 20 of his first 22 pro fights, 15 by knockout. What he lacked in technique, he made up for in power. In a city overrun with Black fighters, he stood out.

I signed Goss, but I couldn't get Pantellas, whose manager, Sam Margolis, wanted Herman Taylor to promote the match. Feldman wanted Lucchese. "The guy (Lucchese) helped us get here when there was no money," Feldman said. "It wouldn't be right to cut him out." Feldman got his wish. My wife felt sorry for me when she saw the video of the press conference on television, but promoters had to compete for the biggest fights and I was fine with it.

That was why having a family member or close friend managing a fighter was key, such as my brother-in-law managing Briscoe. Promotional contracts, where a fighter was signed to one promoter for a series of fights over a period of years, were not in vogue.

Goss outpointed Pantellas over 10 rounds in front of 10,743 fans at the Spectrum. The gate was $70,424. It was the largest local crowd since August 6, 1968, when Emile Griffith defeated Gypsy Joe Harris in the same ring in front of 13,875 who paid $118,389.

Seven days later, North Philly middleweights Lloyd Nelson and Li'l Abner (Perry Abney) met in the eight-round main event at the Blue Horizon. It was the first time I had matched two fighters from the inner city against each other in a main event. It was one of the best fights of the year and right where it belonged, in a small club with a big crowd (1,068).

Neighborhood rivalries had made Philadelphia a great fight town, but by the 21st century, a new crop of fighters, trainers and managers would fail to understand this, jockeying instead for so-called "championship" belts doled out wholesale by sanctioning bodies which collected fees for the alleged privilege.

Nelson and Abner traded bombs. Nelson won 38-37, 37-36 and 38-36 under Pennsylvania's five-point must system. I made $351.11. I scheduled a rematch for six weeks later, but Clarence "Skinny"

Davidson, who managed and trained Abner, signed with Lucchese, forcing Joe Fariello, who trained Nelson, to go along. Abner K0d Nelson at the Arena, Lucchese lost money, and I never spoke to Davidson again.

I promoted at the Arena the first time on Monday, November 2. It was the first season of *Monday Night Football* on ABC-TV and I underestimated its impact. Why would anyone in Philly, I thought, watch a game between the Pittsburgh Steelers and the Cincinnati Bengals? Briscoe scored a sixth-round knockout over Harold Richardson, a 31-year-old New Yorker who had beaten Joe Shaw and light-heavyweight contender Jimmy Dupree. The crowd was 2,217, gross receipts $10,254. I lost $2,101.41, wiping out all I'd made on the three Blue Horizon cards—and more.

That was the first of four straight losers which hit me through December. The 414 fans who saw lightweight Winston Noel, of New York, outpoint Ricky Thomas, of Brick Town, New Jersey, on November 24 at the Blue Horizon, was my smallest crowd to date. Cyclone Hart's December 9 knockout over late sub Jim Davis, of Detroit, drew only 676 customers, despite it being Hart's 16th straight knockout. I'd lost $4,571.26 combined ($31,583.41 in 2021) on the four cards. I asked Dad to lend me $1,500. I told him if I couldn't turn things around, I'd go back to the newspaper business and pay him back the following year.

Chapter Ten
Fight of the Century

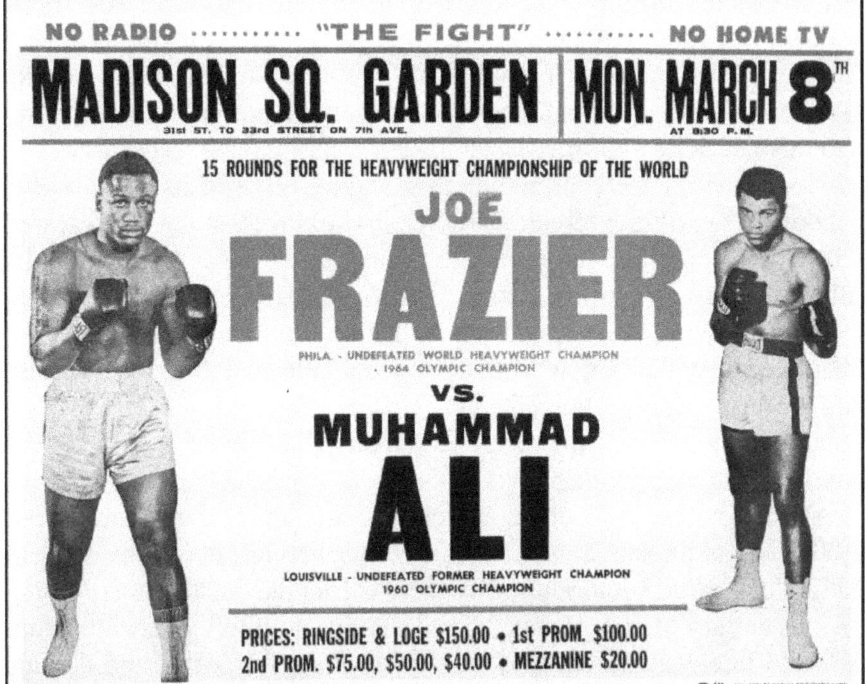

Joe Frazier began training at the Concord Hotel in the Catskill Mountains for his March 8, 1971, fight with Muhammad Ali, but he returned to Philadelphia when 17 inches of snow fell in early February, curtailing roadwork. Fans paid two dollars to watch him at the Cloverlay Gym on North Broad Street. His son, Marvis, collected the money at the door.

I stopped in to ask Yank Durham if one of Frazier's sparring partners, old-timer Don Warner, could fight February 22 at the Blue Horizon. To everyone in the gym, he roared, "I pay my sparring partners more than you can pay for a fight."

A few minutes later, Yank took me aside and told me he had 20 complimentary tickets for the Ali fight and he wanted to make some cash by selling. He didn't want to get caught so he needed someone to do the dirty work. "Whatever you get over the face value, we'll split," he said. One was a front-row ticket for $150 ($1,007 in 2021 dollars). I was 24 years old and not "street smart" so I sold them for their face value and gave the money to Yank.

I wrestled with the front-row ticket. Should I buy it or sell it? It was a lot of money for me at the time. I sold it to Ronald "Booster" McCoy, who ran the Tippin Bar, my favorite hangout, on the Northeast corner of Broad and South Streets. Booster was a fight fan and hustled tickets for me.

Ticket prices were high but this was advertised as, and would become, one of the greatest fights in boxing history. It featured Ali—the People's Champion—returning from exile to reclaim the title that had been stripped from him for refusing to enter the armed forces following his conversion to Elijah Muhammad's Nation of Islam, against Frazier, who had won the title in Ali's absence and had been falsely tagged an Uncle Tom, representing the Establishment. Both men were undefeated and everyone who was anyone wanted to be there.

About four weeks before March 8, Madison Square Garden put 2,000 tickets on sale at $20 each, two per person. I went by train to New York on a Sunday night with two friends. Tickets were going on sale at 8am Monday. A light, but steady snow fell. We were about 50th in a line of hundreds and took turns going for coffee and donuts. When the box office opened, we bought our tickets and left.

When I returned for the fight, I left one ticket at my hotel for a friend—who never showed up—and sat in my $20 seat high atop the Garden. I had binoculars and I scanned ringside, looking for Booster. I spotted him in the company of Frank Sinatra, Aretha Franklin and Diana Ross. "What a jerk!" I thought. "That could have been me."

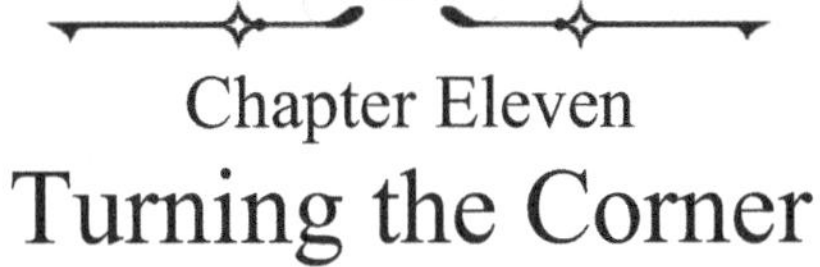

Chapter Eleven

Turning the Corner

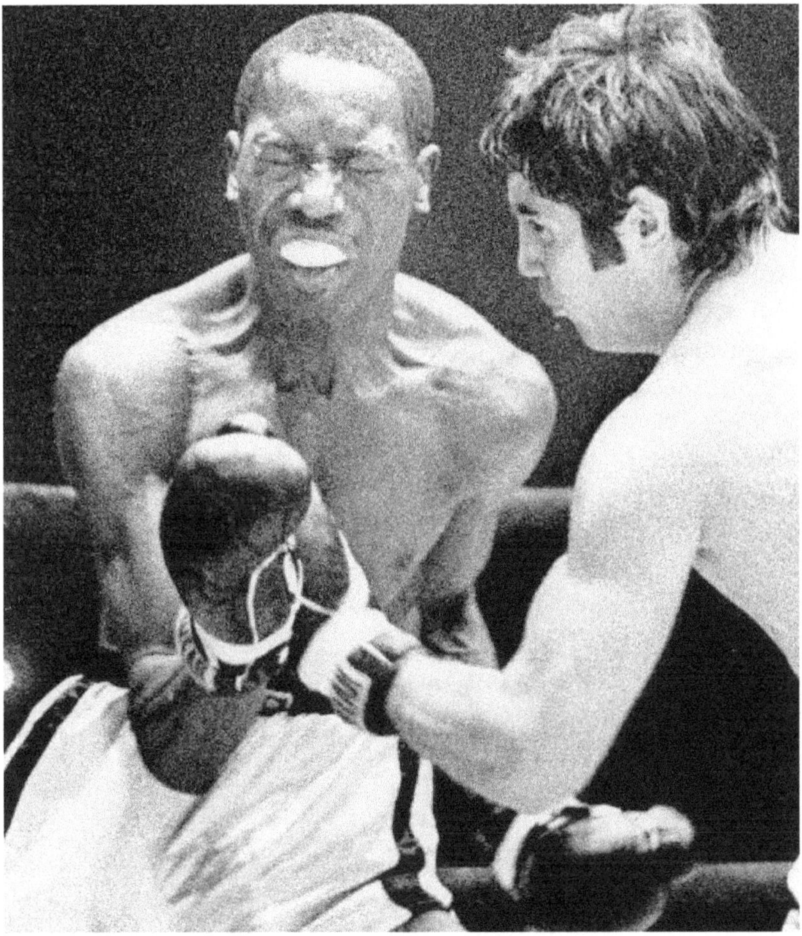

Johnny Bean takes a left from Augie Pantellas in 1971. (Peltz collection)

For the second straight year there were 25 cards in the city. I promoted 15 of them—11 at the Blue Horizon, three at the Arena and my first at the Spectrum. Herman Taylor promoted four, one at the Arena, three at the Spectrum. Joe Frazier ruled after his titanic win over Muhammad Ali, but local fighters were moving up. Bigger venues were needed and the Blue Horizon would suffer. Lou Lucchese ran twice at the Arena but it would be his last year. There was a new promoter in town, ex-lightweight champion Bob Montgomery.

Elliott Miller, of Brentwood, New York, agreed to fight Bennie Briscoe on January 12. Miller was 11-4-4. He came to Philadelphia for the pre-fight physical and press conference. As I got into my car to take him back to the train, Briscoe got in the back. He needed a ride home. Bad idea!

Miller bragged about the tough time he had given light-heavyweight contender Jimmy Dupree in his last fight, even though he had lost. "I ran that bitch out of camp," Briscoe said. All the way to the station, Briscoe mentioned fighters he had beaten up in training camps.

"Are you nuts?" I said after Miller left. "I guarantee you Miller is gonna pull out of the fight." Bennie shrugged.

The next night Freddie Menna, Miller's manager, told me he'd canceled. I cannot recall if I had a signed contract but as Teddy Brenner once said, "Did you ever see a contract fight?"

Menna offered light-heavyweight Ned Edwards. I was desperate so I agreed. Edwards had lost to Red Top Owens, Len Hutchins, Frankie DePaula and just about everyone else. I billed him as 11-8-1 but in the *Daily News*, Tom Cushman wrote: "The book says that prior to 1970, Ned's one victory was over the ever-popular Yucatan Fredericks in Secaucus back in 1969. Logic says that if Briscoe uncoils a left hook, Edwards makes it even money to make it back to New York faster than Elliott Miller did."

My concern was making sure Edwards was no more than 10 pounds heavier than Briscoe. He came to Philly early the morning of the fight and I took him to the Athletic Commission. I told Executive Secretary Bob Patterson that Edwards was starving and needed to weigh early so he could eat. Before he got on the scale, though, I had rolled the balance cylinder, one way or the other as far as I could, so that he would weigh less than 170. I called Patterson, whose eyesight was far from 20/20, and he read off "167 pounds." We said we would be back at noon. Edwards was at least 175. Briscoe was 160.

The fight drew 1,038 fans. I was standing under the balcony on the South side of the Blue Horizon behind five rows of ringside seats. Willie Fisher, Briscoe's friend, was with me. When Edwards took off his robe, the crowd buzzed. He had muscles on top of muscles and looked twice Briscoe's size. Fisher grabbed my right arm and told me I wasn't going anywhere until the fight was over.

When the ring announcer called out 167 pounds for Edwards, everyone laughed. Edwards fired bombs for the first two minutes until Briscoe hit him in the body. "From that point, Edwards had no more business in the ring with Briscoe than a Siamese pussycat has in a lion's cage," Gene Courtney wrote in the *Inquirer*. It was over in two.

Sammy Goss returned February 9 in his first fight since being shockingly stopped the previous November by future World Boxing Council (WBC) junior lightweight champion Ricardo Arredondo, of Mexico, at the Spectrum. Goss destroyed Carlos Zayas, of Holyoke, Massachusetts. I'd advertised Zayas as 25-22-3, but his real record was 16-27-4 with four K0 wins and four K0 losses.

All 1,346 seats were sold ($5,330 gate), but a competitive undercard was followed by an embarrassing main event. Goss won every minute of every round. Referee Ed Marion refused to stop it, even early in the fifth after Zayas' manager, Vito Tallarita, climbed onto the apron and threw in the towel. When Marion finally waved it off at 2:04 of the fifth, fans tossed bottles, cans and paper cups into the ring. It was my second largest crowd and my first riot.

"Put it all together and what you had was a powerful performance by Sammy Goss, a mismatch of the first order by the promoter, a butchered job of refereeing by Ed Marion, and another sordid display by hoodlums who mask themselves as fight fans," Cushman wrote. I never complained to Cushman. If I deserved to be roasted, fine. My $847.70 profit ($5,508 in 2021) was little compensation.

Two weeks later, Mario Saurennann, of North Philly, got off the canvas in the fourth round to knock out C.L. Lewis, of West Philly, in the 12th for the vacant Pennsylvania welterweight title. It was a Blue Horizon classic few people remember, coming two weeks before Ali-Frazier. Hollywood icon Burt Lancaster, who'd been hired to work with Don Dunphy and Archie Moore on the *Fight of the Century* telecast, was there with Frazier's trainer Yank Durham, who managed Saurennann.

Ali-Frazier had everyone focused on boxing and I went back to the Arena, this time with Briscoe against Tom "The Bomb" Bethea, of New York.

Bethea had been just another guy one year earlier. He had lost four in a row when manager Gil Clancy sent him to Melbourne, Australia, for a non-title fight with world middleweight champion Nino Benvenuti, of Italy. It was a tradition for world champions to have non-title or over-the-weight matches. With crowns not at stake, champs could make a few dollars without risk.

Benvenuti was 80-3-1, 30 KOs; Bethea 9-5-1, 4 KOs. Claiming a broken rib, Benvenuti refused to answer the bell for the ninth round. Bethea went from being just another club fighter on the New York circuit to a contender. Ten weeks later, in a world title fight in Umag, Yugoslavia, Benvenuti KOd him in the eighth.

Three weeks before Briscoe-Bethea, I got a call from Flash Gordon, who was at Clancy's Telstar Gym in New York. "Somebody wants to talk to you, Russell, and I don't think you're gonna like it." Bethea got on the phone and said he was not fighting Briscoe for the agreed-upon $3,000. He wanted $4,000. Clancy was out of the country. To save the show, I capitulated.

A week later I was in New York for Ali-Frazier and I stopped by Telstar. Clancy gave me an earful. "Listen carefully, Russell," he said. "When I make a deal for a fighter, I bring the fighter into my office, sit him down and explain everything to him. If he agrees, we have a match. You never should have given Bethea the extra money. It makes me look bad. I would help you out and not take my one-third of the extra money, but I'm going to teach you a lesson. You've got to pay us the entire $4,000."

Clancy was one of the sharpest boxing people I ever knew and he had been the first big-time out-of-town manager who showed me respect. I learned a lesson.

Briscoe-Bethea on March 22 drew 4,453. After six rounds, ringside physician Dr. Alfred Ayella stopped it. Bethea had a lump over his closed right eye. His left eye was a slit and he bled from his nose.

"It was nothing more than a savage street fight: no artistry, no boxing skill, just a test of severe brutality as Briscoe and Bethea fought toe-to-toe and referee Pete Tomasco rarely had to separate them," Courtney wrote.

Augie Pantellas, in his first fight for me, stopped Johnny Bean in six sloppy rounds of the 10-round junior lightweight semifinal. Bean was a 35-year-old from Brooklyn who had lost to some of the best, including world champions Sugar Ramos, Carlos Teo Cruz (twice) and Harold Gomes. His record was 17-27-2 and he had been stopped 14 times, including one 16 days prior by Leo DeFiore in Portland, Maine. The automatic 30-day suspension for anyone knocked out would not be in effect for years.

In the third 10-rounder, Cyclone Hart scored his 18th straight knockout, stopping Canadian Jimmy Meilleur in four rounds. It was the biggest night of my 19-month career. The gate was $26,080. I made $4,315.60 ($28,951 in 2021) and paid back Dad. Briscoe had his biggest payday. His 20 percent of the net gate came to $4,627 ($31,040).

Seven days later in the same ring, Lucchese sold 5,812 tickets ($32,222 gate) when ex-world heavyweight champion Floyd Patterson stopped Roger Russell in nine rounds. It was Russell's first fight since his one-round loss to George Foreman eight months earlier. Lucchese had been promoting since 1962, but when less than 1,000 fans turned out the following month to watch Sammy Goss knock out Beau Jaynes in the first round, he left boxing. Any future plans were dashed in 1973 when Lucchese's son, Louis, was killed in an automobile accident.

Sam Solomon, Hart's manager, wanted Kitten Hayward next. Kitten's career was in free fall. Since beating Emile Griffith late in 1968, he'd lost to Freddie Little in Las Vegas for the vacant junior middleweight title and dropped a rematch to Griffith in Madison Square Garden. A European tour with stops in Paris and Rome netted him one win, two losses and a draw—but let him act in some Spaghetti Westerns and a blue flick. He'd also lost to Alvin Phillips in New Orleans, but he still was Kitten Hayward and he would be the biggest name on Hart's resume.

I picked Kitten up one night, along with trainer Adolph Ritacco, at the Rickshaw Inn across from Garden State (Race) Park in Cherry Hill, New Jersey. The Rickshaw was adjacent to the Latin Casino, the most popular area nightclub of its time where entertainers like

Diana Ross, Frank Sinatra, Liza Minelli, Tony Bennett and Louis Armstrong performed. This was Kitten's world: fast horses, tailor-made suits and big-name celebs.

We drove into Philly for dinner at Arthur's, a steak house in Center City. Kitten insisted on 25 percent of the gate, with a guarantee of $4,000. The guarantee was fine. I should have talked him down to 20 percent, but I was still a fan who wanted to see the fight so I agreed. Hart got the same guarantee plus 25 percent of the gate over $30,000.

I added two more 10-rounders: Briscoe against Carlos Marks, of Trinidad, and Pantellas against Durango Kid, of New York. I charged the same $4, $6 and $8 I had for Briscoe-Bethea.

Jack Fried never came to my press conferences. It irked him to show respect to a kid who had worked under him. He would call the Athletic Commission to ask which fights I had submitted, then write his story to "scoop" the other newspapers. I'd caught on and told commission secretary Patterson I was going to announce Briscoe against Curtis Cokes and Hart against Luis Rodriguez. The *Bulletin* ran Fried's story of the bogus doubleheader which made him look foolish when the *Inquirer* and *Daily News* printed the correct attraction. Maybe I should have tried to smooth things over with Fried, but I was too busy patting myself on the back for the ruse.

Briscoe was not happy fighting "underneath" Hart since he was the bigger name. I made it worse by using big pictures and big names of Hart and Hayward on the poster, relegating Briscoe and Pantellas to smaller type with no pictures.

One Saturday morning I went searching for him on Columbia Avenue. When I found him we drove to Quenzell McCall's house three minutes away. Hayward wouldn't fight Briscoe and I needed Bennie on the card to keep his momentum going. My brother-in-law was the manager, but Briscoe sided with Quenzell so I asked them to do me a favor. They agreed but McCall said, "This will be the only time we ever fight under Hart or any other middleweight in Philadelphia."

A crowd of 6,642 paid $43,057 on May 3 to see Hart's "coming out" party. He demolished Hayward in 60 seconds. A left hook—what else—caught Hayward on the chin with his back to the ropes. He went down, got up and another assault forced referee Zach

Clayton to stop it. It was spectacular. Hayward got $9,612.24 ($62,908 in 2021). Hart got $6,112.24 ($40,002).

Marks knocked an off-balance Briscoe down in the second round—Briscoe's first time down—but before and after that he took a beating. Briscoe pushed him out of clinches, never gave him a chance to set himself and pounded his body and head. When Marks got off his stool for round five, Briscoe was on him. It was over in 31 seconds. Pantellas K0d Durango Kid in two, and one of the all-Philly prelims was a show-stopper as welterweight William Watson drilled Melvin Mayfield with a combination and, as Mayfield was going down, hit him with another left hook, bringing the crowd to its feet. Everyone went home happy.

When I went to the box office, Fried was looking at my contracts. I slammed my hand on the table and grabbed them. It was none of his business and I was pissed. Fried left but wrote that I had become wealthy overnight, seeing only the $4,000 guarantees for Hart and Hayward, not the percentages they had. I'd overpaid, but we had sold out the Arena and I was proud of that. My profit was $4,315.60 ($28,243).

I'd said that a Hayward victory would set up a rematch with Briscoe. Solomon used that as an excuse to take Hart to Herman Taylor for his next fight. I was not happy. I had promoted 16 of Hart's 19 consecutive knockouts. Of the other three, I had produced one opponent and okayed the other two. Taylor was one of boxing's greatest promoters. His career began in 1912. Nearly every heavyweight champion from Jack Dempsey to George Foreman had boxed for him. So had Lew Tendler, Sugar Ray Robinson, Kid Gavilan, Ike Williams, Bob Montgomery, Beau Jack, Harold Johnson….

Like "Bow-Legged" Charlie Brown had warned me: "If you crush the grapes, make sure you drink the wine." Without promotional contracts you needed to trust the manager you were working with. I had trusted Solomon and we had worked well together. But he had been around boxing a long time and he thought going to Taylor was his next step. One day I would be in Taylor's shoes but that was years away. Solomon and I never again would be close and Hart never again mine exclusively.

The Garden's Teddy Brenner, Taylor's long-time pal, delivered veteran Don Fullmer, of West Jordan, Utah, to fight Hart. That card, eight weeks later at the Spectrum, drew 6,796 who paid $42,468. Hart went 10 rounds for the first time. He faded late but his early lead earned him scores of 47-44, 47-43 and 47-43.

The success of my Arena shows led me to the Spectrum. Dad gave me $3,000 in return for 50 percent of the profits. The August 10 card featured Briscoe, Hart, Goss and Watts in 10-round fights. Juarez DeLima, of Brazil, who had beaten Briscoe in 1969 in New York, agreed to the rematch for $3,000. But before contracts were signed, DeLima decisioned contender Tom Bogs, whose record had been 57-2-1, in Copenhagen. This time, Clancy asked for the extra $1,000 because Delima's win had made him more valuable. He was correct.

Hart was matched with Fate Davis, of Akron, Ohio. Davis was a blown-up welterweight and I paid Hart more than I thought he was worth. Solomon insisted that Hart be the main event but the day of the fight I chose the 12-rounder between Goss and Lloyd Marshall, of Newark, New Jersey, which I'd advertised for the vacant North American Boxing Federation (NABF) title. The crowd was 8,642. Briscoe destroyed DeLima in two rounds, Hart K0d Davis in five, Goss whipped Marshall in seven and Watts stopped Junius Hinton, of New York, in five.

I paid Dad back his $3,000. My profit was $11,163.69 ($73,061), by far my biggest payday.

"Where's my 50 percent of the profit?" Dad asked.

"C'mon, Dad, you've got enough money," I said.

"Reds, can you believe this son of yours!" he said to Mom as I sneaked out of the room.

Taylor promoted Hart's September fight against another "big name," Denny Moyer, of Portland, Oregon. Hart dropped Moyer with a left hook in the first round, and they battled until the sixth when they fell through a loose rope and over the press tables onto the concrete floor. Moyer sprained his right ankle and suffered a bone chip in his foot. Hart was temporarily K0'd. Both went for Xrays and Hart stayed overnight in St. Agnes Hospital. It was ruled No Contest.

The injury forced Hart off the annual Deborah Hospital card November 15 at the Spectrum. Matchmaker Jack Puggy wanted Briscoe to fill in against Rafael Gutierrez, a Mexican puncher whose 45-6-3 record included 30 knockouts. Gutierrez had beaten some blown-up welterweights nearing the finish line: Luis Rodriguez,

Curtis Cokes, Battling Torres and L.C. Morgan and several second-tier middleweights. Briscoe was coming off a one-round knockout over Charlie “Bad News” Austin on my October 14 card at the Arena.

A crowd of 7,319 came. Thirty seconds into the fight, Gutierrez knocked Briscoe into the ropes with a big right hand, then down. Thirty seconds later he was down again, on his face. I felt sick. I headed for the tunnel to the dressing rooms. I turned to watch the inevitable and saw Briscoe wade into Gutierrez. Half the crowd wanted referee Pete Tomasco to stop it, the other half wanted Briscoe to clinch. Neither happened! Just as the bell sounded—or a split second after—Briscoe dug a left hand into Gutierrez' midsection—or below—and down he went on all fours.

“I was on cloud nine,” Briscoe told Bill Conlin, of the *Daily News*. “I felt all kind of high and floaty. It felt real good to tell the truth. But I sensed I was in trouble. The last time I went down I got my head together. When the haze cleared away I knew I had to keep him off.”

Gutierrez' handlers dragged him to the corner. McCall grabbed Briscoe—who always stood between rounds—and threw him onto the stool. A revitalized Briscoe banged away at Gutierrez in round two. Gutierrez was bleeding from the eyes, nose and mouth and folded after a pair of left-right combinations. The time was 2:17. Fans poured into the ring. It was a Hollywood ending to a great night but no film exists. Abe Fox had left his camera in New York.

The success of the bigger shows hurt the Blue Horizon. Seven of my 11 cards there lost money, despite being headlined Richie Kates, Boogaloo Watts and Jimmy Young. Then, in the fall, landlord Jimmy Toppi, seeing my success at bigger venues, gave dates to Bob Montgomery, “fronting” as promoter for Joe Gramby and New York booking agent Al Braverman. Marty Kramer made a comeback as matchmaker. Their first show, featuring local featherweight Luis Lopez, sold out, but their next two shows drew 516 and 555. I told Toppi it was hard for one promoter to succeed at the Blue Horizon, let alone two, but he wouldn't listen so I headed west—to West Philly—and Montgomery folded.

Chapter Twelve
The Arena

Pete Tomasco gets the count on Luis Vinales from JJ Harrington. (Peltz collection)

The number of local cards fell to 13 in 1972. I promoted 11 at the Arena. Taylor promoted one there, and the last of the annual Deborah Hospital cards at the Spectrum saw Sammy Goss avenge a loss to Jose Luis Lopez. Joe Frazier twice defended his world heavyweight title in 1972, knocking out no-hope challengers Terry Daniels and Ron Stander. The win over Daniels was on the eve of Super Bowl VI in New Orleans, a practice promoters would try again and again without success. People are more interested in getting hammered at parties than going to boxing matches.

Middleweights ruled Philadelphia, but cracks appeared below the surface. Bennie Briscoe began the year with a pair of brutal knockouts, but Cyclone Hart, not so much. Boogaloo Watts won in Scranton, Baltimore and New York and finished a trilogy with Maryland contender Ralph Palladin, sandwiching two wins around a draw. Watts had not lost since his 1970 West Coast trip. Willie Monroe lost for the first time in his 21st fight when Frenchman Max Cohen outpointed him in Paris in March. Less than six months later, Alvin Phillips beat him in New Orleans.

I had promoted one card at the Arena in 1970 and three in 1971, but it was time to move there permanently. Fighters I worked with had outgrown the Blue Horizon.

The Arena could have been the backdrop for those 1940s film noir boxing movies, like *Body and Soul* and *The Set Up*. John Garfield or Robert Ryan would have felt at home. It opened in 1920 and hosted ice hockey, basketball, wrestling, boxing and the Roller Derby. There was a balcony on all four sides and as many as 20 elevated rows behind the wooden ringside seats. There was no air conditioning. The dressing rooms were primitive—no cubicles—with hooks on the walls for clothes.

Sonja Henie debuted there as a skater after winning a gold medal in the 1936 Winter Olympics. The Roy Rogers Rodeo played the Arena for 20 years. When a young cowgirl died after falling from a bucking bronco, her funeral was held there. Rogers and the Sons of the Pioneers sang *Roundup in the Sky* and everyone rode out to the cemetery. Next door was what would become the WFIL-TV studios where American Bandstand and Dick Clark rose to fame in the 1950s.

Boxing royalty fought at the Arena: Lew Tendler; George Godfrey; Benny Bass; Gene Tunney; Mickey Walker; Tommy Loughran; Primo Carnera; Sugar Ray Robinson; Ike Williams; Joey Giardello; Harold Johnson, and Joe Frazier. It was the city's premier sports venue, even after Convention Hall opened in 1931, two miles away.

Edna Toppi had inherited the building when her husband, Jimmy Toppi, died in 1967. There was friction between her and her stepson, Jimmy Jr., who owned the Blue Horizon. They rarely spoke.

A new middleweight burst onto the scene on February 7—Billy "Dynamite" Douglas, whose punch matched his nickname. His record was 18-6-1, 12 K0s, but he was approaching his 32nd birthday and, despite quality wins over Tom Bethea and Wilbert "Skeeter" McClure, was treading water in his Columbus, Ohio, hometown. Douglas had floored rock-chinned Don Fullmer twice in a 1970 fight there, but had to settle for a draw after a recount of the scorecards.

He had lost 10-round decisions to Jamaican contender Bunny Sterling in London, and to Puerto Rican contender Jose Gonzales in San Juan. He was a Black man with a big punch who needed a new home to showcase his talent.

Douglas' manager was Bruce Trampler, from Flash Gordon's crowd. He'd grown up in Maplewood, New Jersey, and been hooked on boxing since attending the Frazier-George Chuvalo heavyweight fight the summer of 1967 at the Garden. As a freshman at Ohio University, Trampler had hitchhiked 75 miles to a fight card in Columbus to write about Douglas for the student newspaper. Douglas won, but told Trampler he needed help.

Trampler began booking fights for Douglas and became his manager in 1971, the same year he graduated with a journalism degree. *Sound familiar?*

When I called, Trampler was working in Miami Beach for the Dundee brothers, Chris and Angelo. Originally from South Philadelphia, the Dundees had worked the East Coast circuit until the early 1950s when they moved to Miami Beach. Chris promoted and owned the Fifth Street Gym where Angelo trained world champions like Willie Pastrano, Ralph Dupas, Muhammad Ali and Jimmy Ellis. He'd also worked with Carmen Basilio, Jose Napoles and later, Sugar Ray Leonard.

Billy Lloyd, a hard-punching southpaw from West Philadelphia, agreed to fight Douglas. Lloyd, managed by Joe Gramby, was 14-5-2, 12 K0s. He had beaten Alvin Phillips three times, but he was too small for Douglas, having never weighed more than 156 pounds. When Douglas was 162 at the weigh-in, two pounds over, Gramby insisted he sweat them off. Douglas did not even try. Gramby gave me an earful that night and it cost Douglas $200 of his $1,200 purse. But what happened made the fine—and the earful—irrelevant.

Douglas attacked from the opening bell, shook off a hard left and landed four brutal rights which left Lloyd draped over the middle rope, his head on the canvas. It was over in 61 seconds, but Douglas was just warming up. He leaped around the ring and segued into a victory dance which lasted as long as the fight. He had the crowd of 3,437 whooping, a stunning way to say hello to the hard-core Philadelphia fans. Douglas became an instant hit in a new town.

I pounded on Trampler's shoes as he stood on the apron waiting for Douglas to calm down. "We're gonna make a lot of money with this guy," I screamed, but he could barely hear me above the roar.

"Billy wanted to make the early editions of the Columbus papers," Trampler dead-panned to Tom Cushman, of the *Daily News*. "You can't judge Douglas by where he lives. He has the same kind of guns as these Philadelphia fighters. He is an animal in the ring. He belongs in the Philadelphia Zoo."

Douglas added: "I played in the marching band in my high school. I got my own rock and roll band. I love music. Any time I'm happy I dance."

Gate receipts totaled $21,480. Tickets were $4, $6 and $8. Coupled with the January 18 crowd (3,323 paid $20,892), who saw Briscoe knock out Al Quinney, of Buffalo, New York, the year looked promising.

Hart headlined the night Douglas stole the show. Doctors had okayed him as recovered from the injuries from his fall from the ring the previous September. He fought Matt Donovan, a slick boxer from Trinidad whose 16-6-3 included wins over Angel Espada, Ralph Paladin and Carlos Marks. Like Lloyd, Donovan was a junior middleweight and, like Douglas, Hart was a powerful middleweight. It was over in two rounds.

Donovan was managed by George Gainford, who had managed Sugar Ray Robinson. We had agreed on the price by phone, but Gainford showed up in my office one week later to change the contract I had mailed him. Instead of the agreed-upon $4,000, Gainford wanted a new contract for $3,000—and the extra $1000 for himself. Years later, this practice became common, but it was new to me. Whether Gainford also took a "cut" from Donovan's purse, I have no clue.

In the crowd that night was Juan Carlos "Tito" Lectoure, promoter at Luna Park in Buenos Aires, Argentina. We had met earlier in New York to discuss Briscoe-Carlos Monzon that spring for the world middleweight title. But that was a long way off, longer than I knew.

Herman Taylor brought Hart back four weeks later against Nate Collins. Taylor had never promoted a middleweight championship fight and wanted to end his dry spell by getting Hart a shot at Monzon, ahead of Briscoe.

The 27-year-old Collins was 22-13, 15 K0s. He was from California, but it was the lighter-weight Mexican fighters who made big money in Los Angeles, not Black middleweights from Oakland. Collins had won eight of his last nine, beating contenders Andy Heilman, Juarez DeLima and Jimmy Lester, and losing only to Emile Griffith.

Hart started fast, banging Collins around in the first round, knocking him down in the second and dominating the third. Then Hart began to tire.

"It was like a pea shooter destroying a cannon," Gene Courtney wrote in the *Inquirer*, "but the weary Hart, cut over both eyes and bleeding from the mouth, had no artillery shells left. Collins, also bleeding from a cut over the right eye, popped Hart with short jabs and weak right hands and gradually wore him down until the Philadelphian stood by almost helpless, absorbing everything the Californian threw at him."

Ringside physician Dr. Wilbur H. Strickland stopped it after the seventh round. Manager/trainer Sam Solomon said Hart had the flu and he (Solomon) should have postponed the fight. Hart would not fight for more than a year and, when he did, Solomon was gone.

Two weeks later, Douglas was back on my card, topped by Briscoe's first-round demolition of Jorge Rosales, of Mexico. Douglas was not the guy who had won over the crowd in February. Carlos Marks survived a second-round knockdown and an eighth-round battering and led on points. During the ninth round, Trampler came over and said, "It's not your fault (for making the match). Douglas is terrible."

Late in the 10th, a left hook drove Marks into a neutral corner but he appeared to be avoiding Douglas' follow-up shots and was fighting back when referee Frank Cappuccino stopped it with less than 30 seconds to go. Fans pelted the ring with bottles, a chair and other debris. There was a great headline in the Daily News: *Ben's Knockout Party Bottled Up.*

The crowd of 4,638 paid $29,818. Briscoe's 25 percent of the gate was $6,603.35 ($42,000 in 2021), largest of his career at the time.

Trampler never forgave me for putting him in a cheap hotel suite with Chino Govin, a trainer from Cuba who had a fighter on the card. Govin walked around barefoot and only had three toes on one foot.

The Douglas-Marks rematch two months later proved that two out-of-towners couldn't draw. Only 1,722 came to see Douglas win by decision and it cost me nearly half the money I made the night of their first fight.

One month before the Douglas-Mark rematch, I was in Scranton, 125 miles from Philadelphia. Briscoe was fighting Luis Vinales.

Scranton (population 90,000) was a popular fight town in the 1960s and 1970s. The 5,000-seat Catholic Youth Center (CYC) was its premier venue. George Foreman boxed there in his ninth pro fight, light-heavyweight champion Bob Foster defended there twice and Larry Holmes had eight of his first 10 pro fights at the CYC.

Between them, Willie Gilzenberg, Paul Ruddy, Henry Ventre and Snap Nagelberg promoted at least eight cards a year at the CYC. Ventre ran the Briscoe-Vinales card on April 19 as a benefit for the Chic Feldman Memorial Fund benefit. Feldman, sports editor of the *Scranton-Tribune* and a life-long boxing fan, had died at ringside at Madison Square Garden three months before.

Briscoe was a 7-1 favorite over Vinales, a New York-based Puerto Rican. Rated No. 1 at 160 pounds, Briscoe was 29 and had knocked out his last 11 opponents. Vinales, also 29, was 18-17-5. He had scored two knockouts and had been stopped four times, once by Douglas, once by Monroe. But Briscoe was awful—no snap, no drive, nothing—and Vinales won a 10-round split decision (47-44, 44-46, 47-44).

All my work getting Briscoe close to a world championship fight seemed wasted. When I got back to Philadelphia, I didn't go home. I went to the Center City apartment of my friend, Nigel Collins, and spent the day there. I am not sure if I even called my wife. When I went to the office Dad had built for me in his plumbing company building, I kept the lights off and wouldn't answer the phone. When I finally picked up, it was Dewey Fragetta, the international booking agent who had helped put me with Tito Lectoure to negotiate Monzon-Briscoe.

"Where have you been?" he yelled.

"Dewey, I'm so depressed, I don't know what to do," I said.

"Grow up! Now we'll find out what kind of promoter you really are."

I called Bobby Gleason, the 80-year-old veteran who managed Vinales with Bobby Kirk. Gleason (born Robert Peter Gagliardi) had managed featherweight champion Phil Terranova in the 1940s and heavyweight contender Nino Valdes in the 1950s. He ran Gleason's, one of boxing's iconic gyms which had opened in 1937 in the Bronx.

Gleason wanted $10,000 ($65,000 in 2021) for the rematch, but no one was paying Vinales that kind of money in an era of sparse television fights.

I got a call from Woodrow Wilson Larroseaux, a New York-based Cuban who managed welterweight Miguel Barreto. Barreto was trained by another Cuban, Jose Caron Gonzalez, who also trained Vinales. "I can get you Vinales," Larroseaux said, "but he wants $7,000."

Going behind the manager's back was wrong, but I was desperate. Gleason threatened to stop the fight but I scheduled it for June 5 at the Arena. Another problem popped up. I had promised my wife a five-week cross-country car trip starting the end of May, Briscoe-Vinales rematch or not. While Pat and I were on the road, my dad and my brother-in-law took control of the card. If you've been married, you don't have to ask why I didn't stay.

Briscoe failed to show up for the pre-fight physical May 30. Vinales came from New York but no one knew where Briscoe was. Two days later the fight was off. Briscoe had checked into Metropolitan Hospital with a fever and stomach pains and was diagnosed with a mild case of hepatitis. Whether he had this when he lost to Vinales never was substantiated. After being released on June 8, Brisoce could not return to sanitation work until June 30 and could not train until August 1. A proposed July 24 fight with Monzon was scrapped.

The June 5 show went on. Sammy Goss K0d Jose Jimenez, of the Dominican Republic, in seven rounds, and Barreto stopped Adrian Davis, of Washington, DC, in 10. When Cushman asked Dad about his first venture into promoting, he said: "If you have any plumbing problems, call me."

I began working on a new date for Briscoe-Vinales II. Quenzell wanted to go directly to the title fight, but after the July 24 date went kaput, so did an August date and dates for September and October.

Briscoe needed to get down from the 195 pounds he weighed when he returned to the gym. Then Monzon needed to recover from a cut eye sustained in an August defense against Tom Bogs in Copenhagen.

Briscoe-Vinales II was set for October 11 at the Arena, 31 days before the now-signed-and-sealed title fight in Buenos Aires. It was not unusual for fights to be scheduled so close together. Briscoe had not boxed in more than six months and needed work. Besides, with so many postponements, it was not like November 11 was written in stone.

The Arena's biggest crowd of the year (4,765) saw Briscoe hurt Vinales several times, but miss wildly trying to finish him. He was barely ahead, if at all, after six rounds. Mary Ann Seymour, Nigel Collins' wife and a Briscoe fanatic, walked out of the fight and sat on the concrete floor outside the box office, trembling, tears running down her face. I walked into the box office and said to Mom, "I guess we won't be going to Argentina after all."

Just then I heard a roar, ran back to the ring and saw referee Pete Tomasco stop the fight at 2:41 in the seventh after Briscoe landed a series of right hands to knock Vinales down twice.

"People don't realize how much pressure I've had on me," Briscoe told Cushman. "I've waited so long to get a shot at the championship, and then to have it all depend on fighting a boy like this. But I needed a fight and I couldn't fight his sister. I admit I was excited. I've been lying in bed every night wondering if anything could go wrong this time. I kept telling myself it was just a matter of time catching him. But last time I couldn't catch him."

The State Athletic Commission held up $2,262 from Vinales' $7,000 purse and awarded it to Gleason and Kirk. Briscoe got $3,000, but better days were ahead.

Chapter Thirteen

Argentina

Bennie Briscoe was one punch away in 1972. (Courtesy of El Grafico)

When Argentina's Carlos Monzon knocked out Italy's Nino Benvenuti in 1970 in Rome to win the world middleweight title, I was ecstatic. Benvenuti avoided fighting Bennie Briscoe, and no one knew about Monzon. Two years later, Briscoe flew to Buenos Aires to fight him. Boxing had not yet been bastardized by the alphabet groups and world titles still meant something. The middleweight champion was second in popularity to the heavyweight champion. It was a thrill to be there, let alone involved.

Most of Monzon's record (67-3-9, 45 K0s) had been compiled against South Americans and a handful of unranked Americans. When he and Briscoe boxed a draw midway through 1967, it was the first time in 50 fights he had boxed an American-based opponent.

Briscoe signed for $15,000 ($95,000 in 2021) for the November 11, 1972, championship fight. The day of his flight to Buenos Aires, he couldn't find his black-red-green *Black Power* boxing trunks, so he'd bought what Pearson's Sporting Goods had in stock—white trunks with black stripes—in that rectangular box with the cellophane front where you can see the trunks without opening the box. It was a far cry from today when fighters care as much about their ring attire and their ring walks as they do their opponents.

Dad, Arnold and I were met at the Buenos Aires airport by one of the promoter's assistants, Phillip B. Crapper, a descendant of the Crapper family that had perfected the toilet. We snapped a photo of him with Dad and labeled it: *The Plumber and the Crapper.*

When we arrived at the Sheltown Hotel in the middle of the shopping and restaurant district, the first thing cut man Milt Bailey said was, "Bennie is running in the mornings like a deer." Quenzell McCall had not believed Bennie's poor performance against Luis Vinales was due to hepatitis. He suspected—correctly—that Bennie was not doing enough roadwork. McCall got Bennie back on track, so to speak, taking him at 5:30 every morning for a six-mile run. By the time he got to Argentina, Bennie was in the best shape of his career.

I had company in my hotel room. Donald Majeski, who was making $600 a month writing for *Boxing Illustrated*, needed a place to sleep, so my sofa was converted into a pullout bed.

Luna Park, site of the fight, had been built in 1912 as an outdoor amusement park and outfitted with a roof and 22,000 seats in 1934. The Madison Square Garden of South America, it hosted ice shows, the circus, political rallies, the Harlem Globetrotters, concerts, wrestling and boxing. When owners Ismael Pace and Jose Lectoure passed away in the early 1950s, the building was turned over to

Lectoure's nephew, 19-year-old real estate agent Juan Carlos "Tito" Lectoure. Until he retired in 1987, Tito ran boxing cards every Wednesday and Saturday—close to 3,000 cards in 31 years. He promoted 24 world championship fights, many before the alphabets took over.

Every outstanding South American fighter had boxed at Luna Park, dating back to heavyweight Luis Firpo, who ended his career there in the mid-1930s. Luna Park hosted world flyweight champions Pascual Perez and Horacio Accavallo, lightweight contender Justo Suarez, junior welterweight champ Nicolino Locche, light-heavyweight champ Victor Galindez and heavyweight contender Oscar Bonavena. It was difficult to import American boxers due to the low value of the peso but Hall-of-Famers Archie Moore and Sandy Saddler had boxed there.

A 1972 revolution had left soldiers on street corners, brandishing machine guns. A beef shortage had Argentinians eating meat every other week, but we were allowed filet mignon in our hotel. My high school Spanish took time to kick in so the first couple days, Arnold, Dad and I ate ham and cheese sandwiches because I only recognized *jambon y queso o*n local menus.

Briscoe trained at the gym inside Luna Park. There were two regulation-size boxing rings along with a row of heavy bags and speed bags. Fighters who trained there included Monzon, Bonavena, Galindez and Locche. If they needed a last-minute replacement for the twice-weekly cards, I assume they grabbed someone from the gym. The tiny dressing room they gave us, to steal a line from Bud Shrake, of *Sports Illustrated*, "couldn't accommodate a somersault by a dwarf."

As we arrived at the gym one day, a group of boxing fanatics surrounded Briscoe, looking for photographs. Bennie pointed to our car because I had brought 50 postcard-sized photos of him. When I got out, they grabbed at me and at the cards and I couldn't distribute them fast enough. People were pushing and shoving and it got scary so I ran down the street, the mob in pursuit. I tossed the cards into the air and kept running while they gathered like pigeons to pick them from the sidewalk.

Wherever we walked, people came out of stores and office buildings to wave, say hello and take pictures. I don't recall seeing any Black men or women and Bennie stood out with his shaven head and his smile. He enjoyed being a celebrity without ever taking advantage. He struggled to read newspapers, signed his name in slow motion and enjoyed watching American cartoons on his hotel room TV. But he had good values and knew right from wrong and he'd shake his head in disgust when hearing about managers who took advantage of fighters. When his friends questioned his choice of White managers, he said, "Black men will cheat you just as quickly."

Two days before the fight, we had a ceremonial meeting with Monzon and Argentina President Alejandro Lanusse, a former military academy rugby star and amateur heavyweight. Imagine that happening in the United States for a middleweight championship fight.

The weigh-in the morning of the fight was held in the Argentine Boxing Federation indoor stadium. It looked like the Blue Horizon. There must have been 1,500 people crammed inside. I never had seen so many people at a weigh-in and those who could not get in lined the streets, which were blocked off by police to traffic.

We got to Luna Park early that afternoon. Monzon arrived later, gaining momentum from the crowd's cheers as he passed. The fight was shown live on television in Buenos Aires which may have been why only 17,000 seats were filled. Yeah, *only* 17,000!

The three judges were from Argentina so Briscoe wasn't going to win on points. The pace was fast and constant. Briscoe did most of the attacking but Monzon fired back every step of the way.

Besides Monzon, Briscoe's biggest problem was referee Victor Avendano, an employee of Lectoure, whose early warnings inhibited Briscoe from going to the body or pushing Monzon out of clinches. Amilcar Brusa, Monzon's trainer, was permitted to sit on the ring steps in Monzon's corner, but McCall and Bailey had to sit eight feet from the ring. Midway through the fight, an Argentine deputy commissioner grabbed from Bailey's hand the jar with the ointment used to stop the bleeding from a cut Briscoe had sustained. He did not return it for several rounds. These are not excuses. Monzon was the better man.

Briscoe's chance came two minutes into the ninth round when he drove a right into Monzon's jaw just as Monzon threw a right uppercut. Monzon fell into his corner but the ropes held him up. He was half looking into the crowd, right where we were sitting on the first row. I thought he was going to vomit and I jumped out of my seat. Briscoe threw a right to the body but missed a left hook to the head. Monzon grabbed him and Avendano took his time breaking the clinch. Briscoe landed a few lefts but Monzon made it to the bell.

"That was the worst round since I won the title, but I showed I can take it," he later said.

Even though Monzon recovered, Briscoe remained dangerous, and his jab, more like a straight left, always found Monzon's face. In the 15th round, Monzon stood his ground. It was an exciting finish and I had it 10-5 in rounds or 145-140 for Monzon. The official scores were wider: 149-143, 149-139, 150-139. The judge who had it 149-143 scored seven rounds for Monzon, one for Briscoe and seven rounds even. The judge who had it 149-139 scored 11 rounds for Monzon, one for Briscoe, three even. The judge who had it 150-139 scored 11 for Monzon and four rounds even. He did not even give Briscoe the ninth. Please!

"What saved me first (in the ninth round) was I was against the ropes and couldn't go down," Monzon said. "My body was just about out of control, but my mind was okay. I looked up at the clock, watching the seconds and telling myself, 'Boy, this is going to be terrible.'"

There was swelling over Monzon's right eye, and his right hand was very swollen, especially the little finger. "My arms were so tired," he said. "I had to keep moving back and moving my arms all night. It was the hardest fight I ever had."

After the way Briscoe had looked in those two fights with Vinales, no one had given him a chance to go the limit, let alone win. When we got to the dressing room, Dad put his arm around him and kissed him on his forehead. Dad was so proud I thought he was going to cry. He was still holding the 8mm camera he had used to film every minute of every round. Monzon may have been the best I ever saw in person. He had no fear and was one step ahead of a very good Briscoe that afternoon.

"I'm not proud of myself that I lost, but I'm proud that he didn't put me down like he did those other guys," Briscoe said. "And I fought for the world championship. Now that's something not everybody can do, and I might do it again."

I offered Brusa $150,000 tax free, plus South American television rights for a rematch in Philadelphia, but I was pissing into the wind. The next morning we went to Luna Park where Lectoure furnished me with programs, unused tickets and posters from the fight. We flew home, knowing we had been one punch away from the world title and that there could be another chance.

Chapter Fourteen
A Spectrum of Problems

MONDAY NIGHT FIGHTS!

AT THE Spectrum

MON., JAN. 15, 8 P.M.

10 ROUNDS

SAMMY GOSS vs. RAUL CRUZ

TRENTON, N. J.
NUMBER 2 JR. LIGHTWEIGHT

MEXICO CITY
BEAT 4 CHAMPS

10 ROUNDS

NATE COLLINS vs. BILLY DOUGLAS

OAKLAND, CAL.
KO'D CYCLONE HART

COLUMBUS, OHIO
NUMBER 10 MIDDLEWEIGHT

PLUS

FOUR PRELIMINARY BOUTS

TICKETS: $8, $6, $4, ON SALE AT THE SPECTRUM;
ALL CENTER CITY TICKET AGENCIES; TICKETRON OUTLETS

Spectrum

Willie Monroe's fifth-round knockout of California's Indian George Davis on December 5 ended 1972 for me at the Arena. Only 904 customers paid $4,722.32 to see it. It cost me $4,520.23 ($29,000 in 2021), the biggest loss of my career. My total profit from 11 cards in 1972 was $2,065.01 ($13,300 in 2021). The next week, Stephen J. Greenberg, Director of Productions at the Spectrum, called. He wanted me to meet with him and Spectrum president Lou Scheinfeld to discuss a boxing program. Timing....

We met twice and I agreed to a one-year contract to be their Director of Boxing. My salary was $15,000 ($95,000 in 2021) plus 10 percent of any annual profits. I had just turned 26.

Scheinfeld, who had studied journalism at Temple University in the mid-1950s, became a City Hall reporter, then City Editor of the *Daily News*. He quit the newspaper business in 1966 to work with Ed Snider to develop a hockey team and sports arena in South Philadelphia. Scheinfeld named it the Spectrum and went from VP of the Philadelphia Flyers to president of the arena when Snider took control in the early 1970s.

The Spectrum had basketball (76ers), ice hockey (Flyers), rock concerts, the Ice Capades and Ringling Brothers Circus. Scheinfeld wanted to fill its empty Monday nights with boxing.

I stopped by the Arena to inform Edna Toppi. She wished me luck but spun no cartwheels. She got her own license and promoted four cards in 1973, three in her building and one at Convention Hall, showcasing middleweights Boogaloo Watts and Willie Monroe, and light-heavyweight Richie Kates. Her biggest crowd was 2,512 at Convention Hall that summer. After that she gave up.

A December 27 press conference in the Spectrum's Blue Line Club announced the formation of our *Monday Night Fights*. Jack Fried did not attend. He went early and got the press release from the switchboard operator.

My first year at the Spectrum could have been my last. We promoted 16 cards and the only profitable ones were three of Bennie Briscoe's four appearances. The best was June 25 when he knocked out Dynamite Douglas to defend the North American Boxing Federation (NABF) middleweight title he'd won three months earlier, stopping Art Hernandez in the same ring. Briscoe was the No. 1 attraction in town and Douglas had won five in a row here.

The fight drew the largest crowd (9,369) and best gate receipts ($64,565) of 1973. The Spectrum's profit was $14,384.88. Tickets prices were $4, $6 and $8, as they were the entire year.

Our biggest loser—due to initial expenses—was the January 15 opener when junior lightweight contender Sammy Goss K0d Mexico's Raul Cruz, a former title challenger. A short right hand dropped Cruz late in the second round. After winking to his trainer that he was more surprised than hurt, Cruz lost track of time and was halfway up when referee Hank Cisco completed the count. "Quick Count" Cisco had the fastest wave-off in the business. If you got up at 9.9, forget it, you were out.

In the middleweight semifinal, Nate Collins, the first man to defeat Cyclone Hart, quit on his stool after eight rounds against Douglas. Goss was from Trenton, so, technically, all four main-eventers were from out of town.

The crowd was 3,535, ticket sales $21,329. These were good figures for the Arena, not the Spectrum. Gene Courtney pointed that out in his *Inquirer* column and questioned if the talent in Philadelphia could support our program. We lost $10,168.21 ($63,312 in 2021).

Our February 19 card was an embarrassment. Former World Boxing Association (WBA) heavyweight champion Ernie Terrell was scheduled to fight Tony Doyle, of Salt Lake City, whom Joe Frazier had knocked out in 1967 in the Spectrum's first sporting event. Angelo Dundee called six days prior to tell me Doyle had bruised an eye sparring with Muhammad Ali for Ali's fight with Englishman Joe Bugner that weekend in Las Vegas.

Commissioner Zach Clayton complained about Doyle's replacement, Canadian Bill Drover, who had lost seven of his last nine fights. I should have listened but we went ahead. Drover never heard the bell for round two and the press roasted me.

The highlight of the evening came with no one getting hit. Terrell's sister, Jeanie, had replaced Diana Ross as lead singer with The Supremes, who were performing across the river at the Latin Casino. Ernie arranged for her and Mary Wilson, two thirds of the group, to sing the National Anthem.

The 10-round heavyweight semifinal matched 28-year-old Earnie Shavers, of Warren, Ohio, who was 42-2, 41 K0s, against 24-year-old Jimmy Young, of North Philly, who was 7-3, 2 K0s. Young was far from the fighter who would give Muhammad Ali fits in 1976 and beat George Foreman in 1977. Shavers stopped him in three.

There was a fight for control of Shavers between Dean Chance, the 1964 Cy Young Award winner with the Los Angeles Angels, and Joseph "Blackie" Gennaro, a paving contractor from Youngstown, Ohio. Further complicating things, promoter Don Elbaum claimed his signed contract for Shavers to fight George Chuvalo in Ohio pre-dated mine. He sent a process server to the Spectrum. I hid in the mens room to avoid him.

"The last thing Peltz said to me before he disappeared was, 'Jump in the ring and keep your back turned so you can't see the process server if he comes after you,'" Shavers told Tom Cushman, of the *Daily News*. Legal papers were thrown into the ring, thrown out, and the fight, what there was of it, went on. Gennaro had Shavers' $1,000 purse ($6,339 in 2021) held up by the Athletic Commission. Shavers said he got $200 and Gennaro $800 to pay legal fees.

On the March 26 Briscoe-Hernandez card, junior welterweight Mike Everett's opponent failed to show at the weigh-in for their six-round prelim. Mike Laquatra, in town with flyweight Leroy Krienbrook, telephoned Willie Williams in Cleveland. Williams had won 10 of his 39 fights, but this was no time to get picky. No promoter wants to disappoint a fighter who has been training for weeks. We bought Williams a plane ticket and arranged to have him picked up at Philadelphia International Airport, 10 minutes from the Spectrum.

I was at my desk around 6 pm when Williams called.

"Where are you?" I asked.

"I'm in Baltimore," he said.

"WHAT?"

Williams had been asleep when his plane landed in Philly. Some passengers got off, some stayed. When he woke up, the plane had reached its Baltimore destination, 100 miles away. I yelled at him to take a cab and told him I would pay for it. Ten minutes before Briscoe and Hernandez entered the ring, a security guard told me someone was banging on the glass doors, saying he was supposed to fight. I ran to the entrance, let Williams in and sent him to the dressing room.

The cab fare was $80 ($500 in 2021). I don't know if Williams got on a scale, but who cared. Briscoe K0d Hernandez in three rounds, long enough for Williams to get ready for the walkout bout. There was no Hollywood ending. He was knocked out in round two and never won another fight. "Wonderful" Willie retired in 1978 with a record of 10-39-5. He was knocked out 24 times.

There was a new prospect in town, the best since Hart, Monroe, Watts and Young had turned pro in 1969. He was Tyrone Everett, Mike's older brother.

The 21-year-old southpaw debuted as a pro in 1971 in Scranton. In his second fight there, he boxed Ray Hall, a Wilkes-Barre featherweight who was 5-0. Hall was managed by Frank Gelb. Midway through the four-round fight, Gelb's wife, Elaine, whispered, "Frank, I think you're backing the wrong guy." Gelb took her advice and signed Everett.

Everett's next fight was on Herman Taylor's March 7, 1972 card at the Arena, the night Nate Collins knocked out Cyclone Hart. Everett boxed North Philly's Ray Hart (no relation). Hart attacked from the opening bell, throwing wide punches from all angles. He was thick, strong and squat and looked like Arnold Schwarzenegger compared to the reed-thin Everett. It was Ali-Frazier in miniature. In a wonderful display of counter-punching under pressure, Everett nailed Hart at every turn, stopping him 59 seconds into the fourth round.

I was mesmerized. I ran over to Gelb and we made a handshake deal for me to promote Everett.

Everett was schooled by one of the best, but few people outside Philadelphia had ever heard of Jimmy Arthur Washington, known as Jimmy Arthur or Art. When the Passyunk Gym closed, Art built his own at 17th and Reed, also in South Philly. Art had trained horses and fighting chickens in the South. He had been mentored by oldtimer Pop Bates and had worked with Bates' fighters, Percy Manning and Roger Russell.

"When I boxed Ray Hart it was my third fight," Everett said. "Hart had knocked just about everyone out and he was giving me trouble. After the second round I told Art that the pressure was hard on me and I was having trouble. He told me Hart was leg-weary and finished for the night. When I went out for the third, Hart was out of gas. I stopped him in the next round.

"Art doesn't have a big name like Yank Durham or Sam Solomon or Quenzell McCall, but he's just as good. He's younger and he hasn't had a big fighter yet. He's the only trainer I know who runs with his fighters. And he knows what to look for during a fight."

By the end of 1972, Everett was unbeaten in nine fights. He boxed nine times in 1973, eight at the Spectrum. By the end of 1973, he was 18-0, 11 K0s. His "coming out" party was in the semifinal on the Briscoe-Douglas card against Eddie Garces, of New York. Garces (9-4-1) was no stranger to Philly, having gone 1-1-1 with local featherweight Luis Lopez before getting stopped by Sammy Goss eight months prior.

Everett knocked Garces out in the first round. It was the kind of performance in front of a crowd that size that a promoter dreams about. Bruce Trampler, in town with Douglas, congratulated me, knowing the hit this skinny 120-pounder had made.

While *Monday Night Fights* was experiencing growing pains, Cyclone Hart was back, 13 months after his loss to Collins. Herman Taylor matched him with Puerto Rican veteran Jose "Monon" Gonzales in April at the Arena. Gonzalez, approaching his 33rd birthday, was 41-17-2, 13 K0s.

Gonzalez had been in and out of the world rankings for years. Only Dick Tiger had knocked him down and two of his four stoppage losses were due to cuts. He had beaten some of the best 160s in the world: Florentino Fernandez; Luis Rodriguez; Vicente Rondon; Joey Archer; Don Fullmer; Dynamite Douglas, and Hurricane Carter. This was the worst kind of opponent for Hart after a long layoff. Only the Marquis de Sade would have been happy with this match.

Hart had left Sam Solomon after a legal battle and was managed by New York businessman Jim Jacobs, often considered the greatest handball player of all time. Jacobs, and his partner Bill Cayton, were the world's number one collectors of fight films. Hart would be Jacobs' first fighter, but later he would manage Wilfred Benitez, Edwin Rosario and Mike Tyson. Cus D'Amato, a close friend, was brought in as trainer. Hart owed Taylor a fight and D'Amato had failed to sway Jacobs' decision to accept Gonzalez.

“I crawl for no man,” the 70-year-old D’Amato said of the 86-year-old Taylor at the pre-fight physical. “When a man (Hart) is out of action for 13 months, he should get a tune-up. No promoter should jeopardize a drawing card like this guy. You would think that people would improve with age, but his (Taylor’s) chance for that passed a long time ago.”

Taylor fired back: “I won’t let him fight a tune-up here. I don’t make lopsided matches. You should be ashamed of yourself. You put (Floyd) Patterson in with that amateur, (Pete) Rademacher. That’s the kind of fights you want.”

Hart got dropped in the second and third round and the fight was stopped at 1:32 of the ninth. Despite post-fight rumors that Hart would return to Solomon, D’Amato remained his trainer. Only 2,366 paid $14,720 to see the match. Taylor brought Gonzalez back against Monroe in August at Convention Hall, but only 1,775 paid $10,879 to watch Monroe win a 10-round decision. It was Taylor’s final Philadelphia promotion.

Hart returned for me against Thurman “Doc” Holiday on August 6. We put Tyrone Everett in the main event against Jose Valdez, of Mexico. Valdez’ record was 30-26-2 and he had been K0d 14 times, but Everett played it safe. He moved and jabbed, winning nine out of 10 rounds, but drawing boos from the 4,091 fans. It would not be the only time his safety-first style would drive a wedge through our relationship. Hart stole the show when his left hook landed on Holliday’s forehead and the Doc went out 33 seconds into round two.

George Foreman, who had separated Joe Frazier from the world heavyweight title that January in Jamaica, was in Tokyo defending against the over-matched Joe “King” Roman. The Spectrum ran the closed-circuit telecast with Joe Hand on August 31, accompanied by a “live” card featuring young welterweights Alfonso Hayman, William Watson and Jimmy Savage in separate fights, and Li’l Abner in a junior middleweight bout. Hand had parlayed his role at Cloverlay into the closed-circuit television business.

Foreman won in two minutes but there was an interesting side note to our card. Watson survived a deep cut over his left eye in the first round to twice knock down Bobby Haymon, of Cleveland. In the sixth round, Haymon tripped over Watson’s foot, fell out of the ring, banged his head on the press table and was carried out on a stretcher. The bout was ruled a No Decision. Haymon was the older brother of Al Haymon, who would leave the music business and become a major force in boxing in the 21st century.

That was our 11th card of the year and our losses had totaled $14,482.89, or $1,316.62 per, which was not too bad for a startup boxing program. Against my wishes though, we stayed on Monday nights in the fall, competing with *Monday Night Football.* The headliners were Richie Kates, Watts, Briscoe, Hart and Tyrone Everett, but we sold fewer than 12,000 tickets combined and lost $35,686.31, an average of $7,137.26 per card.

The program was in trouble. So was my job. At year's end, we had lost $50,169.20 ($308,000 in 2021). The Spectrum made some money on concessions and parking, often the major source of income at arenas, but no one was happy.

"We took it on for a year and threw everything into it and I'm not satisfied with the results," Scheinfeld told Courtney. "If there is no pickup early in 1974, we'll pretty much be out of the boxing business. There is no way for me to justify another $50,000 loss. If we only break even in 1974, I'll be happy and boxing will go on at the Spectrum.

"We've got five of the best middleweights in the world—Briscoe, Willie Monroe, Bobby Watts, Gene Hart and Stanley "Kitten" Hayward, who recently made a comeback. But none of them want to fight Briscoe or each other. (They) are limiting their income. Fighting each other they'll draw bigger gates. Now they are only getting good records but very little cash. We should not have run on Monday nights against the Monday night pro football games in the fall. It was my mistake but I wanted the continuity—you know, Monday Night Fights on Monday night. We won't do that again next fall."

After our last card December 3, Allen Flexer, vice president and controller, took me to lunch in the same Blue Line Club where we had announced the series 12 months earlier. Flexer was trying to decide if the boxing program was worthwhile. I told him I could turn it around if I could get the local fighters to fight each other. I'm not sure he had confidence in me but he gave me the go-ahead.

Chapter Fifteen

Atlantic City

Tyrone Everett and Frank Gelb in the mid-1970s. (Peltz collection)

While the future of boxing at the Spectrum remained uncertain, Bennie Briscoe was trying for another shot at Carlos Monzon. After winning three times during the first half of 1973, Briscoe signed to defend his NABF title against

Rodrigo Valdes, of Colombia, on September 1. Of all the guys we had a chance to fight during my 10 years with Briscoe, Valdes was the one I never wanted. It was a bad matchup. Valdes could punch, move, was hard to hit cleanly and had a solid chin. A couple of his losses came when he had mononucleosis.

Booking agent George Kanter had been contacted by a promoter in Noumea to deliver Briscoe and Valdes. Noumea was the capital of New Caledonia, which had been military headquarters of the United States in the South Pacific during World War II. Kanter did not look, act, dress or talk like a man who belonged in boxing.

He was born in Belgium, the son of a wealthy manufacturer of women's gloves in Brussels. He'd studied at Harrow, a London boys' school which included Winston Churchill among its alums. He'd graduated in 1937 with a degree in business from Chillon College, a boys' Swiss boarding school, and worked for his father until Germany invaded Belgium and the family fled to New York.

Kanter had been infatuated with boxing since he was 7. After World War II, with many European boxers coming to the United States to fight, Kanter, who spoke fluent French and Dutch, decided to make money booking them. He brought Robert Villemain from France to Philadelphia to box Sugar Ray Robinson in 1950—and fired 17-year-old sparring partner George Benton after Benton made a fool out of Villemain during a public workout the week of the fight. He had asked Benton to go *easy.*

"I couldn't do it," Benton said. "It was the first time my Mom and Pop had seen me box and I didn't want to let them down."

Even with glasses, Kanter could barely see. Like many Europeans, he reversed his thumb and forefinger while smoking cigarettes and, by the time he finished, ashes covered his sport jacket. His live-in companion was named Gigi—perfect.

Silver and gold mining were New Caledonia's main source of income, and the promoters had enough of it to offer Briscoe $30,000 ($185,000 in 2021), his biggest purse yet, and too much to turn down. I couldn't make the trip since I had a card at the Spectrum.

Valdes won a 12-round decision (60-55, 60-51, 58-51), but the fight looked closer on film. Kanter's scorecard (6-4-2 in rounds for Valdes) was used in the Associated Press write-up. After Briscoe picked up an easy win over Ruben Arocha, of Mexico, two months later at the Spectrum, he was offered Tony Mundine in Paris. Briscoe had lost his last three out-of-town fights to Luis Vinales, Monzon and Valdes and I wanted a road win under his belt first. So I turned to Frank Gelb.

Gelb had brought boxing back to Atlantic City Convention Hall that year—in the pre-casino days—with the first fights there since December 7, 1963, when Joey Giardello won the world middleweight title with a 15-round decision over Dick Tiger.

He opened on March 24 when light-heavyweight Richie Kates knocked out Ron Oliver, of New York, in two. Giardello was among more than 2,000 fans at the six-bout card in the 3,200-seat ballroom upstairs, the first of four Atlantic City cards Gelb promoted in 1973.

Gelb had grown up in Wynnefield where his mother had been part of a weekly card game with my aunt. He went to Overbrook High School when Wilt Chamberlain was breaking records there. After two years at the Naval Air Base in Pensacola, Florida, he went to work in his family's furniture business. His dad, Maurice, ran the store at 61st and Market, and he ran the one in Norristown, 15 miles away. Leroy Roberts, a professional boxer and Norristown cop, drove Gelb's delivery truck on his days off.

I had spoken to Gelb before my first card. "You mean you do this for a living?" he asked. That started a lifelong friendship.

Gelb manged some of the best fighters in Philadelphia in the 1970s: Tyrone Everett; Mike Everett; Matthew Franklin; Jimmy Young, and Alfonso Evans. He was concerned about selling tickets to a (Saturday) December 8 card in Atlantic City, so I agreed to finance it. We matched Briscoe with Willie Warren, of Corpus Christi, Texas.

On my way to Atlantic City Thursday evening, I stopped at the 23rd PAL gym. The PAL had two rings, each one a foot off the floor. Briscoe, who was leaving the next day for AC, was boxing Michael "Youngblood" Williams in one. Philly fighters always sparred up until 48 hours before a fight.

Quenzell McCall was all over Briscoe. "What's wrong with you?" McCall asked so everyone could hear. "You look awful. Speed it up. Move your hands. This is embarrassing. How are you possibly gonna win Saturday night?" This was McCall letting everyone know he saw something the rest of us couldn't. Even after Briscoe had knocked out Dynamite Douglas six months earlier, McCall had been quoted, "Bennie was horrible," in a headline over a photo in the

Daily News. Here he was, back at it. I braced for what I knew was coming.

Briscoe stopped sparring, went to the corner of the ring and told assistant trainer Charlie Spicer to take off his headgear and gloves. “Cancel the fight if I look so bad,” he yelled. “Fine with me,” McCall said. Briscoe went up to the second-floor dressing room to change.

I followed and waited for him to calm down. We sat apart on a long bench. I told him a lot of money was invested in the show. He said he was tired of McCall’s act. I suggested he go home, pack his bags, ride with me to Atlantic City and relax. He relented. I took him home and we drove to the shore. We stayed at the Strand Motel, once the pride of the Pacific Avenue strip, less than a block from the ocean, and had dinner there with Edna Toppi, who lived in nearby Ventnor.

I thought it best Bennie and I share a room. In the middle of the night I got up to piss. When I got to the bathroom, someone already had. At breakfast, I said, “Hey, man, don’t you flush the toilet?” He shrugged, which he often did when he didn’t know what to say. I had grown up in a house with a bathroom for Mom and Dad in their bedroom, one for my sister in hers, one for me in mine—and a half bath. Not flushing was foreign to me.

On Saturday morning, Nigel and Mary Anne Collins arrived. When I told them about Bennie’s bathroom habits, they reminded me he grew up in rural Georgia with little or no running water and it cost money to flush. I felt bad. The four of us went for a walk on the Boardwalk. Bennie was a pound heavy and needed to “walk and spit off the weight.”

Mike Rossman, of Turnersville, New Jersey, who had turned pro that summer, ran his record to 6-0 that night when he stopped Lester Camper, of Baltimore, in the last round of their six-round junior middleweight fight. Camper’s handlers, upset over what they claimed was a premature stoppage, touched off a brawl which ended when one of Rossman’s corner men dragged one of Camper’s down the ring steps on his face.

After a slow start, Briscoe found his rhythm and busted Warren up with uppercuts until referee Dick Woerhle waved it off at 1:52 of the seventh round. The crowd was just over 2,000. Briscoe got $1,500, but it would be worth it less than three months later.

Chapter Sixteen

Managers Meeting

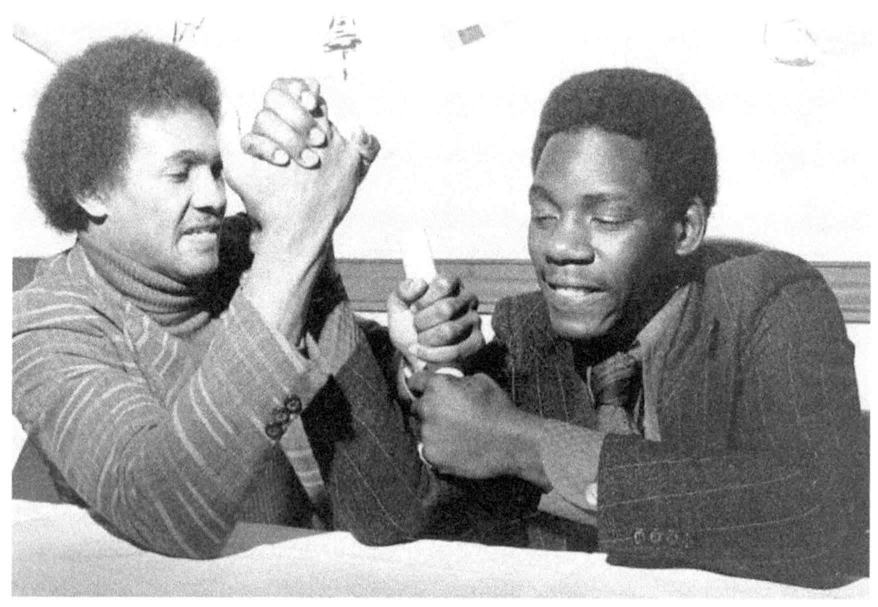

Willie Monroe and Cyclone Hart arm wrestle in 1974. (Peltz collection)

By 1973, there were half a dozen boxing gyms in the city. The newest and biggest was Cloverlay (Joe Frazier's), on North Broad Street across from the North Philadelphia train station. A day after my lunch with Spectrum veep Allen Flexer, I posted signs at each of a meeting at Cloverlay in mid-December, urging managers and trainers to attend.

About 50 people—including a few fighters—did. The meeting ironically was where Yank Durham had held court as trainer and *de facto* manager of Frazier. Yank opposed Philly guys fighting each other. "I will not be destroyed by another Philadelphia fighter, nor will I destroy another Philadelphia fighter," he told Jack McKinney, of the *Daily News,* in 1972. "There's been too much of that in the past."

With his sonic-boom voice, Yank had made himself a larger-than-life character and Frazier's success gave him that platform to shout from. He was born in 1920 in Camden, New Jersey, just across the bridge from Philadelphia. His amateur career ended during a World War II air raid in England when a jeep ran over him, breaking both legs. Yank was in and out of hospitals for two years. He worked as a welder for the Pennsylvania Railroad—later the Penn-Central—and trained fighters in the evening.

Yank was 47 when Frazier beat Buster Mathis for a piece of the world heavyweight title in 1968, 50 when Frazier beat Muhammad Ali three years later. He and Joe were like father and son.

Though he said he opposed Philly vs. Philly fights, Yank had been involved in his share, including Bennie Briscoe vs. Percy Manning and Kitten Hayward, as well as Gypsy Joe Harris vs. Hayward and Johnny Knight. Things changed when Frazier got to the top. In my opinion, Yank thought it would hurt his reputation if one of his fighters, notably Willie Monroe, lost to another Philly fighter, trained by another Philly trainer. His ego couldn't deal with that.

After losing the title to George Foreman early in 1973, Frazier won a 12-round decision over European champion Joe Bugner in July in London. Yank suffered a stroke eight weeks later and died at Temple University Hospital. He was 52.

Eddie Futch took over. Futch first had worked with Yank in 1966 when Frazier knocked out Chuck Leslie at the Olympic Auditorium in Los Angeles. In the dressing room, promoter Aileen Eaton asked Yank about Frazier fighting the following week against Memphis Al Jones, whose opponent had fallen out. Jones was tall—Frazier wasn't—so Yank asked Futch, who said Jones would not be able to take Frazier's body attack. Frazier K0d Jones in one round, then returned and K0d Eddie Machen in 10.

When Frazier got ready to fight George "Scrap Iron" Johnson at the Olympic in 1967, Futch gave Yank a detailed scouting report. Frazier won by decision and Futch became a permanent member of the team.

Futch was born in 1911 in Mississippi, moved to Detroit when he was 5, and boxed as a teenager. He won the Detroit Golden Gloves title in 1933. Joe Louis used him as a sparring partner for speed in the Brewster Center. After a heart murmur ended his career, Futch became a trainer while working as a welder at the Ford Motor

Company. His first major fighter was welterweight Lester Felton, who defeated future champions Kid Gavilan and Carmen Basilio.

Before moving to Los Angeles, Futch trained Berry Gordy, founder of Motown Records. His first world champion was Don Jordan, who won the welterweight title in 1958 by beating Virgil Akins at the Olympic. Futch also had trained heavyweight Ken Norton and welterweight Hedgemon Lewis.

Futch was as low key as Yank was bombastic. Yank was 6-foot-1 and you could hear him from one end of the gym to the other. Futch was 5-foot-8 and you had to get close to hear him. He had been a part of the Olympic Auditorium's storied boxing history and understood the importance of local rivalries. His ego was a fraction of the size of Yank's and he was a big help at the meeting.

There were four or five rows of trainers and managers seated at the gym. I was sitting on the ring apron—outside the ropes—facing them. I told them the Spectrum was losing money on boxing. If I couldn't make fights that drew, the Spectrum would shut down boxing and we would be back at the Arena. The Spectrum was new, nice and clean. The Arena was a relic from a forgotten era.

We'd had too many fights that no one cared about, fights that did not belong in an 18,000-seat building. It was time to make the matches we had been building toward. I was 27. Most of these men had been around boxing longer than I had been alive. They could recite details of the all-Philly fights that had made the city the great fight town it had been. We needed to return to when you had to beat the best to get ahead and many of the best lived in Philly.

Had Yank been alive, I don't know what would have happened. My worst nightmare would have been hearing his voice drown everyone in horror stories of Philadelphia fighters destroying each other. Though I knew I was making sense, the group's positive reaction surprised me. We were about to begin our journey.

From 1974 through 1978, the Spectrum stood alongside Madison Square Garden on the East Coast, the Olympic and the Forum in Inglewood, California, as the four major boxing venues in the country. Many of the best middleweights, light-heavyweights and junior lightweights boxed at the Spectrum during those years.

I was close to signing a 10-round middleweight fight between Kitten Hayward and Li'l Abner. Hayward had returned the week before in his first fight since his one-round loss to Cyclone Hart in 1971, knocking out Dominican Jose Anglada in three rounds at the Spectrum. Tyrone Everett had headlined, but he lacked Hayward's personality and most of the pre- and post-fight newspaper stories centered on Kitten, not the undefeated Everett.

I also had been trying to make a third fight between welterweight prospects Alfonso Hayman, of South Philly, and William Watson, of North Philly. Watson had won the first by decision, Hayman the rematch by knockout. Pop Bates helped me.

Bates was "old school" and he understood what neded to be done. He was born Carey Williams in South Carolina. He was a rum-runner during Prohibition, had been around boxing most of his life, and ran the Passyunk Gym. He had worked with Joey Giardello, lightweight contender Wesley Mouzon and lightweight champion Wallace "Bud" Smith. He often called fighters "dog meat" and once threw me out of his gym when, while working for the *Bulletin*, I went there to interview Augie Pantellas. At the meeting, Bates took Hayman's manager, Jimmy Arthur, by the hand and came to me and they agreed to fight Watson a third time on the Hayward-Abner card.

The plum I was after was Monroe against Hart. Monroe was unbeaten in his last seven fights, including a 10-round draw in Paris with transplanted Italian Fabio Bettini. Futch agreed to let Monroe fight Hart in February. No one from Hart's camp was at the meeting, but talks with manager Jim Jacobs had been encouraging.

Kitten and Li'l Abner were diametric opposites. Kitten was 34 and still liked fast women and faster horses. He was a sharp dresser who spent more time hob-nobbing with singers, comedians, musicians, politicians and businessmen than in the gym. He was 28-9-4, 15 K0s, since turning pro in 1959, and he had beaten some of the best between 147 and 160 pounds. He could box and he could punch and he could set traps. There is no telling how his career would have developed had he worked it. For this fight he trained at Muhammad

Ali's camp in Deer Lake, Pennsylvania. He got his body in shape and, thanks to his host, his mouth.

"I'll be like Secretariat in that ring Monday night," Kitten said at the pre-fight physical. "People are gonna see things they've never seen before. I'm gonna give this boy such a whippin' it'll be a shame. If I don't take this pork chop apart, I'll retire again."

Abner (born Perry Abney) was from a different solar system. He was a quiet, blue-collar citizen and a quiet, blue-collar fighter who walked in a straight line to his opponent and started punching. Abner was 27, married, and worked for Carbonator Rental Service, installing soda systems in bars. His record was 15-7-1, 13 K0s, and although he had knocked out four men in a row, none were named Curtis Cokes, Emile Griffith or Bennie Briscoe, three of Hayward's victims. Abner did his best work against guys who stood in front of him and had cement feet. He was 5-foot-7. Kitten, two inches taller, loved to fight shorter guys.

"When they put you in that 20x20 ring Monday night, you're gonna have to fight," Abner said, accepting Kitten's challenge. "Then we'll find out if you're all mouth."

"Make sure you show up," Kitten yelled.

"I'll be there early."

"If he gets there early enough, he can help you set the ring up," Kitten said, looking at me.

Turning to Abner, Kitten went on: "You better bring Daisy Mae with you because you're going to need someone to wake you up. If I go 10 it will be a miracle. You notice how Abner and Watson go around together just like all those other guys from North Philly. They come together, stick together and Monday night they're going out together."

When Abner refused the referee's instructions to shake hands and walked straight forward at the opening bell, Kitten was the happiest guy in South Philly. "I really got under his skin, didn't I?" Kitten said. "He wouldn't even shake my hand. He couldn't wait to come right to me."

Abner threw one-punch bombs which Kitten avoided for the first two rounds and they went toe-to-toe in the third. In the fourth, Abner connected with a solid left hook to Kitten's body, but was wide open for a right-hand counter and Kitten dropped him. Abner got up but Kitten was a good finisher and referee Pete Tomasco waved it off at 1:44.

"I was going for the kill," Abner said. "I was trying to get the hammer over. When he made that remark about my wife—calling her Daisy Mae—it got me hot. My wife's name is Peggy."

Hayward relished in his success. "They finally saw a little class at these Monday Night Fights," he said in his dressing room. "Look at all these young kids in here. They didn't even know who I was before tonight, but they do now. I know what it's all about now. When you're in shape you can run your mouth, feet and hands at the same time."

As enjoyable as it was dealing with Kitten and Li'l Abner, keeping Hayman and Watson together was a nightmare. Three weeks before the fight, I got a call from Democratic State Representative David Shadding, of South Philadelphia, telling me Hayman had been locked up. The charges included aggravated assault, armed robbery and possession of a firearm without a license. I had to post $1,000 for the $10,000 bail. I needed a terrific card to open 1974 and I couldn't afford to lose the fight.

Without telling anyone at the Spectrum, I picked up Hayman at the Detention Center in Northeast Philadelphia. An ex-Marine, Hayman always had a toothpick in his mouth, even while hitting the bags or skipping rope. He was as quiet as Kitten was talkative. We barely spoke on the ride back.

The next night I went to Jimmy Arthur's gym, a second-floor walkup at 17th and Reed. I brought the contract but Hayman wouldn't sign. Art told me they wanted $2,250, not the $1,750 they had agreed to. I stormed out. I had bailed Hayman out of jail and he was holding me up for more money. But I had no choice. The next day I went back, agreed, and got the contract signed. Hayman later was cleared of all charges except aggravated assault for which he got nine years of probation.

In his *Daily News* story the day after the January doubleheader, Tom Cushman wrote:

"Whatever it was, from the young kids to the guys who have to totter up to the box office windows, they came back to the Spectrum last evening. 'It's our best crowd in over six months,' said promoter

J Russell Peltz, even before learning the official count was 4,707, which made it by far the best crowd over that period of time.

"From start to finish, it also was Peltz' best show since he moved into the Spectrum over a year ago. The prelims were outstanding. Alfonso Hayman ripped out William Watson at 1:07 of the seventh round in an emotional, action-filled semifinal, after which Hayward firmly re-established himself as a headline attraction."

The bottom line showed a profit of $136.85. That is no misprint. It was small but a winner—and only the beginning.

The next day we announced the 10-round bout between Hart and Monroe, who had been on a collision course since their pro debuts in the fall of 1969. Hart was 24-2 with 23 K0s and one No Decision. His knockouts of Doc Holliday and Al Quinney late in 1973 made everyone forget his losses to Nate Collins and Jose Gonzales. People love punchers and Hart was one. Monroe was 26-2-1, 20 K0s, both losses coming on split decisions.

A crowd of 10,127 paid $69,725 to watch Hart-Monroe five weeks later—the best numbers in the program's 14-month history. Each fighter got $10,000 ($57,000 in 2021 dollars) and our $12,928.64 profit ($74,000 in 2021) was second only to the Briscoe-Dynamite Douglas fight. But two men who had 43 knockouts between them failed to produce the expected brawl. Monroe earned a unanimous decision (46-44, 49-42 and 49-41), but refused to engage, and Hart's trainer, Cus D'Amato, had him bobbing and weaving until too late.

The only round Hart dominated was the 10th when he buzzed Monroe. The best punch of the night was a right uppercut from Monroe in the eighth, but he didn't follow up. He moved side to side for 30 minutes and clinched whenever Hart got close. The crowd wanted an execution, not an exhibition.

Daily News columnist Stan Hochman offered this critique: "He (Monroe) made himself and he hurt himself the same night."

The evening's highlight was Ray "Windmill" White, a California light-heavyweight known more for comedic ring antics than serious boxing. White was to have boxed Richie Kates five nights earlier at Convention Hall. Scott A. Charles, who said he was in the record business and managing soul singer Barbara Mason (*Yes, I'm Ready*), had scheduled four 10-rounds fights and had predicted a crowd of 10,000 for a show.

Sugar Ray Seales, 1972 Olympic gold medalist, was on the card, but his opponent had canceled. Charles had one local fighter in a four-round bout and 10 out-of-towners in the others. It made no sense in Philadelphia and less sense five days before Monroe-Hart. Our price was $10 for ringside; his was $12.

Two days before Charles' card, Commissioner Zach Clayton pulled the plug. Charles had failed to post the $10,000 surety bond to guarantee payment of taxes and purses despite Clayton extending several deadlines. Hochman asked me to help White, who was stranded in Philadelphia with a one-way plane ticket.

I had seen White on tape-delayed bouts from the West Coast. Besides his trademark "Windmill punch," he had perfected the "jump shot" punch where he left his feet. He threw punches from behind his back, often threw left and right uppercuts together, and other times simultaneous left and right hooks at his opponent's ears.

White was 35 and had boxed most of the top 175-pounders on the West Coast. His record was 38-14-4, 9 K0s, but wins and losses were not his forte. He was a showman and had guested on TV talk shows hosted by Merv Griffin and Mike Douglas. He agreed to fight Ed Bailey, who was from Miami, but living in Philadelphia. Bailey was 10-9-3, 5 K0s. Two non-punchers so nobody would get hurt.

The only thing hurting was White's back, so I took him to a massage parlor in Center City. The front door had a small square window where they can look out but you can't look in. When no one answered the doorbell, I pressed my face against the window. There was a hard rap on the glass and I jumped back. A less-flattering version of Wonder Woman opened the door. When I told her what we needed, she said in a voice Barry White would envy, "Honey, you're in the wrong place."

Massage or not, White got off the canvas in the first round and went eight rounds to a draw with Bailey. During the second round, the top rope broke. It took 10 minutes to repair. After the fight, White pulled on the overhead microphone to talk to the crowd, but yards of cord came down from under the Spectrum scoreboard. It took another 10 minutes to tie the cord around a corner post so it would not interfere with the rest of the fights.

“Everything I touched tonight fell apart,” White told Cushman. “I hit the ropes, they broke. I touched the microphone, it broke.”

Chapter Seventeen

We'll Always Have Paris

French newspaper depiction of *Le Robot Noir.*

If I could relive one moment of my career, it would be Bennie Briscoe's fifth-round knockout over Tony Mundine on February 25, 1974 in Paris. There have been greater fights I promoted (Saad Muhammad-Marvin Johnson in 1977) or greater awards I received (International Boxing Hall of Fame in 2004), but nothing compares to that wonderful night.

In the 1970s, Philadelphia and Paris were the middleweight capitals of boxing. Philly had Briscoe, Cyclone Hart, Kitten Hayward, Boogaloo Watts, Willie Monroe, Li'l Abner and Dynamite Douglas, the transplanted Ohioan. Paris had Jean-Claude Bouttier, Max Cohen, Jean Mateo and Gratien Tonna. Hall-of-Famer Emile Griffith boxed in both cities and Carlos Monzon twice defended in Paris.

After Briscoe's loss to Monzon in 1972, he'd won five of his next six, losing to Rodrigo Valdes and beating Carlos Salinas, Art Hernandez, Douglas, Ruben Arocha and Willie Warren. International booking agent Dewey Fragetta offered us $17,500 ($100,000 in 2021) to fight Mundine in Paris.

Mundine was from Sydney, Australia. He had knocked out Cohen in four rounds in 1973 at the *Palais des Sports*, the Madison Square Garden of France. Three fights later, back in Paris, he'd clearly won a 12-round decision over Griffith. Mundine was the toast of Europe, appearing in newspapers, on magazine covers and as a guest on TV shows. He was the heir apparent to Monzon.

Our hotel was in the heart of the city. I ate duck l'orange nearly every night because it was the only thing I recognized on the hotel menu. Briscoe ran the streets in the morning and sparred in the afternoon with Li'l Abner and a young light-heavyweight, Matthew Franklin, who would mold a Hall-of-Fame career for himself as Matthew Saad Muhammad.

The week of the fight, Quenzell McCall was concerned about Bennie's weight so we lured Bennie out of his hotel room and McCall went in and disabled the mini bar.

While waiting in the lobby for our ride to the fight, I met Reg Gutteridge, the British journalist doing commentary for European TV. I had been in business less than five years but he recognized me—as I did him—and we spoke briefly. He said: "Mundine is the hottest thing in boxing, in Europe certainly. He can name his price to fight Monzon. Why would he want to tune up with Bennie Briscoe?" I had no answer but a wry smile.

At the *Palais des Sports* we descended a spiral staircase to the dressing room, much too small for Briscoe, Abner and Franklin. A 12-round European junior welterweight title fight opened the card.

Although we were the main event, Briscoe-Mundine was the second fight. I never had seen this and it greatly influenced how I ran shows in the future. The main event does not have to be last. Fans do not want to wait all night to see the featured attraction.

Briscoe-Mundine was a 12-round eliminator. It was as big as it gets without being for a world title. Every major European newspaper was ringside as well as the Associated Press, United Press International, Reuters and the International Herald Tribune. All 4,600 seats were filled. I scampered to the top row of the building. I had my 8mm home movie camera, where you had to change the roll of film after every round.

Briscoe wore the Star of David on his trunks in honor of his Jewish management. As he approached the ring, two Israeli citizens stood, waved their passports and yelled, “Bennie, we’re Jewish, too!”

Mundine, nearly four inches taller than the 5-foot-8 Briscoe, took an early lead, moving side to side and firing. Briscoe never stopped coming. Mundine was on his toes, popping Briscoe with counters. Briscoe occasionally got inside, but Mundine was agile and scored from a distance. Sometimes Briscoe made Mundine miss, sometimes not. Mundine was winning but had to fight every inch of the way.

By the end of round four, Mundine had to be asking himself why his management had made this fight. He was landing his best shots and Briscoe was still there. The pro-Mundine crowd buzzed uneasily.

Mundine moved less quickly in the fifth and Briscoe closed the distance between them. He hit Mundine with a big right hand, then followed him across the ring and trapped the Australian in his own corner. Briscoe whaled away, body and head. Mundine was not punching back. Fans were on their feet at ringside. Some jumped up in front of me. I was so nervous my hands began to shake the camera.

Briscoe followed a barrage of body and head shots with an overhand right and Mundine went halfway through the ropes and onto the canvas. He got to a semi-crouch, his left knee on the canvas, right arm holding the ropes. He could have gotten up, especially since the referee appeared to be counting in fractions, but didn’t. It was over at 2:20.

The Israelis rushed the ring and lifted Bennie onto their shoulders. Jews, then as now, were having a rough time in France and they felt this was their night as much as Briscoe's. Briscoe leaned over and kissed one on the cheek. I went down the steps, shot film along the way and headed to the dressing room. It seemed all of Paris was there.

I looked like I was in Gene Shalit-drag with my curly hair, three-piece plaid polyester suit, and a bowtie a clown might squirt water out of. I climbed onto a file cabinet and filmed the commotion. Briscoe put on his white T-shirt without having showered and I yelled, "Nice shower, Bennie!" and he turned and laughed. I gave the camera to my brother-in-law, and he filmed me as I kissed Bennie on his shaven head. My grin was brighter than the *City of Lights*.

"I feel young again," Briscoe told Tom Cushman on an overseas call. "I was the star from the time I got here. People treated me great. I can't remember being cheered like I was tonight."

Even Quenzell was jubilant. "The other guy was a good fighter," he told Cushman. "He's cute and he can punch like hell, but the pressure took its toll. Bennie forced him to punch every minute and Bennie was catching a lot of punches on the gloves. When Bennie started firing in the fifth round, it reminded me of the guy I've seen in his best fights."

The headline on Cushman's story on the back page of the *Daily News* was: "Briscoe…a Swingin' American in Paris."

We went back to the hotel for a victory meal. We stayed calm because promoter Charley Michaelis and matchmaker Gilbert Benaim were seated near us and we didn't want to gloat. My sister, Bootsie, was there plus two friends, Buzz Marcus and his wife, Ronnie, who had flown there from Philly.

The next day I grabbed every souvenir I could—posters, original photos, newspapers—including copies of *France-Soir*, the Paris daily which had a picture of Bennie standing over Mundine on the front page, headlined: *BRISCOE: LE DEMOLISSEUR*. The photo took up over the front page—that's how big this fight was. When we got to the airport, I felt like I didn't need a plane to fly home.

Chapter Eighteen
Losing the Kitten

Kitten Hayward covers up against Willie Mornoe in 1974. (Peltz collection)

When I got back from Paris, we showcased junior lightweights Sammy Goss and Tyrone Everett in separate 10-round fights on March 11 at the Spectrum. Both won *decisions, Goss over Mexico's Clemente Mucino, Everett over North Philly's Luis Lopez. Tickets were $5, $7 and $10, as they had been for Willie Monroe-Cyclone Hart fight in February. The crowd was 4,820 and Goss and Everett would fight each other, seven weeks later.*

I convinced the Spectrum to support me at the Blue Horizon to develop talent for the big arena. They agreed to contribute up to $500 per card. The rest was on me. Junior welterweight Mike Everett and junior lightweight Jerome Artis each headlined twice, but the biggest crowd was 623 for Li'l Abner's eight-round decision over Juan Rueda, of Puerto Rico, on December 10. The Blue Horizon's resurgence remained years down the road.

Kitten Hayward had agreed to fight the winner of Monroe-Hart but when Monroe won, I should have made other plans. Kitten visited them in their dressing rooms after their fight, telling the sportswriters he was looking forward to fighting Monroe, but he really wanted Hart. One reason was revenge for his humiliating one-round knockout loss three years earlier. The bigger reason was that Kitten did not like to fight tall boxers, and the 6-foot Monroe had at least three inches on him.

As we left Monroe's dressing room, I handed Kitten the contract, but he walked away, saying he needed to think about it.

"Are you a man of your word?" I yelled. He turned around and signed the contract as I held it against the wall. But I should have discussed it with him. I should have matched Kitten with Hart, even though Hart had lost, and I should have saved Monroe for Dynamite Douglas. Hart and Hayward would have been a match fans would have paid to see. Kitten would have talked it up, declaring that there would be more action in one round of him against Hart than in 10 rounds of Monroe against Hart. Instead, his pride made him sign and I was too dense to understand what I had done.

It was not the first time pride had gotten Kitten in trouble. Late in 1966 he was the No. 1 welterweight contender in the world. He had beaten six good men in a row—Percy Manning, Dick Turner, Curtis Cokes, Vince Shomo, Tito Marshall and Bennie Briscoe—but he had not boxed in the 10 months since his war with Briscoe. Manager George Katz wanted him to fight Gypsy Joe Harris, who was unbeaten in 14 fights against unranked opposition. Katz was not impressed with the 20-year-old Gypsy Joe. Kitten was.

"I've been off for 10 months and that young kid is fighting regular," Kitten told Katz.

"What's the matter, are you scared?" Katz said.

Kitten signed, and Kitten lost. He knocked Gypsy Joe down in the third round, but he was cut over both eyes and taking a beating when Katz stopped it after six. Kitten needed 15 stitches. He was out of the title picture and out of action for seven months. Here I was, eight years later, acting like Katz. I went against the blueprint of Teddy Brenner, one of boxing's best-ever matchmakers.

In a 1969 *Sports Illustrated* story, by Jerry Kirshenbaum, Brenner said: "Matchmaking…is not simply a matter of putting the No. 1 and No. 2 men in the ring. Anybody could do that. It is a matter first of determining whether the styles of the two fighters blend. Then you have to decide if it's an important fight. In other words, will the winner move on to a bigger fight? And is it one that I as a fan would want to see? The fans want to see the best fight, and that doesn't necessarily mean the best fighters."

The crowd of 6,095, which saw Monroe-Hayward on April 8, would have been bigger but for people staying home to watch Hank Aaron break Babe Ruth's home run record on TV. The fight was no fight at all. Monroe moved around the ring and never gave Hayward a target. He boxed behind his jab, busted Hayward's face open, and closed his right eye. Ringside physician Dr. Alfred Ayella, Jr. would not let Kitten come out for the seventh.

Kitten lost the fight, and we lost Kitten. We lost him as a fighter, and we lost his wit, his wisdom, his humor, his personality. "I'm gonna hang a sign on my eye that says, 'Closed for the week,'" he joked. It was a great line, but a sad one.

As for Monroe, he finally began to believe in himself.

"I'd never talk bad about Yank (Durham)…I loved him," Monroe told Tom Cushman, of the *Daily News*, "but I have to wonder, if he still was my trainer, if I'd be fighting these guys today. He had one philosophy. Eddie (Futch) has another. All I need to say about Eddie is that he is one of the greatest trainer-managers in the world, and everybody is beginning to learn. I got tired of fighting around the country for $1,000 purses. What's happened recently is like suddenly waking up in front of a gold mine. I think I deserve it because I've been in the business 10 years and I work hard. I was starting to wonder, though, if this time was ever gonna come."

Monroe earned $10,000 for Hart, $10,000 for Hayward. Those two purses combined are worth $114,000 today—calculated solely on inflation—and they were based on ticket sales. There would be more down the road.

If you're going to feel sorry for someone, try Sammy Goss. He turned pro in 1969, won 39 of his first 42 fights, and avenged one of his losses. Despite not carrying a big punch, he had a pleasing style. Early in his career people called him "Little Joe" because he fought like Joe Frazier. By the time he met Everett, Goss had fought on national television, won the USBA and NABF junior lightweight titles, and had headlined at the Blue Horizon, Arena, Spectrum, and Felt Forum and Madison Square Garden in New York.

Yet he never got a chance to fight for the world championship. Ben Villaflor, a Filipino living in Hawaii, and Kuniaki Shibata, of Japan, traded the WBA crown back and forth, while Ricardo Arredondo held the WBC title. In the three years before Goss-Everett, 10 junior lightweight championship fights were held in Japan, four in Hawaii, one in Mexico. There was not enough money to lure Arredondo to Philadelphia for a rematch and he did not draw well enough in Mexico for Goss to go there. Little guys earned big purses in Asia, so Villaflor and Shibata stayed put.

I was close with Goss' managers, Pinny Schafer and Pat Duffy, but I wasn't part of the team. Goss headlined five of my first 15 cards at the Blue Horizon, yet I'd been cut out of his 1970 Spectrum showdown with Augie Pantellas. Brenner used Goss four times in New York, but the Garden never got him a title fight. By the time he fought Everett, Goss had boxed for me 16 times.

It was different with Everett. Frank Gelb and I had a handshake agreement that whenever Everett boxed in Philadelphia, it would be for me. If Everett fought out of town, it would benefit both of us. Gelb was the businessman and I was the boxing man, not that I can recall a single opponent he ever questioned. In fact, several times he suggested opponents and helped me get them.

The 8,628 who came to the Goss-Everett fight represented the third largest crowd since I had become the Spectrum's Director of Boxing. The gate receipts, also the third highest, were $61,965. Monroe-Hart remained number one, followed by Briscoe-Douglas.

I expected Everett to win, but I had no idea how decisively. He knocked Goss down in the second round with a left hook and won every round with the exception of the fourth. At the end of 12, Everett was awarded scores of 59-49 twice and 60-49 under the Pennsylvania 5-point system. I asked Everett not to say anything negative about Goss that would detract from his big win. He ignored me.

"All he (Goss) does is slap," Everett told Cushman. "I can't understand how he got as far up in the ratings as he did. My sparring partner hits harder. I think he was scared the whole fight. He wouldn't even look at me at the introductions. He was looking at the floor."

Goss showed class: "He'll (Everett) make a good champion."

Even though he was just 27, Goss would never again be the same. He would win only four of his next 18 fights and retire in 1981.

We were riding high with five attractive cards and five solid crowds. Spectrum Fights made $14,943.20 ($84,249 in 2021) on Goss-Everett. Then the Law of Averages caught us.

Boogaloo Watts agreed to fight Hart on May 22, but Hart injured his ankle in sparring 12 days prior. By May 18, Hart's ankle was in a cast, and I could not get a decent replacement. Instead of cancelling, I moved the welterweight semifinal between Alfonso Hayman and Roy Barrientos, of Fort Worth, Texas, to the main event. Hayman won by majority decision in a good fight that no one saw. The crowd was 1,526 and we lost $10,839.27 ($61,112 in 2021), our first setback of the year.

Chapter Nineteen

Disaster in Monte Carlo

Princess Grace greets Bennie Briscoe in Monte Carlo. (Arnold Weiss photo)

I got off the plane at the Nice Cote d'Azur International Airport, 40 miles from San Remo, Italy, where Bennie Briscoe was training to fight Rodrigo Valdes for the vacant WBC middleweight title the next day (May 25) in Monte Carlo. Bob Arum, who had worked in the tax division of the U.S. Attorney's Office for the Southern District of New York, had been promoting fights since

1966. He and his European partner, Rodolfo Sabatini, put this one together. Waiting in the car were Bennie and cut man Milt Bailey. The drive to San Remo would take an hour through small villages and over mountain roads.

Bennie wasn't happy. He said that my brother-in-law had cheated him out of a signing bonus four years earlier when he had bought Bennie's contract from Jimmy Iselin. I had no idea what he was talking about. I should have asked if he had gotten a bonus when Iselin bought his contract from Pinny Schafer. He hadn't. Bailey was quiet.

This hornet's nest had been stirred up by Bennie's trainer, Quenzell McCall, who never got along with Arnold. McCall had brought attorney Allen J. Beckman to Monte Carlo to try to break the managerial contract. Quenzell and Beckman had filled Bennie's head with negative thoughts about Arnold while Bennie was training for one of the biggest fights of his life.

This was a Bennie Briscoe I never knew. Missing was the man who had shared a hotel room with me in Atlantic City. Gone was the guy who had smiled when he caught me and Nigel Collins smoking weed in my car one night outside the 23rd PAL. ("Uncle Russ, you guys gettin' down?") This was not the fighter who had reveled in the joy of his knockout of Tony Mundine in Paris. This Bennie Briscoe was sullen and angry and he had his mind made up that he had not been treated fairly.

The week of a fight for a world middleweight title, the camp was split down the middle by lies.

The WBC had stripped Carlos Monzon for turning down an offer to defend against Valdes in Colombia. It made no sense to strip Monzon, but we jumped at the opportunity ($40,000 purse; $226,000 in 2021) to avenge Briscoe's loss to Valdes the previous August. Now, on the verge of Bennie winning a title, McCall, who'd passed on his chance to buy into the management in 1970, had started trouble. He thought Briscoe would win and he wanted to cash in. Briscoe, McCall, Bailey and Beckman were on one side, Arnold and I on the other.

Beckman took me to dinner in a remote bistro outside of San Remo and told me he could break the contract. He said he and McCall would keep me as promoter. That was nice of them. Sure!

The next day, Beckman, McCall, Arnold, his close friend, Buzz Marcus, and I met. McCall asked if Marcus had a financial interest in Briscoe's career, perhaps hoping that some secret deal between them could help Beckman break the contract. Buzz was there as a fan only. The meeting ended with nothing resolved.

The lightest moment of the trip came one morning when Bennie told me he heard a knock on his door late at night. When he opened it, there was a beautiful French girl, completely naked, wanting to enter. He politely declined. I reminded him my room was down the hallway. Bennie also got to visit a famous Philadelphian at her palace. She was Grace Kelly, known as Princess Grace.

The car that took Bennie to the outdoor fight at the Louis II stadium included McCall, Bailey and Beckman. Arnold, my sister, Bootsie, Marcus and his wife, Ronnie, went in a separate car. I went in a van with William Watson, a North Philly sparring partner, and Armando Muniz, another sparring partner who later would fight for the world welterweight title.

Bennie weighed 157½, the lightest he had been since the first Valdes fight nine months earlier. I wondered if the pre-fight turmoil had affected him. He was stunned in the first round and behind after six (59-57, 59-56, 60-55), but still forcing the action. Valdes, badley cut over his left eye, began throwing *Hail Mary* shots, and late in round seven a right hand stiffened Bennie. His body quivered. A follow-up left hook put Bennie on his back. He managed to get up but referee Harry Gibbs waved it off at 2:55.

The dressing rooms at the stadium looked like they came from a second-rate high school gym. There were rusted metal lockers and wooden benches with no backs. When I got there, Bennie sat next to Watson. No one spoke. Watson put his left arm around him and Bennie fell in and cried on his shoulder. Here was Bennie Briscoe, whom the French had dubbed *Le Robot Noir* for his relentless, stoic forward march, weeping. It was the only time in 96 fights he had been stopped and, I believe, the only time he felt someone had taken something from him—manhood, pride.

On the plane home Beckman asked me what was next. He and McCall had counted on big money but Bennie was back to square one and Beckman was scrambling. I said we'd have to see how long it took to get back into position.

Beckman disappeared. The next time I saw him was 36 years later at Bennie's funeral. He was in a wheelchair. I said hello, then left. Arnold refused to talk to him.

Ex-welterweight and middleweight champion Emile Griffith had beaten Renato Garcia (23-0 going in) on the Monte Carlo undercard. After years of trying, I signed Griffith to box Bennie at the Spectrum on October 9. A win would get Bennie back in the running, but he fought like a zombie. He had looked like that in training, too.

After the Griffith loss, McCall questioned Bennie's desire, and the trouble that had bubbled in Monte Carlo boiled over in public.

"This guy (Weiss) is into boxing as a social venture," McCall told Tom Cushman, of the *Daily News*. "We were in Monte Carlo for a championship fight this year and Arnold Weiss was conducting tours of Anzio Beach. He had no concept of what the sport involves when he started, and he hasn't learned anything since."

Arnold saw things differently: "When we came back from New Caledonia after fighting Valdes the first time, Quenzell told us Bennie was washed up. After that he told Bennie not to sign with me again. I think he smelled big money then, and I'm suspicious of his motives now. I know he always wanted to manage the fighter."

Briscoe summed things up perfectly: "When you're a kid, your mom and dad do all the talking and you're never allowed to say anything for yourself. That's the way it was with me and Quenzell. When I started boxing at 16, 17, 18, he started doing my thinking. The thing is I'm 31 now and he still wants it to be the same way. I asked for a new trainer. The thing I resented most was what Quenzell said about me in the papers when I lost (to Griffith), like I didn't try, like I was a bum.

"I don't think it was me that lost interest, I think it was him. How can a man come to the gym in a shirt and tie and stand there and wave at you and think he's doing a job. I know Quenzell's a big man now, and I know he's more interested in Congressman Bill Green (as a liaison to the Black community) than he is in prizefighters. I mean he didn't roll up his sleeves and show me anything new. He didn't give me credit for nothing. I respect him, but I'm human. I want respect, too."

I had been in the middle of the chaos in Monte Carlo and had not handled it well. I was there when Bennie cried, but I never sat down with him and discussed it. After the Griffith fight, he was smarter than the rest of us. Whether Quenzell quit Bennie as Quenzell claimed, or Bennie quit Quenzell as Bennie claimed, their union was over.

Quenzell approached me one day at the Cloverlay Gym and said he would reconsider, but it was too late. Bennie already had talked with George Benton and George had agreed to train him. My relationship with Quenzell would never again be close. Former lightweight pro Sidney "Sweet Pea" Adams came aboard as the third man in Bennie's corner. Bailey remained as cut man.

Benton had boxed Briscoe in 1966 and gave as well as he took until Briscoe's youth—he was 10 years younger—took over. Benton did not answer the bell for the 10th round. Eight years later Benton would train the man who had beaten him. Benton had worked well with Eddie Futch for Joe Frazier against Jerry Quarry that June in Madison Square Garden. He had also worked with Futch in the corner of Willie Monroe.

"At first I said no," Benton told Cushman. "I know Quenzell and I respect him and I didn't want to go messing into that situation. But they kept talking to me, and it was obvious Quenzell was out, and the Cloverlay people said it would be okay, so I finally agreed. I watched Bennie Briscoe against Griffith and I don't think there's anything wrong with him but himself. Self-discipline, which he has never had, and mental peace-of-mind, which he hasn't had recently, is all he needs. I've been around this game so long—I can't remember when I wasn't—that I can sense these things."

Briscoe would become Benton's first fighter as head trainer. It was a new beginning for both.

Chapter Twenty

Back to Broad and Pattison

Willie Monroe grabs Dynamite Douglas on his way down. (Peltz collection)

Joe McGuigan was the son of Jack McGuigan, who had hired a teenage Herman Taylor at the turn of the 20th century to help promote at the National Athletic Club. The National AC, at

11th and Catherine Streets, was one of the world's premier boxing venues in its day. Jack refereed many of the fights he promoted as well as others around the country. Joe, a former referee himself, had been out of boxing for 20 years when he began promoting in 1974. He ran one show at the Arena. Light-heavyweight Richie Kates scored a shocking one-punch, first-round knockout over former world-title challenger Jimmy Dupree, of Jersey City, but the crowd was less than 1,500 and McGuigan sat out the rest of the year.

Boogaloo Watts and Cyclone Hart were from North Philadelphia. They got together on July 15, 1974, but not for long. Their 10-round middleweight fight lasted two minutes and 49 seconds. Watts' left-right combination drove an overly aggressive Hart through the ropes, onto the press tables. By the time Hart got back into the ring, "Quick Count" Cisco had him out. The Spectrum crowd of 5,185 was stunned. Conventional wisdom was that if anyone would score a quick knockout, it would be Hart.

In the semifinal, Mario Saurennann (17-17-7, 3 K0s) rallied in the last four rounds to upset fellow-Philadelphian William Watson (17-3, 8 K0s) by 10-round majority decision. Watson, who had split-decisioned Saurennann three months earlier, suffered a detached retina and never boxed again.

Five weeks later, unbeaten Tyrone Everett was in the nominal main event, a two-round blowout of Blakeney Matthews, a South African who never had been stopped in 52 previous fights (37-10-5 record). It was a performance I believed Tyrone could have displayed at any time. He looked like a future champion, but no one knew Matthews and most of the 7,122 came to see Willie Monroe fight Dynamite Douglas.

Monroe's trainer, Eddie Futch, saw his worst nightmare unfold in the eighth round of a fight Monroe was winning. A left from Douglas landed flush and Monroe grabbed him around the chest, waist, hips, legs and ankles on his way down.

"I am sure that Monroe's knee hit the canvas right away and if that's true then the timekeeper blew it," said Bruce Trampler, Douglas' manager. "The count should have been past 10 by the time Monroe got to his feet."

Trampler argued for a No Contest, but, like most protests, it went nowhere. Scores were 45-44 and 47-44 twice, all for Monroe, now

29-2-1, 21 KOs. He was 28 and ranked among the best 160-pounders in the world.

We switched from Monday nights to avoid conflicts with *Monday Night Football*, in the fall, and changed our name from *Monday Night Fights* to *Spectrum Fights.*

Tyrone Everett starched Jose Luis Madrid, of Mexico, in two rounds on Tuesday, September 10, for his 22nd straight win, but an awful decision spoiled the semifinal. Alfonso Hayman was awarded the split verdict and the Pennsylvania welterweight title after getting undressed by Saurennann for 12 rounds. The only official who scored it correctly was referee Tommy Reid, who had it 58-52 for Saurennann. Judges Dave Beloff (56-54) and Lou Tress (55-54) scored it for Hayman. We would hear more from Tress two years later. The *Bulletin*, *Inquirer* and *Daily News* all had Saurennann winning clearly.

The crowd of 4,425 "booed, stomped and hooted" as Courtney wrote in the *Inquirer*, but Saurennann, whom I'd met in 1965 at Temple when we were students, gave a calm post-fight response all boxers could learn from.

"It's a political thing," he said. "The other fighter is the younger guy, the drawing card. I thought I won it all the way. Offensively, defensively, overall ring strategy, even sportsmanship. In every category. Hayman's an innocent victim. Deep down, he knows I was the better man tonight. I nullified all his advances. I'll go out, have a beer or two. Spend time with my true friends. If I thought I was finished I'd be despondent. But I won that fight and I'll be back in the gym. It's a way of life. I just don't enjoy the shenanigans."

Saurennann was born in Harlem, but came to Philly when he was 4 to be raised by a grandmother who cleaned houses. As a kid he had been a gang member. In 1958, when he was 13, Saurennann was arrested when he was caught with a gun after a street fight. He was expelled from Simon Gratz High School and sent to Morgana State Training School near Pittsburgh for 20 months. He straightened out when he learned that his grandmother had both legs amputated.

"I became the man in the family," he said.

After several jobs, among them car washer and packager in an appliance plant, Saurennann realized he would never get anywhere without an education. He saved enough money to go to Temple High School in 1964 with the help of an anonymous benefactor who gave him and his grandmother $100 a month for living expenses. He learned to speak French and became one of six to win a French Graham scholarship, donated by a wealthy industrialist to aid needy students in the Temple University area. He majored in social welfare there.

Saurennann had started boxing at the 23rd PAL gym when he was 12. He won the Junior National AAU Championship at 132 pounds in 1961. One year later he won the Middle Atlantic AAU Championship at 135 pounds. Power in amateur boxing is not as important as accuracy.

When he failed to make the 1964 U.S. Olympic team, Saurennann rationalized it: "If I'd gone to the Olympics, I wouldn't have started my education." He boxed as a pro from 1965 until 1978 and was 20-21-7. Saurennann was a pure boxer who never was appreciated in his hometown because he wasn't a big puncher—only six knockouts—and he wasn't a showboat, but no one had an easy time with him from 135 to 147 pounds. He was stopped once in 48 fights.

In 2010, Saurennann was diagnosed with Alzheimer's. His neurologist said boxing contributed to its early onset. He had worked for the city's Department of Recreation for 30 years. He and his wife, Brenda, have two kids and live in Philly.

There was one more fight to make. It was between Monroe and Watts, the two survivors of the disjointed mythical Philadelphia middleweight tournament. Watts won a unanimous 10-round decision in a classic boxing match. Scores were 46-45 and 47-45 twice.

"I'd like for them (Spectrum Fights) to bring the old man Griffith back for me," said Watts, now 25-3-1. "I also hope that now business will pick up for me."

As good as he was—and he was very good—Watts never was an attraction at the box office. He was not a street-corner guy. He was a friendly, happy man outside of boxing. He'd worked steadily since he was 15.

Spectrum Fights turned a profit on seven of the 11 cards in 1974, but Watts' postponed fight with Hart (5,185 customers) and the finale with Monroe (4,931) lost money.

The biggest winner at the box office was Monroe-Hart and the biggest loser was Monroe-Watts. One of the four losers was the May 22 card when Hart injured his ankle and we moved the Hayman-Roy Barrientos fight to the main event rather than cancel. We also lost a few dollars on Bennie Briscoe-Emile Griffith since we had to pay Griffith $20,000 ($113,000 in 2021 dollars). We paid Monroe and Watts $10,000 apiece for their fight and when ticket sales totaled only $30,698, we lost $13,664.00 ($77,000 in 2021). Griffith versus Watts was not affordable.

Watts was managed by Sylvia Booker, who signed him after his disastrous West Coast trip in 1970. Sylvia's husband, Clarence, called himself the trainer, but on fight nights the chief second was Jimmy Arthur. Sylvia helped Watts with a down payment on a house and she had a good heart, but she negotiated every fight like it was Ali-Frazier. She tried my patience. Watts should have been an integral part of our program, but Sylvia wanted more than Watts was worth at the box office.

After beating Monroe, Watts did not fight again for 10 months. When he did, he was paid $2,750 for knocking out James Marshall, of Los Angeles, at the Spectrum. Time was wasted. Watts was turning 26 and in his prime.

Chapter Twenty-One
Thrilla in South Philla

Tyrone Everett was too much for Bert Nabalatan in 1975. (Peltz collection)

Tyrone Everett headlined five of the Spectrum's 11 cards in 1975, Bennie Briscoe four. A new promotional group, the Walker Brothers, ran six times at the Arena and did better than Joe McGuigan, who bowed out after two financially draining shows at the Tower Theatre in Upper Darby, just outside West Philadelphia. There were 25 cards in the metropolitan area, seven more than the year before. We promoted six at the Blue Horizon. The 1,027 fans who saw Jerome Artis box a 10-round draw with Sammy Goss there in December was the largest crowd since we'd reopened the building the previous year. I promoted once at the Trenton Civic Center with Goss and once on a bitter cold February night at Club Arlo, a former movie theatre in Camden, where the landlord kept the heat off until the card started and the 385 customers wore overcoats while we hovered around an open stove in the box office. In The Philippines, Muhammad Ali and Joe Frazier waged the Thrilla in Manila, the last great fight for each.

One Tyrone Everett fight would be exciting, the next boring. He was boxing the best in the world at 130 pounds, often not losing a round—often to yawns. He headlined the opening show, but was backed up by Briscoe's return and a 10-round fight featuring future WBA light-heavyweight champion Eddie Mustafa Muhammad (then Eddie Gregory), of New York, who knocked out Steve Smith, of Philadelphia, in four.

The card drew 8,215 and a gate of $60,033. Tickets were $5, $7 and $10. Everett was less than sensational. His opponent, Bert Nabalatan, was a world-rated lefty with a 20-5 record, 15 K0s. Everett said he jammed his left hand two weeks prior in sparring, but he won by scores of 47-44, 49-41 and 49-44. He circled and popped jabs and right hands all night, never moving in until the 10th round, when his lead was insurmountable.

Briscoe got hit more than usual by Lenny Harden, of Rahway, New Jersey. He lost the first two rounds, knocked Harden down in the third and suffered a cut over his left eye in the fourth. They traded power shots the rest of the way while Briscoe grew accustomed to George Benton's teaching. He knocked Harden down twice in the ninth with left hooks and a third ended it at 1:36 of the 10th.

It was Briscoe's 50th victory against 14 losses and two draws. The crowd loved it. When Everett bragged to me about his virtuoso performance, I reminded him that Briscoe stole the show. He didn't say a thing. I was jabbing back at him because he had ridiculed Briscoe after the loss to Emile Griffith three months earlier.

One highlight of the night was a four-round fight between two jockeys. Hungarian-born Paul Kallai decisioned New Jersey's Ralph Baker in a four-round fight watched by their fellow jockeys from Garden State (New Jersey) Race Track. Each man weighed 112.

As sharp as Everett was in March when he knocked out Jose Luis Lopez—who had split two fights with Goss—that's how safety-first he looked in May, waltzing to a 10-round decision over fifth-ranked

Pedro Aguero, of Argentina. A crowd of 6,413 saw the Lopez fight, 6,711 saw Aguero.

Jack McKinney, the hard-nosed Irishman on the *Daily News*, was not an Everett fan. McKinney was a tough man and he liked his fighters that way. He had been close to, and had sparred with, Sonny Liston. He had one pro fight himself and scored a first-round knockout, retiring undefeated.

"Any smart hostess would know better than to invite Pedro Aguero and Tyrone Everett to the same party," McKinney wrote, "because the last time they got together they almost had a fight."

In July, 8,014 saw Everett annihilate Hyun Chai Kim in six rounds. Kim was 23-1 when he arrived from Korea, four months after losing a 15-round split decision to Ben Villaflor in Quezon City for the WBA junior lightweight title. Everett made Kim look like an amateur. The slaughter was stopped in at 1:25 of the sixth round, with Everett yelling at Kim: "I'm mean, man, mean." Kim spoke no English.

McKinney threw his own jabs at Everett: "The undefeated southpaw from South Philadelphia may very well be the best 130-pounder in the world today, for whatever that's worth. He certainly deserves a shot at the world junior lightweight championship, for whatever that's worth. But class? That's only for people who prefer hot dogs to sirloin. Everett displayed his perverted sense of class last night by taunting a beaten, half-blind opponent who might have jumped out of the ring if his handlers hadn't responded to his pleas to throw the towel into it.

"So, after 27 wins, Tyrone Everett still leaves a lot of people with the distinct impression that he is a front runner whose courage is directly related to the recognition of his opponent's ineptness. And from what local fans have seen of the barely warm bodies that have been imported for him, Everett's division must be the most abundantly inept in all of boxing."

In September, Benjamin Ortiz, managed by the people who had WBC champion Alfredo Escalera, almost spoiled everything. Midway through the seventh round, Ortiz unloaded a right which knocked Everett almost horizontal into the ropes. After that, Ortiz pursued and Everett moved left and right and away. The scores were unanimous (48-44, 48-42, 49-43) for Everett, wider than the writers or fans thought. Stan Hochman had it 47-45 in the *Daily News*.

Escalera's manager, Filiberto Lebron, thought if Ortiz could hurt Everett, imagine what Escalera could do.

Everett claimed Ortiz never made weight, even though Everett's manager, Frank Gelb, was there when Ortiz, who was 131 pounds at the initial weigh-in, came back at 128. Everett accused me of not honoring the weight clause in his contract, claiming I was trying to get him beat. He was on the verge of a world-title fight, but our relationship, never great, spiraled downhill. We communicated through Gelb. At one press luncheon, Gelb sat between us, relaying messages.

While that soap opera played out, Briscoe was resurrecting his career. He was held to a disputed 10-round draw by Boston's Vinnie Curto in April, after which I—the so-called unbiased promoter—went ballistic outside the dressing rooms, berating the judges. Mary Ann Collins, Nigel's wife, calmed me down. Briscoe hit Curto with bombs, Curto hit Briscoe with feathers. Scores were 48-42 for Briscoe, 46-44 for Curto, and 46-46.

Kitten Hayward returned in April and knocked out Steve Smith at the Blue Horizon to set up a fight with Briscoe, a decade after their legendary bout which had left Kitten, the winner, in the hospital. Briscoe was 32 and his comeback was gaining traction. Kitten was 36 and he knew the tricks even if he no longer could execute them.

The fight lacked the fireworks of their 1965 war and Briscoe won 47-44 and 46-44 twice. Tom Cushman scored 46-45 for Hayward in the *Daily News*. The crowd of 6,398 favored Briscoe, but not by much.

Briscoe edged the inexperienced Gregory in August. Gregory was 13-1-1, 10 K0s, one over Cyclone Hart in New York, and three straight knockout wins in Philly. Only 23, he was the first dangerous test for Briscoe since Benton took over. It was a stupid fight to make. Briscoe didn't need this young tiger. But I was a promoter first, and sometimes I wore blinders. For two rounds Gregory stayed outside, scoring points, but in the third he decided to stand and trade.

"I was happy as a sissy in Boys' Town when I saw Gregory stop and fight," Benton told Cushman. "I had confidence by that time that Bennie would follow instructions, wouldn't get careless, and that's what happened. When they started firing, Bennie was making him miss, (then) firing back. It was a beautiful round. After that, Mr. Gregory got on his pony and started galloping."

Gregory disagreed: "His eyes were all cut up, too. I was moving so fast he couldn't see me in those late rounds. It was close but I'm sure I won. He's (Briscoe) still there, man. He's not all washed up like they said he was." Referee Tommy Reed voted 46-44 for Gregory, but was overruled by judges Earl Vann (46-44 Briscoe) and Jimmy Brown (49-42 for Briscoe).

When I walked into Eddie's dressing room, he smiled from the rubbing table and bellowed "49-42." He was not wrong. Looking back, I have the same opinion I had that night—the fight was close, but Briscoe dictated the pace. Had it been in Brooklyn, Eddie gets it. But it wasn't.

Jimmy Walker was a local concert promoter. Brother Billy was close with Sam Solomon, who was back with Cyclone Hart after Hart's losses to Willie Monroe, Boogaloo Watts and Gregory. Jim Jacobs remained as manager. Hart scored knockouts over Radames Cabrera, Mario Rosa and Chu Chu Garcia on Walker Brothers cards at the Arena. In August, Hart earned a 10-round decision over Sugar Ray Seales in Atlantic City on the last promotion of Herman Taylor's Hall-of-Fame career. He passed away four years later at 93.

Hart versus Briscoe, a fight everyone had dreamed about years earlier, was back in vogue, but Hart was scheduled to fight Willie Warren on October 14 for the Walker Brothers. Warren was a short, tough guy. Hitting him was like hitting a fire hydrant. He was 41-26-1 and had been stopped only four times in 68 fights, twice on cuts. He had lost decisions to Watts, Monroe, Dynamite Douglas and Yaqui Lopez.

I worried that Hart would fade if Warren survived the early rounds. I didn't want anything to jeopardize the Briscoe-Hart fight. Using the excuse "the end satisfies the means," I went directly to Hart. He was sitting on the ring steps at the Cloverlay Gym one afternoon, taping his hands. He was risking the biggest payday of his career going against Warren.

"It's not that he can beat you," I said, "but he's got a solid chin and he is short and can head-butt you and that would delay the money you will get in the Briscoe fight." Hart told Jacobs to cancel. Jacobs called to say that, without signed contracts, he could not force Hart to fight Warren so we made the Briscoe fight for November 18.

Ticket sales were strong. A few weeks before the fight, I went to the Spectrum box office to deposit ticket money. Blanche McNamee, who worked there, said: "Business must be good because your press is bad." She was referring to a story by Bob Wright, who had left the *Camden Courier-Post* to become the boxing writer at the *Bulletin* following Jack Fried's retirement in 1973.

Wright re-visited the way I'd made the fight. "Twenty years ago, that kind of goings on would have gotten him (Peltz) a new set of teeth," Solomon told Wright. "Peltz put me in the position of having to go back on my word and, by some of the things he told my fighter, he kind of left the idea that I wasn't doin' right by Gene. I don't appreciate it, I can tell you that."

Jimmy Walker was not happy: "I didn't need a written contract because Sam Solomon had given me his word. This isn't the first time we've had problems because of Peltz. He's told other fighters that if they fight for us they won't be fightin' for him anymore. We can't match dollars with him, because we're still getting established. He's trying to keep this a one promoter town—with him holding all the aces."

"I'm going to picket the Spectrum and let all the fight fans in Philadelphia know what kind of person Russell Peltz is," Walker told John B. Rhodes, of *The Philadelphia Tribune*. "He (Peltz) controls boxing in this town and has made it difficult for me to stay in business. Since January, when my brother and I started, he has made it difficult for us to operate. He's (Peltz) slick, he never does things against me directly but indirectly."

Walker led a group of pickets outside the Spectrum on October 21 when heavyweight Duane Bobick stopped Rochelle Norris in two rounds. If the picket line deterred customers it was a good thing because only 4,011 saw a fight in which Norris was suspected of being on drugs, a charge never proven. A bigger reason for the small crowd was Game 6 of the 1975 World Series, the one where Boston Red Sox catcher Carlton Fisk waved his game-winning home run against Cincinnati inside the left field foul pole.

Hart and Briscoe were open at the pre-fight press conference.

Hart: "What you have to understand is that there is more pressure in this fight than in any one I've ever been in. That's because we're so much alike. We specialize in pressure. I'm pressure to him, he's pressure to me. You have to be more alert in a fight like that, but it doesn't mean it won't be a brutal fight because that's exactly what it will be. What is it they say in Philadelphia? Whoever gets hit first goes, right? Well, that's the way it will be. That first clean shot turns the fight."

Briscoe: "You know something, this is the only fight I can remember that I'll just be glad when it's over. I've fought guys just as good, or better, but I know this can't be no less than a very tough night. Hometown boys are always badder than the others. He's a corner boy, I'm a corner boy. We got a lot of the same acquaintances. We train at the same gym. After all, everybody wants to be the champ of the neighborhood."

The fight was a classic. Briscoe shoved Hart to the floor in the second and stunned him late in the third. Hart poleaxed Briscoe in the sixth and they fought after the bell in the third and seventh rounds. There were no knockdowns but Hart was badly hurt from a Briscoe right late in the eighth and he barely survived when Briscoe pinned him in his own corner. At the bell, Hart staggered across the ring to a neutral corner before Solomon and corner man Willie Folk retrieved him.

Benton made a rare mistake before the ninth when he told Briscoe to be wary. Without much pressure on him, Hart cleared his head and came out fresh for the 10th. He poured punches on Briscoe. Most missed or landed on arms, shoulders and elbows, but it was enough to give him the round on two of the three cards. It was a draw: 46-44 Briscoe from referee Pete Tomasco; 45-44 Hart from judge Earl Vann; 45-45 from judge Dave Beloff.

Boxing News, the weekly publication based in England, rated it the second best fight of 1975. The *Thrilla in Manilla* was first and *The Thrilla in South Philla* was next. The crowd of 11,021 paid $74,738. Hart fought for 25 percent of the ticket sales (less city, state tax and commission officials). His purse came to just under $16,000 ($81,000 in 2021). Briscoe fought for 30 percent and his purse came to just under $20,000 ($101,000). Spectrum Fights profit was just under $10,000 ($51,000). They would meet again.

Chapter Twenty-Two

Marvelous Marv

Marvin Hagler under fire from Willie Monroe in 1976. (Zohrab Kazanjian photo)

In the 1970s, the best middleweights in the country wanted to fight at the Spectrum. Marvin Hagler was one. Hagler had moved with his mother to Brockton, Massachusetts, after the urban riots in the summer of 1967 left 26 people dead in his Newark, New Jersey, hometown. After getting roughed up in a street fight, he went to a gym run by Goody and Pat Petronelli, who had begun training fighters in 1969. Hagler had more than 50 amateur fights and won the National AAU 165-pound title in 1973, the same year he turned pro.

By 1976, Hagler was 25-0-1, 19 K0s. He had boxed twice in Maine, 23 times in Massachusetts. His only match outside New England was a 10-round draw with Sugar Ray Seales in Seattle, Seales' backyard. Hagler previously had beaten Seales in Boston. Most of Hagler's fights were promoted by Sam Silverman, who had worked the New England circuit since the 1930s and had promoted 32 Rocky Marciano fights. Hagler needed to break out and Silverman delivered him for a $2,000 purse ($9,400 in 2021 dollars) for the main event on January 13 against Boogaloo Watts.

Hagler trained at the Cloverlay Gym where Joe Frazier told him, "You have three strikes against you—you're Black, you're a southpaw and you're good." Not everyone was impressed. Quenzell McCall told me, after watching Hagler spar, that he would be just another fighter if he were right-handed. What we did not know about Hagler was his self-discipline and determination.

At the press luncheon, Hagler recited poetry:

"The Philadelphia fighters have ducked me so long,
Now Bobby Watts will dance to my song.
But he won't do the Boogaloo,
Only the bump.
I wanted Hart and Briscoe ran;
Willie the Worm crawled in the sand.
Now I've got the best of the whole damn crew.
And they'll finally see what Marvin can do.
The Spectrum crowd is in for a treat,
Cause one of their best is doomed to defeat.
In the city where Rocky took the crown,
Another Brocktonian will go to town."

A crowd of 6,167 watched Hagler lose a majority decision. Referee Hank Cisco had it 46-46, but judges Nate Lopinson (48-44) and Earl Vann (46-44) voted for Watts. I looked at Lopinson and blew him away with the wave you give someone you never want to see again.

On the way to my office, I ran into Spectrum President Allen Flexer. "How could they do that?" he asked. When I saw Silverman, sitting outside Hagler's dressing room, I apologized. He brushed me off, saying he'd seen it before. In the *Daily News* the following day, Stan Hochman wrote it best:

"Marvin Hagler, the fighter from Brockton;
Fought at the Spectrum and barely got socked on.
Boogaloo Watts he did carve;
And guess what happened to Marvelous Marv?"

Gene Courtney's *Inquirer* story headlined: "Marvin Hagler, Welcome to Philly." Courtney opened: "Marvin Hagler, the boxer-poet from Brockton, Mass., disproved the invincibility of Philadelphia's middleweights but he didn't count on the ineptitude of the local judges and, as a result, he sustained the first loss of his career when Bobby Watts got the decision last night at the Spectrum."

Not a single member of the press scored for Watts.

I matched Willie Monroe with Vinnie Curto for March 9. Curto, Hagler's New England rival, had held Bennie Briscoe to that disputed draw in 1975. "Curto will never show up," Pat Petronelli said. "We're gonna keep Marvin in the gym and we'll be ready to fill in as soon as Curto pulls out."

Curto canceled two weeks before the fight. I cannot recall the injury, if any, he used to bail. There was no hesitation on Monroe's part, nor George Benton's (who had replaced Eddie Futch as trainer), in accepting the left-handed Hagler, who could punch, as a replacement for the right-handed Curto, who could not. This is the boxing I remember.

Pat asked for the same $2,000 guarantee, plus an additional 20 percent of the net gate over $33,000. Ticket sales for Hagler-Watts had been $42,349 and Pat thought we would do as well, if not better.

A snowstorm the day of the fight prompted talk of postponing, but the boxers were in town and though some streets were closed, we went ahead. Most of the 3,459 arrived by public transportation, mainly the Broad Street subway. The storm ended by 8 pm, too late to help ticket sales. The gate was $26,552. Hagler got his guarantee and, in my opinion, the only convincing loss of his Hall-of-Fame career. Due to the snow, our film crew never made it. No video exists.

That night we saw the best Willie Monroe. Every round was a battle. He went at Hagler, stood in the pocket, and beat him all the way to Brockton. Monroe's jab was an offensive weapon, not a range-finder. He doubled up with his punches and fought off every Hagler offensive, especially in the eighth round when Hagler stunned him. Scores were 47-44, 48-42 and 49-41.

"A tough decision to accept, but an honest one," Hagler told Tom Cushman, of the *Daily News*. "I thought I fought a great fight tonight. I can see a great future ahead of me, but I still have a few things to learn. I get the feeling he's (Monroe) already learned them."

Monroe told Cushman: "I've known I had the ability. The problem has been I've been neglected ever since I turned pro. First Yank (Durham), then Eddie (Futch). They were always busy elsewhere. After I lost to Boogaloo Watts, I had a talk with myself. Then I went to Joe Frazier and asked if George could train me. Joe said okay. Thank God I got as far as I did before George. He has brought out what I always knew I had in me."

I was in the hallway outside Hagler's dressing room when the Petronellis approached me.

Pat spoke: "Russell, you've got all these middleweights—Monroe, Watts, Briscoe, Hart. Why don't you take us on and we'll cut you in." I said, "What can I do with you if you can't beat the guys from Philly?" That's how I turned down 10 percent of Marvelous Marvin Hagler. Not a smart move!

In the dressing room, Benton was telling the writers that he would not have blamed Hagler if he had quit during the fight. "He could have (quit)," Benton said. "He had opportunities all through the fight and no one would have blamed him. But he's one tough kid. He *is* going to be outstanding."

I should have listened.

Chapter Twenty-Three
Fred and Fredda

Bennie Briscoe breaks down after beating Cyclone Hart. (Eugene Mopsik photo)

Barry McCall, Quenzell's son, got a promoter's license. Between June 1976 and April 1977 he ran 14 cards: 10 at Wagner's Ballroom at Broad and Olney; two at Liberty Caterers on Torresdale Avenue in Frankford; one at Boulevard Pools at Roosevelt Boulevard and Princeton Avenue; one at the Arena. I promoted three cards at the Blue Horizon—all money-losers—and eight at the Spectrum. There were 26 cards in the Philadelphia area and fans were anticipating the city's first world championship fight in eight years and a big rematch.

Wagner's, known for hosting teenage record hops, had 1,050 seats, all on the floor. It lacked the Blue Horizon's intimacy, but it had air conditioning so McCall could promote in the summer. He drew nice crowds with Li'l Abner, Cyclone Hart and Youngblood Williams, but not with lesser names. In small clubs, you can make *some* money with a big crowd, but you can lose *lots* of money with a small one. If you are losing, you need to develop talent you can make money with in the future. McCall developed none and left.

The Walker Brothers sold 4,876 tickets on January 28, 1976, at the Arena when Willie Monroe defeated Carlos Marks for the second time. The reason for the big crowd was the first-ever women's professional boxing match in Pennsylvania. Marian "Lady Tyger" Trimiar, of The Bronx, went four rounds with Gwen Gemini, of Birmingham, Alabama. The bout was ruled *No Decision* since Pennsylvania had not enacted rules for women's boxing.

Trimiar returned in March, but the novelty was gone and less than 2,000 saw her lose to Yvonne Barkley, of Harlem. A February card, featuring Bennie Briscoe against Jose Martin Flores, of Los Angeles, drew about the same.

"I let Bennie fight for the Walker Brothers," Arnold Weiss told Stan Hochman, of the *Daily News*, in 1980. "The crowd was small and they refused to pay me. We met the next day at the commissioner's office. They took the money out of a paper bag and they threw it at me. It went all over the room. There I was, on my knees, picking up the fives and tens. I got out of there in a hurry."

The Walker Brothers promoted five fights in 1976, but never came close to equaling their January crowd. In July, they moved to Convention Hall with Boogaloo Watts, Dynamite Douglas and Eddie

Gregory (Mustafa Muhammad) in separate 10-rounders, but sold less than 1,000 tickets. They left, too.

I had spoken to Chris Dundee about a world title fight for Li'l Abner. Dundee promoted Elisha Obed, the WBC junior middleweight champ from The Bahamas, who was 62-1-2, 44 K0s.

Chris been around boxing since the 1920s and had managed world champions Midget Wolgast (flyweight) and Ken Overlin (middleweight). He had promoted in New York, Virginia, and Washington, DC, before moving to Miami Beach, where he had promoted the first fight between Sonny Liston and Cassius Clay. He had more than a passing interest in Clay's (Ali's) career through his brother, Angelo, and his long-time connections to those who had controlled the business.

Left for dead after knockout losses to Kitten Hayward and Jacques Kechichian in 1974, Abner had resurrected his career by moving down to 154 pounds and being matched correctly. He won seven in a row, five by knockout, and was ranked in the Top 10 by *The Ring*, still known as *The Bible of Boxing*. I don't believe that any publication in any sport ever wielded as much influence as *The Ring*, not even *The Sporting News* for baseball. *The Ring* introduced world rankings in the 1920s and they still carried weight in the 1970s.

Abner got up from a first-round knockdown to stop lefty Bruce Cantrell, of Spartanburg, South Carolina, on the Briscoe-Emile Griffith card late in 1974, a fight which had fans "standing on chairs," according to Bob Wright's story in the *Bulletin*. Abner fought as if defense was a foreign concept. He liked to say, "I'm the guy who ducks the punch after he gets hit."

He won five times in 1975, his toughest a 10-round majority decision over Fate Davis. He liked to fight men with no lateral movement, who stood in front of him and traded punches. His fights often were the most exciting of the evening and he became known as "Mr. Action" after Nigel Collins nicknamed him in Britain's *Boxing News*.

I reached an agreement with Dundee for Obed to defend at the Spectrum early in 1976 but tax problems killed it. The United States and Great Britain (and its possessions) had a reciprocal agreement to suspend the alien tax (30 percent) from being levied on entertainers working away from their country. When The Bahamas gained independence midway through 1973, it nullified the agreement. Dundee could deliver Obed for $35,000, but the alien tax would cost us another $10,500.

Abner knocked out Cleveland's Frankie Kolovart early in 1976 on the Marvin Hagler-Watts card, his eighth win in a row, sixth by knockout. Two months later, underneath Marvin Hagler-Monroe, I matched him with Keith "Voodoo" Averette, of Akron, Ohio. Averette fought like "an awkward, clutching octopus" according to Gene Courtney, in the *Inquirer*. Cushman wrote that Averette "may be the first land crab ever to appear in a Philadelphia ring. Averette moved backwards, grabbed, hugged, punched and used a cotton-like jab to win the decision."

I have no idea why I did this. It was my job to get the right opponent and I failed. One fan verbally abused me at ringside. I deserved it. Abner never again got close to a world title fight. He lost three of his next four and walked away in 1979. He kept his job installing soda machines in bars and restaurants. He passed away at 69 in 2015.

Tyrone Everett had ended 1975 in San Francisco, winning the United State Boxing Association (USBA) junior lightweight title with a 12-round split decision over Ray Lunny III. Lunny was world-ranked, but Everett was better, and winning on the road against a contender enhanced his status. He returned to the Spectrum in February, traded knockdowns with Rosalio Muro, of Mexico, and won a unanimous 12-round decision to retain his title. Cyclone Hart iced Melvin Dennis, of Houston, in three rounds, on the same card.

The Briscoe-Hart rematch was April 6. Ticket prices were $7, $10 and $15 and 11,795 came, our largest crowd yet. The gross gate was $109,360. Briscoe's 30 percent came to $30,000 ($141,000 in 2021). Hart's 25 percent came to $25,000 ($118,000).

WRCP-FM, a local country western station, began broadcasting our main events from ringside, with Del Parks (blow-by-blow) and Skip Clayton (analyst). They didn't have much time to talk. Briscoe trapped Hart on the ropes, went left and right to Hart's body, then followed a pair of overhand rights with a right uppercut and a series of one-twos. Hart went down on his face. It was over at 1:49 of the first round.

At the count of 10, Briscoe dropped to the canvas, knees first, and pounded his gloves several times on the mat. George Benton, corner man Sweet Pea Adams, Monroe and others rushed into the ring to celebrate with him. Had I not been the promoter, I would have joined them.

When Clayton interviewed him, Briscoe cried on the shoulders of George James, who had replaced Milt Bailey that night as Briscoe's cut man.

"I guess you saw me crying in the ring afterwards," Briscoe told Cushman. "That gives you an idea of what this means to me. I'm an old pro who had his head on crooked for so many years, who finally has it straightened out, who owes so much to so many people. My mother, for one. If I ever win the title, she'll be the real champion. And George Benton. He's given me confidence I never had before. When I hit Cyclone tonight, I *knew* he wasn't gonna get up."

Benton was philosophical: "Find an old car that has been taken care of over the years, tune it up, don't push it beyond what it was meant to do, and you'll find you have something that runs better than most of the new models." As good as he was as a fighter, Benton made it to the Hall of Fame as a trainer.

Bailey had been the cut man for both Briscoe and Hart so, as in their first fight, he did not work either corner because that was the way it was. Bailey normally was paid two percent "off the top" of his fighter's purse, but in this case each side paid him one percent. "Off the top" means the gross purse, before deductions for manager trainer, license fees, taxes, anything. George James got two percent for working with Briscoe. I assume Hart's cut man got the same.

Had Hart won the rematch—or even the first fight—the Walker Brothers might have controlled him. Briscoe's victory kept the balance of middleweight power at the Spectrum.

After the fight, I went on a cross-country scouting trip. My wife, Pat, and I had separated the previous June. Marrying at 22 was crazy even though that was the norm. I was focused on my career, not marriage, and Pat didn't like boxing.

My first stop was Indianapolis. One month earlier, Mike Everett had defeated Stormin' Norman Goins on the Hagler-Monroe card. Fred Berns had brought Goins from Indianapolis, our first time doing business.

Berns had grown up in Chicago and studied history at Amundsen-Mayfair College where "tuition was $12 a quarter." As a youngster, he'd gone to fights at the Marigold Gardens and he was at the International Amphitheatre in 1965 when Ernie Terrell beat Eddie Machen for the WBA heavyweight title. Of all the people I've known in boxing, no one had more fun, cracked more jokes, told more stories and laughed more often than Fred Berns.

"That was my attitude," he said. "If you can't get a good story out of it, you've wasted your time. I surrounded myself with oddballs. I was married for a few hours to my first wife, had a daughter, paid child support and drove a U.S. mail truck."

Berns became a policeman after a stint in the Marines.

"I was bored, and in 1961, for the first time, you could legitimately get on the Chicago Police Department without paying someone or knowing someone," he said. "Thousands of people began taking the exam for three dollars and I wanted to show my friends what a great test-taker I was. Nearly 5,000 took the exam the same weekend as I did. It normally took between three and four hours but I was outta there in less than two and ended up number 93 on the list.

"It actually turned out to be a fun job. I rarely wrote a ticket or arrested anyone and didn't even own a pair of handcuffs because in those days they cost $14 and I used to be Jewish and I wasn't gonna use my own money for that. We earned $5,280 a year."

After five years on the force, Berns moved to Indianapolis and married his permanent partner in business and in life, Fredda Neubauer, a Philadelphia native who had moved there in 1948. Fredda got her teaching degree at Indiana University. Berns sold light bulbs for Westinghouse, but in 1968 became a boxing promoter, teaming with Howard Ladin, who owned liquor stores, and later with John Appel, who worked in his family's insurance business.

Bruce Trampler hitchhiked 250 miles from Ohio University to work as matchmaker. Fredda made sure that as much fun as Fred was having, it would be nice to turn a profit now and then. She handled the collections and the payouts.

For the next 40 years, Berns promoted more boxing cards than anyone in the Midwest, dealing with fighters whose names are long forgotten. Occasionally he developed what he called "a real fighter." Goins was one. Later came middleweights Sammy NeSmith and Gary Guiden, and welterweight Harold Brazier, who won 105 out of 124 fights and "would fight Joe Louis if asked," according to Berns.

"The first time I made any money in boxing was from the Joe Frazier-George Foreman closed-circuit telecast in 1973," Berns said.

By 1976, Berns owned more than 50 rental units, mostly houses that helped fund his boxing addiction. Ladin was gone by then and Trampler, who had lived in one of Berns' units, was working in Orlando as matchmaker for promoter Pete Ashlock.

The best fighter in the Midwest, Marvin Johnson, lived in Indianapolis. Johnson needed help but Berns couldn't give it.

"I didn't learn my way around boxing until the 1980s when Brazier came along," Berns said. "That's when I began to learn about ratings, connections and what to do with a limited stable of fighters. I had a bunch of kids fighting for world titles, winning none but having the opportunity and payday of a lifetime."

Johnson, the 1972 Olympic bronze medalist at 165 pounds, had turned pro in 1973. Neither of the two Midwest groups he had signed with had boxing experience, limiting him to 10 fights in three years, nine in Indianapolis or Fort Wayne. He beat contenders Gary Summerhays, Red Top Owens and Ray Anderson, but he was not yet a big attraction and it cost to import solid opposition.

I arrived in Indianapolis in time for the weigh-in for a fight card promoted by Dave Page and the Sons of Italy at the Indiana Roof Ballroom. Page owned a restaurant and a catering hall and he was new at this. Johnson was scheduled for 10 rounds with Harold Carter, of Cleveland. Johnson was 177 pounds. When Carter came in at 189, Johnson was ready to bail.

Johnson and his trainer, ex-heavyweight Colion "Champ" Chaney, huddled with friends. Carter was 17-36-4 and had been knocked out 17 times. I introduced myself and told Champ that "Marvin can knock out Carter in his street clothes." Champ smiled. Carter sweated off four pounds and Marvin knocked him out in two.

I left the next day for Orlando to see Trampler, but stayed in touch with Berns. My brother-in-law was managing Briscoe, Li'l Abner and Baby Kid Chocolate, a bantamweight. Johnson would be a nice addition. Berns convinced Johnson and his attorney, Clarence Doninger, to make the deal and we cut Berns in for 10 percent of any money I made as Marvin's promoter.

After Orlando, I went to New Orleans, Corpus Christi and Los Angeles, but I cut the trip short and flew home to see Linda Sablosky, a high school classmate I was dating. Linda and I had been in the same homeroom for three years. I had had a crush on her but we never spoke—not even hello. A friend of mine, who was handling my divorce, told me Linda was getting her own divorce. I asked her out and the high school nerd and the party girl hit it off.

I was back in Monte Carlo in June. Briscoe was fighting Griffith in a rematch on the Carlos Monzon-Rodrigo Valdes middleweight unification card. We were scheduled as a TV backup in case Monzon-Valdes ended early. When it didn't, Briscoe and Griffith played to a less-than-full crowd at *Stade Louis II*, where Briscoe had been stopped by Valdes two years earlier. It ended in a 10-round draw, but the post-fight stories said Briscoe hurt Griffith in the first, eighth and nine rounds.

"No question he (Briscoe) won the Griffith fight," Benton told Gary Smith, of the *Daily News*. "Won eight out of 10 rounds. He started strong, finished just as strong. Bennie looked like he was 20 years old again in this fight. He's a lot smarter than he was before."

Spectrum Fights returned August 16. Monroe's wins over Marks, Hagler and Felton Marshall had stretched his winning streak to five since the 1974 loss to Watts. David Love, the San Diego middleweight who'd beaten Li'l Abner in 1973, was next. Love was 27-12, 9 K0s, and he had been stopped seven times. Monroe was 34-3-1, 23 K0s. It should have been his 35th win.

Love overcame a shaky first round, stunned Monroe in the second and dropped him in the third. After knocking him down again in the fourth, Love was all over Monroe and Hank Cisco administered a standing eight count moments before stopping it at 2:11. It was a major upset. Monroe was just 30, but he lost as many as he won after that and never again got close to a world title fight

In the co-feature, Briscoe knocked out Mexico's Emeterio Villanueva, the first lefty of his career. Jerome Artis struggled to a 10-round draw with former world-title challenger Jose Fernandez in a junior lightweight match and Baby Kid Chocolate stopped ex-Mexican 118-pound champ Jose Medina.

In the *Daily News*, Jack McKinney called it "the most abundant night of boxing in Spectrum history."

These were good times. The 1976 U.S. Olympic team, led by Sugar Ray Leonard, Howard Davis, Jr., and the Spinks brothers, had captured the imagination of the public, aided by the commentary of Howard Cosell. Many in the crowd of 7,147 had been turned onto boxing by ABC's Olympic coverage from Montreal.

PRISM, the new regional premium cable television channel in the Philadelphia area, broadcast the August 16 card on tape delay. PRISM was the brainchild of Ed Snider, who owned the Spectrum and the Philadelphia Flyers. Lou Scheinfeld had coined the name PRISM (Philadelphia Regional In-Home Sports and Movies), and became its first president.

Having our fights available to subscribers within a 125-mile radius of Philadelphia, along with the home games of the Flyers, 76ers and Phillies, broadened our audience and would help with distribution down the road.

The first *live* boxing event on PRISM was September 14 when Hagler ended his winless streak at the Spectrum, stopping Hart in front of 3,456 customers. Hart went down in round three and refused to answer the bell for the ninth after arguing in his corner with Sam Solomon.

Hart had played a major role in the revival of boxing in Philadelphia, but just 10 months removed from his greatest night—the 10-round draw with Briscoe—his career was over. He was 24.

Hart had two more fights, losing to future world middleweight champ Vito Antuofermo in 1977 at the Arena and to unranked Tony Suero in an ill-advised comeback five years later in Atlantic City. Hart, who'd developed diabetes, later managed his son, Jesse, a world-rated super middleweight.

Mike Everett defeated Dale Hernandez, of Omaha, Nebraska, on the Hagler-Hart card. It was one of Mike's biggest wins, along with an earlier 10-round decision in 1976 over Miguel Barreto, of New York.

Marvin Johnson made his Philadelphia debut against Wayne McGee. McGee was 5-2-1 but had defeated Matthew Franklin (Saad Muhammad) in a six-round fight, drew with him in a six-round rematch and out-pointed fringe contender Angel Oquendo in eight. Johnson went right at McGee and walked into a couple of hard shots, but dropped McGee with three straight left hands. McGee struggled to his feet but referee Charlie Sgrillo stopped it just as the bell ended round one.

Chapter Twenty-Four

The Fix Was In

Tyrone Everett's head meets Alfredo Escalera's teeth in 1976. (Peltz collection)

By the summer of 1976, Tyrone Everett's record was 33-0, 18 KOs. He had beaten four Top 10 opponents at the Spectrum (Sammy Goss, Bert Nabalatan, Pedro Aguero, Hyun Chai Kim) and one in San Francisco (Ray Lunny III). Frank Gelb, who managed Everett, had something special in the 23-year-old southpaw. Everett had won twice in Honolulu, where Ben Villaflor, the WBA champion, lived, but Everett got no offers to fight him. Instead, he was offered an August match against Hugo Barraza in Caracas, Venezuela, with the winner guaranteed WBC champion Alfredo Escalera, of Puerto Rico.

Barraza was from Cartagena, Colombia. He was 26 and his record was 45-6-2, 31 K0s. He had won his last 23 fights and had beaten rated fighters on the road: Susumu Okabe in Tokyo; Raul Cruz in Monterrey; Frankie Crawford in Woodland Hills, California. Barraza would be protected in South America but it didn't matter. Everett was the best 130-pound fighter on the planet.

Hank Cisco went with Gelb to Caracas to serve as a ringside judge. Cisco had boxed professionally in the late 1940s, and had become a referee while working as a policeman in Norristown and a detective in Montgomery County. Gelb had his furniture store in Norristown. He knew Cisco and he was leveling the playing field in Caracas.

The 12-round fight was in a bull ring. The bulls went first. Six were carved up, and a female matador sent to the hospital. The fight, and a steady rain, followed. Each man slipped on the canvas. Barraza was battered around both eyes and Everett had swelling around one. Ringsiders held chairs over their heads in a futile effort to stay dry.

Cisco's scorecard, filled out in ink, began to dissipate from the rain but he put it back together. He scored 120-110 for Everett, which broke down to 10 rounds for Everett and two even. Judge Dimas Hernandez, of Venezuela, had it 118-114 Everett (6-2-4 in rounds). Referee Adam Chavarria, of Mexico, had it 115 apiece (5-5-2 in rounds).

"Tell ol' Peltz to get the money out from wherever he hides it," Everett told Bob Wright, of the *Bulletin*, on an overseas call. "I done my part, now it's up to his people to bring a world championship fight to Philadelphia. Tell him to bid high. After this week, I ain't in no hurry to be travelin' again. You can't eat the food, you can't drink the water, they bring on after the bulls and you gotta fight in a storm."

Bob Arum had been dealing with Escalera and he put the fight together for Puerto Rico, but the coming rainy season and Escalera's lack of popularity in his own country prompted a phone from Gelb to me: "How would you like to do the fight at the Spectrum?"

Escalera got $90,000 ($425,000 in 2021) to come to Philadelphia. Everett got $15,000 ($72,000) for the chance to win the title in his hometown. It was the hottest ticket going. We priced it at $7, $10, $15 and $25 for Philadelphia's first world championship since Joe Frazier-Oscar Bonavena in 1968.

To encourage media attention, we housed Escalera at the Adam's Mark on City Line Avenue, across the street from two of the three local television networks. He trained in the hotel ballroom where we set up a ring, a heavy bag and speed bag.

Filiberto Lebron and Pedro Aponte managed Escalera. They were confident, having watched their fighter, Benjamin Ortiz, perform well against Everett the year before. They said they didn't care about the referee and judges because they knew the WBC would appoint them and Pennsylvania had no control. As the fight neared, the battle over the officials became the focus. It would be one judge from Puerto Rico, one judge from Philadelphia, and a neutral—we hoped—referee.

It took some arm twisting to get Pennsylvania to agree, but Ed Snider, the Spectrum's owner, called the state capitol in Harrisburg and ironed that out the week before the fight. Ray Solis, of Mexico, would referee. Gelb and I checked him out and were okay with it. We assumed the Puerto Rican judge would vote for Escalera so long as he was standing at the end of 15 rounds and we assumed the Pennsylvania judge would be fair. That would be 79-year-old Lou Tress, who had been judging fights since the 1930s.

Commissioner Howard McCall said appointing Tress was his decision, but I believe he was nudged. "Honest" Bill Daly, the only member of the 1950s Frankie Carbo/Blinky Palermo mob not to serve time, stopped by my office the day of the fight to say hello. Daly was tight with ex-referee and former commissioner Zach Clayton. I suspect Daly contacted Clayton, who asked McCall to appoint Tress as a reward for his long service. Tress got the job and he did a job.

I gave Clayton two tickets. He was seated two sections to my right and I was thinking how odd it was to see him so intense during a fight, almost like he had money on it.

The largest crowd (16,019) ever to watch a prize fight indoors in Pennsylvania witnessed the worst-ever decision in Pennsylvania and one of the worst in boxing history. It was a great event, not a great fight. Giving Escalera every break, he won *maybe* five rounds out of 15. Escalera couldn't cut off the ring, couldn't close the distance and walked into shots when he tried. He couldn't have hit Everett with an oar if they were fighting in a rowboat.

Even when he bit Everett's forehead in the 13th round, causing blood to pour down Everett's face, Escalera couldn't score. Everett stood his ground and counter-punched perfectly, drawing cheers from the crowd. When it was over, Escalera applauded Everett and we got ready to crown a new champion. My body was pressed against the ring when announcer Ed Derian read the scores:

"Ladies and gentlemen, the scoring as follows: Judge Lou Tress has scored it 145 Escalera, 143 Everett." Thousands of boos filled the air.

I could not believe Derian had embarrassed himself by reading the score backwards. There was no way Tress could have voted for Escalera. When Derian read that Ismael Fernandez, the Puerto Rican judge, had voted 146-143 for Escalera, I felt like somebody had pulled down my pants in public. It didn't matter that referee Solis scored it 148-146 for Everett. The crowd booed—and booed—and booed. McCall announced that he would review the scorecards. That never happened.

Earlier that evening I had seen Tress heading down the runway leading to ringside. I said hello but he kept walking. Tress was from Wynnefield and an almost daily participant in a late afternoon card game in the 1950s at Krone's gas station at 54th and Euclid, where my uncle, Cy Kramer, hung out—and where Wilt Chamberlain washed cars. Tress even sold life insurance to Frank Gelb and his father Mo. He also had a relative who worked at a race track in Puerto Rico.

Later Gelb and I ran back events the day of fight. He had been visited in his hotel room by Ben Greene, a character from New York who wrote a boxing column in a racetrack tabloid and associated with some of boxing's less pristine people. I had been visited by Daly. There are no coincidences.

How much was Tress paid and where did the money come from? I heard $1,500. The fight had not attracted much action so it must have been for control of the title. Had Everett won, Top Rank and Spectrum Fights would have been partners for his first three defenses. Instead, Escalera began fighting mostly for Don King.

Televised boxing was back on weekend afternoons and Puerto Rico had been a hotbed since homegrown Jose Torres had been light-heavyweight champion in the mid-1960s. From 1975 through 1977, six fighters there had held world titles: Escalera; Angel

Espada; Sam Serrano; Wilfred Benitez; Esteban DeJesus; Wilfredo Gomez.

My guess is that Daly masterminded the deal to help King, though I doubt King was aware.

Daly, who had managed world lightweight champion Carlos Ortiz, twice arranged for Clayton to referee his title defenses, one against Sugar Ramos in 1967 in Puerto Rico, one against Carlos Teo Cruz in 1968 in Santo Domingo. Ortiz stopped Ramos, but Cruz won a 15-round split decision on the votes of judges Carlos Lugo (148-141) and Jose Soto (146-142). Clayton voted for Ortiz (145-139).

In a letter to Gene Courtney published in the *Inquirer* nine days after the Everett-Escalera fight, Clayton defended Tress:

"It is impossible for me to stand by and read the senseless comments destroying a fellow colleague and a very good friend. I had the pleasure of working with Lou Tress in many important assignments when I was a referee. The records will show that he was assigned to more important fights in our state than any other judge in the history of boxing. This is solely because he is one of the most capable and qualified judges in the boxing profession. It disturbs me that so much emphasis has been placed on the decision that Lou Tress rendered in the fight between Tyrone Everett and Alfredo Escalera, the champion. Yet no thought was given to the referee's decision, calling nine rounds even.

"Anywhere in the world where there is an even round in the judgment of the officials, the even round goes to the champion. No reference was made or discussed concerning the referee's judgment. The viewers seemed satisfied that the referee's decision was in favor of Everett, not caring about how he scored various rounds. Never in the history of boxing has any official called nine rounds even. All of those who have criticized Lou Tress should take an honest look at the other officials in last Tuesday's championship fight. Lou Tress has made a great contribution for 50 years to the boxing profession and is respected by boxing notables as one of the outstanding judges in the country. In my opinion, he still is."

Clayton, the first Black man to referee a world heavyweight championship fight, took heat after Ezzard Charles failed to regain the crown in 1952 at Municipal Stadium, losing a 15-round unanimous decision to Camden's Jersey Joe Walcott in their fourth fight. Clayton's 9-6 score was the widest of the officials.

In a poll of ringside reporters, 24 had scored for Charles, 17 for Walcott, who often boxed in Philly. Clayton was criticized by Charles' management and trainer Ray Arcel for interfering with Charles' attack. He constantly told Charles' corner men to remove Vaseline from Charles' face and did it himself when they did not. He warned Charles in three different rounds for low blows and separated the boxers whenever Charles got inside. During the fight, Clayton called Walcott by his "Pappy" nickname.

When my brother-in-law bought Bennie Briscoe's contract in 1970, he was advised by ex-manager Pinny Schafer not to let Clayton referee a Briscoe fight. According to Schafer, in Briscoe's 1967 fight with Luis Rodriguez at the Arena, Clayton had hampered Briscoe by breaking up the action every time Bennie got inside. Rodriguez was managed by Angelo Dundee and Schafer felt Clayton was doing favors for Angelo and his brother Chris, who promoted Rodriguez. Arnold took Schafer's advice.

I had my own Clayton moment. During a 1972 card at the Arena, he motioned for me to sit next to him. "You've got a nice crowd here, young man," he said. "The commissioner sure could use a bag of peanuts." I smiled and left. When I mentioned this to my father, he offered to send one of his trucks to Clayton's house and dump peanuts onto his front yard.

Less than three years after Everett-Escalera, promoter Bob Arum accused Clayton of trying to "fix" the Benitez-Carlos Palomino WBC welterweight title fight in San Juan. Benitez won decisively, but Clayton scored it for Palomino.

"I was there as promoter with Rodolfo Sabbatini," Arum told me. "The three officials all were referees so no one knew who would be the referee and who would be the judges until the day of the fight. If Benitez won, I was going to make him with Sugar Ray Leonard. If Palomino won, he was going to fight Roberto Duran for Don King. Bill Daly was there all week trying to sway the officials to vote for Palomino since he was working with King. Mickey Duff, the British promoter, was there and he was friendly with Jimmy Jacobs, manager of Benitez.

"Harry Gibbs, the British ref, was one of the three officials so Duff spoke with him to make sure he would score honestly. Gibbs was insulted that Duff would think that Daly—or anybody—could get to him. He was going to score the fight on the level. I went to the hotel and spoke with Jay Edson, who became the referee. I told him I wanted an honest fight and an honest decision.

"Edson broke down crying, telling me he couldn't stand the business any longer because of all the pressure. He loved boxing but he wanted to get out and, yes, they had been pressuring him to vote for Palomino. I had been losing money on some shows and I had no site coordinator at the time and I told Edson if he voted on the level, I would hire him full-time for the position. I also told him if he screwed around with the decision he could forget the offer. I tried to find Clayton but Daly had moved him to a different hotel.

"Benitez won clearly but it was a split decision because Clayton voted for Palomino. After the uproar, Clayton said maybe the sun was in his eyes. Me being me, at the press conference, I accused Clayton of being in on the fix, so he sued me. We always have had insurance covering us from defamation suits and the like. Still do today.

"After six months, the insurance company got a call from Clayton's lawyer with an offer to settle for $10,000. The insurance company gave me two options: They could pay Clayton the $10,000 to end the lawsuit or they could pay me the $10,000 and I then would have to take on the lawsuit myself. I told them to give him the $10,000 knowing it would cost me $50,000 in legal fees if I took over. That's how it ended."

I told the newspapers I was planning "to press the (Pennsylvania) commission to have Lou Tress suspended for life on the grounds that he is totally incompetent." I also said that Tress would never again judge a fight at the Spectrum so long as I was Director of Boxing. He never did and he passed away in 1979 at the age of 82.

Spectrum Fights made $16,919.94 ($80,000 in 2021), on Everett-Escalera, but it was little compensation for what would have been made from future championship promotions.

Chapter Twenty-Five
Fallout and Tragedy

Tyrone Everett drawing by Susan Seymour.

The fallout from the Tyrone Everett-Alfredo Escalera fight would hover over boxing in Philadelphia for six months. We were trying to draw fans back after one of the worst decisions in memory. The Philadelphia area again hosted 26 cards in 1977, seven at the Spectrum. Of the five at the Blue Horizon, the only profitable one was December 6 when Marvin Stinson, of North Philly, stopped Mike Montgomery, of South Philly, in a battle of undefeated heavyweights. The card drew 1,253 fans, the most in six years. I lost money on two cards at the Wagner Ballroom and a new venue opened in the suburbs.

Bennie Briscoe returned from Nice, France, late in 1976 after a 10-round draw with Willie Warren and won a harder-than-expected 10-round decision over Karl Vinson on a bitter cold night in January at the Spectrum. Vinson then moved to Philadelphia from Stockton, California, signed with my brother-in-law and trained with George Benton. He won three of his next four fights before a detached retina ended his career.

Briscoe got an offer to fight Jean Mateo in Paris. "Do we really have to go back there?" I whined. This would be our fifth trip to the Paris/Monte Carlo/Nice area in three years and I wanted someplace new. I was spoiled.

Mateo had turned pro in California in 1973, returned to his native France in 1975 and toiled on the fringe of the Top 10. His flat-footed style was perfect for Briscoe, who broke him down. Mateo did not answer the bell for the 10th round. It was so cold in the Pavillon de Paris you could see the fighters' breath in the air.

A third fight with Warren was set for Monday, May 23, at the Spectrum, but Briscoe did not show up at the Cloverlay Gym on Sunday. I got concerned when I couldn't reach him.

Around midnight, I got a call from my uncle, Bob Peltz, who said Bennie had called looking for me and saying he didn't feel well. I said Bennie probably was nervous, which he sometimes was before fights, but the next morning found him resting in Temple University Hospital, where he had been taken by a friend for an appendectomy. We canceled the card. Briscoe would be out of action for two months. I was marrying Linda Sablosky the next month and she came to the Spectrum that afternoon while I answered phone calls about the cancellation.

The new venue was the 69th Street Theater in Upper Darby. The vacant former movie house, with a large balcony, could seat 1,800. We placed the ring on the floor in front of the stage. I had been there with Dad for the 1961 closed-circuit telecast from Miami Beach of Floyd Patterson's sixth-round knockout of Ingemar Johansson in the last of their three fights.

Ex-pro middleweight Marty Feldman was developing a group of suburban kids who trained in a gym over a nearby fire house on West Chester Pike. Ex-cop Eddie Crawford partnered with Feldman to promote at the renamed 69th Street Forum. I made the matches.

There would be 18 cards over the next three years. The March 7 opener reminded me of my early days at the Blue Horizon, except for the color of the participants. Six White kids knocked out six over-matched Black kids and no fight lasted more than three rounds.

Lightweight Micky Diflo, welterweight Mike Picciotti and junior welterweight Victor Pappa all lived in nearby Folsom. Feldman billed them as *Mic, Pic and Vic* and, along with West Philly's Tony "Rocky" Tassone and Darby's Richie "The Bandit" Bennett—both middleweights—and Upper Darby featherweight Kenny Carpenter, they were regulars at the Forum. Bennett appeared on 15 of the 18 cards, Picciotti 12, Diflo 10. All but Diflo and Carpenter would graduate to 10-round fights in Philadelphia and Atlantic City.

Feldman worked out of his store, *Marty and Jack's Wranglers*, within walking distance of the gym. He was built solid and always wore a tight black T-shirt and jeans—a bigger, tougher version of The Fonz from *Happy Days*. Feldman paid me in cash after every fight and since he kept his ledger book in his T-shirt sleeve it was impossible to get exact figures on attendance and gate receipts. Mike Rossman dubbed him "the world's oldest teenager."

In its short-lived history, the Forum hosted the pro debut of Tim Witherspoon, who won the WBC and WBA versions of the world heavyweight title, as well as fights featuring future WBA bantamweight champ Jeff Chandler, Dynamite Douglas and contenders Vinnie Curto, middleweight; Kevin Howard, welterweight; Roger Stafford, welterweight, and Jerry Martin, light-heavyweight.

Four nights after the Forum opened, Frank Gelb teamed with promoter Don Elbaum and TV distributer Hank Schwartz to bring one of the World Television Championships (WTC) cards to the Arena. The WTC was competing against Don King's U.S. Boxing Championships, which were on ABC.

Future middleweight champion Vito Antuofermo, of New York, stopped Cyclone Hart in the fifth round and future WBA light-heavyweight Eddie Gregory (Mustafa Muhammad) got off the floor to win a 10-round split decision (46-45, 47-44, 45-47) over future WBC champ Matthew Franklin (Matthew Saad Muhammad). The Elbaum-Schwartz series had better fighters and fights than King's, but not enough income from smaller television markets to sustain it. The series folded six weeks later.

Six nights after the Arena card, Jimmy Young, who one year earlier had lost to Muhammad Ali in a fight many thought he had won, knocked down and out-pointed George Foreman in Puerto Rico, sending the loser into a 10-year retirement. Gelb had junior lightweight contender Ron McGarvey, of Hillcrest Heights, Maryland, challenging Escalera for the WBC title on the card. When he learned one of the judges was the same Ismael Fernandez who had voted against Everett at the Spectrum, Gelb refused to let McGarvey leave the dressing room until Fernandez was replaced. It held up the ABC telecast and Gelb got his wish, but McGarvey was stopped in six rounds.

On April 7, there was *standing room only* at the Forum. Augie Pantellas was back. He had not boxed since losing a 10-round decision to Miguel Herrera, of Ecuador, in 1971, at the Arena. He had then lost fights to alcohol and drugs.

"The biggest thing in my life is that I have found Jesus," Pantellas told Bob Franklin, of the *Delaware County Daily Times*. "I no longer drink or do sinful things. I am at my best now as a human being. I was lost for 10 years before I found Jesus, even during those so-called glory years. I know it's been six years since I fought, but I don't feel as though I've lost a thing. I think I can still punch as well as I did before and, most of all, I know I'm a lot smarter. I have matured."

Pantellas was 33 and his record was 22-5, 19 K0s. His opponent was Elviro Reyes Jajuja, a Puerto Rican living in Philadelphia. Jajuja was 1-5 but we billed him as 4-3. A 48-seat charter bus arrived from Cobblestones, the Society Hill bar and restaurant where Pantellas had tended bar. Lawyers, doctors and bankers wore tuxedos. The women wore gowns. Everyone smoked cigars and drank champagne doled out by a topless waitress during the 30-minute ride to Upper Darby.

After chants of "AUG-EE, AUG-EE" had subsided, Pantellas stopped Jajuja in the last round of their scheduled eight. The Cobblestones crowd tossed the red carnations they had sported into the ring and boarded their bus for the 30-minute ride back to Society Hill for a midnight breakfast. Pantellas joined them, wearing his hooded sweatshirt and jeans.

Two weeks later I was in Los Angeles with Baby Kid Chocolate, who was fighting on one of the biggest cards of the year, the showdown between two Mexicans, each holding half of the world bantamweight title, Carlos Zarate (WBC) and Alfonso Zamora (WBA). Zarate was 45-0, 44 K0s; Zamora 29-0, 29 K0s. When they couldn't agree on terms to unify the title, they'd settled on a 10-round fight for $125,000 apiece ($545,000 in 2021). No American television outlet was interested.

Chocolate's real name was Ronnie Walker. He had boxed 12 times at the Spectrum, five times at the Blue Horizon and once at Fournier Hall in Wilmington, Delaware, where Gelb and I lost money promoting in 1976 and 1977. Chocolate was unbeaten in 18 fights, but his January win over Socrates Batoto, of the Philippines, on the Briscoe-Vinson card had personified the moniker "walkout bout." People left during it and his box-office value plummeted, so we went on the road.

Chocolate trained at the Main Street Gym in Los Angeles, run by Howie Steindler, the model for the proprietor Burgess Meredith played in *Rocky.* Zarate stopped Zamora in the fourth round in front of what promoter Don Fraser called a disappointing crowd of 14,123. I should be so disappointed! Chocolate was down twice in round three and lost on points to Cubanito Hernandez in what started the backside of his career. He lost seven of his last eight fights and retired in 1983.

Tragedy struck May 26. I was in my Center City townhouse when Mary Anne Seymour, by then separated from Nigel Collins, called. Tyrone Everett had been killed that morning in the rowhouse on Federal Street near 27th where his 24-year-old girlfriend, Carolyn McKendrick, lived with her two children. The *Daily News* reported that 38 cellophane packets of heroin were found there.

According to the autopsy, Everett died from a single gunshot wound. A .30 caliber bullet from a Ruger Blackhawk, a six-shot single action revolver, entered his right nostril, went through his head, through the bedroom window behind him, and was found on the sidewalk across the street. McKendrick and Tyrone Price, admittedly gay and with a lengthy record as a drug pusher, were seen leaving the house by neighbors who'd heard the shot. Rumors circulated that McKendrick had found Everett in bed with another woman—or another man—or a drug deal had gone wrong. The story made front-page headlines.

Everett had won twice in 1977, most recently nine days earlier at the Capitol Centre in Landover, Maryland. He was 36-1, 20 K0s, and negotiations had begun for a rematch with Escalera in Puerto Rico. He and Briscoe had carried the boxing program at the Spectrum. One was in the hospital and one was dead.

I sat on my couch and stared at the wall. In *Godfather II*, Hyman Roth (Lee Strasberg) tells Michael Corleone (Al Pacino): "This is the business we've chosen." I had grown up sheltered from this life, on the White Main Line, one of the wealthiest regions of "old money" in the Northeast section of the country. I had chosen this business…and I kept going.

The funeral was held in the early evening of May 31 at the New Light Beulah Baptist Church at 17th and Bainbridge in South Philadelphia. Thousands lined the streets. Traffic was diverted for blocks while helmeted policeman patrolled the area. Only 1,000 people were permitted inside and less than a dozen were White. Linda and I were there along with the Gelb family. Mayor Frank Rizzo paid his respects. So did Joe Frazier and Briscoe.

Those who couldn't get inside were offering $5 to Frank Talent, the doorman. Talent was one of those guys who'd survived different administrations to become a fixture at City Hall. He was an announcer at boxing and wrestling matches and was known as *Batman* because he dressed up like the Dark Knight at charitable events for children.

The walls were lined with flowers. Above the white casket, which was opened twice during the service, was a large drawing of Tyrone in a boxing pose with wings and a halo over his head. Nurses clad in white walked through the crowd to fan women who were on the verge of fainting. Now and then a woman in the balcony would scream and appear ready to jump. It was the most emotional funeral I ever attended and the scariest.

My fractured relationship with Tyrone had been in the newspapers for years. Promoters never are portrayed as good guys and no one in the Everett family belonged to the J Russell Peltz fan club. No one knew I had told Tyrone that I loved him in the ring before the Escalera fight.

Linda and I had lived lives equally removed from Tyrone's. She had been to her first fight the year before and now she sat next to me in a church full of sorrow, agony, heartbreak and grief.

"I was apprehensive about going and I prayed that it would not be an open casket since Tyrone had been shot in the face," she said. "It was hot as hell in there and we were packed in like sardines. I wasn't sure how I would react to seeing him in the open casket but you really couldn't tell because the undertaker had done a good job."

Mike Everett stood and pleaded for calm. A visiting bishop, Prophet J. H. Baker, scolded the congregation for their overzealous sympathy. Laura Murray quoted him in the *Daily News*. "Let's give this family… respect, he said, to a chorus of Amens. One day death is coming at your door. You're going to be stretched out. Somebody got to come to your funeral. Let's throw our arms around this mother. You had a mother. It hurts; you don't know how much it hurts."

Brother Eddie Everett approached the open coffin, sobbing: "You taught me everything I know. You gave me a will to live. You were like a father to me. I'm going to miss you, Tyrone." Eddie was joined by Mike and their mother, Doris Everett, and this sad chapter was closed, until the trial. McKendrick was charged with murder, a weapons offense and possession of heroin with the intent to sell. She was convicted of third-degree murder and spent five years in prison.

"Tyrone would never do any drugs himself," Mike Everett told Tom Cushman in Cushman's 2009 book, *Muhammad Ali and the Greatest Heavyweight Generation*. "I know him and he couldn't have fought the way he did taking drugs. But he probably was fronting people to buy drugs. Once you start making a little money, you get a little greedy and look for ways to invest it and make some more. That's the life Carolyn was into. That's the life we were leading back then."

People have said that Tyrone's future would have been different had he been declared the winner of his fight with Escalera, but I'm not sure. Tyrone would have made more money but I can't forget what Teddy Atlas once said: "People born round, don't die square."

I had been in the bars and nightclubs where drug deals were made and murders committed, but I was in my 20s and early 30s and boxing was a major sport. My name and picture had been in the newspapers so I assumed people recognized and respected me and that was enough. I never asked about someone's background, their upbringing, their education, their family. I was all business but that was me.

When I was doing research for this book, Eddie Everett sent me this: "Tyrone was different from most fighters. He looked at boxing as a business. He trusted no one. The only person he trusted was my mom and he gave her $10,000 to purchase the Golden Gloves Bar. He had respect for you because you two were alike in many ways. You were the perfect match. Had he won that fight with Escalera, you could have made millions together. The world didn't get to see one of the best fighters in boxing history."

Mike Everett had lost his previous two fights, but Jose Sulaiman, president of the WBC, called Gelb with condolences. Sulaiman said that in the wake of Tyrone's death, he would grant Mike a world junior welterweight championship fight with Thailand's Saensak Muangsurin if Mike won his next fight. Gelb quickly put together a card, in Tyrone's honor, for June 23 at the Arena. Mike defeated

Rocky Ramon, of San Antonio, Texas, in the 10-ound main event. True to his word, Sulaiman delivered.

On August 20, 1977, in an open-air stadium erected on a rice paddy in the Roi-Et Province of Thailand, Mike Everett was stopped in the sixth round.

Chapter Twenty-Six
Recovery

Roberto Duran clocks Edwin Viruet during their title fight. (Bill Lichtenberg photo)

Spectrum Fights ended a four-month layoff following the death of Tyrone Everett, with cards in June, July, August and September. On the national scene, ABC and CBS were fighting to sign the five gold medalists from the 1976 U.S. Olympic team. Sugar Ray Leonard and Howard Davis, Jr., led the way. The release of the first Rocky movie in December, 1976, boosted boxing's popularity, especially in Philly, where much of it was filmed.

Junior lightweights William "Red" Berry, of Trenton, and Jerome Artis, of North Philadelphia, met in one of three 10-round fights in June. Berry (6-2-1, 3 K0s) had upset Ron McGarvey (30-3, 19 K0s) on the Everett-Alfredo Escalera card seven months earlier so I brought him to the Blue Horizon and he'd beaten Gerald Hayes, of Newark, New Jersey, and Alfonso Evans, of South Philly.

Artis had split two amateur fights with Everett. He also defeated Sugar Ray Leonard on his way to the 1972 National AAU 126-pound title. He lost in the Olympic trials to Leroy Veasley, of Detroit. Artis was a mini-Muhammad Ali, but he couldn't walk the walk.

One week before a 1976 main event at the Blue Horizon, he approached me at the Cloverlay Gym with a sling on his left arm. When he saw my face, he broke up laughing. He was a terrific gym fighter, not so much under the lights. He could switch from orthodox to southpaw, but he had little power and less discipline. He out-pointed Berry over 10 rounds and ran his record to 16-1-4, the pinnacle of his career.

Three months later, Artis, already down twice, quit in the second round against Alexis Arguello on the Muhammad Ali-Earnie Shavers card at Madison Square Garden. Artis had no intention of hanging with the Nicaraguan banger, but accepted the fight because of the $12,500 purse ($54,000 in 2021).

"I announced in Flash Gordon's *Tonight's Boxing Program* prior to the Arguello bout that it would be my last as Jerome's manager," Nigel Collins said. "I didn't want people to think I dumped him because he lost to Arguello, which I knew he would. Besides, managing was a bad fit for me. Jerome stayed at my apartment in Deptford, New Jersey, for a few days prior to the fight. He did a few laps around the local high school track and then took laxatives to make weight. Two nights before the fight, I rolled a joint and wrote "Alexis Arguello" on it. After (the fight) he changed into his street clothes, we smoked it in the nosebleed section of the Garden."

Beginning with Arguello, Artis lost 26 of 37 fights and retired at 27-27-4, 9 K0s. He lost 17 of his last 18 as an "opponent" in England, Australia, Italy, Peru, Colombia, Scotland, Venezuela, Canada and Mexico. He was stopped 12 times. A complete waste of talent! Artis died in 1999 from Aids. He was 45.

Many of the 5,449 came to the June card to see Augie Pantellas leap from the 69th Street Forum to the Spectrum. Pantellas had won two straight and was matched with Roberto Quintanilla, a Mexican junior lightweight living in Houston. We found 16 previous fights for Quintanilla, but years later I discovered he was 29-4, 20 K0s, and had been stopped just once.

Pantellas' supporters rejected their pedestrian chartered bus and took three helicopters from Penn's Landing to the Veterans Stadium parking lot across from the Spectrum. There were 49 of them, again dressed in tuxedos and evening gowns, and they paid $32.50 apiece for the fight ticket, flight ticket and a midnight breakfast.

"Half of them could have flown that distance without the aid of a helicopter," wrote Gary Smith, the *Daily News* writer who joined them. "They had gathered at Cobblestones…at 6 p.m. and steadily went about the task of ordering as many rounds as Pantellas was scheduled to fight. Augie beat them, but it was close."

The fight went 10. Pantellas dropped Quintanilla with a perfect shot—pardon the pun—one minute into the first round, but broke his right hand and had to rely on his left for the next nine. Scores were 47-44, 48-45, 49-45. He was out for the rest of 1977.

Junior middleweight Youngblood Williams bled through every round of his 10-round draw with Alfonso Hayman. Dr. Wilbur H. Strickland was a constant visitor to Williams' corner. Hayman's manager, Arnold Giovanetti, screamed that the fight should have been stopped. Williams was managed by Quenzell McCall, whose brother, Howard, was the chairman of the Pennsylvania State Athletic Commission.

The summer and fall of 1977 produced three cards as important as any in the history of Spectrum Fights. They featured four future Hall-of-Famers—Matthew Franklin, Marvin Hagler, Michael Spinks and Roberto Duran.

Before his mother passed away, Matthew and an older brother went to live with an aunt. When Matthew was 5, his aunt no longer could afford to look after both boys and told the older brother to get rid of him. He left Matthew on the Ben Franklin Parkway. He was taken in by Catholic Social Services where the nuns named him Matthew (after the Saint) and Franklin (after the Parkway). He lived in foster care until a Philadelphia couple adopted him. He later began to box, lost in the semifinals of the Pennsylvania Golden Gloves novice division in 1973, and turned pro the next year.

During his years with Tyrone Everett, Frank Gelb thought it would be a good marketing tool to also manage Tyrone's brother, so, in 1976, he bought Mike Everett's contract from Pinny Schafer and Pat Duffy, as well as Alfonso Evans'. Both were trained by Nick Belfiore, a loveable grouch with a loud voice and a big heart. Franklin, also managed by Schafer and Duffy and trained by Belfiore, did not want to be left behind, so he asked Schafer and Duffy to let him go with Gelb. They agreed and Gelb scored a coup Peter Minuet would have envied.

Never one to baby his fighters, Gelb booked Franklin in Italy where he outpointed future WBC light-heavyweight champion Mate Parlov, and in Stockton, California, where he did likewise to future WBC and IBF cruiserweight champion Marvin Camel. Franklin drew with Parlov a second time in Italy and lost a rematch to Camel in Missoula, Montana.

When Gelb asked to see the scorecards at the Camel rematch, officials from the Montana Athletic Commission were AWOL. To appease him, the commission secretary changed the verdict to *No Decision*, but by the time Gelb and Franklin got home, Camel's victory had been reinstated.

Former world light-heavyweight champion Bob Foster, the referee, scored 100-91 for Camel. Billy Edwards, who had trained and briefly managed Foster, worked in Camel's corner. The promoter—at least in name—was the wife of Elmer Boyce, Camel's manager, and Camel worked in Boyce's music store in Missoula. The two judges had it 96-96 and 98-96 for Camel.

"Matthew won eight of the 10 rounds," Gelb said. "From now on we're going to stay away from these Cowboys. We felt just like Indians at a massacre out there."

By mid-1977, Franklin was 15-3-2, 9 K0s, and looking for a big fight. Marvin Johnson was available. Johnson had knocked out Tom Bethea in April in Indianapolis and he was 15-0, 12 K0s. Franklin, after losing the close one to Eddie Gregory in March, had changed his style from boxer to slugger.

The WBC and WBA were the only major alphabet groups then—but that still was two too many. *The Ring* was enough. Johnson was

No. 7 in the WBC, No. 3 in the WBA. The July 26 brawl would turn out to be the greatest fight I ever saw in person and I am proud to have promoted it. It was for the vacant NABF title.

Bill Livingston nailed it best in the *Inquirer*: "This one came right out of the blood-plasma unit, the same folks who brought you Ali-Frazier reddening the dawn skies in Manila. The same script that gave the world Graziano-Zale and before that, Christians and lions. Loser gets a thumbs down. This fight had it all over everything but the neutron bomb."

Johnson's philosophy: "When the bell rings, you start fighting." Pace was not in his vocabulary. No one went down for 11 rounds. At the start of the 12th, referee Ozzie Saddler had Johnson ahead 53-49; judge Harold Lederman had Franklin ahead 51-48; judge Paul Harris had it 51-51. Johnson's tank was empty.

A series of Franklin right hands 30 seconds into the 12th, punctuated by a right uppercut, drove Johnson across the ring. He grabbed the second rope from the top with his left hand and tried to hold on as he was getting hit, but he sagged to the canvas and Saddler waved it off at 1:12. The crowd erupted. Mike Everett was first into the ring to grab Franklin's waist and dance around him. Corner man Jimmy Hayes, an ex-pro heavyweight, leaped cleanly over the ropes, followed by the not-so-agile Belfiore, who fell to the canvas trying to emulate Hayes.

When I later went to the Penn Center Inn to check on Johnson, he was sprawled on the floor in the hallway outside his room. Kelse McClure, Indiana Boxing Commission chairman, found the room key and we lifted Marvin into his room and onto his bed.

Only 6,459 paid to see the most brutal local fight since North Philly welterweights Charley Scott and Garnett "Sugar" Hart ruined each other in their 1959 classic at Convention Hall.

The next month we drew 8,169—tickets were $6, $8 and $12—for the finale of the Marvin Hagler-Willie Monroe trilogy. Hagler had avenged his 1976 loss to Monroe early in 1977 in Boston, stopping him in the 12th round in front of crowd of 4,400, largest ever to watch boxing at the Hynes Auditorium.

The quickest way back to the Top 10 for Monroe was to beat Hagler again. Monroe wanted 10 rounds, Hagler 12.

"We signed for 12 rounds and that's what we are going to fight," said co-manager Pat Petronelli. "If it's not for 12 rounds, we're not coming. I know Monroe wants 10 rounds because he can't go 12. Monroe gets weak in the late rounds. My fighter can go 15 easily." Monroe agreed to 12.

The jab that had worked for Monroe in their first fight never found its mark. He looked unsure of himself and was off balance, reaching with his punches. Hagler was moving his head and body and he landed half a dozen left hands. After round one, Benton tried to calm Monroe. "Settle down, relax," he said. "The jab will take care of it. Don't be in a hurry and don't try to prove nothing."

Monroe landed a decent right-left combination in round two, but Hagler shook him with a hard left and Monroe clinched. After referee Tommy Reid separated them, Hagler backed Monroe into the ropes and landed a perfect right hand and Monroe went down. He got to his feet, but swayed so badly Reid stopped it at 1:46.

"I wish he had gotten up," Hagler said. "I wanted to put his lights out for good. I hate to say that about the man but when he decisioned me...he didn't make an easy time of it. So I wasn't going to show him no mercy."

It was the end of Monroe's days as a contender. Boogaloo Watts had suffered the same fate four months earlier when David Love K0d him in four rounds in San Antonio, snapping Watts' 13-fight win streak and ending his days as a title threat.

Michael Spinks, who won the middleweight gold medal at the Montreal Olympics, knocked out Jasper Brisbane, of North Philadelphia, in two rounds that night, his fourth straight win as a pro. He weighed 166 pounds to 173 for Brisbane, who was 5-0-1. "It started out tough and maybe everybody thought it was gonna go the other way," Spinks said. "Then there was a real change."

Don King needed a site for the WBA lightweight championship fight between Robert Duran, of Panama, and Edwin Viruet, a Puerto Rican living in New York. Viruet was 27 and had lost twice in 28 fights, once by 10-round decision to Duran two years prior in a non-title fight at the Nassau Coliseum in Uniondale, New York. We made a deal with King for Saturday afternoon, September 17.

Network television's policy was that no advertising could appear on the canvas or corner pads except the promoter's name or logo or the name of the venue. I wanted to get exposure for the Spectrum on ABC. King shipped his canvas with his logo in the center but I had it stashed across from the Spectrum at what was then JFK Stadium. The signature from the receiving person was unreadable.

Rich Giachetti, who worked for King, spent the morning of the fight trying to locate the canvas. After he gave up, King was forced to use our canvas and our logo. King accused me of "trickeration," but I feigned innocence. Maybe King got the last laugh because Spectrum Fights lost $1,241.67 on the card.

We held the weigh-in at noon Friday in the Blue Line Club. Other than heavyweights, boxers always weighed-in the day of the fight, but both camps had agreed since the card was a 3 p.m. start. Viruet and Duran both had trouble making 135. We had an oversized scale, like at carnivals where the hustler guesses your weight or you win a stuffed animal. After an early morning workout, Duran was 134 ½.

Paddy Flood, who managed Viruet, was more than two hours late driving from New York. Viruet barely had his feet on the scale when corner man Al Braverman yanked him off, but his 135 pounds were official. Flood argued that Duran would be 140 by fight time and Viruet would still be 135, but the weights stood.

There was a fight over the officials, too. Howard McCall, Athletic Commission chairman, wanted local officials since neither fighter was from Pennsylvania. It made sense, but this was boxing, and the WBA threatened to walk away. If it did, ABC would follow.

Late Friday afternoon I saw Spectrum owner Ed Snider leaving the building and I brought him up to date. Snider did a U-turn and called Pennsylvania Governor Milton Shapp, who solved the problem by letting the WBA appoint the referee and one judge. Still, ABC was nervous about the weigh-in fiasco. They were recuperating from the bad publicity King's United States Boxing Championships earlier in 1977 had brought.

Saturday morning, I met at the Sheraton Hotel with Howard Cosell and the ABC television staff to smooth over the issues, but I left wondering if the fight would go on. I tried to stay positive—not my forte—but it wasn't until the first off-TV fight began that associate producer Alex Wallau told me ABC was back in. I was so drained that Wallau had to tie my necktie at ringside.

Duran won a tactical fight by scores of 71-65, 73-65, and 73-68. I was disappointed with the fight and the crowd. Only 7,910 paid, but those who did witnessed another Matthew Franklin slugfest in the semfinal. Less than eight weeks after his war with Marvin Johnson, Franklin was defending his NABF light-heavyweight title against 37-year-old Dynamite Douglas.

For the first four rounds, Franklin was pitching and Douglas was catching. Midway through round five, Franklin ran into a right hand and went down. When he got up, Douglas pinned him on the ropes and pounded him for more than a minute but referee Hank Cisco did not step in.

In round six, Franklin hurt Douglas with a right hand and began unloading but could not drop him. Cisco stopped it at 2:44. The crowd booed straight through the announcement. I screamed that Cisco "should never be allowed to referee a fight in which Frank Gelb has an interest" because of their close relationship.

"From ringside, it appeared Douglas was capable of continuing at least a bit longer," Bob Wright wrote in the *Bulletin*, "but it also seemed obvious that Franklin had recovered from the fifth-round beating he'd absorbed and was in better shape than his older foe." Wright added that "Douglas does have a history of playing possum."

Cisco told Wright: "He's (Peltz) got a lot of nerve. The doctor (Alfred Ayella) had come to me at the end of the fifth round and told me both guys were in such bad shape, I should stop the fight at the first opportunity." Wright added that "Dr. Ayella confirmed telling Cisco both fighters must be watched very carefully but he did not recall telling Cisco to stop the fight at the first opportunity." Gelb threatened to sue if I didn't recant. I did.

Eight weeks after his appendectomy, Briscoe K0d Sammy Barr, of The Bahamas, on the Franklin-Johnson card and qualified to fight his old nemesis, Rodrigo Valdes, for the middleweight title that Carlos Monzon had vacated. Bob Arum and King appeared to monopolize network boxing and Arum sold the match to CBS.

With European co-promoter Rodolfo Sabbatini, Arum made a deal with Casino di Campione on the Swiss-Italian border near Lake Como. Quaint European towns and villages were paying site fees to promoters for internationally televised fights to boost tourism. The ballroom for the fight could only hold 500 people but the casino was the largest in Europe.

Two men disguised as Valdes and Briscoe went 15 slow-motion rounds on November 5. Valdes won 146-144, 148-143 and 149-142. The audience, mostly European high rollers, made little noise other than polite applause for a good punch or a defensive maneuver. Benton had guided Briscoe through 13 fights—nine wins, four draws—to the brink of the world title. There would be more big fights, but Bennie's career was winding down.

Chapter Twenty-Seven

Biggest Year Ever

Richie Kates staggers after final shot from Matt Franklin. (Peltz collection)

I was involved in 22 of the 23 cards in Philadelphia in 1978. A new promoter, Nancy Sciacca, of New York, ran once at the Blue Horizon and drew 481 customers, not much worse than any of the seven I promoted there that year. The 69th Street Forum stayed busy and continued to outdo the Blue Horizon, but the Spectrum was the place to be. Light-heavyweight replaced middleweight as the hot division and it was a big year for Matthew Franklin, Marvin Johnson and Mike Rossman. It was the last big year for Bennie Briscoe, and his most lucrative.

If the 1977 fight between Franklin and Johnson was the greatest I ever saw in person, Franklin vs. Richie Kates—seven months later—was not far behind. Kates was born in Savannah, Georgia, one of 11 children in a family that moved to South Jersey before he was a year old.

"My parents were sharecroppers and I learned about hard work when I was a kid," Kates said. "No one gave us anything. I worked at a local Acme in Bridgeton, (New Jersey), sweeping floors, stocking shelves. One of my friends in school told me he was training at a boxing gym and I said, 'How are you going to be a fighter when I can beat you up?' So I started going to the gym. I won the South Jersey Golden Gloves in Atlantic City and then I lied about my age and turned pro when I was 16."

Franklin, 23, was the NABF light-heavyweight champ even though the 24-year-old Kates claimed his one-round knockout over Jimmy Dupree four years earlier had earned him that title. Franklin was 18-3-2, 11 K0s. Kates was 34-3, 19 K0s, and two of his losses to Victor Galindez for the WBA title. Franklin and Kates each got $7,500 ($32,000 in 2021). The 12-rounder was scheduled for Tuesday, February 7, but Philadelphia's worst snowstorm in a decade forced a postponement. The Spectrum had an open night that Friday—rare in those days—so we moved it.

"I'm so sick and tired of the name Franklin," Kates told Lee Samuels, of the *Bulletin.* "He (Peltz) put us up in the Franklin Motor Inn, we're near the Franklin Parkway, and the other day we drove by the Franklin Institute. I can't stand it anymore."

Franklin was three pounds heavy at the morning weigh-in and spent 90 minutes in the men's room at the Spectrum, running hot water to generate steam. He bathed his body in cocoa butter, shadowboxed to sweat and made 175.

It was the biggest local light-heavyweight match since 1961 when Harold Johnson knocked out Von Clay in their NBA title fight at the Arena. Johnson made a rare public appearance for this one and what he saw was far removed from his counter-punching style of working behind the jab and probing for openings.

Kates was down in the second round, but referee Charley Sgrillo ruled it was a push. Kates had a solid third, and in the fourth landed a right that dropped Franklin on his face. Franklin got to his feet as the bell rang, rallied in the fifth and floored Kates with his own right hand. Kates was saved by the bell, too. He tried to con his way through the sixth on unsteady legs, but Franklin landed a series of rights—and a slight push—and Kates went down. When he got up, another right hand sent him lurching through the ropes, bent over, head first. Sgrillo stopped it at 1:35.

"It was the most savage fight in Philadelphia in more than a decade," Gene Courtney wrote in the *Inquirer*. "They fought like Neanderthals throwing rocks at each other. They staggered and slumped and survived vicious punches and knockdowns. And when it was over, Matt Franklin emerged as the North American Boxing Federation light-heavyweight champion and Richie Kates was taken to Metropolitan Hospital for observation."

Despite their success together, Franklin wanted to divorce manager Frank Gelb, claiming Gelb had too many interests and was spending too much time with his other fighters, even though Tyrone Everett was gone, brother Mike's career was fading and Jimmy Young's contract had been sold. By the time of Franklin's last two Spectrum fights that year against Dale Grant and Yaqui Lopez, I was dealing with his attorney, Harry Rubin.

Bob Arum offered Franklin a shot at Galindez on the Ali-Leon Spinks II card in September, but Franklin turned it down. If he beat Galindez, he would owe Arum three title defenses and since the deal would have been signed while Gelb was his manager, Gelb would have shared in the money. Franklin said his contract with Gelb ended in October. Gelb said Franklin had signed a two-year extension.

It was not a good year for managers. After a grueling 10-round decision over Roman Contreras in March, his second win of the year, Augie Pantellas said he was getting short-changed. He had earned a total of $5,500 for the two fights, which was more than the Spectrum had.

Pantellas complained about Marty Feldman's 25 percent cut, but that was less than most managers took, especially one who also was the trainer. Pantellas had a sweetheart deal but didn't know it.

"Twenty-five percent of everything I do for five years? It's ridiculous," Pantellas told Gary Smith, of the *Daily News*. "I'm not forgetting my roots. Jesus brought me back to life. Marty didn't do nothing. If they (Peltz and Feldman) are gonna be punks, I'm not gonna fight anymore. If I wasn't a Christian, I'd say some beautiful words about these men."

Feldman said his contract with Pantellas was for sale for $7,500—to no takers.

"When he (Pantellas) came to me (late in 1976) he looked like death," Feldman told Lee Samuels, of the *Bulletin*. "His skin was gray-colored. I said stick with me, come to the gym and work out—not to fight again but to live again. He had a bad liver and a bad spleen and he was washed up as a fighter. So he trained, took the right kind of vitamins, ate nourishing food and when he took a three-hour physical a few months later at Jefferson Hospital, he passed with flying colors. That's when we decided to go fight again. "

By September, everyone had kissed and made up and Pantellas fought Bobby Chacon at the Spectrum. The former WBC featherweight champion was 38-4, 35 K0s, but on tapes he looked like he had slowed down. Wrong! Chacon put on the best performance ever at the Spectrum by a visiting fighter. He floored Pantellas twice and stopped him in the seventh round.

It's hard to figure why only 4,081 paid to see it since many of Chacon's West Coast fights were televised to the East Coast on tape delay. Pantellas had one more fight, avenging his 1970 loss to Sammy Goss by earning a unanimous 10-round decision the following January at the 69th Street Forum, and retiring. He was 28-6, 20 K0s, three weeks short of his 35th birthday.

After Feldman passed away in 2017, Pantellas was remorseful: "Marty was the best trainer around. I can't believe I said those things about him. I wouldn't ever want anyone else in my corner. I was the highest paid fighter in Philly in the late 1960s, other than Joe Frazier. I made $18,000 ($125,000 in 2021) for my first fight with Sammy Goss in 1970. Kitten Hayward told me he never made that kind of money, not even when he beat Emile Griffith at the Spectrum. I cannot imagine how good I could have been if I had lived a clean life back then.

"If I just had a drink now and then or just smoked some weed, I would have been fine but it was the hard stuff that hurt me. I'd stagger into the gym after a weekend down the shore in Margate (New Jersey) and I'd be wasted. If I was cool I could have been champion. I was stupid. I was messed up before the first Goss fight. I had hepatitis and my skin was gray and my doctor didn't want me to fight but I went ahead, anyway. (Ricardo) Arredondo became world champion and I had him on the floor."

After boxing, Pantellas opened a successful hot dog stand outside the Delaware County Courthouse in Media, a borough 13 miles west of Philadelphia. He's still at it today and is as well-known there as the people who frequent the courthouse.

On March 21, Curtis Parker, a 1977 National Golden Gloves champion, fought Clarence Jody White, of Trenton, in a middleweight prelim at the Blue Horizon. Parker, 19, was 3-0, 2 K0s. White, a former New Jersey Golden Gloves champion, was 28. He had been stopped by Frank Fletcher in his pro debut nine months earlier.

For two rounds it was war and the crowd gave them a standing ovation. Parker took over in the third and I wondered why referee Cal Freeman or White's corner let it continue. White's chief second, Bobby Williams, waved the towel at 1:19 of the fourth.

After the first round of the main event between local middleweights Ernie Singletary and Jerome Goodman, someone told me that White, after asking to lie down and rest, was unconscious in the dressing room. When I got there, Dr. Floyd Carson was pounding and massaging White's chest, trying to revive him. It was not yet mandatory to have ambulances standing by, but one arrived within minutes. White was attached to a resuscitator, placed on a stretcher and taken to St. Joseph's Hospital five blocks away. He was pronounced dead on arrival at 11.05 p.m.

I had gone with Jay Seidman, Director of Promotions at the Spectrum, to his apartment two miles away. I called the hospital, but when the woman who answered said she could talk only to immediate family members, I knew White was gone. Married with one son and another child on the way, he worked full-time as a security officer at Trenton State College and helped train amateurs at the Trenton PAL. He was paid $150 to fight Parker. Freeman walked away from refereeing.

"It never should have happened," Parker said. "Was he (White) in top shape? I don't know. I remember walking around the ring with him after the fight was stopped. The crowd was cheering. When he died, it was terrible. I gave my purse ($128 net) to his family. For a few weeks I thought about not fighting again, but I got back in the ring three months later."

Was there anyone to blame? I had checked on White to make sure he was training at the Trenton PAL. He was. Did I make a fair fight? Parker was the prohibitive favorite. Had it ended earlier, would White have survived? No one gets hurt in a quick fight because it ends before one fighter takes a sustained beating.

Fighters get hurt in competitive fights and this one was competitive for two rounds. Benny "Kid" Paret died after being stopped in the 12th round by Emile Griffith in 1962, but he had floored Griffith in the sixth and it was a battle. It was the same when Deuk Koo Kim died after being stopped in the 14th round of his 1982 fight with Ray Mancini. Parker-White could have been stopped in the third or in the corner before the fourth, either by the ringside physician—who did not enter the ring to check—or by White's team. It's speculation.

I put one foot down in front of the other and soldiered on. The following week my brother-in-law and I were in Kansas City. Briscoe was fighting 24-year-old lefty Tony Chiaverini, who was 21-3 and had won his last 10, nine of them there. Briscoe had lost on points to future champ Vito Antuofermo in February in Madison Square Garden, but his name still meant something and more than 10,000 packed the Municipal Auditorium, the largest crowd in Kansas City since Joe Louis K0d Natie Brown there in 1937.

Briscoe was one of a handful of Black men in the building, fighting in front of an all-White crowd in a predominantly White city. The only other Black men were George Benton, Milt Bailey, referee Eloda Morrison, and legendary three-time undisputed world champion Henry Armstrong, who was introduced before the main event. There were a few racial slurs from ringside during preliminary fights.

Briscoe's purse was the same $20,000 ($85,000 in 2021) he got for Antuofermo. Chiaverini lacked speed and movement and stood in front of Briscoe. Big mistake! At times, Chiaverini put his head on

Briscoe's shoulders and tried to match punches. Bigger mistake! To steal a line from Howard Cosell, it was like firing spitballs at a battleship.

Chiaverini, his right eye completely shut, his left eye on its way, motioned the referee at 1:05 of the eighth to stop the fight. Judges John Romano and Bill Easton each had Briscoe ahead by only 68-67. Perhaps they had filled out their scorecards in advance. Ex-pro Ron Marsh, the only judge paying attention, gave Briscoe every round. It would be Briscoe's last major victory. It felt good winning a big fight on the road, especially at this stage of Briscoe's career.

The next day we flew to Indianapolis. Marvin Johnson was boxing Eddie Davis, of Hempstead, New York, 10-0-1, 5 K0s. The Tyndall Armory held 1,891, but people sat in the aisles and stood along the walls to watch Johnson stop Davis at 1:24 of the seventh round.

John Bansch, assistant sports editor of the *Indianapolis Star*, quoted me: "Marvin has more raw talent than any fighter in the world. He hasn't touched the surface. He still flies through the air at times. He still keeps his head too high. If he ever sees his full potential he could be world champion. I believe we've seen only 50 to 60 percent of his potential."

Back home, the *Daily News* headline read: "Peltz' Properties Punched Out." The new crop of local talent we were was hoping to develop—middleweight Rudy Donato, lightweight Smokin' Wade Hinnant and welterweight Skinny Jimmy Rothwell—lost 10-round decisions on April 10 at the Spectrum.

The only fight worth watching was Donato's loss to Archie Andrews. Donato was a good right-hand puncher from the Frankford section who lacked confidence. Andrews was an overachiever from South Philadelphia who upset three prospects that year—Guy Gargan, Donato and Rocky Tassone—before losing his next five fights and retiring. Rothwell's 10-round loss to Victor Abraham was a dreadful match between two counter-punchers I never should have made.

The biggest disappointment was Hinnant, who had fast hands and a crowd-pleasing style. He was 19 and his 12-0 record included wins over Johnny Copeland and Norman Goins, tough guys from the Midwest. He knocked Rufus Miller down in the second round, but the action stalled and the visitor from Paterson, New Jersey, got the split decision. When Hinnant came back to the dressing room, he said, "Get him for me again." I sat there knowing what the old-timers would say: "You just had him for 10 rounds."

Hinnant was born in Nash County, North Carolina. He'd moved to Philadelphia when he was 8 and ran track for the ABC Recreation Center in North Philadelphia.

"If you didn't come in first place in track, you didn't get a medal or trophy," he said. "I found out that if you came in second or third in boxing, you still got a trophy and trophies were good for impressing the girls, so that's why I started boxing. I had about 40 amateur fights but I never won any titles. I'd get to the finals and I'd always come up short. I was in 10th grade at Ben Franklin High School when I turned pro."

After school one day, 16-year-old Hinnant got a call from his trainer, Walt Headon, who asked him to turn pro that night at the Arena. He won a four-round decision and got $125.

"I took that money and I went out and bought a lot of clothes the next day," he said. "After that I sparred with Tyrone Everett and one day I was sitting on the steps of my house, looking at the *Stop* sign on the corner, and it seemed blurry. An eye doctor told me I had a cataract in my left eye. He convinced me to have surgery, but that made it worse.

"My mom knew there was a problem, but not the full extent of it. I didn't fight again for six months and I dropped out of high school in 11th grade. I knew math percentages and I thought that would help me in business."

Hinnant went to training camp in 1976 to help Lou Bizzarro prepare for his title fight with Roberto Duran.

"I started seeing black spots in my left eye," he said. "I was supposed to fight on the card in Erie, but the doctor turned me down and told me I had a detached retina. I got another operation that November, but they didn't have the technology back then and the doctor said it was irreparable. But as long as I was fighting in Philadelphia, everything was okay."

After losing to Miller, Hinnant out-pointed Mike Everett and lost a majority decision to future WBC world junior welterweight champion Bruce Curry. He was scheduled to box the following July at Steel Pier in Atlantic City, but his license was denied by the New Jersey Athletic Commission after his pre-fight physical. Years later, when I asked him how he had been allowed to fight in Philadelphia, he didn't want to talk about it.

"The scariest thing about my fights was passing the eye exam," Hinnant said. "I didn't want anyone to know, mainly because I didn't want to be looked at differently. After I couldn't fight anymore, I was bitter for a long time. I was mad at God and at some of the other fighters from my gym, who made fun of me, saying, 'He ain't Smokin' no more,' and I was mad at the newspaper reporters who broke the story. The headlines read something like, 'Wade Hinnant is just another one-eyed fighter.'

"I stayed in the house for two weeks after that. It broke me. I was always told that the newspapers will build you up and then break you. I was painfully shy and quiet back then. I internalize a lot of things. Looking back, I would do it again."

Michael Albert DePiano was born in 1956 in South Philadelphia, but his family moved to Turnersville, New Jersey. When he turned pro after 30 amateur fights, his dad billed him as Mike Rossman the "Jewish Bomber." Jimmy DePiano's wife, Celia Rossman, was Jewish, and DePiano knew that a Jewish fighter would be an attraction. "I wanted Michael to be a lawyer or a doctor, never a boxer," Celia said.

Rossman turned pro at 17 as a junior middleweight. He didn't lose until his 23rd fight when Mike Nixon earned a 10-round split decision in Nixon's Binghamton, New York, backyard. Rossman K0d Nixon three months later in Las Vegas and won two out of three from Mike Quarry while growing into a light-heavyweight. He was close to a world title fight in 1978 when Yaqui Lopez stopped him after six rounds on March 2 at the Felt Forum.

I had been the promoter or matchmaker for seven of Rossman's first 15 fights. After that, his dad worked with Teddy Brenner at Madison Square Garden, catering to New York's Jewish population. Rossman boxed 10 times at the Garden, often on cards featuring Joe Frazier, Jerry Quarry and Muhammad Ali.

After losing to Lopez, I matched Rossman with Lonnie Bennett, of Los Angeles, on May 24 at the Spectrum. Bennett had lost to John Conteh for the WBC world title in 1975, but he had beaten Dynamite Douglas in 1976 and Lopez in 1977. He had been stopped in his last two fights, but he was 28-5, 24 K0s. A crowd of 9,331 paid $79,933 to see it.

A right hand knocked Bennett down early in round two. When he got up, Rossman drove him into a corner and dropped him again. Bennett got up but Rossman hung him up on the ropes and referee Frank Cappuccino stopped it at 1:41.

Bennie Briscoe scored his 50th knockout that night, stopping Jersey's Bob Patterson in five rounds. Marvin Johnson won a 10-round decision over Houston's Johnny Baldwin in the only fight that went the distance. Jeff Chandler K0d Mexican Jose Luis Garcia in five. We got 25 rounds out of 48 scheduled and everyone went home happy.

Rossman fought for me in July in Atlantic City against overmatched Matty Ross, of Lowell, Massachusetts. Ross was 13-1 but his fights were in New England and he was not Marvin Hagler. It was over in two. I would see Rossman in September in New Orleans.

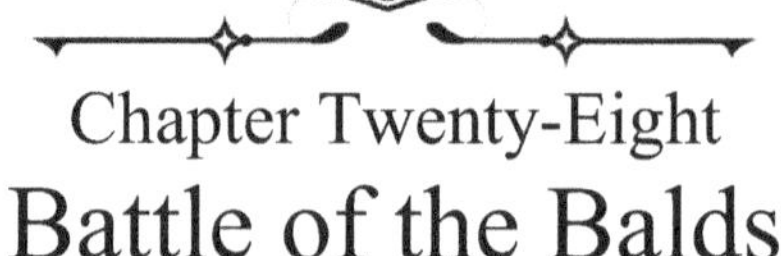

Chapter Twenty-Eight

Battle of the Balds

He was right; we had fun. (Peltz collection)

By the summer of 1978, Marvin Hagler had become Marvelous. He had lost two of 41 fights and twice avenged the one to Willie Monroe. He would catch Boogaloo Watts down the road. He had not been invited to Don King's U.S. Championships the year before and boxing politics would keep him from becoming world champion for another two years. Hugo Corro, of Argentina, had relieved Rodrigo Valdes of the world middleweight title, but he wasn't going to get in the same country, let alone the same ring, with Hagler. The biggest middleweight fight on the planet was coming to Philadelphia.

Promoter Rip Valenti offered Bennie Briscoe $20,000 to fight Hagler at the Boston Garden, but the fight belonged at the Spectrum where Hagler "made his bones" and where Briscoe would get much more than $20,000. Hagler made the fight a personal vendetta. He claimed Briscoe had dissed him when he came to Philadelphia for his earlier fights.

"We were trainin' at Frazier's gym for Watts or Monroe—one of the fights here—and some remarks were made," manager Pat Petronelli told Bob Wright. "I really don't know exactly what was said, but Marvin's had a thing for Bennie ever since."

"I never said nothin' about the boy," Briscoe said. "I never cared about him. I didn't think I'd be fightin' him 'cause he's southpaw. You know, he be goin' around with his head bald just like me. Well, there ain't but one Bennie Briscoe. He gonna find that out Thursday."

"I don't like him and he don't like me," Hagler said. "I'm going to give him the beating of his life, make him retire."

"He's scared," Briscoe said. "He's talkin' like that, but inside he's just hopin' to God he can get one over on me."

It went like this the week of the August 24 fight. We scheduled an outdoor boxing exhibition at JFK Plaza in Center City, but both refused to spar. That was left to others on the card. When Hagler and Briscoe got into the ring to be taped for interviews for the evening news, KYW-TV had to "bleep" Briscoe close to a dozen times.

"How's he gonna do all this stuff to me," Briscoe said between bleeps. "A man ain't gotta talk about what he gonna do. You just go do it. Some of my corner boys come down here to see me and lots gonna see this thing on television. I can't let him make me a fool in front of my folks."

The contracts said each fighter had to bring two pairs of different-colored trunks to the weigh-in. Briscoe and Hagler each brought burgundy velvet and no way was I going to ask them to flip a coin. I had two Black men with shaven heads and nearly identical trunks. Briscoe's had a white Star of David and Hagler's a thick white waistband. I cannot imagine what it looked like from the top rows. The crowd was 15,302, largest indoor crowd ever in Pennsylvania for a non-world championship fight.

Hagler won what he'd labeled the "Battle of the Balds," 47-44, 48-43 and 49-43. He survived a cut over his right eye by choosing to stick-and-move and counter. That is what you do when you're 24 and approaching your prime and your opponent is 35 and past his.

"I knew the other guy was gonna fight like he did—moving and firing as he went," Benton told Tom Cushman. "If he stands there with a guy like Bennie, he gets K0d. If Bennie stays outside, he gets K0d. So I told him to stay inside, figuring that with the kind of pressure Bennie can put on, Hagler would have to stop and fight eventually. The main thing was, Bennie wasn't gonna get hurt that way. He followed the plan to perfection, fought a helluva fight, did every damn thing I asked him to do...but the other guy is young, strong and awfully good."

Hagler got $15,000 ($65,000 in 2021), his best purse yet. Briscoe received 30 percent of the $145,308 gate. His paycheck, in excess of $40,000 ($170,000 in 2021), was the third largest of his career. Adding in the $1,750 fee from the Boston Garden, where the fight was televised on closed-circuit, Spectrum Fights realized a profit of $47,487 ($202,000), its best night ever.

It was Hagler's last fight in Philadelphia. He returned in 1983 as world champion for Briscoe's retirement party at Palumbo's in South Philadelphia. When he spoke, he said he came to Philadelphia for the experience, "certainly not for the money," looked at me and everyone laughed. He never forgot those first three $2,000 purses and I never forgot that I had turned down 10 percent of his contract.

I'd see Hagler every June at the Hall of Fame in Canastota and we'd reminisce. He was a good man and it was a shock when he passed away suddenly in 2021 at the age of 66. He was one of few remaining from the times when boxing was real. He had been living in Italy for more than 30 years.

Three weeks later after Hagler-Briscoe, I was in New Orleans. Muhammad Ali was trying to regain the heavyweight title from Leon Spinks, Mike Rossman was fighting Victor Galindez for the WBA 175-pound title, and Marvin Johnson was going against local star Jerry Celestine in a 10-round contest. Ali and Johnson won but the drama was in Rossman-Galindez.

Galindez was from Argentina. He was just under 5-foot-10, thick and strong. He fought like a bull, had been champion for nearly four years, but he always complained about head butts and low blows. He got the benefit from WBA officials in close fights, twice against Yaqui Lopez, once against Eddie Gregory, once against Richie Kates. He was prone to cuts but he had made 10 successful defenses. Few gave Rossman a chance, even though it took Galindez three trips to the scale to make 175.

That night, the 22-year-old Rossman fought a perfect fight. He got inside, answered every Galindez flurry with his own and busted up the champion's face until referee Carlos Berrocal stopped it 55 seconds into the 13th round. The more than 60,000 in the Superdome couldn't have asked for a better performance. Rossman had trained at Ali's camp in Deer Lake, Pennsylvania.

Back in the dressing room, he went to the shower and I smelled marijuana. I pulled back the curtain and saw him and younger brother Andrew smoking a joint. Now that's a celebration!

Bob Arum had options on Rossman's first three defenses and wanted the first in New York, but Jimmy DePiano, Rossman's father and manager, wanted it at the Spectrum. We guaranteed Arum no worse than "break even" and to split any profit 50-50. Ringside was $50, high for Philly, especially in December. We had charged $15 for Briscoe-Hagler. Regardless, a crowd of 11,205—including Sylvester Stallone—came to see Rossman fight European champion Aldo Traversaro, of Italy.

Rossman was cut on the left cheekbone and had a bloody nose after five rounds. He took control in the sixth and a right uppercut-left hook combination ripped a nasty gash near Traversaro's hairline.

Blood gushed and referee Jesus Celis stopped the fight. Traversaro needed 12 stitches.

Three nights earlier in Marsala, Sicily, Marvin Johnson had won the WBC version of the title by knocking out Mate Parlov, of Croatia, in the 10th round. Arum also promoted that fight, but I stayed in Philly for Rossman-Traversaro, missing the first of "my fighters" to win a world title. I watched on television with Stan Hochman in a hotel near the Spectrum. When it ended, I screamed, ran out and drove home to celebrate with Linda.

The Rossman-Traversaro gate was $236,144. It should have meant a nice profit. A few days later Spectrum President Allen Flexer told me most of the $7,087 profit came from ad sales in the souvenir program.

"How is that possible," I asked? "We paid Rossman $100,000 and Traversaro $25,000."

"Rossman's father got $50,000," he said.

When I spoke to him for this book, Flexer did not recall the conversation. But I never forgot it. Perhaps the $50,000 was DePiano's one-third of his son's contract as manager and he never took a "cut" from the official $100,000 purse. Perhaps he was hiding it from his management partner, Vincent Carlesimo, a former Villanova University football player then in the olive oil business in Verona, New Jersey.

DePiano had been on boxing's fringes for more than 30 years, always looking for the big break. His family had owned bars in South Philadelphia, but he loved boxing and did odd jobs for promoter Jimmy Toppi at the Olympia at Broad and Bainbridge. He lost a lung at 16 when he was shot during a street fight. After serving in the Air Force, he managed a few fighters who'd gone nowhere. When his son won the world championship, he basked in the glory. His cigars and jewelry made it seem he'd stepped out of a Damon Runyon novel.

Two years earlier, after Rossman had defeated Mike Quarry in Las Vegas, we changed planes in Chicago on the trip home. As we boarded, DePiano remarked that he could blow up the plane if he felt like it. Security personnel halted everything, emptied the plane, and made us wait 90 minutes to re-board. DePiano's voice had a sandpaper quality and he had no censors. He managed his son on a

50-50 basis. If father-son relationships were bad for boxing, this was Exhibit A.

Rossman was scheduled to defend against Galindez in February, 1979, in Las Vegas, but the fight was canceled. Galindez had demanded that the WBA, not Nevada, appoint the officials. It came down to the wire but with ABC-TV televising, viewers saw Rossman walk into the ring and Galindez walk out of the building. The challenger went unpunished and won the title back two months later in New Orleans, stopping Rossman in the 10th round.

Losing again five months later to little-known Ramon Ranquello, Rossman seemed bored. He signed for a rematch in February, 1980, but backed out the week of the fight, claiming he had the flu. Commission Doctor Frank B. Doggett found no symptoms and Rossman was suspended indefinitely by the New Jersey State Athletic Commission. Michael Spinks subbed and K0d Ranquello in six.

Everything came apart. Rossman argued with his father over money he thought he had been cheated out of. DePiano allegedly sold his half of his son's contract to co-manager Carlesimo. When Carlesimo did not pay him on time, DePiano threatened to put a lien on his son's purse.

"Sometimes when family is involved in business, it's the worst," Rossman told Lewis Freedman, of the *Inquirer*. "I didn't make no money. I didn't make money like I should have as champion. What do I need a manager for? My manager never did nothing for me. A couple of times in my career if I'd had a good manager, things might have been different."

Rossman returned that summer and boxed at Resorts International, the first Atlantic City casino to host televised boxing since gambling had been legalized four years earlier. He outpointed Don Addison, then knocked out Al Bolden in the 10th round of a fight he was losing. Two 10-round decisions over Luke Capuano at the Conrad Hilton Hotel in Chicago followed.

Frank Gelb was trying to sell a match between Rossman and Richie Kates. It would have been a terrific local attraction but no TV network was interested. I offered Dwight Braxton and CBS-TV bought it. We did the fight in May, 1981, at Resorts. Rossman got $120,000, Braxton $20,000. Ex-pro Wesley Mouzon and Quenzell McCall were handling Braxton and they knew it would be his big chance. Rossman went down from a left hook in the seventh and did not get up. He retired afterward.

Less than two years later, Jimmy DePiano died from pancreatic cancer at 59. He had complications from a blood clot that traveled to his lung, but the cancer did it. Linda and I went to the funeral in Turnersville, New Jersey. Celia, his wife, wept as she told me her husband was a good man and that he loved me.

When I offered my condolences to Michael, tears ran down his cheeks. Two weeks earlier his dad had called me from his hospital bed to make me promise to "take care of my son." When I shook Rossman's hand, he told me he was going to fight again—for his father—and he wanted me to work with him. I thought he was simply saying something nice and it would not amount to much.

One month later Linda and I visited Rossman and his wife, Maxine, at their Turnersville home. I asked Linda not to mention him fighting again. We sat at their kitchen table for two or three hours. We talked about their young son, life in general, maybe some recent fights. Every now and then the phone rang. Michael picked it up and, without saying a word, handed it to Maxine.

When it was time for us to leave, he said, "I cannot believe you," meaning that he could not believe I did not prod him to resume fighting. We spoke a few days later and he was back in the gym. Willie O'Neill was his new trainer.

Rossman boxed four times for me in 1983, all in Atlantic City. His first was in April at Resorts against Charlie Smith, a journeyman from Norfolk, Virginia.

"He (Peltz) might not buy you a cup of coffee, but he's a good matchmaker, a good promoter," Rossman told Thom Greer, of the *Inquirer*. "He's done a lot for a lot of guys in Philly. I can talk to him and get straight answers. I can talk to him about other things besides boxing. He's a good guy. I'm just trying to surround myself with better people."

O'Neill was training Rossman and Jeff Chandler at the Percy Street Gym in South Philadelphia. I held the lease on the gym. Rossman was out of sync but he stopped Smith in the 10th round. The bigger problem was locating Smith the night of the fight. He had weighed in that morning, but when I got to the dressing room he wasn't there and he wasn't in his hotel room. Someone said he'd driven to Philadelphia to visit relatives.

It was 7.30 and the card started at 8. I paced back and forth at the entrance to Resorts. Smith pulled in at 8. There was no reason to berate him—but I did. He apologized and went to his room to get his equipment. People have no idea what promoters go through. Years later, when I was spending winters in Florida, I would fly back to Philadelphia a week or 10 days ahead of my fight cards. Someone asked me why. "Don't the fighters just show up?" he asked. You can't even respond to that question.

Rossman was better in June when he K0d Army Lieutenant Al Fracker in six rounds at the Playboy Club & Casino. I had a one-year deal with PRISM to televise monthly cards in Atlantic City. The ballroom was packed.

Playboy employed several ex-boxers to serve as greeters, including former champs Rocky Graziano (middleweight) and Paddy DeMarco (lightweight). When DeMarco popped his head into our office, I called out, "The Brooklyn Billy Goat," hoping he would be pleased someone not only recognized him but also knew his nickname, one he had been stuck with for, shall we say, occasional head-butting. He wasn't pleased, but nobody got hurt.

In August at the Sands Casino, Rossman out-pointed ex-University of Pittsburgh football player Robert White. After rallying to knock out Henry Sims, of Chicago, in the same ring in November, Rossman said, "I made you look like (legendary promoter) Tex Rickard tonight." I envisioned Rossman challenging for the world light-heavyweight title. He was 4-0 on his comeback and he knew White fighters attracted television.

He signed to fight Roddy MacDonald, of Halifax, Nova Scotia, in February, 1984, at the Sands. It was on a network of cable and pay stations put together by Lou Falcigno, a major player in the closed-circuit television business. This was perfect for Rossman, who would win and be 5-0 and ready for something big.

Two weeks before the fight, he came to my Philly office, sat on the floor and said he couldn't fight. He'd been drinking and couldn't be ready. We put in a new main event and rescheduled him and MacDonald for May. One week before the rescheduled date, Rossman cut his chin sparring. He got three stitches, kept training, and it didn't reopen. O'Neill said he could cover it and Rossman grew a small beard to hide it.

I was in my hotel room at the Sands when my office manager, Pat Doris, called me to get down to the weigh-in. The commission doctor wouldn't let Rossman fight. When I pleaded with deputy commissioner Roy Johnson, he told me Rossman didn't want to. I ran after Rossman and offered him more than the $17,500 he was getting. "You've got no juice left," he said, and kept walking.

Jimmy Hill, a trainer who had a preliminary fighter on the card, called his other fighter, Stanley Ross, in Philadelphia, to fill in. Ross was 8-5-1, MacDonald 25-4. Ross K0d MacDonald in three rounds and was paid $5,000. It was the last fight Ross would win. He lost his next 10 and retired.

Rossman was in the casino that night but he had no reaction when he heard MacDonald had been knocked out. A month later I got a call from John Baskerville, who ran my gym on Percy Street. He told me Rossman was coming to train. I told him Rossman was not welcome. He never fought again.

He was 27 and his record was 44-7-3, 27 K0s. He had talent but couldn't control his demons. He got a job with the Roofers Union in Atlantic City. Years later, after we reconciled, I told him he could have fought Marvin Johnson in 1986 for the WBA light-heavyweight title.

"And how would that have changed my life?" he asked.

Chapter Twenty-Nine

End of the Line

Willie Monroe covers up against Curtis Parker in 1979. (Peltz Collection)

The number of local cards dropped to 17 in 1979, six at the Spectrum, our fewest ever. Three promoters went one and done—Nancy Sciacca at the Blue Horizon, Mitchell Berger and Butch Lewis at Convention Hall. My three Blue Horizon cards excited no one, but the 69th Street Forum sold out two of its five. Network television had renewed its love affair with boxing and Marvin Johnson and Matt Franklin would fight again, this time in Indianapolis with a market small enough for TV to "black out" the area.

I didn't realize the impact casino gambling in Atlantic City—approved in 1976—would have on boxing. Maybe I didn't want to. My contract with the Spectrum was ending January 31. I had agreed to co-promote, with Bob Arum, the Johnson-Franklin title fight with ABC televising it. That did not sit well with the Spectrum since I had planned the fight while my contract still was in effect.

"We have a good relationship with Russell," Spectrum president Allen Flexer told Tom Cushman, of the *Daily News*. "One thing I would like to point out…the boxing program does not consist of one man. There are many, many people involved." When asked if boxing would continue at the Spectrum if I left, Flexer answered, "Certainly. Regardless of the impression created by the media over the years, what we have here is a boxing program, not a one-man show."

Flexer had been an accounting major at Temple, class of 1963. After graduating, he worked for the Van Heusen clothing company, first in Philadelphia, then in Manhattan. When the Spectrum advertised for a new business manager, Flexer applied. He interviewed with five different executives, including owner Ed Snider. Hal Freeman, the interim president, called him on a Friday night to offer the job. When Flexer wanted the weekend to think it over, Freeman was flabbergasted.

"The Spectrum offer was $5,000 a year less than I was making at the time, working at ABC Trucking in New York," Flexer said. "I had played basketball at Lincoln High School and I loved sports and I loved music so the job would be a perfect fit. I had use of a company car at ABC Trucking but would not at the Spectrum. And I was running a knitting mill and pulling in about $5,000 a month so I had a lot to think about. My wife, Shelly, didn't want me to take the job but I thought there was a bigger upside at the Spectrum."

Flexer started in the fall of 1971, more than a year before I got there. I never took advantage of his business skills and he never had time to learn the inner workings of boxing. With his knowledge of business and my knowledge of boxing, Spectrum Fights could have been bigger. We might have gone national by signing the talent that had boxed for us. Flexer dealt with the Flyers, concerts, Ringling Brothers Circus and Disney on Ice, and the 76ers. Boxing was not a priority. It did not generate the income of these events.

When Bennie Briscoe caught the flu the weekend before his January 15 fight with David Love, the card was postponed until February 5. Some people at the Spectrum questioned if I had delayed Bennie's fight to force contract negotiations in my favor. That stung. But I agreed with Flexer and Stephen Greenberg, director of productions, to a new two-year contract with a substantial raise. After that, nothing went right.

Tyrone Everett was gone and Briscoe was 35. Augie Pantellas' comeback had been derailed by Bobby Chacon. The careers of those once-young middleweights—Cyclone Hart, Willie Monroe, Boogaloo Watts—were in the rear view mirror. Frank Gelb, a pleasure to work with while he managed Everett and Franklin, was focused on Atlantic City as a promoter and *de facto* casino boxing representative. He was fighting to control Franklin's career—fighting in court, not in the ring. The television networks didn't want to talk to anybody but Arum and Don King unless you offered them an Olympic gold medal winner.

We lost $44,788.89 ($165,000 in 2021) on the six cards in 1979, not much less than we lost on 16 in 1973, our first year. And that figure did not include my $40,000 salary.

Our troubles started with Briscoe's illness. He was 166 pounds on February 5, four over the contract limit, and had to run in the cold to take off two and pay Love a penalty for the other two. Late in a fight he was losing, the elastic wore out in his burgundy velvet trunks and George Benton had to wrap silver electrical tape around Briscoe's waist to keep them from falling down. It was that kind of night and that kind of year and we would need more than silver electrical tape to fix our problems.

The March 20 Spectrum card fell apart after main-eventers Chacon (bruised right hand) and Jerome Artis (strained back) withdrew. We pushed it back to March 31 and moved Thomas Hearns against Alfonso Hayman from the semifinal to the main event. But Hearns caught the flu which delayed things until April 3.

This was Hearns' first big fight outside Detroit. He was 20 and had knocked out all 17 opponents, including a first-round K0 over Skinny Jimmy Rothwell. He had boxed once in Tennessee and 16 times in Michigan, 12 of them in Detroit before crowds as big as 10,000. Emanuel Steward, former amateur Golden Gloves champ, was his manager and trainer. Hearns was the best thing to happen to Detroit boxing since Joe Louis.

Hayman was 30 and his record was 20-15-5. He was coming off a pair of wins in Virginia Beach—not exactly the capital of boxing—but had lost 12 of his last 17 and was far from the world-ranked fighter of five years earlier. It was okay for a semifinal, but nothing more.

Hearns trained at the Cloverlay Gym, now renamed the Joe Frazier Gym. Five days before the fight I got a call from Steward's lawyer who wanted to renegotiate the $5,000 contract Hearns had signed since he was now in the main event. The lawyer threatened that Hearns would leave town unless.... So I agreed to $6,000 plus 50 percent of the net gate over $50,000, but told the lawyer what I thought of him.

Though he had been stopped six times, Hayman became the first to go the distance with Hearns, but he did not win one round. Hearns hurt both hands and Steward blamed me for using the less expensive G&S gloves, not the Everlast or Reyes gloves he had stipulated in an addendum to the original contract. Since Hearns had not signed the revised one, we paid him only the $5,000. I had informed Spectrum executives earlier and no one objected.

Steward appealed to Howard McCall, the Pennsylvania commissioner. Steward showed McCall a copy of the addendum, said we did not use the agreed-upon gloves, did not play the theme from *Rocky* when Hearns entered the ring as he'd also stipulated, and had not paid the extra money.

McCall ruled that since Steward was reading from the addendum to the original signed contract, he would enforce *it*—not the unsigned one—so we paid Hearns $5,000. I was wrong but I felt Steward was taking advantage of us by demanding extra money. The crowd was 5,479 and the bottom line showed a net of $751.05, our only profitable card of the year. With Hearns' extra $1,000, we would have lost money. Steward and I later made peace. He and Hearns went on to Hall-of-Fame careers.

Hayman lost four of his next five. On December 23, 1980, he was in courtroom 378 in Philadelphia City Hall for a bail hearing after pleading guilty to the October 16 robbery of $4,500 from Robbins Jewelers on Castor Avenue in Northeast Philadelphia. He had been released on $5,000 bail since he had contracts for December fights in Detroit and Italy, but when he returned from overseas the judge raised the bail to $25,000. Hayman would have to spend the holidays behind bars.

After placing his hands behind his back to be handcuffed, Hayman punched Sheriff's Deputy Jack Wright in the jaw, pulled a .357 magnum from his jacket and waved it as spectators screamed and ran. Hayman ran down the stairs and out of the building but was subdued by two plainclothes officers at 17th and Market, three blocks away. Chief Inspector George Fencl, who was in the courtroom for another case, had called police radio with a full description. Five months later Hayman was sentenced to 5-10 years for the robbery as well as assault by a prisoner, escape, aggravated assault and a weapons offense.

After Hearns-Hayman, I was in Indianapolis where Fred Berns and I worked with Arum on the April 22 Johnson-Franklin WBC light-heavyweight championship match, which had been postponed from February when Johnson suffered a hairline fracture of the jaw. He was getting $150,000 and wanted to prove his value by making his first defense against Franklin. Fighters like Johnson no longer exist.

"This is not a mandatory fight," Johnson explained at the press conference. "Why did I pick Matthew Franklin…because he deserved it. Secondly, he beat me before and I don't think he'll do it again. I want it to go down in the record book that Marvin Johnson beat Matt Franklin."

Years later, Marvin told me: "I had some hard fights and there were some guys I could have left alone. But I had the mindset to be the best and the way to prove that is to beat the best. If someone beat me, I had the ego to want to fight him again to prove I was the better man. I wanted to beat everyone you put in front of me."

Franklin had strained a muscle in his right leg two weeks earlier. The night before the fight, he went to a hospital in Indianapolis—

under an assumed name—for X-rays and whirlpool treatments which did the trick.

The second Franklin-Johnson fight, in front of 8,395 at Market Square Arena, was as brutal and furious as the first—four rounds shorter. Johnson got off to his usual quick start and, by the end of the fifth, Franklin was bleeding from his nose and mouth, the area under his right eye was swollen and he was cut over both eyes.

Things changed late in the sixth when Franklin forced Johnson into backing up. Johnson changed strategy in the seventh, circling behind his jab, and Franklin hurt him with a straight right hand. Franklin jumped on Johnson in the eighth, missing as many as he landed, but a short right floored Johnson. When he got up unsteadily, referee George DeFabis stopped it.

Johnson called DeFabis "an amateur referee" but it was the right call. Franklin led on two scorecards (68-67 and 67-66), Johnson (68-65) on one. It was the kind of fight which could give boxing a good name. When he got fitted for a championship belt, Franklin announced he would now be known by his Muslim name, Matthew Saad Muhammad. "Saad means good future and Muhammad means worthy of praise," he told Cushman, "so, as you can see, the name has been good for me already."

Franklin converted to Islam. Bilal Muhammad became his manager and made all the boxing decisions with the help of Akbar Muhammad—later a Top Rank vice president—and Murad Muhammad, who became the promoter of record once Arum's options ran out. Gelb went to court for his $11,250 share of Franklin's $50,000 purse and the Indiana Boxing Commission ruled in his favor. His two-year extension was ruled valid. He would be paid from Saad Muhammad's purses until late in 1980.

Johnson defeated Carlos Marks in September in Indianapolis to set up a fight with WBA champion Victor Galindez in November in New Orleans. Arum had hooked up a two-city card on ABC-TV, linking it with Marvin Hagler's 15-round draw with middleweight champion Vito Antuofermo and Sugar Ray Leonard's 15th-round knockout of WBC welterweight champion Wilfred Benitez from Las Vegas. Fighting in their shadow, Johnson's 11th-round knockout of Galindez, a future Hall-of-Famer, never got the accolades it deserved.

Johnson hurt a tiring Galindez in the 10th round and trainer Champ Chaney told him to set Galindez up with his jab and get him out of there with the overhand left. It worked. Johnson got $50,000. Galindez got $150,000 plus TV rights to Argentina. Benitez got $1.2 million and Leonard $1 million. Antuofermo got $150,000, Hagler $40,000.

That summer, it was time for middleweight Curtis Parker to step up so I reverted to the Philly-versus-Philly formula and matched him with Willie Monroe.

Parker often was compared to Joe Frazier. Both were short, lacked the reach to be effective from mid-range and had to fight inside. Both could punch, would not back up, and believed they could impose themselves on anybody. Both took a good punch, were fearless and didn't care who they were fighting. Parker came in more directly than Frazier and he lacked Frazier's head and upper body movement. Frazier relished making his opponent miss while giving the illusion he was right there. Parker often absorbed his opponent's best to get inside and fed off them being demoralized by not being able to slow him down.

"I never wanted to take my opponent's best shot in order to land one," Parker said. "It may have looked that way but I never was willing to get hit. If I had to do it all over again maybe I could have been more of a boxer, but I was short for a middleweight."

Monroe and Parker were headed in opposite directions. Monroe was 33, Parker 20. Monroe wanted to box and pick his spots to lead Parker into mistakes, but Parker was too energetic and he took punches to work Monroe over. Monroe knew the formula to neutralize Parker, but he was out-worked and overwhelmed.

The unanimous scores for Parker (48-44 twice and 49-43) did not reflect the competitiveness of the fight. At times, Monroe reminded you of the fighter he once had been, but he couldn't beat the clock. It was the unbeaten Parker's 13th win and our best card of the year.

For Monroe, the end was near. He lost two of his next three and quit in 1981. He was 35 and worked briefly as a referee. He also drove a truck for the *Inquirer* and worked in maintenance for the Philadelphia Housing Authority. He later suffered from dementia, developed prostate cancer and passed away in 2019 at his home in Sicklerville, New Jersey. He was 73.

"My dad didn't talk much about his career," said April Monroe, one of Willie's two daughters. "I remember going to a couple of his fights but I was so young I fell asleep before they were over. We'd go running together on Kelly Drive and he taught me about breathing while running. I wanted to have a pro fight but he was against it. One was scheduled in 2003 but never came off."

I was enthusiastic about the Spectrum's future, but Parker was not a street guy. He was from Frankford, six miles from North Philly. He never drew the crowds Briscoe or Hart drew even though he had a Philly style. He also didn't have the local rivals Briscoe or Hart had and he came along when boxing was headed to Atlantic City.

On the Parker-Monroe card, light-heavyweight Jerry "The Bull" Martin knocked out Willie "The Bull" Taylor, of New York, in eight rounds. Teddy "The Irish" Mann, of Forked River, New Jersey, stopped Li'l Abner in six. It was Abner's first fight in 29 months and his last. Only 4,548 paid, maybe because it was a Monday night in July.

The three winners returned in September in front of 7,104, our largest 1979 crowd. Parker knocked out Elisha Obed, a ghost of the junior middleweight champ who nearly had defended against Abner in 1976, in the seventh round. Martin stopped lefty Leo Rogers in three, but everyone was talking about Mann vs. Briscoe. Since losing to David Love, Briscoe had won in DC and Atlantic City.

Mann (born Theodore Manschreck), 28, a former drug dealer and user, was 18-1 and had beaten Richie Bennett for the mythical Irish middleweight title. Two months after fighting Briscoe he would beat Rocky Tassone.

Mann's father had been killed in a car crash and Mann once received 38 stitches in his head from slamming into a pole, driving drunk after an all-day binge.

"The last time the cops came for me, the house was surrounded by about 15 or 20 police cars," Mann told Cushman. "They didn't want me to slip out the back door, I guess. Anyhow, they found 25 pounds of marijuana in the house and $10,000 in my bank account and they took everything." Mann served time in the Ocean County Jail and turned to boxing. Manager/trainer Carmen Graziano helped him stay clean by keeping him in the gym.

Mann did not punch hard enough or move well enough to disrupt the aging Briscoe, whose jackhammer jab, as Bob Wright wrote in the *Bulletin*, controlled the action. The decision was unanimous. There was talk of a Parker-Briscoe match but Briscoe meant too much to me to serve him up to Parker, regardless of the potential gate. Some people at the Spectrum took exception but they would have to live with my decision.

Parker had trouble holding off Gary Guiden on our last show of 1979. Guiden had been scheduled to fight for $400 on November 18 in Muncie, Indiana, but when Love canceled out (sprained back) five days prior to his November 14 date with Parker, Guiden jumped at the chance to earn $5,000. Guiden was 28-4, 24 K0s, and I had seen him fight in Indianapolis.

Even though Parker dropped him twice with body shots in round two, Guiden survived, ripped open a cut over Parker's right eye and staggered him with a right in the third. Both men landed well in the fourth. Parker dropped Guiden with a three-punch combination in the fifth and hit him when he was down. Referee Charles Sgrillo could have given Guiden extra time to recover, but didn't. Sgrillo gave Guiden a standing eight after Parker knocked him into the ropes and a third knockdown ended it at 2:55.

The crowd was a disappointing 5,325, but Parker's future was bright. He would gradate from PRISM to NBC.

Martin was fortunate to get the 12-round split decision over Jesse Burnett, of Los Angeles, to retain the NABF light-heavyweight title he had won that summer, and add the USBA belt as well. A right hand in the last round wobbled Burnett and swung the scores in Martin's favor. The decision (115-114 Burnett; 117-115 and 115-113 Martin) was not greeted kindly.

Souvenir program editor Flash Gordon called that night's eight-rounder between junior welterweights Victor Pappa, of Folsom, and Arseneo Green, of Allentown, one of the greatest fights ever at the Spectrum. Pappa, down in the fourth and fifth, was saved by the bell at the end of the fifth. He dropped Green just as the bell ended the sixth. In the seventh, Pappa's right ended the fight and fans leaped from their seats. Despite winning, Pappa had to be carried back to his corner. No video survives.

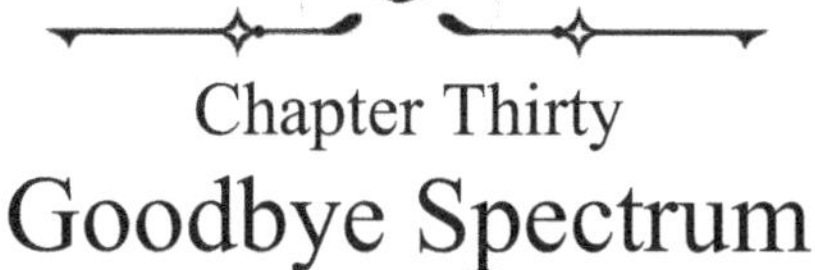

Chapter Thirty

Goodbye Spectrum

Emile Griffith, Bennie Briscoe and Marvin Hagler in 1983. (Pete Goldfield photo)

There were 12 boxing cards in the Philadelphia area in 1980, the fewest since the 11 in 1968. Five were by Impact Promotions, a new group headed by Claude Benner, a friend of sports agent Mark Stewart. Stewart, who once represented Philadelphia Flyers ice hockey coach Fred Shero, purchased the Arena in 1980 for $100,000 and renamed it the Martin Luther King Arena. The 69th Street Forum closed in February after its second card of the year. Michael Margolis, a 26-year-old newcomer, folded after one show at the Wynne Ballroom, an old movie theatre in

Wynnefield. The Blue Horizon went dark. Everyone was heading to Atlantic City.

Most of Atlantic City's 1979 cards were on the Boardwalk in a theatre at Steel Pier. Resorts International had purchased the aging amusement park and used it for storage, but kept the theatre open. The rest of the grounds would reopen years later, again as an amusement park.

Frank Gelb paid me $50 a show to help make matches and serve as the color analyst on the Tuesday night cards, which PRISM televised locally and, via satellite, to Los Angeles, Denver and cities in the Southwest. By the time I drove to Atlantic City and had dinner, it was a losing proposition, but some of the headliners were my fighters, like Bennie Briscoe, Jerry Martin and Jeff Chandler.

Briscoe had looked awful losing to Clemente Tschinza, of The Congo, in December, 1979, in Liege, Belgium, the so-called handgun capital of the world. Tschinza was 42-13-5 and quick. Briscoe fought as if he was in quicksand.

Knowing this, Marty Feldman wanted his middleweight, Richie Bennett, to fight Briscoe in January at the 69th Street Forum. I thought it would be an easy night for Briscoe. Bennett was 21-2-2 against mediocre opposition. He was tall and lanky and had been shut out by Teddy Mann five months before Briscoe defeated Mann almost as decisively. Briscoe may have slipped, but not that far. The match sold out, but Bennett won a 10-round split decision. I thought Briscoe had been robbed, but if he had to struggle with Bennett, it was time to retire. He looked every bit like a boxer two weeks before his 37th birthday.

I loved Bennie and Bennie loved me and anyone who didn't know that either wasn't around or wasn't paying attention. I didn't want him to take any more punches after 162 fights, amateur and pro. When he refused to quit, I did the wrong thing for the right reason. I wrote boxing commissions, asking them not to license him. Bennie ripped me in the press, but besides the punches he was taking in fights, he was getting hit in sparring. Arnold released him from his managerial contract and George Benton walked away as trainer.

George James, a boxing veteran, took over as manager and trainer. Bennie beat Bennett in a rematch that summer at the Arena but lost four of his last seven and retired at the end of 1982. Arnold had set up a Keogh (retirement) plan by putting away a percentage of Bennie's earnings. Had Bennie not withdrawn the money after the split, it would have been worth at least $225,000 when he turned 65.

Angelo Dundee stayed when Muhammad Ali fought Larry Holmes and Trevor Berbick. I should have stayed with Bennie and looked after him, but George James picked the right opponents, men with no power. When I re-read the newspaper stories years later, I felt even worse. I never should have gone public. Bennie was hurt and I was sorry. By 1982, we had made peace. I still called him "Old Man" and he still called me "Uncle Russ" and he cried when speaking about our relationship at his retirement dinner in 1983. He finished at 66-24-6, 53 K0s.

I cannot explain why we had the relationship we had. People said, "Never fall in love with a fighter, he'll break your heart," but Bennie never broke mine. I was a White kid from the Philly suburbs and he was a Black man from rural Georgia. We had central air conditioning in our house in 1954, but I'm not sure Bennie's even had indoor plumbing before he moved to North Philly in 1957. I was 23 when we took over his career—he was 27. I saw him as someone who needed a break but also as someone who could take me to the next level, though I never treated him as a commodity. I lived and died during his fights—not for financial rewards, but for him to achieve his dream of being world champion. Maybe he saw me as someone who cared about him beyond business. We never discussed it. Harold Johnson may have been my boyhood idol but Bennie was my heart. I bled for him.

Bennett, just 21 when he beat Briscoe, went 3-4 in his next seven fights—including the loss to Briscoe in their rematch—and retired in 1983. In April, 1991, he died from a drug overdose. He was 32.

Jeff Chandler, a 5-foot-7, 118-punder with a narrow head and pointy ears, had packed in more than 1,800 fans at the 69th Street Forum in the fall of 1979 when he knocked out Baby Kid Chocolate in nine rounds for the vacant USBA belt. It was South Philly over North

Philly and it solidified Chandler's claim as the best bantamweight East of Chicago.

When he boxed the following February at the Spectrum, it marked the first time 118-pounders had headlined at a major Philadelphia venue in 39 years. Chandler added the NABF bantamweight title to his collection, scoring two knockdowns in the ninth round and stopping Javier Flores, of Salt Lake City, in the 10th.

"A scientist needs no one staring over his shoulder," Gary Smith wrote in the *Daily News*. "How many were there when Salk sacked polio, when Pasteur punched out rabies? The smallest fight crowd to stagger into the Spectrum in the last six years saw Jeff Chandler take apart Javier Flores like a Nobel Prize winner dissecting a pinned-down rat.

"It was brutality with precision, one of the sharpest boxing exhibitions that no one has ever seen. Only 2,708 sat in Chandler's hushed laboratory but Joltin' Jeff just shrugged it off. 'Lotta people gonna be sore tomorrow that they missed it,' he said after his 10th-round KO. Javier Flores will be sore, and he had the best seat in the house."

Chandler's dressing room was mobbed with well-wishing fans and pros. Some compared him to Tyrone Everett.

"I'm more aggressive than Everett," Chandler said. "The best thing I can say about my punching is, 'Ask my opponent.' I'm hitting shots right now where I'm supposed to. Both knockdowns were single shots, not combinations. I'm ready for the championship. The champ is no better than this guy."

I wondered if Philadelphia would warm up to a bantamweight, even one of its own. Flores came in at 24-4-3, 17 K0s, and had never been knocked down or stopped. He had been in and out of the world rankings, but Chandler ruined him. Flores won just two of his next 15 and retired in 1984. Spectrum Fights lost $4,757.64 that night, but it would be the last time. Before the end of 1980, this skinny little kid who was paid $2,500 for a 12-round fight and could attract only 2,708 into the Spectrum would become a world champion.

Almost unnoticed on the undercard was Boogaloo Watts, who had his last local fight, stopping Fred Johnson, of New York, in the third round of the scheduled 10-round co-feature. It was Watts' third win in a row, but less than three months later he was K0d by Marvin

Hagler in in the second of their nationally televised rematch from Portland, Me.

Watts won his next four, but left boxing after being stopped in four rounds by Mark Kaylor midway through 1983 in London. He was 39-7-1, 22 K0s, the last of the three young middleweights to retire. Cyclone Hart's career (30-9-1, 28 K0s) had ended in 1977, save for one comback loss in 1982. Willie Monroe (40-10-1, 26 K0s) was gone by 1981. They would be missed.

David Love owed me a fight with Curtis Parker and national television was interested. Ferdie Pacheco, known as the "Fight Doctor" for his work in the corner with Muhammad Ali, had been hired by NBC to choose fights to enable the network to compete with ABC and CBS. Pacheco broke the virtual monopoly that Bob Arum and Don King had on network boxing. He gave opportunities to me, Dan Duva, Murad Muhammad and Phil Alessi. Once again, timing is everything.

Frank Gelb, the only licensed boxing promoter in Atlantic City, represented Resorts International. He offered me a $40,000 site fee to put Parker-Love in its 1,300-seat Superstar Theatre on March 9, a Sunday afternoon. NBC paid $30,000. There was no cost for rent, security, ushers, advertising, ticket sellers, ticket takers, hotel rooms or meals. We paid the fighters, their travel, insurance and the commission officials. Resorts kept the ticket sales. There was no way to make this work on a Sunday afternoon in Philadelphia so Spectrum Fights went to the seashore.

That day, Parker celebrated his 21st birthday and, instead of candles, he blew out Love, ending the Californian's jinx over Philly fighters—Li'l Abner, Monroe, Watts and Briscoe—knocking him out in the ninth round for the vacant USBA middleweight crown. Parker was paid $13,000 ($45,000 in 2021 dollars), Love $15,000 ($51,000). Spectrum Fights cleared $21,175 ($72,000).

Later that month, Marvin Johnson, in his second stint as light-heavyweight champion, lost the WBA title in his first defense, this time to Eddie Gregory, who then became Eddie Mustafa Muhammad.

Johnson had a knack for losing world titles to men who changed names and religions afterward. Gregory was the mandatory challenger but he was a free agent and Arum couldn't get options.

"I was in Arum's office," Eddie said, "and he offered me the minimum, $50,000, for the fight. He told me it was his only offer and if I didn't agree he would move past me to someone else. I had confidence in my ability to beat Marvin so I accepted."

Johnson got $175,000 for the fight, televised by ABC-TV from the Stokely Center at the University of Tennessee in Knoxville. Eddie hurt Marvin with body shots, some of which lifted Marvin off his feet. It was over in the 11th round. Arum, a Talmudic Scholar, labeled the show the *Passover Night Massacres* since it fell on the Jewish holiday.

Arum's WBA heavyweight champion, local hero John Tate, was knocked cold by Mike Weaver in the 15th round of a fight Tate couldn't have lost on points. As part of the same three-city television hookup, Sugar Ray Leonard K0d Dave "Boy" Green in Landover, Maryland, and Larry Holmes K0d Leroy Jones in Las Vegas.

By then, Arum had closed a deal with a new cable television company, ESPN, to televise weekly boxing from four different sites. A tournament would crown champions in different weight classes with purses better than what many fighters, outside the Top 10, had been earning. I was in charge of Atlantic City; Dan Duva ran Totowa, New Jersey; Ernie Terrell had Chicago; Mel Greb had Las Vegas. The first card was April 10 in the 400-seat Rutland Room at Resorts. Arum tabbed me "the best matchmaker in boxing." The story hit the papers and the shit hit the fan.

Ed Snider, who owned the Spectrum, also owned PRISM. ESPN was a competitor. I was called to a meeting in Snider's satellite office at 15th and Locust in Center City on Monday, April 7. Allen Flexer, Stephen Greenberg and Larry Rubin, director of public relations, were there. Snider accused me of not being a team player. I *had* been a team player, but Atlantic City casinos were here to stay and I was under contract at the Spectrum for another 10 months and no future beyond that.

Flexer said I only asked for advice when I had a problem, referring to the Parker-Love fight having been tossed out of Resorts 10 days ahead of time because the casino had failed to file paperwork with the Casino Control Commission. I'd scrambled for an alternate site in Philly or AC, but Resorts resolved the issue and we were back in the Superstar.

Rubin complained I made fights he had trouble selling to the media. Snider said: "Anybody can sell a fight between Muhammad Ali and Joe Frazier. It's your job to sell the fights you're given." I appreciated—and never forgot—that.

"If you're not happy, we'll let you out of your contract," Snider told me.

I didn't say a word, much as I had not said a word 10 years earlier and one block away when Jack Puggy had said Briscoe's contract was for sale. When the meeting ended, I called my attorney, Stuart Lundy. He had me draft a letter to Flexer which said, "This is to confirm—based on our conversation of Monday, April 7, 1980—that I am terminating my contract with Spectrum Ltd., dated February 2, 1979." Copies were sent to Snider and Greenberg.

I resigned effective at 6 pm on April 9 and drove to Atlantic City for the opening card the next night of the ESPN boxing tournament. The 60-mile ride was a breeze. I no longer had the security of a steady paycheck, but I was excited about going back out on my own.

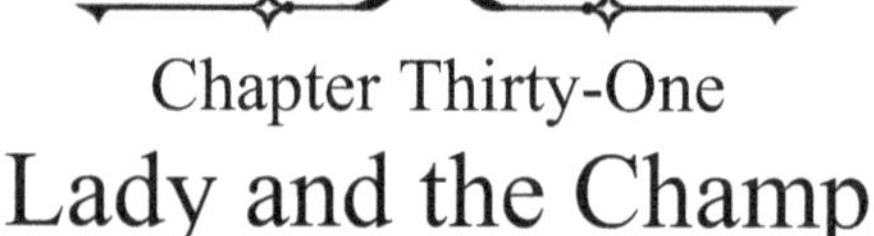

Chapter Thirty-One

Lady and the Champ

Jeff Chandler, Willie O'Neill and K.O. Becky. (Pete Goldfield photo)

Arnold Giovanetti became Joey Giardello's advisor in the late 1950s. They were South Philly guys even though Joey was born in Brooklyn. Joey was 5-foot-10 and walked around at 180 pounds, even when he was middleweight champion of the world.

His face showed all 133 fights from his 16 years as a pro. Arnold was 5-foot-7, 140 pounds, good looking and a charmer. Joey turned pro in 1948 and had his share of managers but he kept Arnold in for five percent because Arnold was his friend and Joey liked having him around. If you pissed Joey off, he'd break your face. If you pissed Arnold off, he'd call Joey.

I met Arnold in 1967. I was 20. He was 31. He and Mike Goffredo, a talent promoter known as the *Mayor of South Philadelphia*, got me hammered one night at a suburban dance club. I had to be at the *Bulletin* at midnight but who cared. Arnold's stepfather, Sam Molitieri, was a boss on the waterfront. After Arnold graduated from South Philadelphia (Southern) High School, Molitieri got him an office job at Front and Snyder Avenues.

In the mid-1970s, Arnold managed Alfonso Hayman and Jeff Chandler. He'd stop by my Spectrum office every Wednesday with an Italian hoagie from the Red Top luncheonette at 12th and Moore. Arnold lived on South Broad Street, within walking distance of the Spectrum and Veterans Stadium.

On Wednesday, August 10, 1977, Arnold did not show up. I called his home and Terry answered. Terry (Teresa Mary Mercurio) owned a beauty salon at 12th and Wolf. Linda and I had been guests at their lavish April wedding at the Venus Lounge at Broad and Reed. A Mummers String Band made a cameo. Terry said Arnold would call me when he got home. He never did.

Arnold had been on his way to meet Hayman at 19th and Reed to collect his share of the purse from a Hayman fight in Santo Domingo. Hayman said he never showed up. Arnold had stopped at a bank and an auto body shop in South Philly. That was the last anyone saw him. His white Cadillac Eldorado was found in a parking garage at Philadelphia International Airport, but no airline had any record of him buying a ticket. Center City private eye Mike Phillips offered a $5000 reward for information, but Arnold's disappearance went unsolved.

Chandler wanted Willie O'Neill to take over. O'Neill was a 5-foot-5 walking encyclopedia of Philadelphia boxing. A James Cagney look-alike, he had been around boxing since the 1920s when he'd befriended Benny Bass, who held the featherweight and junior lightweight titles.

In 1940, when he was 24, O'Neill and Frederick J. "Angel of Death" Tenuto were arrested in the shooting death of 41-year-old James Decaro at the San Francisco Club at 8th and Latonia. Tenuto was convicted of first-degree murder. O'Neill, who was shot in the back, was convicted of second-degree. They were sent to Eastern State Penitentiary in Fairmount, but O'Neill was transferred to Philadelphia County Prison (Holmesburg) in Northeast Philly.

After his release in 1952, O'Neill joined Local 542, International Union of Operating Engineers, as an "oiler" for bulldozers, front-end loaders and other heavy machinery. In 1953, he and six other men were charged with beating Theodore McCarty, another union member, in an elevator at the Broadwood Hotel. Even though McCarty was taken to Hahnemann Hospital, Magistrate James T. Donnelly called the incident "just a brawl" and dismissed the case.

O'Neill didn't think Chandler should be managed by an ex-con. He suggested his wife. K.O. Becky, as she was known, was described by Stan Hochman as "only slightly bigger than a ripe pineapple and just as sweet. She is 4-8 and 89 pounds and has a voice like 14 miles of gravel road."

Becky called herself "a midget, a pixie, a Jewish shamrock." She was born Rebecca Birenbaum in 1924 in South Philadelphia, the youngest of Philip Birenbaum's seven children. She worked in vaudeville as Tiny Baron with the South Philly nightclub act of comedians Al Fisher and Lou Marks. She was the National Jitterbug Queen of Madison Square Garden in the mid-1940s, around the time she married Nicholas Gallelli.

When television killed vaudeville during the early 1950s, Becky became a housewife. After Gallelli died of a heart attack in 1961, she became a waitress at Nick's Roast Beef, a South Philly landmark at 20th and Jackson. She met O'Neill there and they moved in together with Becky's sons, Phillip and Joey, and daughter, Denise. They got married in 1974 and were regulars at boxing matches.

Fighters who trained in South Philly were regulars at the O'Neills' South Broad Street home. They went to discuss strategy with Willie and they also went to eat Becky's cooking.

Chandler boxed six times at the Spectrum in 1978, moving from six to eight to 10 rounds. He appeared on cards headlined by Mike Rossman, Bennie Briscoe, Matthew Franklin and Marvin Hagler. He won four by knockout and two on points, beating Hispanic opponents whose walk-in styles made them perfect fodder.

Working with Becky and Willie was a dream. I chose the opponents and promoted the fights. Becky handled public relations. Willie helped in the gym, even though Nick Belfiore had replaced Pat Paterson as trainer.

Chandler's 10-round victory over Davey Vasquez, of New York, in April, 1979, opened eyes. Vasquez had been the best bantamweight on the East Coast for a decade, twice losing 12-round decisions to future world champion Enrique Pinder, of Panama. Vasquez may have been past his prime, but no American-born bantamweight had dominated him the way the 5-foot-7 Chandler's speed and power did.

At first, Chandler had rarely spoken. He went about his training quietly and diligently and seemed like someone you'd want to cuddle. Attitude set him apart. Midway through 1979 I told him he was to fight Jose Resendez, a .500 fighter from Los Angeles. "Can't you get me anyone better?" he asked. I did. Later that summer at Steel Pier, after a third-round knockout over inept 5-foot-2 Texan Alberto Cruz, he said, "Don't ever embarrass me like that again in front of my fans."

When I would be asked by a 21st century manager to "get me six wins in a row," I would think of Chandler.

When, in 1980, Atlantic City became the East Coast boxing capital, Chandler found a new home, winning three times at Resorts—twice on ESPN—to solidify his world ranking.

Muhammad Ali Professional Sports (MAPS) offered us a WBA world title fight with champion Julian Solis, of Puerto Rico. MAPS had come onto the scene, paying exorbitant purses, more than Don King and Bob Arum. No one could understand where the money came from and their fight cards were drowning in red ink. Ali's only connection was his name.

Chandler challenged Solis on November 14, 1980, at the Jai Alai Fronton in Miami. Solis was 23, unbeaten in 23 fights. Chandler was 24 and unbeaten in 24. The last American-born bantamweight champion had been Manuel Ortiz, of Corona, California, in 1950. Since then, the 118-pound title had been owned by fighters from

South Africa, Mexico, Central and South America, Europe, Australia, Asia and Puerto Rico.

In the first round, Chandler knocked Solis down with a left hook. He dominated the fight until referee Carlos Berrocal stopped it at 1:06 of the 14th. I thought Linda, six months pregnant with our second son, would deliver on the spot. Chandler's fans stormed the ring as did Belfiore, who was crying. K.O. Becky had become the first woman to manage a world champion. The calmest person was Willie O'Neill, who looked like he was strolling down South Street on Sunday.

"Ecstasy," Chandler told Hochman. "I knew I had won the championship. I was bringing it home to Philly."

A clause in Chandler's contract stipulated MAPS had to inform him in writing within thirty (30) days that they were "exercising the option" to promote his next two fights. When 30 days passed without any correspondence, I told Becky and Willie we were free to do our own thing. They said they would not screw the people who had delivered the title fight. I apologized and stored their response in my memory. It came in handy 37 years later.

Ex-champ Jorge Lujan, of Panama, would be Chandler's first defense. We put the fight in Philadelphia on Saturday afternoon, January 31, in the 2,500-seat ballroom of the Franklin Plaza Hotel. CBS would televise. I hoped Philadelphia could return as a major fight town and I scheduled a card a week earlier at the Blue Horizon.

"I love the ballroom—it's a really nice, classy place," Chandler told Rich Hoffman, of the *Daily News*. "But I don't know...about the people. February first last year, I fought at the Spectrum (against Javier Flores) and a lot of people didn't come out because it was cold. I don't know what's it's gonna be like January 31st. If the weather's not good, people will stay away again. If Russell Peltz is going to stay here in Philadelphia, promote here in Philadelphia, based on these two fights, he'd better not bet on it.

"I don't know. Philly as a fight town, it's...deteriorating. It's dying as a fight town. Nobody wants to stage fights here. It costs promoters money to stage fights, and the people aren't coming out. The promoter's paying for the whole show. The gyms are full of guys who are drying up, not fighting at all. And when they do get to fight, they've got to go away, overseas, something like that. These guys have got to have some kind of fights. Here."

MAPS had sent me $10,000 for expenses. Joe Hand was my partner in the live gate while MAPS kept the television money and paid for the main event. The night before the fight, Mort Sharnik, boxing consultant at CBS, called. MAPS' assets had been frozen after it was discovered they had been funding their business with money embezzled from Wells Fargo bank. MAPS' boss, Harold Smith, was really Ross Eugene Fields, who, along with co-conspirators Sammy Marshall and Ben Lewis—Wells Fargo employees—had siphoned more than 21 million dollars from the bank. Sharnik asked me to take over and CBS would guarantee the purses.

Thankfully, MAPS' check to me cleared.

Lujan now demanded his $20,000 in cash. It was Saturday and most banks were closed, but Hand contacted a Center City attorney who had cash on hand. Hand took a briefcase of it to Lujan's dressing room. Lujan took a peek but didn't count the money. When Hand and I settled, there was a $5,000 charge from the lawyer for the right to borrow his cash for 24 hours. Not a bad gig!

Chandler weighed only 113.5 pounds. He was stale and Lujan was worse. Not many solid punches were landed, but Chandler grabbed a unanimous decision (146-143, 146-142, 148-143) from three Puerto Rican judges. We were far from sold out. Chandler's critique of Philly fans was on the money. Two days later, Hand and I took a train to New York to collect the rights fee from CBS.

MAPS asked us to honor a commitment it had made for the Chandler-Lujan winner to defend again Eijiro Murata in April in Tokyo. The purse was $150,000 ($460,000 in 2021), more than double what Chandler got for Lujan. Murata was unbeaten in 19 fights and had drawn in a title fight the previous June in Tokyo with WBC champ Lupe Pintor.

Japanese promoter Shigeji Kaneko had won 51 of 62 fights in the 1950s. He had beaten junior lightweight champion Flash Elorde four times, and lost to another great, featherweight champ Sandy Saddler. Jeff trained at a gym run by ex-bantamweight champion Fighting Harada. Trips like this were a godsend, but Linda couldn't go since it was four weeks after our son, Daniel, was born.

I took a three-hour train ride to Kyoto, once the capitol, where I walked the hillsides and loaded up on c*hatchkas.* In Tokyo, bicycles were everywhere and parked in lots as big as car lots in Philly. At night, Becky and I walked the neon-lit Tokyo streets, staring into the restaurants which displayed sushi dishes in the windows so visitors would know what was available.

Korakuen Hall provided stiff pillows at ringside, no chairs. Sitting or kneeling on them was difficult. In the first round, a Murata right hand sent Chandler into the ropes into a near horizontal position, but he stayed on his feet. Years later, after a rule change, it would have been a knockdown and Murata would have won the round, 10-8. In 1981, it went 10-9 for Murata. Chandler gained control down the stretch but another big right hand nailed him in the 15th.

I headed to the dressing room, fearing the worst. I did not speak Japanese, but when I heard the announcement, I knew it was a draw. Judge Fernando Viso, of the USA, scored it 147-146 Murata; judge Humberto Figueroa, of Panama, 145-142 for Chandler; referee Ernesto Magana, of Mexico, had it 146-146. Had the knockdown rule been in effect, it would have changed Magana's card to 146-145 Murata, and the title would have stayed in Japan.

Two months later, Bob Wright, now sports editor of the *Bulletin*, called to tell me Chandler had been arrested after being stopped by police after making an illegal U-turn in South Philadelphia.

When Chandler reached into his glove compartment for his driver's license, four packs of a powdered substance and three marijuana joints fell out. He was arrested for possession of a controlled substance, driving without a license and making an illegal U-turn. He was arraigned and released on his own recognizance. An August 11 hearing was scheduled, conveniently after Chandler's July 25 title defense at Resorts against ex-champ Solis.

The rematch lasted half as long as the original. CBS televised it and Chandler led 59-57, 58-57 and 60-54 after six rounds. In the seventh, he caught Solis with a right hand and Solis' face bounced off Chandler's right shoulder as his body fell backward to the canvas. The time was 2:58. It was the first time *Sports Illustrated* featured Chandler. He was paid $86,000 for the fight, but took home a little less than $10,000. He never had filed income tax returns and the IRS was at the weigh-in. For the rest of Chandler's career, we had to escrow a certain amount of money from his purse to guarantee tax payments.

At the August 11 hearing, Common Pleas Court Judge I. Raymond Kremer gave Chandler six months non-reporting probation. No drug counseling, no drug testing. If he stayed out of trouble, his record would be expunged. Hochman wondered why Kremer, who had attended fights at the Spectrum and occasionally covered them for United Press International, did not recuse himself. Hochman also questioned the representation of Chandler by James J. Binns, chairman of the Pennsylvania State Athletic Commission.

For the December rematch with Murata at the Sands in Atlantic City, Willie O'Neill became the chief second. Becky told the press that Belfiore's contract had run out as co-manager and she was in control, but I never knew Belfiore to have a contract. I believe Willie took over the training for the Solis fight and Belfiore got upset and quit.

Chandler ruined Murata with uppercuts and a one-sided fight was over at 1:52 of the 13th round. "Before today I was an arm puncher, a gladiator," Jeff told Rich Hoffman of the *Daily News*. "Willie O'Neill changed that. It was a 180-degree turn."

Chapter Thirty-Two
ESPN Begins

Dwight Braxton fires on Johnny Davis in 1981 ESPN match. (Peltz collection)

The Atlantic City years represented my Chapter III. AC was perfect. I could concentrate on making matches and leave promoting to the casinos. The monthly cards at Resorts let me develop fighters and pay them better. Our son, Matthew, was nearly 2 and I was spending a lot of time in Atlantic City so Linda and I purchased a second home in Ventnor, two miles from the casinos and one block from the beach. Bob Arum paid me $3,000 per ESPN card and I did others on my own. It was a good time for boxing. It was a good time for me.

When ESPN kicked off its middleweight tournament, Arum questioned my including a southpaw from Southwest Philly, Frank Fletcher, as well as his opponent, Ben Serrano, from Warminster, Pennsylvania. Fletcher was 4-2-1, Serrano 1-2-1. I told Arum not to worry. I had paid Fletcher $100 for a four-round fight two years earlier at the Blue Horizon, and Serrano $125 for a four-round fight at the 69th Street Forum. Now they were going eight rounds for $1,000 apiece.

Fletcher won by decision and his career took off. He knocked out locals Jerome Jackson and Caveman Lee to win the East Coast end of the ESPN tourney, all in the 400-seat Rutland Room at Resorts. He was paid $2,000, $3000 and then $4000, plus a $1,000 bonus for crushing West Coast champion Randy McGrady. Fletcher became known as "The Animal." His prize was a $10,000 payday against a Top 10 opponent.

Inquirer boxing writer Lewis Freedman sketched Fletcher: "With a scar on his nose, a sometimes toothless grin, and the flat-footed, rather bumpy boxing style, he is no beauty. He is no contender for Miss America, but he might be a contender for the world middleweight championship."

Fletcher was not a big puncher and he was not a great boxer, but he was relentless. He was like a bad flu—you couldn't get rid of him. You could hit him with one punch, two punches, even three and he was still there, firing back. It was hard to think of a more exciting lefty. Fletcher came from a fighting family. His uncle, Dick Turner, had been a world-rated welterweight until his career was cut short in 1964 by eye problems. Younger brother Anthony, as an amateur, had beaten three future pro champions: Johnny Bumphus, (WBA junior welterweight); Ray Mancini (WBA lightweight); Frankie Randall (WBC junior welterweight). Another brother, Troy, would win the Pennsylvania bantamweight title.

"I've always been the black sheep of the family," Fletcher said. "I was always getting into trouble with the law, and then I said to myself that I was going to make things better through boxing. I was still getting into trouble, though, but thanks to my uncle Dick Turner and Rev. (Elvin) Thompson, they keep me disciplined."

Marty Feldman, co-manager with Thompson, moved Fletcher into his home in suburban Broomall, training him, feeding him, watching him. Feldman notified the police not to arrest Fletcher if they noticed a Black man running through the neighborhood at 6 in the morning. It paid off. Fletcher knocked out the WBC's No. 6 contender, Slammin' Sammy Nesmith, of Indianapolis, in December, in six rounds, this time in the 1,300-seat Superstar Theatre at Resorts.

Fletcher's rise was one of my many feel-good stories in the early 1980s. Curtis Parker's crushing knockout of David Love in March had earned him another NBC appearance in May, but I chose the wrong guy. I matched him with Mike Colbert, a slick boxer from Portland, Oregon. "Road Runner" was his nickname. I must not have been paying attention.

Colbert was 29-4-1, 9 KOs, and had gone 10 rounds with Thomas Hearns. Willie Reddish was a wonderful trainer for Parker, but I slipped up, trying to please Ferdie Pacheco, NBC's boxing consultant. I had this exciting, walk-in styled action fighter and I should have matched him accordingly. Pacheco, like many TV executives, wanted fighters with good records, regardless of style. Colbert turned the fight into a track meet. After 12 frustrating rounds, Parker was awarded a decision that only the referee and the two judges thought he deserved. Not one of the eight boxing writers at ringside agreed.

Pacheco pushed me into matching Parker with Dwight Davison on a prime-time NBC card in August after aggressive lefty Mustafa Hamsho pulled out. It was a co-promotion with Gil Clancy, then matchmaker at Madison Square Garden. Pacheco had turned down action fighters like John Locicero and Nesmith as replacements.

Don King claimed he had the rights to Davison, so, to avoid aggravation, Clancy sold his interest in the show to King and I did the same. King was the former Cleveland bookmaker who was convicted of second-degree murder in 1967 after stomping to death an employee, Sam Garrett, who owed him $600. He got into boxing in 1970 after befriending Muhammad Ali and he later rivaled Arum as the most powerful man in boxing.

Pacheco said I should have "stood up" but he was the one siding with King to get the fight done. Years later, friend and Hall-of-Fame promoter/matchmaker Don Chargin cautioned me, "Don't let television dictate how to match your fighter."

Davison was from Detroit. He was 26-0, 20 K0s, and, at 6-foot-1, had five inches on Parker. Parker never cut the ring off and reverted to a throwaway jab and launched sweeping hooks and overhand rights from long range which Davison avoided. Davison took over in the fourth with an assortment of uppercuts. Parker had a good 10th round but the judges had it right, 97-94 and 97-93 twice, for Davison.

I asked Parker to step back and fight on ESPN against someone he would look good against, but Reddish said no. I thought it was Parker's decision to keep fighting tough guys but years later he said that wasn't true. Reddish hooked up with Murad Muhammad as promoter and Parker lost back-to-back fights to Hamsho and Wilford Scypion and never got back to where he had been. He was 23-3 when I promoted his fights, 6-6 elsewhere.

"Will was old and I guess he wanted to make the money and I left the business up to him and his son," Parker said. "I should have stayed with you. You were a good promoter and you were a big part of my career and you helped me get started. I don't think Will was sharp enough to deal with Murad Muhammad. You and I should have stayed together and you could have done better for me."

We did hook up later, but every time Parker scored a solid win, he left and lost a fight he never should have accepted. "Life is a ride and my boxing career was a joyride," Parker said. "I had a good time. But I could have trained a little harder, done more roadwork. Sometimes I got lazy."

Parker worked full time in the cafeteria at The Hospital of the University of Pennsylvania, setting up the food lines and making sure everything was clean and working well. He moved to maintenance—plumbing, carpentry and electrical work. He saved his money and raised four daughters and bought his mother a house. "I did everything for mom," he said. "She was my real manager and my promoter. She brought me up. My dad wasn't there and my mom did both jobs. Everything I did in life was for her."

Away from Atlantic City, Jerry "The Bull" Martin was doing well. Despite his narrow victory over Jesse Burnett late in 1979 and his dreadful 10th-round stoppage of 40-year-old Dynamite Douglas three months later on the last card at the 69th Street Forum, Martin was rated among the best 175-pounders. George Kanter, then working with King, needed someone to fight unbeaten James Scott, who was locked up at Rahway State (New Jersey) Prison for armed robbery. Martin accepted.

Before Scott *went away*, he was 11-0 and had beaten contenders Ray Anderson and Burnett. Rahway had a boxing program and Scott convinced the warden to allow television cameras inside to air his matches. HBO was first and Scott shocked everyone late in 1978 with a 12-round decision over the future Eddie Mustafa Muhammad, ranked No. 1 by the WBA. Scott beat his next five opponents, among them Richie Kates, Jerry Celestine and Yaqui Lopez.

Martin got $40,000 to fight Scott on NBC on Memorial Day weekend. It was hot inside the prison and, as we walked through each section, you could hear the prison bars slamming shut. Martin's dressing room looked like a cell for solitary confinement.

About 45 minutes before the fight, Don King's men showed up with an option agreement giving King the rights to Martin's next three fights if he won. If Martin didn't sign, King threatened to cancel the fight. I should have called his bluff but Pacheco waved the old loyalty flag in my face, reminding me again of everything he had done for me. We signed and it was a mistake.

At the introductions, I looked at Scott's corner and Pacheco was his cut man. Nothing like the old conflict of interest! But it didn't matter. Martin dropped Scott in each of the first two rounds and outmuscled him the rest of the way, fighting like his "Bull" nickname and winning 7-3 and 6-4 twice on the rounds system.

Martin, manager/trainer Leon Tabbs, cut man Milt Bailey, ex-pro Jimmy Savage and I had dinner at an outdoor restaurant in the area. Some of Martin's countrymen from Antigua came over and spoke passionately about what we had done for their friend. Their speeches capped one of the best days of my boxing life. Six years before, Martin had been locked up as an illegal alien. Tabbs had spent $1,000 to bail him out and get him papers. Now he was on the verge of becoming a world champion.

When Arum learned King had options, he was not happy. He would have done the same thing—but when the contract was negotiated. What followed drove a wedge into our relationship. The battle between King and Arum was as much about ego as about money. At times they would outbid each other just to get a fight on television, even if it meant losing money. This was one of those.

Arum wanted Martin to challenge Mustafa Muhammad for the WBA title he had won from Marvin Johnson, but we were signed to King, even though he could not produce that fight. I asked Arum for a "hold harmless" agreement, meaning if King sued us, Arum would assume responsibility for defending us and paying any judgement. He had no choice.

Martin got $60,000 ($205,000 in 2021). He was 26, far removed from the person who earned $100 a week cutting sugar cane in Antigua before coming to the United States.

The fight with Mustafa Muhammad was televised by CBS from the Great Gorge Playboy Resort in McAfee, New Jersey. One week earlier in the same ring, WBC champ Matthew Saad Muhammad had come from behind to knock out Yaqui Lopez in the 14th round of *The Ring* magazine's *Fight of the Year*.

I was confident, but 30 seconds into the fight I knew we had a problem. The aggressive, relentless Martin, who had pushed and bullied Scott, had been replaced by a tentative, probing Martin, who was overwhelmed by the occasion and let the champion dictate the pace.

Mustafa Muhammad was one of the great underachievers of his generation. He had an incredible boxing IQ and if he thought he could beat you, he fought like the excellent fighter he should have been his entire career. If not, he got cautious and outhustled.

As he'd done against Marvin Johnson four months earlier, Mustafa controlled the pace and he broke Martin down and dropped him twice in the fourth and once in the 10th with a right hand over Martin's jab. Martin got up but referee Tony Perez stopped it at 2:25. At the time, Judge Harold Lederman scored it 85-85, but judge Eva Shain and Perez had it 88-82 and 87-83 for the champion. It was a long ride home.

Another light-heavyweight had arrived. Dwight Braxton, from Camden, was 27 and no one paid attention to him at Joe Frazier's gym until 1980 when Wesley Mouzon took over. Mouzon had been a brilliant prospect in the 1940s. By the time he was 19, he had knocked out Bob Montgomery and boxed a draw with Ike Williams, two Hall-of-Fame lightweight champions. Mouzon had suffered a detached retina sparring the week before the 1946 rematch with Montgomery for the title. The promoter and the boxing commission turned a "blind eye" and a deflated Mouzon, knowing it would be his last fight, was stopped in eight rounds. Braxton would give him the world title he never won.

A booking agent wanted someone to fight Theunis Kok, a 22-year-old lefty from South Africa, who had won all eight of his fights, seven by knockout. We sent Braxton and his 5-1-1 record to Durban early in 1980 and he KO'd Kok in the 10th. I was accused of sending a ringer, one agent claiming I had substituted David Braxton, a junior middleweight from Detroit who was 12-0. No one believed a boxer with one knockout and seven fights could do that.

Braxton had spent time in Rahway for armed robbery. "I am not proud of the past but I am proud that I've gone straight," he told Tim Panaccio of the *Philadelphia Journal*. "I never saw the sun except for three months the whole time I was in jail. I swear I'll never go back."

He was a 5-foot-7 Joe Frazier with a more deliberate and conventional right hand. He didn't utilize head and upper body movement as effectively. Braxton's aggression was more subtle. He attacked in spurts. Frazier was more constant bell to bell. Braxton worked off his jab to get inside while Frazier got there more on making his opponents miss.

Sportswriters ridiculed the ESPN tournament, calling the Rutland Room at Resorts "TV's studio by the sea," but the fighters loved the steady work and the money. We entered Braxton at 175 pounds and he scored four knockouts to win it all.

"I've been doing it all my life," he told Tom Cushman, "and I've always had a knack for it. I'll fight anybody, at any time, for any amount of money—because that's the way I am. But the tournament is the best thing that ever happened to me. Before I was always told that matches couldn't be made. Suddenly I've come a long way in a short time and now I can see that I'm gonna go all the way.

"Today, tomorrow, the next day, look good to me. To some of you I may not have the experience to fight Top 10 guys, but I know more about what I can do than anyone else. When I think today about what's ahead of me, all I can do is smile."

Chapter Thirty-Three
Leonard-Duran I

LE STADE DU PARC OLYMPIQUE
MONTREAL
CHAMPIONNAT DU MONDE
DES POIDS MI-MOYENS C. M. B.
SUGAR RAY
LEONARD
VS.
ROBERTO
DURAN
VENDREDI 20 JUIN 1980 A 20h00
PARTERRE OUEST $150.00
TAXE INCLUSE – NON REMBOURSABLE
VALIDE SI REMISE

The biggest fight of 1980 was shown on a giant screen at the Arena. WBC welterweight champ Sugar Ray Leonard vs. Roberto Duran was the most anticipated boxing match since Muhammad Ali-Leon Spinks II. Every arena in the country—including the Spectrum—carried it on closed-circuit TV from Montreal.

Joe Hand, the ex-cop who had bought stock in Joe Frazier after the 1964 Olympics, was in charge. Hand had become an officer in Cloverlay, Inc., the group which managed Frazier, and began dabbling in closed circuit. I'd met him in 1969 when Cloverlay purchased tickets for Willie Monroe's pro debut. We'd worked together on the closed-circuit telecast at the Arena for the Carlos Monzon-Bennie Briscoe fight in 1972.

Hand controlled most of the East Coast for big closed-circuit TV fights. I often worked for him, and I deserved combat pay for some of the places he sent me.

Camden Convention Hall was in one of the most crime-ridden cities in America and he sent me there for Ali-Frazier II in 1974. We decided to admit, free of charge, any Camden policemen in uniform. There must have been several hundred cops in the 85,000 population because the place filled up with Men in Blue. Either that or there was a fire sale that day on uniforms.

For the first Leonard-Duran fight, I ran the Arena in West Philly, the first event there since Mark Stewart had bought the building one week earlier. It had not been used in over two years. I spent the day in the box office selling every one of the 5,000 available seats. Fight managers Gary Hegyi and Ivan Cohen worked with me. Every hour one of them would take the cash to a bank around the corner.

Around 7, the power supply transistor, a $130 item, blew, and the projector went down. We would have had a backup but, with so many venues around the country showing the fight, we couldn't find one. Mechanics tried to fix it while I was on the phone to Hand's office. Doors would open at 8 and the fans, who lined up outside, were not happy to learn of our problem.

About 9, they shattered the glass and broke down the doors. Hand located John Ianieri, of Willow Grove—30 miles away—who had a projector. Hand phoned me in Stewart's office where some people were crouched under desks, with the lights off, fearing what would happen if the fans found them.

"Russell, I'm watching the Action News telecast on Channel 6," Hand said. "They just interviewed a man who said if they don't let us in we're going to tear this building apart brick by brick." I cursed him and hung up.

Ianieri, with a police escort, reached the Arena at 10 after an 80-mile-per-hour race from Willow Grove. By this time the building was packed with a pissed-off crowd. Hand called again, asking me to check on the program sales. "WHAT?" I yelled. I hung up again and stayed in Stewart's office.

The signal came on in the middle of the semifinal between heavyweights Trevor Berbick and John Tate. By then, some fans had left, but those who stayed were happy. A day or two later, one of the newspapers printed Hand's home address for those wanting a refund. He had police block off his street from customers.

Chapter Thirty-Four

The Early 1980s

Tony Braxton takes one from Frank Fletcher in 1982. (Peltz collection)

I was involved in just six of 66 cards in Philadelphia from 1981 through 1983. I promoted once at the Spectrum in 1981, but only 2,394 saw light-heavyweight Jerry Martin stop late sub Leon McDonald, of Deerfield Beach, Florida, in seven rounds. A new wave of promoters was led by Joe Verne, of Huntington Valley, who was in the wholesale furniture business. In those three years, Verne promoted 23 cards at the Golden Eagle Caterers—which could seat

1,500, all on the floor—and two at the Blue Horizon, working with Barry McCall, who returned as promoter and matchmaker. Ex-pro Harold Moore ran eight cards at the Blue Horizon. Impact Promotions had three cards at the Arena before it was damaged by fire in 1981. Another blaze destroyed it in 1983.

The Golden Gloves Center, a second-floor walkup at 6th and Moore in South Philadelphia, opened and closed in one night in 1982. I ran the card with Frank Cariello, who had been involved with Sammy Goss' career and later would run the Pennsylvania Golden Gloves where he treated fighters like family. The city almost shut us down when we forgot to apply for an amusement license. They should have—we lost $4,907.59. When the toilets didn't work, girls jumped up and squatted on the sinks to urinate.

I also promoted twice at the Brandywine Club, a log-cabin-like night club in Chadds Ford, 25 miles west of Philly, where the ring was so small inside the ropes—14 feet, instead of the usual 18—that fighters could hear the instructions across the ring from their opponents' trainers.

Bob Arum got rid of me as the Atlantic City promoter of his ESPN cards in March, 1981. He felt he should have been involved with Frank Fletcher and Dwight Braxton since the ESPN tournament had benefitted both. He was not wrong but we never discussed it. I wasn't good at working for people and Arum replaced me with Bruce Trampler.

But, like I've said…timing.

I got a call from Bill Weidner, president of the Sands in Atlantic City, offering me his 800-seat Copa Room. That call began a five-year relationship.

"Philadelphia was a hotbed of boxing talent in the '80s and some fighters developed a local and regional following," Weidner said. "Boxing was very popular with our key—primarily male—Philadelphia, northern New Jersey and New York ethnic clientele. Televised boxing allowed the Sands to expand its market reach and improve the attractiveness of its events for our core customers."

After hosting dozens of my fights, Weidner partnered me and the Sands with Sylvester Stallone in 1984, initiating *Tiger Eye Boxing*, a monthly series whose slogan was "a chance, we just wanna give fighters a chance."

Frank Fletcher was the hottest television fighter of the early 1980s. His straight-ahead style resulted in weekend bloodbaths at the Sands, his permanent home. NBC-TV was there with Marv Albert doing blow-by-blow alongside analyst Dr. Ferdie Pacheco. Ring announcer Ed Derian (born Setrak Ejdaharian) got as much air time as the fighters and every seat was filled.

Once Fletcher left his dressing room, sounds of "Animal, Animal" reverberated in the Copa Room. People clapped to the upbeat music the Sands had recorded. Drums pounded in the background. Mother Lucille, the toughest Fletcher, patrolled the stage next to the ring, yelling instructions, and waving a stuffed tiger in one hand and a cigarette in the other. Fletcher had graduated from ESPN and his purses grew from $12,500 to $150,000 in less than two years, more money than some world champions got.

After a year by myself—for awhile without an answering machine—Pat Doris, who had worked at the Spectrum in promotions, came on board. She handled the books, did the paperwork, helped coordinate weigh-ins, and made life easier. I never was good at delegating authority so she took over.

Fletcher won the vacant USBA middleweight title in June, 1981, outpointing Norberto Sabater. He successfully defended the next year against Tony Braxton, Clint Jackson and James "Hard Rock" Green, all on NBC. All were slugfests, but none compared to Fletcher's fight against fellow-Philadelphian Ernie Singletary in the summer of 1981 on PRISM.

Singletary had turned pro in 1974, working part time as a carpenter to supplement his ring earnings. He was 29, jealous of Fletcher's sudden rise. He was 24-2, 7 K0s, but Fletcher got the attention. Singletary had boxed mostly in small clubs, from Fournier Hall in Wilmington, Delaware, to the Goodwill House Fire Hall in Bristol, Pennsylvania. He had headlined at the Blue Horizon and Wagner's Ballrooom as well as the 69th Street Forum and the Tower Theatre. He had won in South Africa, lost in England and won five times on Spectrum undercards.

Fletcher was making top dollar while Singletary was earning minimum wage. Fletcher's USBA title gnawed at Singletary.

Fletcher was No. 6 according to *The Ring*, Singletary No. 15, and he didn't like that, either.

"It bugs the hell out of me to see someone take the shortcut when Ernie Singletary takes the long way around," Singletary said at the press conference. "I've paid my dues for this fight…Fletcher hasn't. He took a shortcut in all those TV fights. They call him 'The Animal' but I'm the 'Animal Tamer.' No 11-2-1 TV fighter is gonna beat me. I thought that belt he has should've been around my waist a long time ago."

Fletcher: "I'm walking around with *his* belt? The only way he could get a belt like mine is if somebody gives him one or he goes out and buys one. He could go to my co-manager Marty Feldman's (jeans) store and he'd show him a whole rack of belts so he can select one for himself."

Pride and disdain drove Singletary to the best performance of his career, but it was not enough. You've read about fights that could have taken place in a phone booth—this was one.

"For boxing haters, all the people who think the sport is barbaric, a film of this one would confirm their most deep-seated fears," Rich Hoffman wrote in the *Daily News*. "The action was truly vicious at times, with both men slugging away at close range, rocking each other repeatedly before Singletary lost any punching power he had in the later stages. And when it was over, both guys were a mess. Dresden looked better in 1945."

Singletary had a split lip and his right eye, completely closed, was a swollen, pulpy target for Fletcher's left hooks. Fletcher was cut around both eyes and bled from his mouth. Ringside physician Dr. Paul Williams told referee Paul Venti to stop it after the seventh. Fletcher led on the round-by-round scorecards: 4-2-1, 5-2, 5-1-1.

"They should have yelled 'hike' at the start of every round instead of ringing the bell," Lewis Freedman wrote in the *Inquirer*. "Frank 'The Animal' Fletcher and Ernie Singletary made like offensive and defensive linemen every time they heard a clang last night. They pushed and shoved and they smashed each other's faces for three minutes every round."

When the medical staff placed Singletary on a stretcher in his dressing room to take him to Atlantic City Medical Center and photographers began snapping pictures, Charles Singletary, Ernie's brother and manager, ordered everyone to leave. He made Ernie walk to the ambulance.

Fletcher was no better off. “I hurt so bad I was crying in my hotel room,” he told Lee Samuels, of the *Bulletin*. “My right eye hurt so bad I couldn't stand it. I had a headache which wouldn't go away. So I called up my manager, Marty Feldman, in his hotel room, and said, 'Marty, I got to get out of here.' “

Marty and I found Fletcher face down on the floor in his room. We couldn't get an ambulance so we put him on a cot and rode with him to the hospital in a police wagon. The attending physician said if we’d waited any longer, Fletcher could have died. He got five stitches around his right eye and didn’t fight for six months.

Singletary boxed four months later, losing a 10-round decision to Thomas Hearns on the Muhammad Ali-Trevor Berbick card in The Bahamas. He retired in 1984. Fletcher was the only man to stop him in 32 fights. He later worked construction in Maryland, but lost sight in his right eye, which had bothered him for most of his career. He raised four sons and three daughters and still lives in Maryland.

Fletcher was in line to fight Marvin Hagler but street life was a problem. Three weeks after beating Hard Rock Green late in 1982, he was arrested on disorderly conduct charges for shoving a police officer who had seen him shouting and cursing on the street in Southwest Philadelphia. The case was thrown out of court. So was another, after Fletcher was handcuffed in front of his house following a domestic dispute.

Arum offered us a title shot with Hagler, but Fletcher had signed to fight Wilford Scypion for me on NBC in February, 1983. Fletcher got $150,000 to fight Scypion, half of what he would have received against Hagler. I’d failed to realize that the three men Fletcher had beaten in 1982—Braxton, Jackson and Green—were blown-up junior middleweights.

Scypion was 5-foot-11, a strong, solid middleweight. He was 25-3, 10 K0s, and never had been stopped. He’d lost decisions to Green, Dwight Davison and Mustafa Hamsho, but he smothered Fletcher and used his strength inside to win a unanimous 12-round decision (6-5-1, 7-4-1, 8-3-1). Scypion got Hagler—and was K0d in four.

Marty and I rationalized the decision to fight Scypion by saying Fletcher would have been locked up again had we waited until May for Hagler. And after Fletcher stopped unranked Curtis Ramsey in July, Arum again offered Hagler—if Fletcher could beat Juan Roldan, an Argentinian slugger, in the semifinal to Hagler's fight with Roberto Duran in October in Las Vegas.

Fletcher got $90,000 to fight Roldan. Two days prior, Marty told me Fletcher, a 3-to-1 favorite, didn't have it anymore. Marty wanted to go halves on a $30,000 bet on Roldan, but I lost my nerve and didn't do it. Roldan knocked Fletcher cold at 2:58 of the sixth round. When he came to and the doctor asked him where he was, he answered, "At the Sands in Atlantic City." We would have split $90,000 on the bet.

After beating fellow-Philadelphian Jimmie Sykes, Fletcher was stopped in his last two fights by John Mugabi and Curtis Parker and retired in 1985. The week before we flew to Florida to fight Mugabi, we had to bail him out of jail after another domestic dispute. He was 31 and his 18-6-1 record included 12 K0s. He had made over half a million dollars and lost it all. I had suggested we take 10 percent of his $100,000 purse against Green and put it into a bank which he couldn't touch without my signature. He agreed, but the day we were to meet at the bank, he said, "Listen, Russell, I'm a big man. I don't need you or anyone to tell me what to do with my money."

An aggravated assault charge got Fletcher 5-10 years in the State Correctional Institution in Dallas, Pennsylvania, where he was stabbed by another inmate. He was released after five years, some of it spent in solitary confinement. When he got out, he was shot in the backside by an "unknown assailant" in West Philadelphia. Fletcher had trouble staying out of jail. He was released for the last time in 2015 with major health issues.

Frank's younger brother Anthony, a southpaw lightweight, was 18-0-1 midway through 1984 and had beaten future champs Livingstone Bramble and Fred Pendleton. After a draw with Frank Newton in June, 1984, Anthony was diagnosed with Bells Palsy, normally the result of a viral infection which causes one side of the face to droop. He also had retinal surgery and did not fight again for two years. When he returned he went 6-4 and retired in 1990 after Oba Carr stopped him at The Palace in Auburn Hills, Michigan.

Anthony had been arrested in 1987 on drug charges after a policeman saw him toss a green plastic bag—containing 22 $10 bags of cocaine—from his car. When the cops tried to search him, he broke loose but was caught after a three-block chase and arrested for possessing a controlled substance. Police said he was a member of the Junior Black Mafia, "a Philadelphia-based African-American organized crime syndicate."

In 1989, he survived being shot four times while sitting with a friend in a car after leaving a South Philadelphia playground watching a basketball game. His friend was killed.

He later was sentenced to death for the March, 1992, killing of 26-year-old Vaughn Christopher, who allegedly owed him money for drugs. He also pled guilty to a 1999 robbery charge for beating a 14-year-old boy and stealing his gold rings valued at $140. He was released from prison in 2021—after years on death row—when a federal judge ruled he had ineffective counsel in the Christopher case.

Dwight Braxton was moving up but our association fizzled after he beat Mike Rossman in 1981. He signed with Murad Muhammad. I had a poorly written contract and Quenzell McCall and Wesley Mouzon, his managers, were upset over the disparity in money from the fight. I think McCall enjoyed leaving, perhaps payback for when Briscoe left him.

Braxton outpointed what was left of James Scott at Rahway Prison in September and three months later K0d Matthew Saad Muhammad in the 10th round to win the WBC title at the Playboy Hotel & Casino. Saad had been five pounds heavy at the morning weigh-in for the 5 pm fight. He ran on the beach to shed the weight but he was a shell of himself that afternoon.

In the rematch eight months later at the Spectrum, Saad was stopped in six rounds by Braxton, now known as Dwight Qawi. Hard fights had caught up with Saad and he won only seven of his last 20 and retired in 1992.

In retirement, Saad squandered his money—one purse had been $500,000—and sold his trunks, robes, championship belts and trophies. By 2010, he was in a homeless shelter in Philadelphia. Linda and I saw him early in 2014 in Center City. He called to us, got out of the car he was riding in, and hugged us like old times. He had that same kid-friendly smile on his handsome face. He passed away that May from complications of ALS.

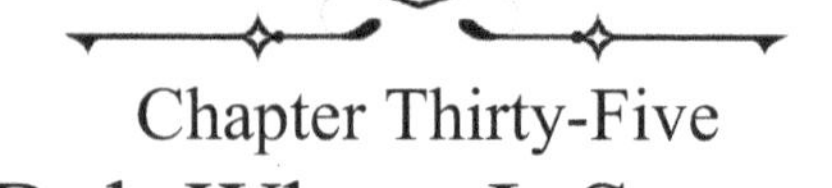

Chapter Thirty-Five

Bok Where It Started

Jeff Chandler's uppercut finds Johnny Carter's chin in 1982. (Peltz collection)

The biggest local fight of 1982 was Jeff Chandler against Johnny Carter, former classmates at Bok Vocational High School. Chandler had narrowly lost to Carter in his second amateur fight and figured if he could do that well against an experienced boxer, why fight for trophies. He turned pro in 1976, one year ahead of Carter.

In 1978 at the Blue Horizon, Carter had scored a six-round decision over John Glover, who twice had lost to Chandler. When he did not return his unsold tickets, we deducted their value from his paycheck. Carter made an ethnic slur and that ended the discussion—and our relationship.

Bob Botto, known as "Big Bob from the Mob," became Carter's manager. He was 6-foot-4, 300 pounds, wore a baseball cap and always had a cigar in his mouth. When he held court at Ponzio's diner on Route 130 in Brooklawn, New Jersey, you could hear him in Manhattan.

Botto grew up in South Philly, moved to Woodbury, New Jersey, and opened a meatpacking and slaughterhouse business when he was 20. He claimed he went to Hollywood for a role in *The Untouchables*, but came home when the TV series was canceled. He manufactured sausages at his plant in Mount Royal and sold them at his supermarket in Swedesboro.

Heavyweight Leroy Diggs shopped there and asked Botto to manage him. When Diggs took Botto to the Passyunk Gym to meet his trainer, Jimmy Arthur, the visit became a fire sale. Botto bought the contracts of Carter, welterweight Leroy Jefferson and heavyweight Randy Mack. I wouldn't use Carter, so Botto looked to an old friend.

Tony Torcasio had become the casino manager at the Tropicana in Las Vegas after executive positions at the Aladdin and MGM. Torcasio left Vegas in 1977, but he had friends there and he helped broker deals for Botto to sell his sausages to several casinos and get fights for Carter.

From January, 1979, through May, 1981, Carter won 15 out of 16 fights, 14 in Las Vegas, 13 at the Silver Slipper Casino. The Silver Slipper had boxing every Wednesday in a 500-seat ballroom. There was no television but several top fighters boxed there early in their careers: Earnie Shavers; Ken Norton; Rodrigo Valdes; Ray Mancini; Roger Mayweather; Freddie Roach.

Carter became world-ranked and business overruled my personal feelings. Teddy Brenner once said: "I don't mind if you hold a grudge against someone, but it shouldn't be a lifetime sentence. There always should be room for parole."

I made a two-fight deal with Botto and, four weeks before Chandler K0d Eijiro Murata in their rematch at the Sands, I matched Carter with the only man who had beaten him, Sergio Castro, of Pomona, CA. Carter K0d Castro in the eighth. Chandler was next.

Frank Gelb offered an $80,000 site fee to put Chandler-Carter at Resorts and I called the New Jersey State Athletic Commission to reserve March 27, 1982. Commissioner Robert W. Lee said Don King had that date at the Playboy for Wilfredo Gomez, of Puerto Rico, against Juan "Kid Meza" Mexico, for Gomez' WBC Super Bantamweight title. Lee would not allow two fight cards on the same day in the same city, but I reminded him of his rule that the promoter who turned in the signed contracts first got the date. He agreed.

I told my driver, William Bishop, to be at Lee's office in Trenton with the contracts by 6 the following morning. Bishop called me at 9 am and put me on the phone with Lee's secretary, who had my contracts and no one else's.

When I called Lee to confirm, he told me King's secretary had contracts delivered to his home in Fairlawn the night before. Lee said it was not unusual for promoters to mail or deliver things there. I told Lee he was playing games and sued him and the Commission.

There was a hearing in Flemington—50 miles from Philadelphia—where Bruno Richard Hauptman had been convicted in 1935 for kidnapping and murdering Charles Lindbergh's infant son. People still think Hauptman was innocent—not a good omen, I felt, for me.

When the judge noticed that King's contracts had not been signed by either Gomez or Meza, I thought we were good. But he ruled in Lee's favor, a decision that made the one in the Tyrone Everett-Alfredo Escalera fight look legit.

"I didn't play any favorites with this thing." Lee told Lewis Freedman, of the *Inquirer*. "People are trying to make it out as something shady. This just isn't worth it to me for my credibility."

Lee left the Commission the next year, established the International Boxing Federation (IBF), and was its president until 2000, when he resigned after being convicted of money laundering, tax evasion and interstate travel in aid of racketeering. The judge gave him 22 months and fined him $25,000. He also had to pay the IBF $50,000 in a separate lawsuit and accept a lifetime ban from boxing.

None of that helped me in 1982. The Chandler-Carter fight was 33 days away, no time to appeal. I booked the 3,500-seat Pennsylvania Hall at the Civic Center in West Philadelphia, paying for rent, ring, security, setup, cleanup, ticket takers, box office, ushers, advertising, hotel rooms, meals—everything that Resorts would have covered—and without the $80,000 site fee I would have received. The semifinals of the *Final Four* of college basketball's *March Madness* were that afternoon, televised live into Philly from New Orleans.

Dave Bontempo, of the *Atlantic City Press*, skipped the Gomez-Meza fight at the Playboy Club and came to Philadelphia. His story that morning began: "This is the fight that Atlantic City lost."

The crowd was 2,417, the gate $33,756, my profit $17,501.96. At Resorts, it would have been five times that. Chandler got $150,000 ($420,000 in 2021), Carter $50,000 ($140,000). It was Chandler's biggest payday yet and Carter's career-best.

It was the first world bantamweight title fight between Americans since 1947 when Manuel Ortiz, of Corona, California, regained the crown from Harold Dade, of Chicago.

Carter won the first two rounds, but by the third Chandler had closed the distance. At the end of the fifth, Carter's left eye was closing, and he was cut on his right cheek. He trailed 48-47, 49-47 and 49-46. Trainer Jimmy Arthur scolded Carter, telling him he was fighting Chandler's fight, but Carter kept fading.

In the sixth, with his back to the ropes, Chandler landed a right uppercut and two left hooks, sending Carter to the canvas. He got up but Chandler jumped on him and referee Frank Cappuccino stopped it at 2:28. Irony: In King's fight at the Playboy, Gomez K0d Meza in the same round as Chandler (6th) and at the same time (2:28).

"It was a way to show the people in Philadelphia that I was for real because it was partially divided," Chandler told Rich Hoffman, of the *Daily News*. "He was a legitimate contender and a lot of people just weren't sure who to pick. But I am a true champion. Yes, it is, the most satisfying. As a titleholder, beating the No. 1 man (Eijiro Murata) last December was the most satisfying. But being from Philadelphia—this was the most satisfying. It gives me more respect at home."

The WBA ordered Chandler to fight Miguel Iriarte, of Panama. Iriarte couldn't spell F-I-G-H-T if you spotted him the F-I-G-H, but he was ranked No. 1 by the Panamanians who ran the WBA, Elias Cordova and Rodrigo Sanchez. They made Frankie Carbo and Blinky Palermo look like Mister Rogers and Donald Duck.

Cordova had been president of the WBA from 1974 to 1977 and chairman of its ratings committee from 1979 thru late 1982. He and Sanchez flip-flopped positions. Cordova appointed Sanchez ratings chairman in 1974 and Sanchez replacied Cordova as president in 1979. Sanchez passed away inn 1982, one month before the fight.

Iriarte was 12-1-1, 8 K0s, having beaten only one fighter with double digit wins. His last three fights had been against men who were 0-0, 0-1 and 0-3. We laughed at his videos. No major network would touch the fight, but Dan Duva added it to his monthly cable series, which included PRISM. Resorts hosted.

Chandler was 1.4 pounds heavy and the yahoos the WBA sent to supervise the fight whooped it up, thinking Jeff would lose the title on the scales. It took Chandler two hours and two more trips to the scale to make 118. Then he toyed with Iriarte, knocking him out in the ninth round. "The WBA embarrassed me by making me fight this guy so I wanted to embarrass them by taunting him and showing everyone how unqualified he was," Chandler said.

Chandler's career-best performance was in March, 1983, when he outpointed Gaby Canizales, of Laredo, Texas, over 15 rounds in an ABC-televised fight from Resorts. Canizales was 24-1, 19 K0s, and eventually would become world champion. But not this day! Chandler withstood his body attack and won by 145-141, 147-140 and 148-140. He was featured on the cover of *The Ring* magazine in July, 1983, as "the best fighter nobody knows."

Michael Spinks was defending his WBA light-heavyweight title against Eddie Mustafa Muhammad, the man he won it from, on Saturday afternoon, July 16, 1983, in Washington, DC. Mustafa

Muhammad was two pounds over the 175-pound limit that morning and refused to lose the weight, claiming the scale was wrong. After agreeing to a non-title, over-the-weight match, Spinks changed his mind and the card was canceled.

I was at our summer home in Ventnor when I got a call from George Krieger, Vice President of Programming at HBO, which was to televise the fight. He said ABC had purchased the delayed rights and had planned to show it one week later. HBO was not as popular as it would become and the fight would have been seen by many more people on ABC, which now had a hole in its schedule.

I contacted Ed Sobel, manager of Oscar Muniz, a bantamweight from Pico Rivera, California, who was 35-3-3, 22 K0s. I had been talking to him about a world title fight but that was out of the question on short notice. My offer was a 10-round non-title fight in seven days. Then, fighters *stayed* in shape; now they *get* in shape.

Sobel, a wholesale office furniture dealer on the West Coast, accepted for $20,000 ($55,000 in 2021). I located Chandler, who was staying with his girlfriend at one of those less-than-stellar motels on Admiral Wilson Boulevard in Camden. He was either separated or divorced from his wife, Charlotte.

"Would you like to make $100,000 ($275,000 in 2021) next Saturday in a 10-round fight?" I asked. "Are you in any kind of shape?" I had seen him running the previous week along Philly's East River Drive. "Let's go for it," he said.

I called Bob Iger, head of ABC Sports, at his weekend home in Sherman, Connecticut. Iger later became head of the network and eventually Executive Chairman and CEO of the Walt Disney Company. His wife said he was jogging and would call me back. When he did, he asked me how I found out but I kept quiet.

ABC paid $200,000 ($535,000) for the Chandler-Muniz 10-rounder. Bill Weidner and Rob Goldstein, who ran the Sands, said the showroom was booked for the evening, but they could accommodate me in the afternoon. On short notice, I got a $20,000 site fee and I put the card together in a few days.

Chandler was not in top shape. He weighed 121.75 pounds, same as Muniz. The action was a back-and-forth but Chandler lost by taunting Muniz, sticking out his tongue, yapping after the bell on occasion and waving his right hand. He did this to stall for time and it turned the crowd—and perhaps the judges—against him. By the

10th round, nearly everyone in the room—who had cheered Chandler when he was introduced—was yelling "OSCAR, OSCAR, OSCAR." All three scorecards were 5-4-1 in rounds, two for Muniz, one for Chandler.

"Each experience in the ring is a learning one," Muniz told Bill Livingston, of the *Inquirer*. "This time I learned what to do with a talker. I wanted people to know Oscar 'The Boxer' was here to fight."

Dad was at the fight. He was disgusted with the way Chandler clowned and taunted Muniz. "You really think Jeff won that fight?" he asked. I said yes but it was a hollow yes. It was a marked contrast from how proud Dad had been of Bennie Briscoe in 1972 after the fight with Carlos Monzon. This would be Dad's last fight. He died five days later, at 69, from a heart attack. Mom had passed eight years earlier, at 59, from emphysema.

In Chandler's hotel room, the lights were out and he was sitting on his bed with his back against the headboard, his legs stretched out in front of him. He was smoking a cigarette, something I never had seen him do. A couple of his friends were sitting on chairs. We spoke for a few minutes but he showed no emotion, staring straight ahead. His dream of staying undefeated was over. The $50,000 ($135,000) I made on the fight was little compensation, but I had a saleable rematch.

Five months later, Chandler stopped Muniz in seven rounds in the same ring, sending him to the hospital with cuts under both eyes and a possible broken jaw. In between the two Muniz fights, the WBA ordered us to fight Murata a third time, so we went back to Tokyo, the only place it made sense. Chandler scored three knockdowns and won in the 10th round.

Chandler was 27 and in his prime. His record was 33-1-2, 18 KOs, and he had defended his title nine times. He twice had earned $210,000—the biggest purses then for a defending bantamweight champion—and twice he had been the subject of articles in *Sports Illustrated*. He also had developed a cataract in his left eye.

The WBA insisted he fight Edgar Roman, a Venezuelan contender who had been stopped by light-hitting Julian Solis and recently had gone 10 rounds with a fighter who was 0-7. Network television wasn't interested. I spoke with the WBA and was told that if I paid a Venezuelan promoter $3,000 to use Roman on his card in the interim, Chandler would be allowed an optional defense. I delivered the check in Las Vegas the week I was there to see Marvin Hagler defend his middleweight title against Juan Roldan.

Richie Sandoval, of Pomona, California, was available. Sandoval was solid, but not a big puncher despite having 15 knockouts on his 22-0 record. I didn't think he was strong enough for Chandler. ABC televised on Saturday afternoon, April 7, 1984, from the Sands.

The day before the fight, Willie O'Neill asked me to his hotel room. “I've got bad news,” he said. “Jeff can't fight tomorrow. His left shoulder has been bothering him and he can't even put on his shirt without help.”

I've always been a big believer that the show must go on, so I called Dr. Frank Doggett, the Chief Medical Physician for the New Jersey Athletic Board. In his office, he shot Chandler's left shoulder with cortisone to make it mobile again. I had no idea that Chandler had been unable to use the arm for two weeks but it would not have mattered.

Joe Gramby told me that one night in 1942, future lightweight champion Bob Montgomery had vomited in the dressing room at the Arena an hour before he was fighting Maxie Shapiro. His tonsils had not been completely removed three months earlier. When I asked Gramby why he didn't pull Montgomery out, he reacted as if I had cursed his wife. “You must be joking,” he said. “I would never do that to a promoter.”

So I took charge and the fight was on.

Chandler's timing was off and Sandoval ran over him. Chandler was knocked down in the 11th round for the first time in his career and referee Arthur Mercante stopped it at 1:20 of the 15th.

I do not regret going through with the fight. Chandler did not argue. I assumed he thought he would be okay—we all did. His $210,000 purse ($570,000 in 2021) may have been a factor. I later learned that the New Jersey commission was getting ready to lift his license due to the cataract in his left eye and one forming in his right eye.

“I didn't do too much in that fight,” Chandler told Elmer Smith, of the *Daily News*, three months later. “I tried to take him out early. Then after that didn't work I thought I would get him in the later rounds. But there was no authority to my punches. It just wasn't there. I'll take the blame for that. I just couldn't get myself ready.

The only thing I was doing in training was my running. I did that faithfully. That's why I could go the distance.

"When the referee stopped the fight, my physical body was fine. But I wasn't able to think my way through that fight. The pain killer that was in my arm was in my head, too. I'm not trying to take the credit away from him. That's why I didn't mention it at the time. He fought an extremely smart fight. But without that pain killer in my arm, or some foreign substance affecting me, Richie Sandoval don't beat me."

Ironic that Gaby Canizales, the man Chandler had dominated in 1983, would end Sandoval's career in 1986, brutally knocking him out in seven rounds to win the title.

Chandler never boxed again. Six months later, Dr. Richard Ellis removed a traumatic cataract from Chandler's left eye and inserted a clear plastic replacement. He saw the new cataract forming in Chandler's right eye and said Chandler had a retinal problem in his left eye which had been repaired earlier. "Not only shouldn't he fight," Dr. Ellis said, "but anyone who has had that type of surgery should not even rub their eye hard."

Dr. Ellis was an attending physician at Wills Eye Hospital and had lived on my street in Bala Cynwyd when I was growing up. I was not happy but I respected Dr. Ellis and his hospital. Chandler never told anyone he was getting the operation. He said he didn't want me to know because he thought I would persuade him not to have it done. He made the right decision.

When New Jersey and Pennsylvania announced they would not license the 28-year-old Chandler, the rest of the country followed. He may have been the best fighter I ever had and he was still learning when he had to leave. He was voted into the International Boxing Hall of Fame in 2000. He and his wife, Diana, a certified nursing assistant, live in Newark, Delaware.

Chapter Thirty-Six

They Also Served

Down goes Sugar Ray Leonard. (Courtesy Worcester Telegram & Gazette)

Welterweights Bobby Joe Young and Kevin Howard never fought for a world championship, but they should have. Their 1982 matchup was the kind of fight you rarely see today. Had they come along 10 years later when world titles were available at roadside flea markets, they could have had one of those green or red plastic belts like everyone else.

North Philly's Howard turned pro in 1978 and lost twice in his first 17 fights, a pair of 10-round majority decisions to Roger Stafford, who was to fight Sugar Ray Leonard for the welterweight title in 1982—except Leonard underwent surgery for a torn retina. Howard had boxed for me early in his career and later on cards promoted by

Top Rank in Atlantic City, and by Impact Productions at the Arena—then known as the Martin Luther King Arena.

A basket of flowers reunited us. In the summer of 1981, Howard's manager, Frank Ward, had suffered third degree burns over 50 percent of his body when the car engine he was cleaning exploded from a gas leak in the carburetor.

"I was in St. Agnes Hospital burn center for more than three months," Ward said. "I had seven skin grafts. A few boxing people visited me—a friend of (commissioner) Howard McCall's, (trainer) Slim Jim Robinson, Mark Stewart—and they all said, 'It doesn't look like you're gonna make it so do you want me to take over your fighters?' Here I was, wrapped up like a mummy, and they wanted to take my fighters. You sent me flowers."

After Howard outpointed Dickie Ecklund early in 1982, we signed a promotional contract. The first time I matched him was against Young. Dr. Ferdie Pacheco wanted the fight on NBC as the semifinal to Jeff Chandler's WBA bantamweight title defense against Johnny Carter in Pennsylvania Hall.

Young was from Steubenville, Ohio. He had lost his 1980 pro debut to three-time New York Golden Gloves champion Pedro Vilella, then won 14 straight, 13 by knockout, the last six for me. He was managed by Carmine Castellano, of East Northport, New York, who owned secretarial services and was in medical research.

Howard was 1.4 pounds over the 148-pound limit at the weigh-in the night before. We told Young's people to give him an hour.

"When we got back," Carmine Castellano, Jr., said, "we were told Howard already had re-weighed and made 148. The commissioner confirmed it. My dad was upset and he thought you had pulled one over on him. I'm not sure he believed Howard made the weight."

During the fight, blow-by-blow announcer Marv Albert questioned matching two young prospects. Young was 23, Howard 22. "Wouldn't it make more sense to wait and let them fight down the road in a bigger fight?" he asked. "Not necessarily," Pacheco replied. "It takes a great promoter and Russell Peltz likes to go for it. There's nothing to say they won't meet again down the road."

The first four rounds were even but, in the fifth, Howard accidently thumbed Young in his left eye, hampering Young. Howard's left eye also had swelled but he took over and won by 10-round majority decision (46-46, 47-46, 48-45).

The loss to Howard and the situation with the weight strained my relationship with Castellano. We continued together and Young won his next five fights, but after he lost to Nino La Rocca in 1983 in San Remo, Italy, we split. Four years later, Young became the only man to beat Aaron Pryor, stopping him in seven rounds in Sunrise, Florida. Young retired in 1989 after being K0d by Simon Brown.

The Kevin Howard who beat Bobby Joe Young was the best Kevin Howard I ever saw. He was the underdog and the purses reflected it. He got $5,000, Young $15,000.

Howard kept winning, but with less discipline. Four months later he had to be coaxed into showing up at the weigh-in the day of his fight with Dominican Mao De La Rosa in Atlantic City. He weighed 159.5 pounds, more than 11 over the contract weight. He would have caught a hefty fine but De La Rosa was six pounds over himself. Howard knocked De La Rosa down in the first, but it took him eight more rounds before winning by knockout.

Ranked No. 9 by the WBC and on a seven-fight win streak, Howard boxed Marlon Starling on April 23, 1983, at the Hartford (Connecticut) Civic Center. CBS televised it. In 28 fights, Starling had lost only to future Hall-of-Famer Donald Curry and would win the WBA and WBC versions of the welterweight title. Howard had to make 147 since the fight was for the vacant USBA and NABF titles.

At ringside, Mary Ward, Frank's wife, told me Howard had lost 30 pounds in the last six weeks. He made 146.5, the first time he had been under 147 in over two years. But he was drained. Starling knocked him down in the first and won big (60-48, 59-49, 58-51).

Howard split his next two fights but was chosen to be Sugar Ray Leonard's first opponent for his comeback in 1984. Leonard had been out 27 months following his surgery. The $100,000 purse, twice what he got for Starling, was Howard's career best. When their February date was delayed until May due to another eye operation for Leonard, Howard K0'd Indiana's Bill Bradley at the Sands.

The night before the Leonard fight, Linda and I had dinner with Allen Flexer, and his wife, Shelly. Flexer still was President of the Spectrum but also President of SMG, an arena management company. He had worked with the city of Worcester, Massachusetts, to construct and operate the Centrum, site of the fight. He questioned my decision to let Howard fight Leonard. "All Howard has to do is put up a good fight," I said. "If he does, his value will skyrocket."

In the fourth round, HBO blow-by-blow announcer Barry Tompkins said, "I have a hunch…that Sugar Ray Leonard feels he has Kevin Howard in his pocket." Fifteen seconds later, he added, "I really believe that Sugar Ray…thinks he can take him at any time." As Tompkins was finishing, Howard threw a punch and Tompkins screamed, "and a right hand from Kevin Howard puts Sugar Ray Leonard right on the seat of his pants."

It would have been one of the biggest upsets in years. Half the people were on their feet, but Leonard survived the round. When he hurt Howard in the ninth, referee Dick Flaherty stopped it with 32 seconds left. The crowd didn't like what they felt was a premature stoppage. Flaherty had it closest at 77-76 for Leonard. The judges had it 78-74 and 79-74.

Howard's performance opened doors, but he closed them, including an $80,000 offer to fight Thomas Hearns. "I thought the offers weren't enough," he said.

Ward's take: "Kevin got friendly with James Hope and he started listening to him and not to me." Hope owned a steak and hoagie shop and he had befriended Howard months prior to the Leonard fight. Ward blames Hope. Howard blames Ward. Accusations of drug usage still reverberate from both sides.

Howard didn't box again for 11 months. When he did, he lost a 10-round decision to Robert Hines at the Sands in Atlantic City. I paid him $75,000 less than he was offered for Hearns. Ward held up his end of the purse. He collected $1,795 and split from Howard.

"My mom had died about a month before I fought Hines," Howard said. "I took the fight out of frustration." Howard lost two of his next three fights and retired in 1986. He was 25.

Earl Hargrove's criminal record was as long as his boxing record. Between 1971 and 1979, Hargrove spent more time in prison than out. Street fights, armed robbery, attempted murder. He ran with the 7th & Emily gang in South Philly.

"It was the environment I grew up in," Hargrove said. "Street gangs were a way of life. My dad always told me that if I ever got into street fights, to bring home a sample—an eye, a nose or an ear."

Hargrove almost took his dad literally. He got as far as ninth grade at Bartlett Junior High before being sent to Glen Mills. A reform school for "bad boys," Hargrove called it. A more professional definition was "youth detention center for juvenile delinquents." It held 12-through-21-year-olds in Delaware County, 30 miles outside Philly. Glen Mills lost its license in 2019 after claims of child physical, emotional and sexual abuse.

Hargrove learned to box at his next stop, Camp Hill State Correctional Institution—followed by stints at Western Penitentiary and Holmesburg Prison in Northeast Philly. He was held at Holmesburg in 1978, while awaiting trial for the armed robbery of the *Soul Gents* teen social club in South Philadelphia, but was released in 1979. His next stop was the Percy Street Gym, run by Ivan Cohen, who was in construction.

"I liked boxing because you could hit someone and not get locked up for it," Hargrove said. Gary Hegyi, who worked in the Philadelphia Traffic Court system, became his manager. Hegyi was from Northeast Philadelphia and he had been matchmaking and booking fighters since the mid-1970s. He took Hargrove to Joe Frazier's gym and had George Benton train him.

Hegyi got Hargrove fights in Virginia, New Jersey, Massachusetts and Pennsylvania. Within two years he had knocked out 15 opponents. Five were making their pro debut and seven were winless. Only one had more victories than defeats.

Bob Connelly, who was in the vending machine business, began promoting in the suburbs. Connelly was from Phoenixville, 28 miles outside Philly, and he staged Hargrove's next five fights against slightly better competition. By the time Hargrove boxed for me early in 1983, he had knocked out 20 straight, 16 within three rounds.

He made it 21 straight when he K0d Greg Stephens, of San Diego, in two rounds at Resorts, netting him an NBC-televised semifinal on May 22, 1983, at the Sands. Jeff Chandler outpointed Hector Cortez, of Ecuador, in the non-title main event.

Don King, the fighter from Indianapolis—not the promoter from Ohio—was in the opposite corner. Carlos "Panama" Lewis, King's chief second, verbally abused Hargrove at the weigh-in and again during the ring introductions. Lewis' ploy worked, sort of. Hargrove wanted to decapitate King, and floored him with a right hand 30 seconds into the fight. Then King got up and went to war.

When Hargrove returned to his corner at the end of the round, Benton blew his cool: "You think you're fightin' a great fight, huh? Well, you ain't fightin' shit. You're not fightin'. Now listen, man, I want you to box this guy. You're not fightin' worth a damn. Now that's not fightin'. Now listen to me, man! I never taught you how to box like that. Now listen, you get out there and fight like you know how. What the hell, are you crazy? Now box this guy. I don't want you to go out there and throw punches like you're a fuckin' nut."

Benton's tirade didn't make air, but I got a "dirty copy" of the fight, which includes the corner talk between rounds while viewers are watching commercials. It was not the usually reserved Benton I knew. Hargrove was a street fighter and he stopped King in the ninth round—the best performance of his career, despite Benton's comments. Two fights later, Hargrove met Mark Medal, of Jersey City, for vacant IBF junior middleweight title on March 11, 1984, also at the Sands.

Medal was 22-1, 19 K0s, against better opposition. He weathered bombs for three rounds, turned things around in the fourth and stopped Hargrove 49 seconds into the fifth. Hargrove's $45,000 purse was the biggest of his career.

Hargrove fought sporadically for the next 11 years, losing five of his last 13 fights, then quit and went into business for himself. His company, *Earl Hargrove Painting & Power Washing*, does quite well. His three daughters and one son are college graduates.

Chapter Thirty-Seven

Early IBF Champs

Robert Hines pops Matthew Hilton in 1988. (Chris Farina photo)

Dissatisfied with the way things were being run and unable to get Bob Lee elected president, a group of United States boxing commissions broke from the Latin-controlled WBA in 1983 after a nasty convention in Puerto Rico. They formed the International Boxing Federation (IBF), with offices in East Orange, New Jersey. Lee became president. Just what boxing needed—another alphabet group. The WBA, formed in 1921 as the National Boxing Association, always played second fiddle to The Ring magazine and the New York State Athletic Commission in determining world champions and rankings. The WBC was formed in 1963 when foreign managers and promoters complained the WBA was then American-controlled and Latino fighters got scant recognition. Despite our previous problems, Lee was easier to deal with than the people who ran the WBC and WBA.

The emergence of the IBF made "world" titles easier to come by. This mess had started in the mid-1970s when the WBC began stripping champions not defending against contenders it designated. The first time it affected me was in 1974 when Carlos Monzon was stripped and Bennie Briscoe met Rodrigo Valdes for the vacant WBC middleweight belt. The days of dominance by *The Ring* and the New York State Athletic Commision were fading.

It became more about money and pseudo-celebrity than hard-earned glory. Call me a romantic but that's what boxing was for me. The dream of winning a world championship in one of eight or 10 weight classes put you atop Mount Everest, but the birth of the IBF opened smaller summits to scale, and, by the end of the decade, the World Boxing Organization (WBO) brought meager hills.

Nine new weight classes and four champions in each. Imagine baseball, football, basketball and ice hockey without playoffs. You'd have dozens of teams calling themselves world champions. Who would care? That's what happened to boxing.

Even the pride of being a contender lost its value. With a possible 40 Top 10 contenders in each weight class—WBC, WBA, IBF, WBO—what would happen to the iconic scene from the 1954 movie, *On The Waterfront,* when Marlon Brando, as ex-pro Terry Malloy says, "I coulda been a contenduh." Now, not only could Rod Steiger, so could Eva Marie Saint.

Many of the important fights on the East Coast of the 1980s would take place in garish casino ballrooms, in nightclub-like settings. High rollers, with their wives or girlfriends, would sip cocktails or down shots, watching the action from upholstered chairs and u-shaped booths. Missing was the excitement of standing-room-only at the Blue Horizon, an overflow crowd at the Arena, 15,000 at the Spectrum, 17,000 in Luna Park. Missing was the smoke, obscuring the light.

Atlantic City competed with Las Vegas for the biggest fights of the 1980s. Casinos by the ocean fought each other in an attempt to gain national television exposure and lure gamblers. In Las Vegas, big fights were in makeshift outdoor stadiums erected on casino parking lots. In Atlantic City, Mike Tyson and Michael Spinks drew close to 22,000 to their 1988 bout at Convention Hall.

Philadelphia hosted 172 boxing cards in the 1980s, 29 fewer than the previous decade. Atlantic City hosted 841. Promoters from all over the country flocked to share the pie.

Charlie "Choo Choo" Brown scored two knockdowns, was down once himself and fortunate to get a 15-round split decision over Melvin Paul, of New Orleans, to win the first IBF lightweight title on January 30, 1984 at the Sands in Atlantic City. A group of cable systems aired the fight, including PRISM. Brown was paid $12,500, Paul $7,500.

North Philly's Brown got by on slick movement and solid power, in the ring or in the streets. I remember on the way to our hotel in 1979 in Washington, DC, driving past him as he stood on a street corner eating fried chicken from a fast-food restaurant as his pre-fight meal at 2 in the afternoon. He still won by knockout. When he fought Paul he was 27 and in his prime. His record was 23-2-1, 16 K0s, but he lacked the discipline for world-class competition.

Three months later in the same ring, Harry Arroyo, of Youngstown, Ohio, stopped him in 14 rounds to take the title. Brown got $30,000 for the NBC-televised fight.

Brown's last big chance came late in 1984 in Belfast, Northern Ireland, but he was blown away in three rounds by ex-WBC junior lightweight champion Cornelius Boza-Edwards. "I put him in retirement after he lost to (Anthony) Cobra Williams at the Blue Horizon (in 1986)," said manager Fred Jenkins. "He was doing drugs and getting high all the time. He kept fighting later without me."

After losing to Williams, Brown dropped his next 10 fights, eight by K0, and retired in 1993, years after boxing commissions should have denied him a license. He finished at 26-16-2, 18 K0s, having lost his last 11 fights. Those late-career beatings may have helped him wind up in a wheelchair.

Gary Hinton was a former gang leader from the Mantua section of West Philadelphia, a predominantly working-class Black community with drug warfare rampant. He was managed and trained by Marvin "Toochie" Gordon and Frank Taylor at the Executioners Gym at 60th and Vine. Hinton lost to Brown in 1980, but his work ethic earned him a better career. Hinton got a shot at Aaron Pryor's IBF junior welterweight title on March 2, 1985.

The left-handed Hinton was a blue-collar fighter. His previous 10 fights had been in Atlantic City ballrooms. He was not a big puncher and never had earned over $7,500 for a fight. He was smart, calm and awkward and he beat a steady stream of fringe contenders to become one himself by building the same 23-2-1 record as Brown.

Pryor, from Cincinnati, was 35-0, 32 K0s. He had beaten future Hall-of-Famers Antonio Cervantes and Alexis Arguello and his fights had been on network television and Pay-Per-View. He had boxed at Caesars Palace in Las Vegas and the Orange Bowl in Miami. He was in another galaxy.

I was in-house promoter at the Sands and we had a deal with Sylvester Stallone's *Tiger Eye Boxing* for monthly cards. No one gave Hinton a chance against Pryor, who had given up his WBA title and retired in 1983, only to return in 1984 and win the first IBF 140-pound belt.

"We had all kinds of problems selling Hinton to the Network," I told Dave Bontempo, of the *Atlantic City Press*. "First, CBS passed. The problem was, 'Who is Hinton and why isn't he rated anywhere except maybe the IBF?' He's got no wins over major names and has strategic fights. He's a nine-to-fiver.

"Selling Pryor helped us sell Hinton. Pryor has been the most exciting guy in the business. He hadn't fought in nine months and yet his picture was on the cover of major boxing magazines. Pryor had struggled over Nick Furlano (to regain the title)."

Bob Iger still headed ABC sports. He, Alex Wallau and Jim Spence decided which fights to buy for the network.

"We thought Pryor was a dangerous fighter and we were afraid of a short fight," Iger told Bontempo. "Russell Peltz told us we ought to take another look at the fight. When we did, it became apparent that maybe Pryor wasn't the same Pryor he'd been in other fights and that Hinton could make a fight of it. We were willing to roll the dice.

"A bad fight is something you have to be sensitive to because if you do put on a mismatch you not only get 8,000 people tell you how lousy it was but you get branded as the network that puts on the mismatches. The people will turn that off."

Hinton was paid $50,000—a career best—and started fast. It was anybody's fight until Pryor decked him with a right hand early in round 14. Hinton got up but lost a 15-round split decision (141-143, 146-139, 141-143). It was Pryor's last solid performance. Drugs had consumed him and he did not fight again for more than two years. When he did, he lost to Bobby Joe Young, won three more fights, and retired in 1990.

In 1999, the Associated Press voted him the best junior welterweight of the 20th century. Pryor got clean in 1993 and stayed that way until he passed in 2016.

With Pryor gone, Hinton flew to Lucca, Italy, in 1986 to fight for the vacant IBF belt. Lucca is a town of less than 100,000 in Italy's Tuscany region. It was visited by Caesar and conquered by Napoleon and known for the medieval city walls which still encircled it. It was within easy distance of the Leaning Tower of Pisa and the village where Carlo Collodi (born Carlo Lorenzini) wrote *The Adventures of Pinocchio*. The town fathers wanted exposure from European television to boost tourism.

Hinton won the title in the Palazzo Dello Sport, scoring a unanimous 15-round decision over Reyes Antonio Cruz, of the Dominican Republic. He got $28,000. Like Brown, he would lose in his first defense—for a purse of $42,500—when Joe Manley K0d him six months later in the less picturesque Hartford (Connecticut) Civic Center. Hinton was idle for the next 18 months and we split. He returned in 1988, won four in a row but retired after being stopped by ex-WBC champ Saoul Mamby in the summer of 1989, five days short of his 33d birthday.

A decade later, Hinton showed up in my office and gave me his IBF championship belt, his robe and trunks. I never heard from him again.

Robert Hines grew up in the Raymond Rosen housing projects at 23rd and Diamond in North Philadelphia, next door to Bernard Hopkins. At 15, Hines moved in with his girlfriend in South Philadelphia and used her address to go to South Philadelphia High School. He flunked the 1979 school year when he was traveling with the local amateur boxing team, but he graduated in 1980.

Hines was a pleasing southpaw, though not a swarmer like Marvin Johnson or Frank Fletcher. He was flat-footed and threw quick, short, compact punches. Brittle hands were a problem. I marveled watching him dominate *Ms. Pac-Man* in the game room on fight days at the Sands.

He was managed by Seymour "Sam" Ingerman, whom I labeled the *Bingo King of Philadelphia* because he operated several bingo parlors. I wanted to sign Hines out of the amateurs in 1980, but when Ingerman insisted on having a lawyer present, I backed off. Lawyers scared me.

Hines went with Dan Duva and Main Events and won his first 17 fights, 12 by K0. I'd watch him spar Fletcher at the Upper Darby Fire House gym. Fletcher was an NBC-TV star, but the way Hines handled him you couldn't tell who was the sparring partner.

In his 18th fight, Hines stumbled. He was 23 and ranked No. 8 by the WBA when he faced Ricardo Bryant in the spring of 1984 at the Sands. Bryant, a laborer at the Drakenfeld Chemicals plant in Washington, Pennsylvania, never was serious about boxing. He was 10-5 and had lost four of his last five, two by knockout. Hines led early but Bryant began landing right hands and stopped him in the seventh round.

"That fight hurt me on the inside but I never let it out," Hines told Dave Bontempo. "I thought I could do everything, even take on Marvin Hagler. I felt like I couldn't lose. I was in the best shape of my life. Then I got cocky. I let my head down, did a little bit of showboating like Sugar Ray Leonard and got caught. That fight taught me a lot. The biggest thing it did was tell me not to underestimate anyone. You've just got to stay alert."

Duva released Hines from their promotional agreement, and Ingerman and I got together—this time with Ingerman's attorney—and we signed a promotional contract.

"I met Sam in 1980," Hines said. "He was managing (welterweight) Roger Stafford and he came to Joe Frazier's gym to watch us spar and I tore Stafford's ass up. Sam signed me after that. I was with (trainer) Al Fennel my whole life. I had 178 wins and 11 losses as an amateur. Won three Philadelphia Golden Gloves titles but I always hand trouble with my hands."

Hines boxed for me April 8, 1985, at the Sands, his first fight since Bryant. His opponent, Kevin Howard, had not boxed in 11 months since losing to Sugar Ray Leonard. Neither the *Daily News* nor the *Inquirer* was there. The *Bulletin* had ceased publication in 1982, one year after the *Philadelphia Journal*. Tom Cushman had left for the West Coast in 1980.

Hines dominated Howard and earned a 10-round decision. I brought him back July 1 and he was held to a 10-round draw by James "Hard Rock" Green in the same ring. Green was managed by Lou Duva, Dan's father, and he had been up and down the junior middleweight and middleweight ratings.

"I was disgusted after the Green fight," Hines said. "I thought I won but I thought the Duvas pulled one over on me with the judges and I stopped going to the gym after that. I made money working for Sam in his bingo parlors. He had one in Manayunk, one on Frankford Avenue and one at 52nd and Market. I would go around and collect the money from the players. I was known as the 'cash collector' there.

"I stayed out of the gym for the rest of 1985 and most of 1986. Then one day late in 1986 I was gambling on the street corner at 11th and Louden in Logan. Al Fennel drove by and got me in his car to go to the gym because Sidney Outlaw needed some left-handed sparring for his fight with John David Jackson at the Blue Horizon. I lit up Outlaw that day and some writers were there and they asked me why I wasn't fighting any more. So I decided to go for it again, all the way up to the world title."

Hines K0d Ismael Negron, of New York, in seven rounds on March 31, 1987 at the Blue Horizon. He went unbeaten in his next five fights, won the USBA title at 154 pounds and became mandatory challenger for Matthew Hilton, of Montreal. Hilton was a strong, thick, walk-in banger who was 29-0, 23 K0s. Bob Arum outbid me for the fight and put it at the Las Vegas Hilton as part of a triple header on November 4, 1988.

A 4-1 favorite, Hilton struggled to make the 154-pound limit and the fight almost was canceled 24 hours prior to the weigh-in with Hilton still at 159. Hilton made the weight, but his struggle with the scales was kept from the Hines camp.

The night of the fight, Hines checked into his dressing room, but went back to his hotel room to get a shot of lidocaine for his sore hands.

Hilton knocked Hines down in rounds two and three. He was throwing wide shots and while some were landing—several low—Hines was countering with short, crisp, inside uppercuts. Hines was hurt in the second, more surprised than hurt in the third, and took control as Hilton tired. His comeback had Hines crying when he was awarded a unanimous 12-round decision (116-110, 114-111, 112-111). He earned $125,000, which was $124,000 more than I had paid him when he boxed Negron 19 months earlier.

That same night, Michael Nunn defended his IBF middleweight title by beating Juan Roldan on points and Thomas Hearns got off the floor and squeezed by with a majority decision over James Kinchen for the first World Boxing Organization (WBO) super middleweight title.

Hearns had signed to challenge Fulgencio Obelmejias, of Venezuela, for the WBA super middleweight title because Arum wanted Hearns to win a fifth "world" title before Sugar Ray Leonard, who was to fight Donny Lalonde for another promoter the following week in Las Vegas for the WBC super middleweight and light-heavyweight belts. When Obelmejias suffered a cracked rib in sparring and had to cancel, Arum was desperate.

Earlier that year, disgruntled Puerto Rican and Dominican businessmen had walked out of the WBA convention in Venezuela after a disagreement over rule interpretations. They formed the WBO, which no one took seriously until Arum had them approve Hearns-Kinchen for its vacant 168-pound belt. I was at the Hilton pool the day before the fight when Ed Levine, a real estate attorney from Florida, told me Top Rank had flown him and other WBO officials to Vegas to supervise. I shook my head.

Less than two weeks later, the Nevada State Athletic Commission reported that Hines had tested positive for lidocaine, illegal in Nevada but not on the IBF's list of banned substances. Hines and I flew to Las Vegas for a hearing. Lidocaine was not a performance enhancer so Hines kept his title but was fined $750.

Hines defended on February 5, 1989. It was the first boxing card at Trump Castle in Atlantic City. I should not have rushed him. I should have let him rest his sore hands but the NBC-TV money was appealing and everyone was scrambling to get one of the few available network slots. Despite a 39-0 record, no one took challenger Darrin Van Horn seriously. He was from Kentucky, which meant basketball, not boxing. He was 22 and had scored 25 K0s but his opposition suggested nothing to fear.

"I should never have fought Van Horn," Hines said. "My hands were hurting me. I talked it over with Sam and we didn't think much of Van Horn and the money was good ($150,000), so we decided to go through with the fight and get my hands operated on after that. I was hoping I could get fights with Hearns, (John) Mugabi and Leonard. I was confident going into the ring against Van Horn, but by the third round my hands were hurting so bad I just couldn't do anything." Scores were 116-112, 118-111, 118-110, all for Van Horn.

Two fights later, Brett Lally, of Northville, Michigan, stopped Hines in five rounds for the vacant North American Boxing Federation (NABF) junior middleweight title on June 25, 1990, at Harrah's Marina in Atlantic City. "I hardly trained for that fight," Hines said. "If I couldn't beat a guy like Brett Lally, there was no point in going on. My hands were hurting me and the future did not look too good, so I quit."

Hines was 29. His record was 25-3-1, 17 K0s. He began training fighters. He does better today, teaching cardio and boxing basics to white collar professionals.

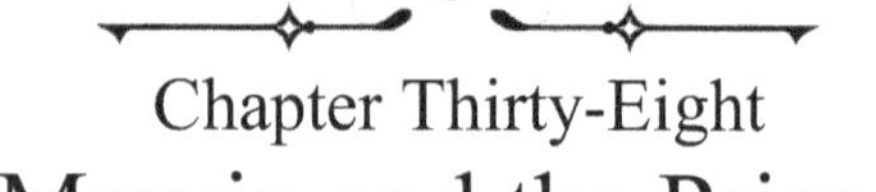

Chapter Thirty-Eight

Marvin and the Prince

Marvin Johnson (left) en route to second win over Eddie Davis. (Peltz collection)

Two light-heavyweight champions met late in 1984, though neither held a title at the time. Marvin Johnson went 10 rounds with Prince Charles Williams at the Tyndall Armory in Indianapolis, Johnson's hometown. ESPN was there, but the telecast did not register with Mr. and Mrs. Nielson. Smart money said Johnson was over the hill and Prince Charles would never climb it.

Johnson, approaching his 27th birthday, had looked more like 57 when Michael Spinks flattened him in the fourth round of their 1981 fight in Atlantic City. Spinks' right to the body and half-left hook, half-left uppercut to the head snapped the three-fight win streak Johnson had compiled after losing his WBA title the year before. Johnson suffered a mild concussion. While doctors worked on him, the loud speakers in Resorts' Superstar Theatre played *Another One Bites The Dust,* by Queen, in a display of poor taste.

I wondered about Johnson's future. He was raised as a Hoosier in the Midwest. He had a Southern-like accent and spoke as if he carefully scripted each word. He did not renew his manager's contract with my brother-in-law and did not fight for 13 months. He came back and took it slow for two years, winning five fights against less-than-stellar opposition in Illinois, Indiana and The Bahamas.

Then Clarence Doninger, Marvin's attorney and later Athletic Director at Indiana University, called. He wanted to hook Marvin up with me alone this time—without a manager. I was promoting monthly cable-televised cards at the Sands in Atlantic City and Marvin became a regular in 1984, beating Eddie Gonzales, Jerome Clouden, Johnny Davis and Eddie Collins. We accepted an offer from Top Rank to fight Prince Charles on ESPN in November, and 1,683 crowded into the Tyndall Armory.

Prince Charles was born in Columbus, Mississippi, but had lived with his grandmother in Mansfield, Ohio, since he was 5. He played center on his 7th grade basketball team at John Sherman Junior High, but got interested in boxing after following his older brother to the gym. He had 34 amateur fights, losing to future pro Tony Ayala in the 156-pound semifinals of the Junior Nationals in 1977.

He turned pro the next year at 16, but was stalled at 12-3-2, 8 K0s, when he arrived in Indianapolis. Every round was a battle and he stunned Johnson in the 10th. The scorecards, all for Johnson (99-91, 99-90, 100-89), did not tell the story. When I later noticed how upset Prince Charles was, I thought, "Did this man actually think he could come into Indianapolis and win?" That attitude reminded me of Jeff Chandler.

"I thought I could beat Marvin," Prince Charles said. "I was young (22) and I was strong and I was training in Grand Rapids, Michigan, with heavyweights, Tony Tucker and Buster Mathis, Jr. They couldn't hurt me so I didn't think Marvin could, either."

In the following weeks, I spoke with Gerry Stapleton, who managed Prince Charles. I recommended Marty Feldman as a new trainer and she agreed. I put Prince Charles on the Aaron Pryor-Gary Hinton championship card at the Sands and he won a six-round decision over Marcus Jackson, of Hartford, Connecticut. On Feldman's advice, I signed him.

After beating Prince Charles, Johnson won five more fights through the end of 1985. Only Eddie Davis posed a threat. Dennis Rappaport, a New Yorker who managed Davis, had been known as one of the "Whacko Twins" (with Mike Jones) for driving promoters and TV networks crazy with their demands when they managed heavyweight contender Gerry Cooney and 1976 Olympic lightweight gold medal winner Howard Davis, Jr.

Rappaport was a high roller and the Sands wanted his action so we made a deal for Davis to fight Johnson again on April 21. There was no television and Johnson won by knockout, putting him in line for another fight with Spinks, by then the undisputed champion.

When Spinks defeated Larry Holmes, becoming the first light-heavyweight champion to win the heavyweight title, the WBC, IBF and WBA each scrambled to find a 175-pound champion. Agreeing to one championship fight made too much sense.

J. B. Williamson, an Indianapolis neighbor of Johnson's, won the WBC belt with a 12-round decision over Prince Mama Muhammad, of Ghana, at the Forum in Inglewood, California. Slobodan Kacar, of Yugoslavia, won the IBF's with a 15-round decision over Eddie Mustafa Muhammad in Pesaro, Italy.

The WBA light-heavyweight title fight got the most attention when ABC televised Johnson's fight against Leslie Stewart, of Trinidad, on February 9, 1986, in Indianapolis. Stewart was 25 and unbeaten in 18 fights with 11 K0s. His biggest win was over Lottie Mwale, who had defeated Johnson eight years earlier in Yugoslavia.

"Pops," Johnson's new nickname, was two months short of his 32nd birthday. Besides Mwale, only world champions had beaten him—Matthew Saad Muhammad (twice), Eddie Mustafa Muhammad and Spinks. Market Square Arena got behind the promotion and 8,173 fans chanted *Mar-vin, Mar-vin,* drowning out a calypso drum brought in by West Indian countrymen to support Stewart.

Johnson's one gear was "drive" and he was in it the entire way. Stewart refused to surrender, but Johnson stayed one punch ahead. Stewart was cut over both eyes and, when he got rocked in the seventh, the fight was stopped after 56 seconds. Everyone in the building rose and cheered Johnson, who became the first man to win the light-heavyweight title three times. He led by 58-57, 59-55, and 60-55, but it would be his last great fight.

Linda called from home to say that Marvin had praised me in his post-fight interview with Al Michaels. He said I had believed in him when everyone else had turned their backs and all young fighters should sign with me because I was "a fair man."

Marvin got $75,000 ($180,000 in 2021), Stewart $50,000 ($120,000) and the TV rights to Trinidad. ABC paid us $125,000 and Market Square Arena kicked in a $75,000 site fee. There was income from overseas television, led by Italy with $10,000. France, Norway, Argentina, Puerto Rico and Costa Rica also contributed.

I paid my partner, Fred Berns, $10,000. My profit was $45,443.25 ($109,000). That would offset some of the losses from the recent years at the Blue Horizon. This was how boxing worked for me. You invest in club shows which usually lose money, hoping to develop a future star to help you recover your losses and turn a profit.

His third time as champion, Marvin finally made a successful defense, stopping Jean-Marie Emebe on cuts in 13 rounds seven months later in the same ring. Emebe was from the Cameroons and was 24-2, 20 K0s, but Marvin led 115-113, 117-115 and 117-114. A syndicated television network, put together by co-promoter Sam Glass, carried the fight. Marvin again was paid $75,000. This time, the crowd was half the size as February 9, and since syndicated television did not pay the same as ABC, the card lost $27,000, half of which was mine.

Stewart won five fights after losing to Johnson and became the mandatory challenger. Berns flew to the WBA headquarters in Venezuela to bid on the fight against Jim Cavo, the Florida businessman who managed Stewart. Berns went to bluff Cavo into increasing his bid since we knew the rematch would be cost prohibitive in the USA.

Cavo's winning bid was $265,000. Marvin's 80 percent (WBA rules) came to $212,000 ($488,000 in 2021), largest of his career. Berns and I agreed to 10 percent for our work.

The rematch, Trinidad's first world championship fight, was at its National Soccer Stadium in Port-of-Spain, Saturday afternoon, May 23, 1987. It was boiling hot; then a monsoon swept through; then it was dry again. There was drumming, constant cheering and singing from the crowd of more than 25,000.

The night before, a WBA official said, "Marvin has been a great champion but he's held the title long enough and it's time for new blood."

John Bansch, of the *Indianapolis Star*, wrote in his post-fight story that one of the ringside judges stood and applauded when Stewart entered the ring. I didn't like the way referee Bernie Soto separated the fighters when Marvin got inside. He warned Marvin for holding but Stewart's went unnoticed. None of this made a difference. Marvin was down twice in the first round and took a beating for the next seven. I told Champ Chaney—on the advice of ABC's Alex Wallau—to stop it before the 9th.

Marvin had won 16 in a row since Spinks in 1981. His record was 43-6, 35 K0s. I wrote to him and told him I loved him and his wife, Delores, and said his health was more important than his bank balance. He was 33, never boxed again and worked in the Marion County (Indianapolis) Sheriff's Department for over 35 years before retiring late in 2020.

I didn't see Marvin again until 1999 when, working for ESPN, I invited him to a Berns card at the Farm Bureau Building in Indianapolis. He wore a white-on-white suit, signed autographs and enjoyed being Marvin Johnson again. The next time I saw him was in 2018 when he and Berns were inducted into the inaugural class of the Indiana Boxing Hall of Fame in Carmel, Indiana. His speech was insightful and funny and the best of the day.

"You were hard to read," he told me. "I couldn't look at you and know if you were on my side or not. You always seemed to be neutral and I guess that's what promoters were supposed to do—be neutral."

When I assured Marvin I was with him every minute, he was happy to hear it.

There was an addendum to my Indianapolis story. Seventeen years after Marvin's last night, my youngest son, Daniel, entered the 2004 Indiana Golden Gloves. He finished runner-up in the 165-pound Junior Open division. He was a senior at Indiana University and, in keeping with the tradition of great Jewish fighters of days gone by, he never told his mother.

After the loss to Marvin, Prince Charles won 21 straight fights over eight years. The win over Marcus Jackson was the first of six at the Sands, the biggest a 10-round decision over Jeff Lampkin, avenging a knockout loss. He won the vacant USBA title in 1986 with a 12-round decision over James Salerno, of Orlando, Florida, and became No. 1 challenger for the IBF world title, which Bobby Czyz had won by stopping Slobodan Kacar.

With Stapleton's blessing, I sold half my promotional contract to Berns, who was backed by Richard Espovich, a lawyer from Alexandria, Virginia, and Chris Middendorf, an art dealer from Washington, DC, newcomers in boxing. Losses at the Blue Horizon were draining and I got $25,000 for 49 percent of my contract.

Prince Charles defended the USBA title in the summer of 1987 at the Blue Horizon with a second-round knockout over Miami's Joe Dolphin, who had lost 10 out of his previous 24 fights. The card cost me $7,686.73 but it kept Prince Charles at No. 1.

The fight with Czyz was part of a triple header on Showtime Pay Per View, outdoors on October 29 at the Las Vegas Hilton. Michael Nunn K0d Darnell Knox for the vacant NABF middleweight title and Thomas Hearns stopped Juan Roldan for the vacant WBC middleweight title in the main event.

Prince Charles got $60,000 and earned every penny. Two right hands from Czyz dropped him just before the end of round two. Early in round three he was knocked sideways into the ropes. Referee Carlos Padilla called it a knockdown even though that rule had not yet been approved by the IBF. Czyz was ready to pounce when Padilla pulled him away and counted.

Linda said, "It's not your fault. You got him here. You did everything you could."

As if he heard her, Prince Charles turned the fight around. He nailed Czyz with uppercuts and jabs for the last two minutes of the round and stayed with the jab, the double jab and the uppercut. Czyz' right eye swelled, closed—and the fight was stopped with him in his corner after the ninth round. Prince Charles, a 4-1 underdog in

Vegas, was the new champion. Scores were 89-83 and 88-84 for him and a ridiculous 85-85 from judge Dalby Shirley, one of many controversial scorecards in his career.

The TV announcers were Tim Ryan, Gil Clancy and Marvin Hagler. Clancy set the standard which all others tried—or should have tried—to emulate. He had one of the sharpest and most analytical boxing minds I ever knew. He commented early on Prince Charles' ability to use the jab.

Feldman did not work the corner. He had applied for Social Security disability. Walking up the steps and into the ring would not have been a good look. I got him a seat in Williams' corner at ringside and he gave instructions from there—both to Prince Charles and Billy "Smiley" Hayward, the chief second.

"Marty taught me all about the jab," Prince Charles said, "but at first I couldn't understand his technique. He told me that sometimes I would have to 'eat a jab' to get my jab off. I looked at him like he was crazy but when I sparred it began to work. I really think I had the third best jab of my era, behind Larry Holmes and Ali. Marty always was concerned about his fighters and he looked after them. He made sure you did your roadwork and he turned my career around."

The win over Czyz should have opened doors, but with Sugar Ray Leonard, Roberto Duran, Thomas Hearns and Mike Tyson around, network or Pay-Per-View opportunities were scarce.

We spent 1988 in France. Prince K0d Jim Shavers in a non-title fight in Paris and made successful defenses against Ricardo Caramanolis in the ski resort town of Annecy, and against Rufino Angulo in the wine district of Bordeaux. He was not happy with the $10,000 he got for Shavers, the $90,000 for Caramanolis, or the $100,000 for Angulo. So the Berns group paid me another $26,000 and now owned 75 percent of the promotional agreement.

I walked away after Prince's third defense, a 10th-round knockout of Czyz in their rematch. Arum paid him $175,000 for the fight, part of back-to-back weekend cards televised by ABC from Atlantic City. I couldn't deliver the big money and neither could Berns, Espovich or Middendorf. Contacts had expired and Prince signed with New York-based promoter Cedric Kushner, but still was confined to title fights against second-tier or aging names like Frankie Swindell,

Mwehu Beya, James Kinchen, Vincent Boulware and Freddie Delgado.

Most of the fights were held in small towns in Italy and in smaller casino ballrooms in Atlantic City without the benefit of network or major cable television in the United States. The fight with Delgado, of Trujillo, Puerto Rico, was held in Williamson, West Virginia, a town with a population of 5,000. The site, the Williamson Field House, catered to high school basketball games and concerts.

Prince deserved better: "I was making about $100,000 a fight. Cedric was keeping me busy and I liked that even though the money wasn't great. I defended the title five times in two years and I had one 10-rounder, but then I broke my right hand twice and I didn't fight at all in 1992. Then Cedric sold me down the river.

"I went to Germany to fight Henry Maske in March, 1993. When we got there, Cedric told me he made the match in Germany because he thought I was finished after breaking my hand twice. He said, 'I'm Jewish and you're Black and the Germans don't like either of us. Even if you knock him out, they'll throw water on him to revive him.' The night before the fight I called my wife, Cynthia, back home, and told her I lost. She asked me how I lost if the fight had not yet happened. I told her what Cedric said."

Prince said he got $100,000 for the Maske fight, which seems low, considering how popular the unbeaten Maske was and how much money was available in Germany. Scores were 116-111 (twice) and 118-110, all for Maske. Williams won his next three against mediocre opposition and then got his biggest payday ($260,000) to challenge James Toney for the IBF world super middleweight title on July 29, 1994, at the MGM in Las Vegas.

"Jackie Kallen managed Toney and I had gotten to know her when I trained In Michigan," Prince Charles said. "I called her myself and that's how I got the fight."

Feldman devised strategy to get inside and smother Toney. It was the same strategy he had used two years earlier when little-known Dave Tiberi, of New Castle, Delaware, lost a controversial 12-round split decision to Toney for the IBF middleweight title in Atlantic City. The strategy worked early, but Toney took over and stopped Prince Charles with 15 seconds left in the 12th round. By then, all four sanctioning bodies had agreed to 12 rounds for world championships. Toney led 105-103, and 106-102 (twice). Prince retired three fights later early in 1996 and works at youth center gyms in Mansfield, teaching kids to box.

Feldman was a *mensch.* After Prince and I split, he paid me 10 percent from his 10 percent trainer's fee. He did this, he said, because I had gotten him in as trainer. If Prince got $100,000 for a fight and Feldman's end was $10,000, he gave me $1,000. I mentioned this at his funeral in 2017 and his younger son, David, said he never knew. What other trainer would do that? Perhaps when he had taught me there is no such thing as 99 percent loyal, this was an example of what he meant.

Chapter Thirty-Nine

Casino Days Were Taxing

Live All The Action!

The Sands Hotel and Casino is Atlantic City's World Class Resort.

504 Luxurious Rooms and Suites • Complete Meeting and Convention Facilities • Exciting Casino Action • Big Name Entertainment
Superb Dining • Health Club • Pool • Championship 18 Hole Golf Course nearby • Special hotel package plans available.
For Information and Reservations call toll free (800) 257-8580. For special group rates call the Sands Sales Dept. at (609) 441-4150.

Artists Conception of Remodeling to be Completed in
Spring 1984

Sands
HOTEL & CASINO/ATLANTIC CITY
Indiana Ave. & Brighton Park
Atlantic City, NJ 08401

Promoting at casinos in Atlantic City came with problems. Once you did a certain dollar amount of business, you had to apply for a casino license. According to its website, the Casino Control Commission (CCC) "promotes public confidence and trust in the credibility and integrity of the gaming industry as an independent licensing authority." The Division of Gaming Enforcement (DGE), which investigates all license applicants, reports to the CCC, as does the New Jersey State Commission of Investigation (SCI), which investigated mob influence. Both groups looked into boxing in 1983. Once their interim report was published early in 1984, the DGE denied my application. My problem was taxes, not gangsters.

I appealed, and we went to court. I had just signed a two-year contract as the "in-house" promoter at the Sands, and the first of two $125,000 annual bonus payments was delayed, pending my license.

In New Jersey, promoters are taxed on tickets sold and television revenue, which—along with license fees from boxers, managers, trainers, matchmakers, promoters—funds the State Athletic Control Board. This also is true in Pennsylvania. (Philadelphia adds a city amusement tax on tickets sold).

Since nearly every casino boxing card in Atlantic City in the 1980s was televised—except for the weekly ones at the Tropicana—state tax on TV income was substantial. From 1977 thru 1983, Bob Lee had served as Deputy Commissioner, then Acting Commissioner. He'd told me I could deduct expenses for television production and pay the TV tax on the net. In court, he denied saying he gave me, or any promoter, that authority.

In June, 1986, the CCC voted 4-0-1 to overrule the DGE's denial of my license. I was free to do business with the casinos. According to the ruling, I had been misguided on the tax situation and that I actually had overpaid taxes by $77,000.

"We didn't contest any facts from the law judge," Carl Zeitz, a commissioner, who voted in my favor, told Dave Bontempo, of the *Atlantic City Press*. "We interpreted them differently. In my 15, 16 years at looking at state government, I've never seen anything like this. It was a tremendous bureaucratic screw-up. The individual (Peltz) was caught in the middle of it. The incompetent way the government dealt with him was more offensive than anything."

The ruling came one week before my Sands contract was due to expire and enabled me to pursue the $250,000 owed me. In court, the Sands' attorney argued that since my contract never had been fully executed, they did not have to pay me. The judge asked him if I had delivered monthly shows there for the last two years. Yes. He asked if they had paid me a monthly salary for last past two years. Yes. He asked if they had reimbursed me for expenses for the last two years. Yes.

There is a term in legalese known as *doing business*. Since the Sands hired me to promote fight cards for two years, paid me a salary for two years and had reimbursed me for two years, they had abided by the terms of the contract and that meant that the $250,000 bonus was part of that contract. The judge suggested they settle. I walked away with half the bonus money.

By 1986, things had begun to slow down in Atlantic City. Weekly cards at the Tropicana had boosted the resort.

"We ran at the Trop from late in 1981 until 1986," said Don Elbaum, the in-house promoter with Teddy Menas. "Then a new general manager came in and wanted to go in another direction—away from boxing—even after he saw that the Tuesday night casino 'drop' was triple what it was on Mondays and Wednesdays."

Boxing in AC went from a high of 144 cards in 1985—the last year the Trop ran weekly—to 80 the following year and to 48 in 1988.

I was busy at Resorts, the Sands and Harrah's Marina in the 1980s. ABC, CBS and NBC were frequent weekend visitors, especially during the 1982 NFL strike when they scrambled to fill weekend slots. The exposure Atlantic City casinos got in the early 1980s was crucial to their growth, but halfway through the decade oversaturation had taken its toll.

That same month I got my first show on USA Network from the Blue Horizon. Timing is everything!

Chapter Forty

Call from Dan Duva

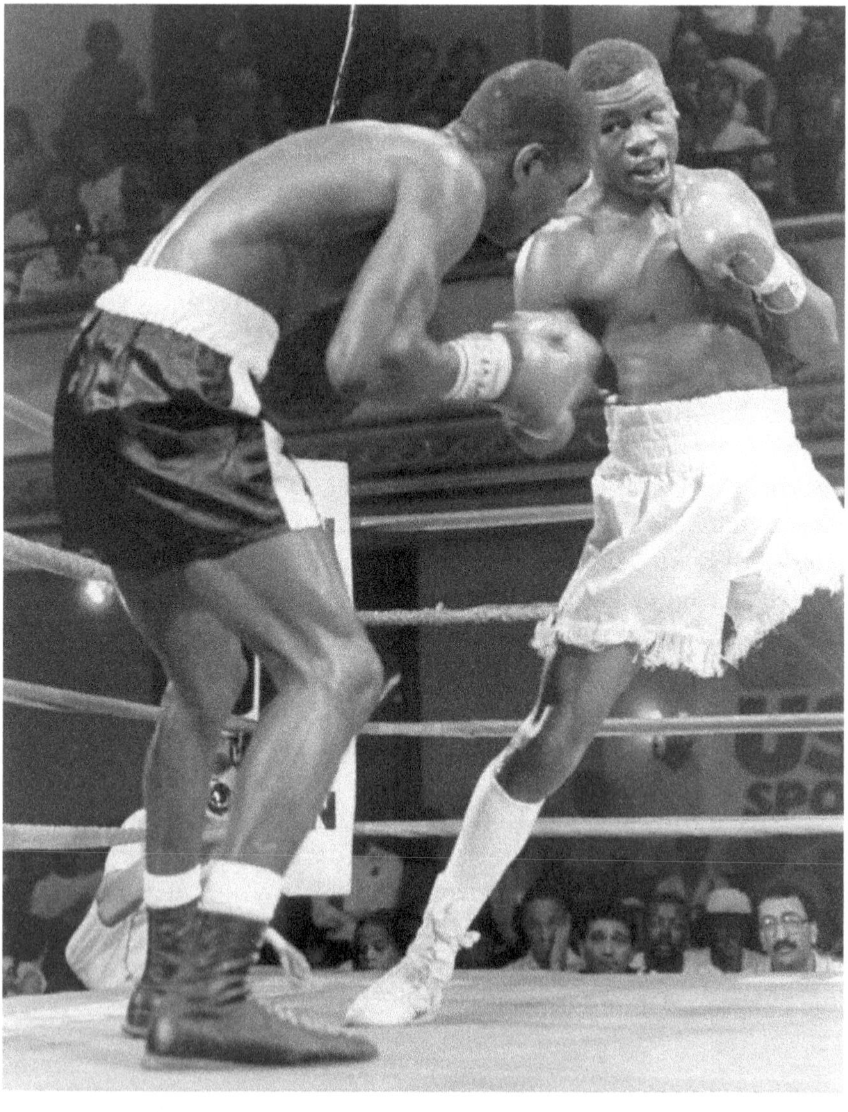

Buttons Kearney eyes Marvin McDowell in 1986. (Charles Baltimore photo)

Joe Verne promoted two cards in 1984 at Golden Eagle Caterers, then left boxing. Barry Shapiro, who was in the scrap metal business from South Philly, ran seven times at Champs Camp, a former bowling alley and miniature golf course on Frankford Avenue. Local headliners Rockin' Rodney Moore and Myron Taylor boxed on two of his cards. So did future IBF junior welterweight champion Joe Louis Manley. "Barry never made any money," said Lee Schley, matchmaker and manager. "We gave away a lot of tickets." With Joe Hand, Bob Connelly and Quentin Ellis in the mix, there were 29 cards in the Philadelphia area that year, the most since the 35 in 1962.

Harold Moore joined us in 1984 to help make undercards. We were running more than 30 shows a year. I don't know how we did it. We were in Atlantic City, at the Blue Horizon and other spots like the Zembo Mosque in Harrisburg or the Covered Wagon Inn in Wayne, Pennsylvania.

Moore had boxed professionally as a middleweight from 1948 thru 1951. The highlight of his 3-5-1 career was September 10, 1951, when he defeated Jimmy Franklin, of Reading, over six rounds at Shibe Park in front of 15,595 who had come to see Strawberry Mansion's unbeaten welterweight Gil Turner stop former world lightweight champion Ike Williams in the 10th round. Moore worked for Local 427 Streets Department, Sanitation Division. His mom nicknamed him "Spits" because, as a youngster, he spat when he spoke.

"Sanction fees for amateur boxing were expensive so Spits would get all the coaches together and he'd run 'gym workouts' at different gyms," said Anthony Boyle, a pro lightweight. "He would match fighters according to their ability and he made sure no one got hurt. If a fight got too rough, he would slow it down. He knew how to match amateurs before he got into matchmaking for pros. His goal was not so much about wins and losses but to make us better fighters."

Moore promoted seven times at the Blue Horizon between 1982 and 1983, including Bennie Briscoe's last fight, a 10-round loss to Jimmie Sykes, of West Philadelphia. Moore had worked with Ron Katz, matchmaker at Top Rank, and with promoters in Maryland. He convinced me to return to the Blue Horizon. Our March 6, 1984 card was my first there in three years. Local welterweights Jimmy Muse and Roberto Mendez headlined and 705 fans paid $7,050 ($10 a ticket). We lost $2,775.75 but we were back.

From then until mid-1986, we ran 26 boxing cards at the Blue Horizon—and lost money on each. The total deficit was $67,202.26 ($165,000 in 2021), an average of $2,584.70 per card. The only future world champion on those cards was Steve Little.

Despite losing to Hugh Kearney early in 1986 at the Blue Horizon for the Pennsylvania welterweight title, and to Robert Hines two years later in Atlantic City for the USBA junior middleweight crown, Little persevered and, in 1994, in England, upset Michael Nunn to win the WBA super middleweight title.

One of 18 children, Little grew up in Reading, 60 miles from Philly. He sold used cars to supplement his boxing income, or maybe it was the other way around. He died at 34 in 2000 from colon cancer, less than a year after he was diagnosed. He left behind his wife, Wanda, and six children ranging from 9 to 17.

Other fighters on those cards included heavyweight Jesse Ferguson, light-heavyweight Vaughn Hooks, middleweight Tony Thornton, junior welterweight Rodney Moore and Boyle. Ferguson, Thornton (three times) and Moore (three times) challenged for world titles, but came up short.

Despite box-office losses, Philadelphia again was becoming a boxing hub. Five of the cards drew more than 1,000 customers. The biggest crowd was February 19, 1985, when Troy Fletcher, of Southwest Philly, and Brian "Boogaloo" Jones, of North Philly, met for the vacant Pennsylvania bantamweight title. The place was packed, proving Jimmy Toppi's saying that "people will go up a blind alley to watch a fight if it is one they want to see."

Fletcher, youngest of the fighting Fletchers, was 23, and his record was 8-0-1, 2 K0s. Jones was 20 and he was 8-0, 2 K0s. When I went upstairs during the second or third prelim, it was hard to move because of the crowd. When I went back down, we still had tickets to sell and had not touched those for standing room. We couldn't figure it out until someone said a man was outside selling our $10 tickets for $5.

I sent Pat Doris, my office manager/vice president, out to buy one. It had the same number as the ticket of the guy who had told us about the scalper. Our tickets came from a cheap printing company and were easy to reproduce. I don't know how many people were in the building but our paid crowd was 1,201, our gate $12,010. We lost $1,497.54 despite having one of the biggest Blue Horizon crowds in years. If we had sold 150 of those counterfeit tickets we would have broken even.

Fletcher got off the floor to win a unanimous decision by scores of 55-54 (twice) and 58-52.

In 1980, professional boxing became one of the first major sports to get air time on cable television. ESPN's weekly series had given Bob Arum a head start on developing fighters who could move on to bigger fights on bigger networks. On October 1, 1982, USA Network jumped in. Though it became better known as USA's *Tuesday Night Fights*, it televised fights on Wednesdays and Fridays in the early years.

Dan Duva, who had a law degree from Seton Hall, was one of three promoters who had a contract with USA. Duva, one of ESPN's four original on-site promoters working with Arum in 1980, was chosen by Sugar Ray Leonard's advisor, Mike Trainer, to promote the 1981 welterweight unification fight between Leonard and Thomas Hearns in Las Vegas.

Duva had a USA date on June 25, 1986, but was busy in court and his company, Main Events, was working on other promotions. He asked me to take the date, a Wednesday, on tape delay, and he gave me the $2,000 rights fee. This would be the first nationally televised fight from the Blue Horizon since 1964 when ABC televised Kitten Hayward's knockout of Curtis Cokes. The call from Duva would impact my business for the rest of the century. Just as Atlantic City was slowing down, this propped me up. Again, timing is everything!

Johnny Carter had won eight of nine since losing to Jeff Chandler in 1982. He was a contender at super bantamweight and I matched him with Juan Veloz, a Puerto Rican living in New York City. Carter was 31-3, 20 K0s. Veloz, who had lost two in a row and had not boxed in a year, was 9-6-2, 1 K0. It didn't look like much on paper, but Carter tired down the stretch and lost a 10-round split decision.

USA's announcers were Al Albert and Randy Gordon. Albert described the Blue Horizon as "everybody's old-time boxing movie." He compared it to Ebbets Field and the Polo Grounds, "except that the Blue Horizon is still standing."

In the six-round super bantamweight TV opener, John Farina, who worked as a bartender in suburban Ardmore, boxed Keith Jenkins, of North Philadelphia. Farina was 5-0-2, 1 K0. Jenkins was 0-7-1, had been stopped four times, and had lost twice to Farina on points. The TV screen showed—and the announcers claimed—that Jenkins had one win, but that was incorrect. Promoters tend to fib a little. Gordon complimented me during the telecast for making a competitive match and not being a slave to fight-by-fight records. Farina won by decision and the fight got a standing ovation.

When I watched it again doing research for this book, I got chills, knowing the TV exposure had put the Blue Horizon on the map. We drew 922 customers and lost $2,700, but USA executives were watching and liked what they saw.

Duva gave me another slot in July. The rights fee was $3,000 this time and he kept $1,000. Kelvin Kelly and Lionel Byarm met for the vacant Pennsylvania light-heavyweight title, which Kelly won with a unanimous 12-round decision. Kelly and Byarm were paid $1,500 each and, despite virtually no pre-fight publicity in the newspapers, the crowd was 1,155 and we made $1,209.57, my first Blue Horizon profit in nine years.

We were hustling by word-of-mouth, ads in the *Daily News* and a mailing list. Maureen Sacks, who replaced Pat Doris in 1986, would reduce the 22x28 old-time posters to postcard size and bulk-mail them to over 3,000 people. Maureen also handled bookkeeping, ticket sales and insurance policies. She paid the fighters and worked the box office the night of each fight. She was calm and professional. For her, it must have been like being in the eye of a hurricane. I met her in 1972 when we both worked at the Spectrum and she came to work with me on a part-time basis in 1983, full time from 1984 until 2014.

I did another USA card December 9, my 40th birthday, when Marvin Garris defended his Pennsylvania lightweight championship by stopping Anthony Williams on cuts in the seventh round. I lost $2.54, but got to watch the delayed telecast on New Year's Eve, celebrating because I had given USA three solid cards in a great atmosphere and hoped to get my own deal. I did.

Rob Correa, vice president for Entertainment and Sports Programming, made the Blue Horizon a regular stop for live USA boxing, beginning March 31, 1987. Robert Hines K0d Ismael Negron, of Newark, New Jersey, in seven rounds. A crowd of 1,230 paid $13,196. USA paid $6,500 and Italian television chipped in $1,000. We had income from program sales, program ads and Blue Horizon T-shirts. Our profit was $4,974.23 ($12,500.00 in 2021), the most I had made at the Blue Horizon.

I promoted 10 fights at the Blue Horizon that year, seven on USA. We lost money on the three non-televised cards and three USA cards, but bigger crowds, bigger gates and bigger rights fees were ahead.

People who had heard or read about the Blue Horizon were getting an up-close-and-personal look at the storied building. Television exposure would turn the Blue Horizon into the hottest fight club in the country.

When I had promoted there from 1969 to 1971, ringside seats were reserved and the balcony was general admission. This time, everything was general admission, first-come, first-served. We started at $10 in advance, $12 at the door, increased to $11 and $13, and kept going.

When Vaughn Hooks took Kelly's state title by stopping him in six rounds on October 1, 1987, we sold 1,499 tickets. It was the largest Blue Horizon crowd since opening night in 1969 and one of the Top 5 ever. Hooks and Kelly each were paid $2,923.31, based on 20 percent of the $17,119.00 gate after taxes. Our profit was $3,267.31.

"At 6 pm on fight night, the building came alive," said Sean O'Grady, the ex-WBA lightweight champion who replaced Gordon as USA analyst in 1987. "Fans gathered in front and talked boxing. It was their version of tailgating. When the doors opened, it sounded like a train was approaching as fans rushed, pushed and jockeyed for position to get the first few seats in the balcony. Those coveted seats were only five feet from the ring post, where the fans felt like they were a part of the action. You could see, sense and smell every punch."

Hugh "Buttons" Kearney was a Blue Horizon regular. When he was born, his mother said he had a nose like a button. He had gone to West Philly High and had won 103 out of 110 amateur fights. After Kearney's fourth pro fight, Raymond Munson, who had been close with Sonny Liston, introduced Kearney to "Nick" Nichols, who owned the 421 Club at 56th and Wyalusing.

"I had signed a contract with Jimmy Beecham and Marty Feldman and they didn't pay me anything at the time, but they said if I was dissatisfied I could get out of the contract," Buttons said. "When Mister Nichols came along they said I misunderstood them and they got Nichols to pay them $10,000 to release me."

A 1990 Pennsylvania Crime Commission report described James Walton Nichols as "the largest Black numbers operative in the city of Philadelphia, with a territory covering West Philadelphia and parts of Southwest Philadelphia. At its peak in the mid-1980s, Nichols' operation grossed between $8 and $10 million annually and employed over 40 numbers writers."

"I didn't know anything about him, only that he owned some bars and some clubs," Buttons said. "Nichols didn't know much about boxing, but he had a lot of money and people with a lot of money could get things done in boxing. I figured he could move my career along and that's why I signed with him."

Buttons boxed from 1983 through 1988. All of his 21 fights were in Philadelphia or Atlantic City—12 at the Blue Horizon—five televised by USA. By the end of 1987, he was 17-0-1.

He was to box Juan Rondon, of Venezuela, on April 28, 1988, at the Blue Horizon, but Rondon canceled a week before and booking agent Johnny Bos got me Jorge Maysonet, a Puerto Rican living in the Bronx. Maysonet was 15-2, 15 K0s. The night before the fight, Bos predicted that "the first time Maysonet hits him (Kearney), the fight is over."

That "hit," a straight right hand eight seconds after the opening bell, left Buttons stiff as starch. Maysonet followed with a straight left and Buttons went out in 20 seconds.

"I had seen some video on Maysonet and even though he had a lot of knockouts he didn't look like a big puncher to me," Buttons said. "A lot of people told me not to take the fight. I thought I could outbox him but I got caught before I had a chance to warm up. After the fight I felt kind of down in the dressing room. Mitch Allen was screaming at Munson for making us take the fight. Mitch had replaced Jimmy Beecham as my trainer and he was not happy. I figured I would have to start over and get back to where I was."

Buttons won his next fight but future IBF junior middleweight champion Vincent Pettway ended his career October 6, stopping him in two rounds at Pennsylvania Hall.

"I knew Pettway could punch, but he had been knocked out by a guy I had beaten (George Leach)," Buttons said. "The morning of the fight, after breakfast, I threw up right in the middle of the street and a friend of mine wanted us to call Nichols and tell him to call you (Russell) and let you know I wasn't feeling well. I told them not to, even though I threw up again later. I thought I would be ok by that evening. I should have boxed Pettway but I decided to go after him, fight him toe-to-toe and that was a mistake. I was 23 and I decided to retire.

"It didn't seem like anyone was looking out for my best interests. Nichols was paying me $300 a week while I was fighting so I didn't have to work but he didn't know much about the business and I didn't think you (Russell) were looking out for me. We didn't have a contract but you were promoting my fights and I felt if you were going to put me into those kinds of fights, well, I just thought I needed better guidance. So I quit. I never heard from Nichols after that."

Buttons had odd jobs for three years before going to work for SEPTA (Southeastern Pennsylvania Transportation Authority). Frank Friel, his cut man and assistant trainer, had gotten Kearney a job with SEPTA in 1983, but Beecham had asked him to quit so he could concentrate on boxing.

"I was cleaning buses and working the fuel lanes when I first worked there," Buttons said. "I was filling up the buses with gas and sending them back out on the street. When I went back in 1991, I did whatever they asked me to do. I retired from SEPTA in 2013 with a pension and now I'm working for First Transit at Philadelphia International Airport, driving buses back and forth from the employees lot to the terminal.

"My wife and I live in Elkton, Maryland. I have five sons. Boxing made me the man I am today. Being responsible, fighting for and taking care of my loved ones and challenging anything in my path that's wrong. It's much like life. If you slip some you're gonna get hit some. I did not win the world title I chased but through it all people still remember my face."

Maysonet parlayed three more wins at the Blue Horizon into a title fight with IBF welterweight champion Simon Brown early in 1980 in Budapest, Hungary. He was stopped in three rounds. It was the first world championship fight behind the Iron Curtain and Laszlo Papp attended.

Papp had won Olympic gold medals in 1948 in London, 1952 in Helsinki, and 1956 in Melbourne. He beat future Hall-of-Famer Jose Torres in the 1956 junior middleweight final and boxed professionally from 1957 to 1964. He won the European middleweight title and was unbeaten in 29 fights. Negotiations were underway for a shot at Joey Giardello's world title in 1964 when the Hungarian government revoked his exit visa, claiming professional boxing was not permitted in Communist Hungary and Papp was avoiding the issue by fighting in Austria, Germany, France, Demark and Spain. He never boxed again.

North Philly light-heavyweight Andre "Thee" Prophet turned pro at 19 in 1987 and had 13 fights in 12 months, 10 at the Blue Horizon. He was 12-0-1, 11 K0s. He was 6-foot-2 with an 80-inch reach. When I watched him spar IBF champion Prince Charles Williams it was like watching a real fight.

"He was a big, strong kid," Prince Charles said. "I think he had a good shot to win the title." Nigel Collins, editor-in-chief of *The Ring* magazine, said, "It looks like you've finally found a puncher who can put people in the seats."

Prophet was trained by Dwight Triplett and George Benton. He outgrew the light-heavyweight division and manager Scott Kendall thought the heavyweight division and Mike Tyson were in the future, but at 5:20 am on August 13, 1988, Prophet and 18-year-old Tres Kelly were killed when their motorcycle was struck by a hit-

and-run driver at 22nd and York in North Philly. Prophet left behind a son and a daughter. Prophet was 20.

It was Philly boxing's second motorcycle death in two years. Two-time National Golden Gloves champion James Shuler was killed March 20, 1986, when his motorcycle collided with a tractor-trailer at 11th and Wallace. Shuler had bought the motorcycle that day with some of the $250,000 he had earned 10 days before, fighting Thomas Hearms, his first loss as a pro after 22 wins. Hearns offered to place the NABF belt he had won from Shuler in the casket, but Shuler's family declined, saying Hearns had earned it in the ring. Shuler was 26.

Chapter Forty-One
Freddy J

Choo Choo Brown and Fred Jenkins in 1984. (Peltz collection)

Champs Gym and the 23rd PAL produced a lot of talented fighters in the 1960s and 1970s. The Cloverlay Gym on North Broad Street, later known as the Joe Frazier Gym, took over in the mid-1970s. Another gym in North Philly, the Athletic Recreation Center at 26th and Master, operated under the radar. I first became aware of the Rec in 1975 when Smokin' Wade Hinnant turned pro.

Fred Jenkins ran the Rec. He was called "Herk" because, like Hercules, he was the strongest—and he says meanest—kid in the neighborhood.

"I worked at a grocery store at 26th and Girard when I was 12," Jenkins said. "Things were slow one day so I went to another store at 28th and Girard. When I got there, I saw this guy grab an old lady's pocketbook. I chased him but I couldn't catch him and I fell.

"Someone called the cops and they grabbed me, thinking I was the guy who took her pocketbook. I told them they had the wrong guy. I didn't have the pocketbook but they grabbed me anyway. They found the old lady and she said I wasn't the one but the cops told her I *was* the guy. They kept insisting it was me so she finally agreed.

"They sent me to Glen Mills because I had gotten into trouble a few times before. I got out when I was 15 and they put me on extensive probation. I had to report once a week. I went to Overbrook High School in West Philly and my first class was at 7.15 in the morning. I had to leave my house at 6 and take two buses to get there on time. If I cut school, they were gonna to send me back to Glen Mills."

Jenkins gravitated to the Rec in 10th grade. Stan Williams, who later trained WBA cruiserweight champ Nate Miller, trained him. Jenkins had 20 amateur fights and turned pro in 1974, the year he graduated from Overbrook. He debuted as a junior middleweight, against another newcomer, Moses Robinson, on November 11 at the Blue Horizon. At the weigh-in, Jenkins decided not to fight.

"I found out that morning that Moses had been in the service," Jenkins said. "He was a good guy and I only wanted to fight bad guys."

Jenkins sat at a desk in the commission office while I pleaded on one side of him and Nigel Collins, his manager, on the other.

Williams finally convinced him to fight and Jenkins knocked out Robinson in less than two minutes.

"I was living in Camden when I fought Fred," Robinson said. "My father was in the service and I was born at Fort Sill in Oklahoma where he was stationed. I enlisted in the Army and I went to Vietnam when I was 18. I was there for 11 months, 25 days, until I got wounded—my hand—at Pleiku. I came home and eventually got a job with Penn Central (railroad) as a mechanics helper. I stayed there for 34 years and retired in 2008."

Robinson was a better trainer than fighter. His prize pupil was southpaw light-heavyweight Eric Harding, who beat world champions Montell Griffin and Antonio Tarver and lost to another, Roy Jones Jr.

Three months after beating Robinson, Jenkins boxed Tyrone Freeman at the Spectrum. Freeman had won only three of 13 fights, but Jenkins wasn't throwing many punches and I couldn't understand why. Neither could Nigel, who was covering for *The Ring* magazine. After the fourth round, Nigel climbed into the corner to prod Jenkins, but nothing worked and Jenkins lost on points. It was the last fight Freeman won. He boxed two draws and lost 11 times in his next 13 fights and quit in 1981.

"When I was a little kid, I had this friend named Tyrone," Jenkins said. "We hung out together. He taught me how to shine shoes and we went *paper junkin'* together. We'd collect paper on the street and bundle it up and take it to the junk yard. We'd get 25 cents a pound, sometimes less.

"One day when I was 6, the gate to the swimming pool at the Rec was open and I jumped in the water, but I couldn't swim. Tyrone ran after me and pulled me out. As soon as my feet hit the ground, I ran home. I never knew his last name. So when I got to the weigh-in and saw it was the same Tyrone, how could I hit him? He saved my life."

Jenkins retired after one more fight and began training fighters. He managed and trained Charlie "Choo Choo" Brown, the first world champ from the Rec.

"Charlie Brown had all the talent in the world, but the streets ate him alive," said Al Mitchell, who worked with Jenkins in the 1980s and later moved to Michigan and coached three U.S. Olympic teams. "Choo Choo was a real Philly fighter but he loved the girls and he loved to drink. The same thing happened to Jerome Jackson. He couldn't survive the streets."

By the time he was 20, Jackson had beaten two middleweight contenders, Teddy Mann and Gary Guiden, and had lost to two others, Sammy Nesmith and Wilford Scypion. "He had a kidney transplant when he was in his 30s," Jenkins said. "That's what did him in." Jackson passed away at age 55.

"The Rec wasn't in the best neighborhood, but it was a refuge for some of the kids," Mitchell said. "We tried to show them what was right and what was wrong. It kept them off the streets for a while. So many talented kids came through our gym. Brian Jones and Andre Sharpe Richardson could have made it big, but they got locked up. There was only so much you could do. We lost so many guys to drugs or gang wars. It was rare to find guys like Marvin Garris and Rodney Moore who survived the street life."

Garris was the Pennsylvania lightweight champion in the mid-1980s. His 15-9-1 record looks more impressive when you see the list of world champs and contenders he faced: Fred Pendleton; Sammy Fuentes; Lester Ellis; Roger Mayweather; Gert Bo Jacobsen, and Micky Ward.

"I had both my parents and they were strict," Garris said. "I had a full-time job when I was fighting, part owner of a paper recycling company. Rodney worked, too. He was a disc jockey and worked for Home Depot. Maybe that's what kept us out of trouble."

Moore was a study in determination. He turned pro in 1983 and waited 10 years for a title shot. He was 2-3 before he turned things around and won 33 of his next 37. Moore was known as the *King of the Blue Horizon*, where he boxed 22 times. His breakout win came in 1992 when he knocked out Sammy Fuentes, of Puerto Rico, in two rounds on USA Network. Fuentes had lasted nearly 10 against Julio Cesar Chavez seven months earlier in Las Vegas for Chavez' WBC junior welterweight title.

"Something just clicked on inside me," Moore told Mark Kram, Jr., of the *Daily News*. "I just decided that this is what I wanted in life and I started chasing it. Getting as close (to a title shot) is like a dream."

It was still two years away. Moore's unbeaten streak reached 20 when he got off the floor twice in the first round to win a 10-round split decision over Tony Baltazar, of Los Angeles, at Pennsylvania Hall. Lynn Carter scored it 94-93 for Baltazar, but judges George

Hill (97-91) and Ron Greenley (96-91) gave it to Moore, now ranked No 3 (WBA), No. 4 (IBF) and No. 7 (WBC).

Moore's streak ended five months later when Ramon Zavala, a Venezuelan with a 13-7 record, upset him in 10 rounds at the Blue Horizon. Guy Richardson had it 98-92 for Moore, but judges Bill Nealon and Tommy Reid scored 96-95 for Zavala.

Moore rebounded with a second-round knockout of Louie Lomeli and signed to fight ex-WBA lightweight champion Livingstone Bramble on January 26, 1993, at the Blue Horizon. For the first time, the Blue Horizon sold out ahead of time. Tickets were $17 in advance, $20 at the door, but none were available that night. We experimented with reserved ringside seats, making the first five rows *Golden Ringside,* and charged $30. We piped the telecast in on a big screen in the downstairs ballroom and charged $10 a ticket to about 25 customers.

More than a few people came that night for the pro debut of featherweight Mike Rafferty, whose dad, Fran, was a polarizing figure on Philadelphia's City Council. The elder Rafferty, a former amateur boxer and Army veteran, twice got into fistfights with community activist Milton Street over whether or not Mayor Frank Rizzo should be allowed to seek a third term.

The younger Rafferty stopped Joey Intrieri, of South Philly, in two rounds. Intrieri later became known as Joey Eye, one of the best cut men in boxing.

Bramble was 32. It had been seven years since his championship days, but he had won three of his last four and was still a big name. Moore won 98-93, 98-92, 99-93. The USA rights fee, ticket sales, program income and minor sponsorships brought in $63,097. Our profit was $11,390.82 after we paid Bramble $12,000 and Moore $6,000.

Four months later, Moore boxed Charles "The Natural" Murray, of Rochester, New York, for the IBF belt vacated by Pernell Whitaker, who'd moved up in weight. Murray, promoted by Top Rank, was 28-1. Cedric Kushner and I ran the card at Trump Castle in Atlantic City with a small overseas television hookup.

"This is the most important fight of my career," Moore told Robert Seltzer of the *Inquirer.* "When I see people who knew me in the early days, they say, 'Man, I can't believe you stuck with it and got a title shot.' Well, I look in the mirror and I can't believe it, either."

Moore also was insightful about his future. "He (Murray) came out of the amateurs with the red carpet rolled out for him, with the backing of a big-time promoter (Bob Arum)," he told Bernard Fernandez, of the *Daily News*. "He had every advantage. Even if he loses he's not going to be too far away because of the connections he has. Now, if I lose, I'll be buried. I don't know how long it will be, if ever, before I get another chance. That's why I'll be fighting like my whole career is on the line. I'm going to be like a hungry lion that's been let out of its cage."

Fred Jenkins was an early believer in Moore: "You could see Rodney had talent, but he really didn't go all out when he fought. He was the kind of kid who wasn't a born fighter. He would have to be a *made* fighter. (After 15 amateur fights) I told him not to turn pro so soon, but he was in a hurry. He wanted to be a neighborhood hero."

Moore abandoned his body attack midway through the fight and Murray took the unanimous decision, 115-113, 116-112 and 118-110. Each fighter got $50,000.

Moore never boxed for me again. He took an advance on a fight Mike Acri, a promoter from Erie, Pennsylvania, and I had lined up for him and disappeared. One day I got a phone call from ex-pro Dorsey Lay, who told me Moore had signed with Don King. Lay felt badly but knew the business. Blinky Palermo had managed him.

This may have been the first time—in my experience— when a fighter began to manage the manager, especially when there was no written contract between them. It would not be the last. Jenkins stayed with Moore, who won five out of seven fights with King, both losses coming in world title fights. He was K0d by Frankie Randall in 1994 and Felix Trinidad in 1996. I was at the Trinidad fight in Las Vegas. Moore reportedly got $140,000. When I woke up the next morning, Jenkins had slipped an envelope with $5000 in cash under my hotel room door.

"When people help you out you can't forget them," Jenkins said. "Everything isn't perfect but you have to respect the fact that you got some help. In order for Rodney Moore to be Rodney Moore, he needed all those fights you gave him at the Blue Horizon and Atlantic City. That's how he got the fight with Trinidad."

Moore was 32 when he retired in 1997.

Jenkins continued to manage and train fighters, including stints with welterweight David Reid, lightweight Zahir Raheem and heavyweight Malik Scott. He transformed Bryant Jennings from a basketball and football player into an unbeaten heavyweight contender. Jennings was 19-0, 9 K0s, and lost a competitive 12-round decision to Wladimir Klitschko for the WBA/WBO/IBF title in 2015. But Jenkins had no written contract and Jennings signed with a a new manager, new trainer and went 5-3. Jenkins also trained Jesse Hart, two-time world-title challenger at 168 pounds and son of Cyclone Hart.

In 2017, when our first-born son, Matthew, passed away at 38, a victim of the opioid crisis, Jenkins was the only boxing person we asked to be a pallbearer at the funeral. (Marty Feldman had died four months prior). Jenkins had known Matthew since he was born and had accompanied Linda and me to central Jersey two years earlier to pick him up from the police station after his car had hit a tractor while he was high on drugs. When I asked Jenkins why he had made himself available on short notice so late at night, he said, “How could I not?”

Chapter Forty-Two

Punching Postman

Ref Joe Cortez pulls Tony Thornton off Karama Leotis in 1990. (Peltz collection)

Tony Thornton was a good fighter and a better person. We got along because he was outgoing, which I wasn't, and we shared the same sense of humor—dry and needling. The first time we spoke was after his 20-second pro debut on June 15, 1983, at the Playboy Casino. He came to the office where we were paying the fighters and bragged about all the people who bought tickets to see him. He acted as if we had known each other for years.

Thornton won NCAA boxing championships in 1979 and 1980 at West Chester State College, outside Philly. Joe Gramby managed him. I never had a promotional contract and Gramby's contract with

Thornton had run out in the late 1980s. Gramby was 78 when he died on February 19, 1991. Thornton had moved from middleweight (160 pounds) to super middleweight (168). He was 31 with a record of 26-4-1, 21 K0s, and ranked in the Top 10. Two of his losses had been to future world champions Doug DeWitt and Steve Collins.

The day of Gramby's funeral, Thornton drove to my office from his home in Glassboro, New Jersey. He asked me how I wanted to handle his career. His purses had been between $7,500 and $10,000.

"'I'll manage and promote you for 10 percent," I said.

"Sounds good to me," he said. We shook hands and he left.

Then I thought about the deal. I was going to be manager *and* promoter for 10 percent. I called him.

"What's up, boss?" he said.

"Tony, I think I sold myself short," I said.

"I think you did, too. Whaddya think is fair?"

"Twenty percent."

"Fine with me!"

That phone call was our contract. After 50 years in boxing, it's a struggle to name a handful of fighters who would have responded that way.

Thornton's next fight was May 16 for Top Rank at Harrah's Marina against Merqui Sosa, whose only loss in 20 fights had been a 12-round split decision to James Toney. Thornton hurt his right hand—a career-long problem—but earned a 10-round split decision (97-94, 94-96, 96-94). Three wins later he was ranked by everyone from No. 1 to No. 4. In the fall of 1992, we flew to Glasgow, Scotland, to fight Chris Eubank for his WBO world super middleweight title.

I went with Dr. Frank B. Doggett, chief physician for the New Jersey State Athletic Control Board. Thornton had brittle hands and a sore shoulder and he paid Dr. Doggett's way. Thornton was a full-time mailman, and the weight of the mail bag on his shoulder didn't help.

The 26-year-old Eubank wore a bowler hat, riding boots, and carried a silver-tipped cane. He was 32-0, 18 K0s, and part of a group of world-class middleweights and super middleweights from England and Ireland, which included Nigel Benn, Michael Watson and Steve Collins, and later, Joe Calzaghe.

When Thornton entered the ring, he took off his robe to reveal the plaid Scottish kilts he wore over his trunks. He removed them before the bell rang. Eubank entered to Tina Turner's *Simply the Best.* A near capacity crowd of 10,000 filled the Scottish Exhibition Centre. The atmosphere was electric. It was all you could ask for in big-time boxing.

Nick Halling, reporting for Britain's *Independent* newspaper, wrote that "the flamboyant champion seemed flattered by verdicts of 117-112, 116-113, and 115-113. Most ringside observers had little more than a round separating them, with some giving the edge to Thornton. The judges saw it differently, giving the American scant credit for a wholehearted performance which forced Eubank to concentrate for the full 12 rounds."

When promoter Barry Hearn's paymaster came to the dressing room, Thornton told him, "Give the money to Russell," a rare expression of a fighter's trust. Thornton had pissed before a commissioner came for a urine sample. Two hours later, when Thornton still couldn't piss, the commission accepted a letter from Dr. Doggett on Thornton's behalf and we left. It was an expression of trust I may or may not have shared.

Four wins later—the biggest over future world-title challenger John Scully at the Blue Horizon—Thornton was in Tulsa, Oklahoma, late in 1993, challenging James Toney for the IBF version of the 168-pound title. In the main event, Michael Bentt knocked out Tommy Morrison in the first round for the WBO heavyweight title.

Toney was one of the best of his generation. He boxed professionally from 1988 to 2017, middleweight through heavyweight. He had a "tough guy" persona. A high school football star, he turned down a college scholarship because, he said, he didn't take orders well. He won 116-112 and 118-110 twice, but said Thornton was so nice he couldn't generate any animosity toward him.

After that, I stopped hearing from Thornton. I never believed in pushing a fighter into the gym. If you had to, something was missing. In the fall of 1994, Thornton called and said two Philadelphia attorneys wanted to manage him. They told him I had run out of "juice." I told Thornton to get $5,000 for himself—

nothing for me—and I would walk away. When they refused, I told him $2,500. Again they refused.

So I matched Thornton with Lenzie Morgan late in 1994 at the Blue Horizon. Morgan was from West Virginia—not a boxing stronghold—and his 12-12-2 record included five knockout wins, two knockout losses. Thornton was out of sync, the fight was terrible and he was lucky to win a split decision. Scores were all over the place: 100-90 and 97-93 for Thornton, 96-94 for Morgan.

Six weeks later, Thornton was back against Daren Zenner, a Canadian living in Port Chester, New York, for the vacant USBA super middleweight title. The Blue Horizon was in the middle of six-year run of consecutive sellouts and fans complained about having to watch Thornton again after the Morgan fight. Zenner was 14-1-2, had knocked out four straight, and had lost only on points to future WBA light-heavyweight champ Lou Del Valle.

Thornton looked terrific. He knocked Zenner down with a left hook and stopped him at 2:49 of the second round. He moved into the No. 1 mandatory challenger spot for IBF champion Roy Jones, who had won the title from Toney the year before. They met September 30, 1995, at the Civic Center in Pensacola, Florida. Two weeks prior, Thornton had injured his left shoulder but no way was he walking away from a career-high $250,000 purse ($445,000 in 2021).

I was promoting a card that week in Atlantic City so I sent Linda ahead with Thornton, trainer Wesley Mouzon, cut man Leon Tabbs and Thornton's dad. Linda said the sight of a White woman having breakfast with four Black men drew stares in Pensacola. Jones was a 30-to-1 favorite. At the pre-fight meeting with HBO, analyst George Foreman asked Thornton how he planned to beat Roy Jones. "You tell me," Thornton said.

On his way to the Civic Center for the fight, Thornton looked like a man on the way to a party he didn't want to attend. He made Jones miss a lot, but he couldn't sustain an attack. Jones was too quick and too good and he knocked Thornton down with a wide left hook just as the bell rang to end the second round. Early in the third, Jones landed a right and trapped Thornton in a neutral corner, unloading a slew of medium-to-hard punches, many landing on gloves or shoulders or arms. Referee Brian Gary told Thornton to fire back, but his shoulder hurt and he couldn't. Gary stopped it after 45 seconds.

Thornton never boxed again. He was almost 36 and his 37-7-1 record included 26 knockouts. I thought about those two lawyers who wouldn't pay $2,500 to manage him. They would have had a nice return on their investment.

We stayed in touch. Every time he came to my office, he'd ask why there were no pictures of him—or posters from his fights—on the walls. He took a boxing card of himself to a trophy dealer and had it placed inside a piece of Lucite on a wooden plaque, with his name inscribed, and gave it to me.

Thornton eventually became a customer-service supervisor at the Bellmawr (New Jersey) Post Office. On August 30, 2009, he was killed when his motorcycle was hit by a bus as he crossed the Ben Franklin Bridge from Philadelphia into New Jersey. He left behind daughter Ashley and Tony, Jr. He was 49. I miss him!

Chapter Forty-Three
Away from Home

Glenwood Brown (left) gave Meldrick Taylor fits. (Hinda Schuman photo)

When ESPN began televising weekly cards in 1980, they originated from Las Vegas, Atlantic City, Chicago and Totowa, New Jersey. The Atlantic City and Las Vegas cards were from casinos, Totowa and Chicago from arenas. By the end of the '80s, 10 more Atlantic City casinos would bid for fights. In the 1990s, Foxwoods, in Ledyard, Connecticut, led the next wave into boxing, along with the South. Until television discovered the Blue Horizon in 1986, the best local talent went on the road. Out-of-town promoters swooped in to sign Philly guys as they did in other cities. You could watch a fighter from Boston box one from Dallas in a casino in Mississippi—not the best way to develop a hometown following.

Dan Duva signed the best of the 1984 US Olympic boxing team—Tyrell Biggs, Meldrick Taylor, Mark Breland, Pernell Whitaker and Evander Holyfield. Biggs and Taylor were from Philly. Biggs, the heavyweight gold medalist, won 30 out of 40 pro fights, but never boxed here. He was 15-0 when Mike Tyson KOd him in seven rounds for the world title in 1987 in Atlantic City. Biggs lost nine of his last 24 and retired in 1998.

It took five years and 23 fights before Taylor, the featherweight gold medalist, boxed in Philly. As IBF junior welterweight champ, he met Jaime Balboa, of Mexico, in a non-title fight. Balboa was 42-9 and was chosen for his "Rocky" surname, but he pulled no upset. He lasted until the fifth round, but only 1,827 came to Pennsylvania Hall for what we billed as *The Homecoming.*

Taylor had won 25 in a row when he met WBC champion Julio Cesar Chavez in a title unification in 1990 in Las Vegas. In one of boxing's most controversial endings—with two seconds left in the 12th round—Taylor got up from a knockdown, but looked at his corner instead of referee Richard Steele, so Steele stopped it. Taylor led on two scorecards (107-102, 108-101) and trailed on the third (104-105).

Taylor won the WBA welterweight title in 1991, and defended in Philly early in 1992, surviving two knockdowns to outpoint Glenwood Brown, of Plainfield, New Jersey, at SRO (3,200) Pennsylvania Hall. As a fading ex-champ in 1996, he made the last Philly appearance of his 47-fight career, losing a 10-round split decision to Darren Maciunski on a Bob Connelly-promoted card in the less-than-full Blue Horizon.

It was the same with the other Olympians. Breland, welterweight gold medalist, who was from New York, had three of his 39 fights there. Whitaker, lightweight gold medalist, was the busiest at home, with 14 of his 45 fights in Virginia—10 in Norfolk, two each in Virginia Beach and Hampton. Holyfield, light-heavyweight bronze medalist, boxed four times in his Atlanta hometown out of 56 pro fights.

"Breland fought on undercards in New York a few times early in his career, but he really did not move the box office," said Kathy Duva, wife of Dan Duva and a Hall-of-Fame promoter herself. "His early fights were grouped with the other Olympians as part of the deals with ABC and USA. New York was prohibitively expensive.

Dan saw Atlantic City as an extension of the New York market. He tried putting Mark in Northern New Jersey, Brooklyn and South Carolina, where Mark's family originated, but couldn't make any of those options work financially.

"Whitaker was selling out in Virginia and Dan concluded that secondary markets work better than big cities where costs were much higher and media attention more difficult to come by. Atlanta was different. We couldn't sell tickets there for Holyfield, despite help from local businesses. It was a tough place to market."

Two of Holyfield's most memorable fights were at the Omni in Atlanta. The first was his 15-round split decision over Dwight Qawi for the WBA cruiserweight title in 1986. Qawi had lost to Michael Spinks in a light-heavyweight unification (WBC/WBA) fight in 1983, but moved up to claim the cruiserweight belt in 1985.

After Holyfield won the world heavyweight title from Buster Douglas in 1990, I got an assist for his 1991 defense. He was to fight Francesco Damiani, of Italy, and HBO would televise. Holyfield held the WBA, WBC and IBF versions. Damiani, the ex-WBO heavyweight champion, wasn't given much respect. Few paid attention to the WBO, fewer to its ex-heavyweight champion.

Around two weeks before the fight, I got a call from Dan Duva. He was concerned that Damiani, complaining of a foot injury, would pull out, and asked me to get the erratic, but dangerous, Bert Cooper, as a replacement. I did nothing for several days, but after hearing more rumors about Damiani, I called Rick Parker, who handled Cooper. I made him an offer and put him in touch with Duva.

Damiami canceled and Cooper was *thisclose* to knocking Holyfield out in the third round, which would have set the boxing world on its ear. Holyfield rallied to win in seven. Newspaper accounts say Cooper got $750,000, more than my offer. A few days later, Dino Duva, Dan's brother, sent me a $5,000 check. I thought it would have been more, but, then, all I'd done was make a phone call, start the dialogue, and put the two sides together.

A few weeks later, Dan was in Philly for a pre-fight press conference for the Taylor-Brown fight. We had breakfast at the Franklin Plaza Hotel.

"Did you get a check from Dino for the Cooper fight?" he asked.

"Yes," I said.

"How much was it for?"

"Five thousand."

"Really? I'm going to tell Dino to send you another check for $5,000."

That's the kind of guy Dan Duva was.

"We didn't make any real money on the fight," Kathy Duva said. "We did it to get everyone paid—including Evander—so that we could all recoup what we had already laid out in anticipation of the (Mike) Tyson fight, which had been cancelled. I also remember that being one very long night. Nobody wanted to be there—including Evander—because the cancellation…was such a tremendous letdown."

I was promoting at the Blue Horizon and in Atlantic City and working with Main Events when they came to Philly. My business was a two- or three-person operation and I couldn't sign everyone and some talent went elsewhere.

Calvin Grove was from Coatesville, 39 miles west of Philadelphia. He won the Pennsylvania Golden Gloves title at 125 pounds, turned pro in 1982 and won his first 20 fights, 11 by knockout. I was involved in 16, either as promoter or matchmaker.

In his 21st fight, Grove met future IBF bantamweight champion Kelvin Seabrooks at the Sands. He was knocked down in the second round and when I went to his corner, manager John Traitz chewed me out for making such a hard match. Grove knocked Seabrooks down in the fifth and won a 10-round decision, but it was our last fight together. He signed with Josephine Abercrombie, a multi-millionaire from Texas, and began fighting at the Atlantis Casino (formerly Playboy) in Atlantic City.

Abercrombie had founded the Houston Boxing Association and housed her boxers, free of charge, in an apartment complex and had them train in a state-of-the-art gym. She gave them healthcare insurance and profit-sharing benefits.

Bob Spagnola, an accounting major from Lehigh University, became Grove's new manager. A former amateur boxer, Spagnola was a two-time state wrestling champion from Connecticut and wrestled briefly at powerhouse Lehigh. After college, he moved to Houston and became involved with professional boxing. "Bob

Spagnola was the best thing that ever happened to me in boxing," Grove said.

Grove was 33-0 after winning the IBF world featherweight title in 1988 in France, getting up from a knockdown in the fourth to stop Antonio Rivera, of Puerto Rico, in the same round. After outpointing Myron Taylor at the Sands, he lost the title in a Mexicali bull ring when he was knocked down three times in the 15th round and lost a majority decision to Jorge Paez (142-140, 143-140, 142-142). It was one of the last official world championship fights—from a recognized sanctioning body—scheduled for 15.

Early in 1990, Grove moved back to Coatesville to be near his four sons. "More than anything, Calvin was a father," Spagnola said. "Family meant a lot to him."

Grove boxed for me three times as an ex-champ. Besides beating Julian Solis, he was K0d by Bryant Paden at the Blue Horizon. After he beat John Brown in 1995 at Caesars Atlantic City, I told the press that "Calvin Grove would have been a tough 'out' for any featherweight or junior lightweight in history." Grove, approaching his 33rd birthday, said, "That's the nicest thing you ever said about me."

Grove won 14 of his last 22 fights before retiring in 1998. Nine were against past or current world champions. He defeated Solis and Troy Dorsey at the Blue Horizon and Jeff Fenech and Lester Ellis (twice) in Australia. He also lost a unanimous decision to Azumah Nelson in a WBC junior lightweight title fight in Las Vegas.

He once was quoted as saying that "all fighters are whores and all promoters are pimps." He laughed when I reminded him. "Sometimes I do things without thinking," he said, "but it was just a foolish line. I didn't mean it."

For some in our business, it was not the worst analogy.

Chapter Forty-Four

A Word from the Mob

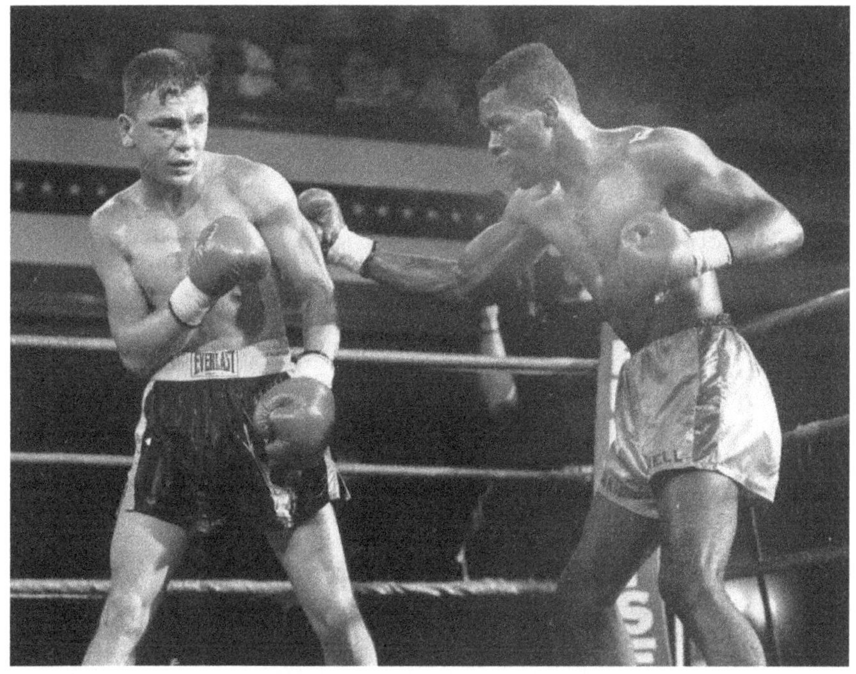

Anthony Boyle (left) and Frankie Mitchell battle in 1992. (Hinda Schuman photo)

Frank "Blinky" Palermo died in 1996, at 91. Let's hope he does not have a "return clause." Being around him was like being around the devil. I cannot think of anything positive about him. When people tell me something nice he did, I remind them Al Capone had soup kitchens for the unemployed during the Depression. Palermo once ran Philadelphia's numbers racket and, from the 1940s through the early 1990s, he raped the souls and bank accounts of dozens of fighters. He worked alongside Frankie Carbo, a member of Murder, Inc., often mentioned as the man who killed Bugsy Siegel.

Palermo was involved when Jake LaMotta took a *dive* in his 1947 fight with Billy Fox, the Philadelphia light-heavyweight he managed. Lightweight champion Ike Williams, also managed by Palermo, claimed he never got paid from two title defenses in the 1940s, and later told a Congressional investigation he had gone *into the tank* against Chuck Davey, a popular White fighter from Michigan who had a large TV following in the 1950s.

Johnny Saxton, also with Palermo, won the world welterweight title twice on questionable decisions over Kid Gavilan and Carmen Basilio in the 1950s. When he couldn't do it publicly, Palermo grabbed pieces of fighters through intimidation. In 1961, he and Carbo were convicted of undercover managing and extortion and each sentenced to 25 years after being prosecuted by U.S. Attorney General Robert Kennedy. Carbo died in prison but Palermo was paroled in 1971 after serving less than eight.

After his release, Palermo befriended Steve Traitz, business manager of Roofers Local 30-30B. Traitz, who ran the Montgomery County Boys Club, was convicted of racketeering and bribery and imprisoned from 1987 to 1994. His sons, Steve III and Joey, also served time in prison in the union corruption case. In the early 1980s, pros from the Boys Club had compiled impressive records.

Palermo applied for a boxing manager's license in 1978 in Pennsylvania. He said he wanted to help young kids. He probably would have been licensed had Tom Cushman not found out. Cushman's and Stan Hochman's campaign in the *Daily News* put so much pressure on the State Athletic Commission that Palermo withdrew his application before the three-member board voted. Palermo claimed he had no interest in professional boxers, but anyone with half a brain—and there were plenty of them in boxing—knew Palermo was calling the shots for heavyweight Jimmy Young.

"Inviting Blinky Palermo back into boxing is like asking a reformed drunk if he'd like a job as a taster in a winery," Cushman wrote.

Steve Traitz disagreed. "Blinky took care of his fighters," Traitz yelled at Hochman after Palermo withdrew his application. "Now, Philly has the best gyms, the best trainers and guys like Peltz give their fighters a bowl of soup and two coffees."

Fox got a job setting up pins in a New York bowling alley. Williams lived in poverty in a rooming house in Los Angeles. Saxton wound up in a state mental hospital, saying "no one ever gave me more than a couple of hundred dollars at a time." Palermo sure took care of his fighters.

Frank Gelb managed Young, a heavyweight with little power but solid technical skills. Young boxed for me six times in his first 11 fights, but when he was stopped in three rounds by Earnie Shavers in 1973, that was it for me. Young's fights were tedious and he never caught on in Philadelphia.

"One time we fought Randy Neumann at Madison Square Garden," Gelb said, "and the fight was so bad that (matchmaker) Teddy Brenner came down to the ring and said, 'Gelb, if Young doesn't start throwing punches you'll never get another fight at Madison Square Garden.' That's what I was up against."

Gelb took Young on the road, three times to London, once to Venezuela where he upset Jose Luis Garcia, and once to Maryland where he got off the floor to draw with Shavers in their rematch. Early in 1975 in Hawaii, Young upset Ron Lyle, who had lost only to Jerry Quarry in 32 fights. Young was paid $4,000, his career high at the time.

"Even after beating Lyle, I still couldn't move Young," Gelb said. "Don King had all the heavyweights. I put Young in a fight in Scranton and one at the Arena in Philadelphia, but I couldn't pay him the kind of money he deserved after beating Lyle. Bob Brown was my partner. He was Young's trainer and he was frustrated. One day Brown came to visit me at my father's furniture store at 61st and Market. He wanted me to sell Young's contract. I never spoke with Jimmy about it. I asked Brown, 'Whaddya gonna do, make a deal with Don King?'

"I got a call from a guy with a raspy voice who wanted to know if he could buy the contract. I didn't know this man but he said I soon would. Then Brown shows up at the store with Blinky Palermo. I had heard his name but I didn't really know who he was. I never read boxing books. So eventually I sold Young's contract to Blinky. The next thing I knew Young was being managed by Jack Levin, who owned the largest electrical supply business in the area. His store was across Market Street from my father's in West Philadelphia."

Through his connection with King, Palermo got Young a title shot against Muhammad Ali and later a fight with George Foreman. Young narrowly lost to Ali, upset Foreman and lost a 15-round split decision to Ken Norton late in 1977. Norton later was designated heavyweight champion by the WBC when Ali refused to fight him a fourth time. Many felt Young beat Norton but suffered from a backlash due to the rumors that Palermo was involved. With or without a license, Palermo discarded Young when the heavyweight fell out of the big time.

After Jeff Chandler made the first defense of his WBA world bantamweight title in 1981, Palermo visited Chandler's people, K.O. Becky and Willie O'Neill, at their South Philadelphia home. He offered them $50,000 in cash to leave me and go with a promoter of Palermo's choosing. I did not have a contract, but Willie and Becky said, "Thanks but no thanks."

A few weeks later, when O'Neill took Chandler to the Montgomery County Boys Club for sparring, he saw Palermo and said hello. Palermo waved him off with that get-out-of-my-face hand gesture and turned away. O'Neill grabbed Palermo by the shirt collar, pushed him up against the wall, and said, "You may have these kids fooled that you're some kind of tough guy but if you ever do that again, I'll knock the shit out of you right here in front of them." Palermo put his hands up and claimed O'Neill had misunderstood him.

I didn't hear much about Palermo for several years after that.

In 1987, I began promoting Frankie Mitchell, an undefeated lightweight who had moved to Philly from Columbus, Ohio. By the middle of 1992, Mitchell had boxed for me 13 times and had won the North American Boxing Federation (NABF) title. His fights had been on USA Network and SportsChannel and he'd challenged Brian Mitchell, of South Africa, for the WBA world junior lightweight title, a match I'd made with promoter Cedric Kushner late in 1990. Mitchell lost a unanimous 12-round decision (116-113 twice and 117-113) in Aosta, Italy, his first setback in 26 fights.

Two fights later, Robert Seltzer wrote that Mitchell was addicted to cocaine. The story hit the front page—not the sports page—of the *Inquirer*, on January 14, 1992, the day Mitchell was defending his NABF lightweight title against fellow-Philadelphian Bryant Paden at the Blue Horizon.

"Cocaine clogs your mind, messes with your thinking, man," said Mitchell, adding he'd been clean for six weeks. "It can ruin your life. You get high, then you come down, and you're back to where you started…nowhere. I can't tell you I'm gonna get off the drugs for good, and I can't tell you I'm not. All I can tell you, is that I'm not on them now, and I'm gonna try to keep it that way."

Mitchell went missing three days before the fight and had been in the gym only once the week before. After Jimmy Arthur, his trainer, located Mitchell, we put them in a hotel with instructions for Jimmy not to let him out of his sight. Mitchell owned nothing but the clothes he was wearing, but he beat Paden by unanimous 12-round decision (117-111, 118-113, 119-113). No one could understand it. He got $6,000 for the fight.

"They only test you after fights," Mitchell told Bernard Fernandez, of the *Daily News*. "Lay off the stuff about a month before the fight and you're going to test clean. (I won) because everybody thought I was a bum, washed up. I may be an old man, but I still can fight."

Greg Sirb, executive secretary of the Pennsylvania State Athletic Commission, said: "We can't discipline a fighter merely for saying he takes drugs. Admission of guilt is not guilt. You have to flunk a drug test." When I spoke to Sirb for this book, he said today he could do random drug testing "if there was probable cause, but I'm not sure we could have done it in 1992."

Mitchell was managed by Dean Rosenberg and Bruce Gross, who said they knew nothing about Mitchell's addiction. Rosenberg was from suburban Huntington Valley and was in the check-cashing business with his father, Joe. Gross was from Wynnefield and his family owned a deli/restaurant at Broad and Cumberland, one mile north of the Blue Horizon. Rosenberg's dad knew Palermo and that was how Rosenberg and Gross got the fighter, but I never spoke to Palermo in any dealings for Mitchell and never had seen him at any of Mitchell's fights until….

When Mitchell defended his NABF lightweight title against Anthony Boyle on June 16, 1992, it was a hot local fight which sold out the Blue Horizon. USA paid $35,000 for the rights and the gate receipts were $24,300 from a crowd of 1,243. During one of the prelims, someone said Palermo was sitting in the West press section in view of the main USA cameras. I got him to change seats.

Mitchell won in the 11th round and there was talk about fighting WBC junior welterweight champion Julio Cesar Chavez for $125,000. I thought it was suicide, but since I had paid Mitchell $10,000 to fight Boyle, second only to the $17,500 he got to fight Brian Mitchell, it made sense. Promoters normally got a minimum of 20 percent of the total monies available when one of their fighters boxed for another promoter. Most took more.

I had promoted 15 of Mitchell's 18 fights since he had moved to Philadelphia but I had no contract at this time. Rosenberg and Gross were my friends. They and their wives had been at the Bar Mitzvah of our oldest son, Matthew. We went out socially.

Rosenberg said Palermo now was calling the shots and the best I could get was $10,000. Then I got a call from Rosenberg's father, who said I never did anything for Mitchell and was not entitled to anything—and that's what I got. Gross said there was nothing he could do. I never dealt with either one again.

Chavez K0d Mitchell in four rounds in Las Vegas. Three months later, Levander Johnson K0d Mitchell in two in Lake Tahoe. Mitchell split his next two fights and retired. Rosenberg and Gross never managed another fighter and I never again ran into Palermo.

When I made Mitchell-Boyle, it was a better match for me than for Boyle.

"There were some disappointments in my career and some good points as well," Boyle said. "If I had someone who was more of a promoter for his fighters than he was for the fans, things could have turned out better." We both laughed but we knew it was true. "You were more of a fan and you wanted to make good fights and I understand that," he said, "but if you had looked out for me more, things might have been better, but I would guess a lot of fighters talk that way about their careers."

Boyle was not wrong. There were things about his career I should have handled differently. I *was* a fan's promoter, not a fighter's promoter. That mindset was instilled in me as a fan and during my early years in business when we had so many terrific fighters and only the best survived, a time when we had only 10 divisions and one champion in each.

Gary Hinton, who won and lost the IBF world junior welterweight title in 1986, told David Bontempo, of the *Atlantic City Press*: "The way I'll win the title is stay away from Peltz. He puts me in wars."

Boyle was from the Kensington section of Philadelphia, a largely working-class Irish Catholic community. His mom and dad split in 1983 when Boyle graduated from North Catholic High School. Bob Boyle worked construction and had taught his son to box. Joan Boyle was a hairdresser and her son's biggest fan, but she never watched him box—amateur or pro. She'd pace the lobby or the street, smoking cigarettes.

As an amateur, Boyle won 134 out of 142 fights. He was invited to the 1984 U.S. Olympic Trials, but a scratched cornea ended that. He won his first 17 pro fights, one over former bantamweight contender Johnny Carter. In his 18th fight, future IBF world junior lightweight champion Troy Dorsey stopped him with seven seconds left in the 10th round. It was the semifinal to the Robert Hines-Darrin Van Horn championship card early in 1989 at Trump Castle in Atlantic City.

NBC televised Hines-Van Horn. Kevin Monaghan, who succeeded Ferdie Pacheco at NBC, had spoken to me about Boyle fighting Tracy Harris Patterson in May. I hadn't been able to get tapes of Dorsey, who was 7-2-2 and coming off a 10-round draw with 14-8 Rogelio Lopez. The only available video was of one of his brothers. I was told the brothers had the same style and I gave the tape to Boyle.

I had a popular White featherweight who sold a lot of tickets, was unbeaten in 17 fights, on the verge of a network TV date, and the best I could do was send him a tape of his opponent's brother. Boyle and I joke about it, but it must bother him as much today as it bothers me.

"It took me a long time to get over that fight," Boyle said. "I had a sinus infection, but I didn't want to pull out because things were coming together in my career and I thought I could overcome it."

Two fights later, Boyle fought ex-WBA bantamweight champ Julian Solis, who was 33 and had lost six of his previous eight. The wins had been over fighters with records of 1-2 and 1-4. Solis had not knocked anybody out in three years, but he had experience from 49 fights. Boyle's corner complained of head butts and punches after the bell but, as always, protests get nowhere. Boyle was down in the fifth and didn't answer the bell for the seventh. He trailed by one point on two cards, two points on the third.

Boyle returned a year later and won five in a row before fighting Mitchell. Despite losing, he still had a chance to crack the Top 10. Ex-pro Wesley Mouzon had become his trainer, following Tommy Forte, Jimmy Beecham and Jack Costello. Boyle won his next three and challenged Carl Griffith, of Lorain, Ohio, for Griffith's USBA lightweight title. Victory would put Boyle in the IBF Top 10.

Griffith was 27-3-2, 12 K0s. Boyle was 25-3-2, 12 K0s. I cannot recall the last time two White fighters had headlined at the Blue Horizon. But April 12, 1994, the place was packed. For the first time, every seat was reserved, $30 for ringside, $25 for the balcony. USA paid us $42,500 and the gate receipts totaled $25,838. Boyle and Griffith each got $9,000 and our profit was $16,374.17.

The fight started slowly and in Griffith's favor. Boyle came alive in the sixth round and fought his way back, cutting Griffith in the 9th and finishing strong. All three scores were 115-113, two for Griffith, one for Boyle, who dropped to his knees. "In any other city, they give it to the hometown guy," he said. "Why not here?"

Seven months later, Griffith parlayed that win into a high-paying fight with Oscar De La Hoya for the WBO lightweight title.

Boyle lost two of his next three and retired after John Lark stopped him in 1995 at the Blue Horizon. He finished at 26-6-1, 12 K0s. "I wish Mister Mouzon had been with me from the start," he said. "I learned more in my short period with him than I learned total before he came along."

Linda and I were at Boyle's 1997 wedding to Maureen Divirgillio. They have three sons. Boyle drove tow trucks while he was boxing and later started K & A Auto Salvage, Inc., one of 10 companies who have contracts with the City of Philadelphia to remove abandoned vehicles and deliver them to the police department.

Chapter Forty-Five

My Blue Heaven

Tony Green and Rudy Zavala battle at the Blue in 1994. (Hinda Schuman photo)

In the 1990s, the Blue Horizon was in a zone. It didn't matter who headlined. We matched prelim kids who were 3-6 against guys who were 4-7 and fans kept coming because they were competitive. Fighters who sold a lot of tickets had to wait their turn. Many fighters expect soft touches because they bring customers, but when every card sells out, who cares? No fighter came to the Blue Horizon to pad his record. Fans wanted good fights, not slaughters of second-raters. "It was boxing's Ring of Dreams," USA announcer Al Albert said. "Whenever we were at the Blue, we came to understand that the true soul of boxing had always been there."

Season-ticket holders came from Ohio and Kentucky. A Michigan couple planned a vacation around a Blue Horizon fight. The ring was 15 feet, 9 inches inside the ropes, more than two feet smaller than most and three inches under Pennsylvania regulation. Credit goes to handyman Mark Kondrath, who extended the turnbuckles on the ropes in each corner of his ring to minimize the available space inside.

"It was an honor to fight at the Blue Horizon," said Hall-of-Fame bantamweight champ Orlando Canizales, who ended his career there. "The place was always packed and the ring was small. It was like fighting in a phone booth."

We were a small club with big fights and everyone wanted to box at 1314 North Broad Street. It was a dream for a promoter and matchmaker. One night, Alan Gelb, Frank's oldest son, said, "Russell, you haven't given a single fighter a break. Every fight is a war." I said, "Look at the crowd! This is what people want."

Jimmy Toppi sold the Blue Horizon in 1987 to Ross Collette, pastor of New Horizons Church. The ballroom on the first landing housed Collette's services. The upstairs auditorium had boxing and other big events. I never had a contract with Collette and his wife, Kaye. The only interference came from their college-age daughter, Angela, who questioned the clothes—or lack of—on the round-card girls, so our ladies dressed more conservatively.

The years with Collette, from 1988 to mid-1994, were wonderful, as they had been with Toppi. I had a one-hour show on WIP All-Sports radio, Wednesdays, 11pm to midnight, from 1989 through 1992. We talked current boxing, boxing history and we gave away a pair of fight tickets if a caller could answer our trivia question. I played radio clips of Don Dunphy calling fights from Madison Square Garden. Old-timers, who went to bed early, set their clocks so they could wake up and listen.

The Blue Horizon was a USA staple. In 1989, USA hired Brad Jacobs as Program Director. Jacobs lived in Tampa and had been matchmaker for promoter Phil Alessi in Florida. Alessi promoted there and in Atlantic City. Jacobs gave Hall-of-Famer Michael Buffer his first ring announcing gig, a card on October 1, 1982, at the Playboy in Atlantic City. ("I begged him to destroy the tapes," Buffer said. "I was quite dreadful.) Jacobs chose which fights USA bought and we got along well. He tolerated my whining.

"The Blue Horizon was the heart and soul of USA Tuesday Night Fights," Jacobs said. "You could always count on terrific fights and amazing nights. The grittiness and raw bare bones atmosphere were the attractive part. We staged events all over the world and in every venue you could imagine, but The Blue always felt like home."

Other promoters couldn't match our success. Top Rank came to the Blue Horizon when Atlantic City was not available. The busiest were Luddy DePasquale, who was in the new and used car business in New Jersey, and his brother, Peter, an advertising exec in New York. They had promoted in North Jersey, primarily to develop the Toledo brothers, Frankie and David, a pair of southpaw featherweights from Paterson. Frankie later won the IBF title.

At the Blue Horizon, Luddy and Peter partnered with local manager Rob Murray to promote two dozen shows from the end of 1994 through the middle of 1998.

"We never really made any money," Luddy said. "That wasn't our goal. We were running shows as an investment. We wanted to develop and move our fighters."

Welterweight Tony Martin, who lost a 10-round decision in his last fight to Julio Cesar Chavez in Las Vegas, and heavyweight Terrance Lewis, were their prize pupils. Lewis beat Al Cole and fought some of the best big men of his era, including Greg Page, Michael Moorer, Hasim Rahman and Andrew Golota. Luddy and Peter left boxing promotion midway through 1998 to concentrate on Lewis and to devote more time to their regular businesses.

The Blue Horizon was a fight fan's nirvana. Fighters on their way up to world titles fought there—Arturo Gatti, Fernando Vargas, Eric Lucas, Vincent Pettway, Frankie Randall, Bernard Hopkins, Nate Miller, Vivian Harris, Prince Charles Williams, Alfred Kotey, Gary St. Clair, Julio Borboa and Antonio Tarver—as did fighters on their way down from world titles—Canizales, Tim Witherspoon, Livingstone Bramble, Buster Drayton, Dwight Qawi, Bronco McKart and Bonecrusher Smith. Sometimes they fought each other.

In the history of the Blue Horizon, three undisputed champions boxed there—Harold Johnson as ex-champ in 1963, Curtis Cokes as future champ in 1964, Bernard Hopkins as future champ, seven times in the 1990s, twice for me.

The Blue Horizon's biggest crowd was September 10, 1991, when Witherspoon, former WBA and WBC heavyweight champion, knocked out Art Tucker in three rounds. The official paperwork says the crowd was 1,385, but more than 2,000 crammed into the building. Tickets were $15 in advance, $20 at the door, and you literally couldn't move. Our buddy, Frank Talent, man about City Hall, knew the Fire Marshall.

Dennis Rappaport managed Witherspoon and he had made a deal with USA—and USA with me—to put the fight in the Blue. USA paid Rappaport for Witherspoon and Tucker, and paid me $25,000 for everything else. Ticket sales were $20,570 and our profit was $14,467.87 ($30,000 in 2021).

Reserved seating was the big difference. White-collar regulars from the Spectrum and Arena days didn't want to stand in the lobby at 6 pm and run upstairs for good seats when the doors opened. They wanted to have dinner with friends or business associates, and have seats waiting. We experimented in 1993 when Rodney Moore fought Bramble, reserving the first five rows on the West floor. Slowly we covered the entire floor and, in 1994, the balcony. After that, every show sold out.

The night Charles Brewer defeated Frank Rhodes on March 12, 1996, we announced Ivan Robinson would headline 10 weeks later against Sammy Mejias, of Puerto Rico, for Robinson's USBA lightweight title. No one knew Sammy Mejias from Sammy Davis, Jr., but tickets were gone the next day. USA paid us $60,000 and, combined with gate receipts of $48,357.10, sponsorship money and souvenir program sales, we made $30,644.67 ($52,000 in 2021).

There were nights, with PRISM or SportsChannel, we made a fraction of that, but we kept moving. Business was so good I stopped printing posters, a mistake for nostalgic reasons. We continued to mail the poster-like postcards. The only posters printed after 1996 were for the Brewer-Joey DeGrandis IBF world title fight in 1997.

Not every headliner was world-ranked. Eric Holland, a junior middleweight from North Philly, had turned pro in 1986, winning one of his first nine fights. He was 8-13-3 when he upset crosstown rival William "Hammer" Jones by eight-round decision late in 1992. Jones was 19-0, 15 K0s. I thought he was going places, but Holland won by 78-75 and 77-75 twice.

When USA's card fell apart for Phoenix, Arizona, on June 1, 1993, Jacobs needed a venue on less than one week's notice. I agreed to do it at the Blue Horizon with Bonecrusher Smith in the main event so long as USA covered expenses. Smith, then 40 and six years removed from his WBA heavyweight title, K0d Donnell Wingfield, of Cleveland, Ohio, in two rounds. Holland turned his career around in the semifinal against Scotty "The Body" Smith, of Little Rock, Arkansas, who was 22-0-1, 18 K0s.

Art Dore, who managed Smith, was from Bay City, Michigan, and, in 1979, had helped start the *Toughman Contest*, which became an international success.

"There were certain guys around town who had the reputation of being (bad dudes)," Dore told Lee Thompson, of MLive.com. "They were the guys who would walk into a bar and people wouldn't even look at them—they didn't want to give them a problem. We said, 'Let's put all these guys together and see who is the toughest of 'em all.' That's what we did. We got all of those guys, plus some other guys who thought they were just as tough. And that was the best damn show ever."

The Toughman slogan, *Are You Tough Enough*, helped launch the careers of Mr. T, Tommy Morrison and Butterbean. Dore ran more than 100 cards a year and *Toughman* ran as a series on Showtime, FX and FOX Sports.

"Scotty (Smith) was from Little Rock and we did a lot of *Toughman* shows there," Dore said. "He always wanted to try it, but I knew he'd never make it because he was too small. When he decided to try boxing, he moved to Michigan."

When Smith got to the Blue Horizon, only two of his 23 opponents had more wins than losses. USA previewed the fight with head shots of him and Holland and their records. "I think I'll be the crowd favorite because I'm undefeated and I'm good looking," Smith said, staring into the camera.

After the fight, USA again showed Smith's face. He no longer was undefeated and no longer good looking. Holland battered him for 10 rounds (97-93, 98-94 and 97-93). USA paid for the main event and gave me $35,000 to cover the rest of the card. Holland and Smith each got $3,000. We sold 73 tickets and made $8,487.78.

I began to match Holland with aggressive guys. Boxers gave him trouble. He was 5-foot-6, thick and a good body puncher. The win over Smith was his second of seven straight at the Blue Horizon, including his first knockout when he stopped Hammer Jones in the ninth round of their rematch, ending Jones' career at 19-2, 17 K0s.

When Holland outpointed Tyrone Haywood, of Washington, DC, midway through 1994, it got him to 15-15-3, 1 K0. It didn't matter that Haywood was 4-17-2 going in. Holland had reached .500 and the crowd gave him a standing ovation. He was one of theirs. After he outpointed another USA favorite, Jesse James Hughes, of Mobile, Alabama, in the summer of 1994, he was ready for a Top 10 opponent.

"I never wanted to be known as the best fighter with a losing record," Holland said. "I'd rather be known as a winning fighter and this has been a long time coming. I guess perseverance really does pay off."

Curtis Summit, of Fayetteville, North Carolina, ranked No. 9 by the WBA, signed to fight Holland on October 11, 1994, the first main event of Holland's career. Holland trained in Palm Springs, California, helping Meldrick Taylor get ready for his rematch with Julio Cesar Chavez on September 17 in Las Vegas. Taylor got a six-figure purse to fight Chavez and Holland was to get $500 a week for four weeks of sparring. He said he only got paid for two. When Holland got back to Philly, he had lost his job as a UPS driver.

"I guess UPS figured they'd let me go because I was out of town so much," Holland told Robert Seltzer, of the *Inquirer*. "That wouldn't have been so bad if I'd have gotten paid for sparring. I was looking for another job and I just couldn't focus." I'd given Holland $1,000 to help out, and he told Seltzer: "He (Peltz) really came through for me. Now my head is clear and I feel good about fighting again."

Summit was 24-7-2, 14 K0s. It would have been nice for Holland to win and get ranked, but Summit won 96-95 and 96-94 twice. Summit got $7500, Holland $6,000. The Blue Horizon was sold out but my records show only 953 in attendance. Then again, boxing promoters aren't known for giving correct attendance figures.

One win and four months later, Holland left town without saying goodbye.

"I was working security for a grocery store in West Philly," he later told me. "Some dude came in one day and was giving the cashier trouble. He threatened me so I hit him and knocked him down. The dude got up and left, but someone called the police. There were witnesses who said I did the right thing, but I thought the guy was gonna come back with some friends for revenge so I stayed away from the store for a few days.

"Then I decided to quit the job altogether. I got behind on my rent and I was about to get kicked out of my apartment. I didn't want to ask you for any more money because you had helped me once and you had a lot on your plate so I left Philly and drove to New Mexico to stay with my parents."

Holland went to New Mexico State University in Almogordo and got his EMT Certification, but the boxing bug bit him and he never put his degree to work. He won only five of his last 22 fights and retired in 2003 with a record of 22-33-3. About a year after he left Philly, he sent me a letter. Inside was a check for $1,000.

"I was going to pay you back if it took the rest of my life," Holland said. "I had never run into any promoter or any person in boxing who would do that for me. I never forgot that."

Holland worked in construction for years, then, in 2019, got a job marketing and advertising for *World Peace*, a smoke shop in Almogordo.

Tony Green was a street fighter. Whenever there was a disturbance in their West Philly neighborhood, he and his brother, David, would settle matters.

"Tony's boxing career started on a bet," said Dave Wilkes, Tony's uncle. "Tony wanted money to go to the movies and I bet him he couldn't last in the ring with a boxer. I told him I would give him one dollar for every round he could last with a boxer. That was my way of getting him in the gym. Every time he came back to the corner I asked him if he wanted to stop and he would ask me how many dollars he had made to that point. He would say that's not enough and he would go another round.

"He only made six dollars that first time because he made three guys quit after two rounds each. My plan worked because Tony and David both came back the next day. I saw the determination, guts and ability to learn that I already knew Tony had. He was obedient because he wanted to be the best at whatever he did. David kept fighting in the street."

Wilkes owned a moving and hauling business, bought houses, rented rooms, and ran an entertainment company. After Green, a featherweight, won 12 amateur fights, 11 by knockout, Wilkes called me and we worked together from Green's first pro fight in 1987 until his last in 1996. Green boxed 24 times at the Blue Horizon, most by any pro. Rodney Moore had 22, Anthony Boyle 18.

Green was 10-1-1, 7 K0s, midway through 1990 when he boxed Harold Warren, of Corpus Christi, Texas, in an eight-rounder at Harrah's Marina. Warren was 10-4, 4 K0s, and coming off a pair of losses, but a listless Green lost on points.

I needed someone to fight Fernando Rodriguez, of Allentown, 22 days later at the Blue Horizon. Rodriguez was 7-0, a difficult southpaw no one wanted to fight. I didn't think Green took the Warren fight seriously so I thought, "The hell with him." But Green knocked Rodriguez out of the ring with two left hooks and the fight was over in 17 seconds.

"I was pissed when Tony lost to Warren," Wilkes said. "His head wasn't into it. Atlantic City made him starstruck and it took his mind off what had to be done. I had no idea the Rodriguez fight was punishment. One thing I learned from (ex-pro) Jimmy Beecham is when you are close to your fighter, most fighters take on the attributes of their trainer. I thought I couldn't be beat and I instilled that way of thinking in Tony so it didn't matter who was in the other corner.

"People always warned me about not fighting certain fighters, that I shouldn't let Tony fight this guy or that guy because it was a tough fight. I would say, 'Good, I like the ones that can fight.' I transferred my confidence over to Tony."

Green won 12 of his next 13, including a 10th-round knockout of former world-title challenger Myron Taylor, older brother of Meldrick, for the state title in 1991. It was the end for Taylor, a National Golden Gloves champion who had turned pro in 1980, gone unbeaten in his first 15 fights and challenged for a world title. He retired at 29-9-2, 16 K0s, and later worked for Service Champ, an auto parts warehouse.

By the time Green boxed Rudy Zavala, of Rosemead, California, on June 14, 1994, he was world-ranked. Philly was in the middle of a heat wave. When the USA telecast opened, Al Albert told the television audience: "Well, it's 94 degrees, the humidity is about 183 and we've worked up a sweat. A punch has not yet been thrown."

Between the packed house and the television lights, it had to be 120 degrees at ringside. Zavala (22-3-2, 18 K0s) was a former USBA and NABF super bantamweight champion. Green was knocked down 30 seconds into round two and when he got back to his corner, Wilkes was in his face.

"Tony didn't even know where he was for two or three rounds," Wilkes said. "I didn't let him sit because I knew he might not get back up. I wanted to keep his legs active. At some point you have to scream at a fighter to keep him pumped up or to be sure he does what you say."

Green literally wobbled out of his corner at the start of round three, but he rallied in the fifth and one of his left hooks cut Zavala's right eyelid. It was a war down the stretch and Green's left hooks to the body were the difference. Ex-pro Bobby Grasso had it 95-94 for Green. Judges Alfreda Armstrong and Sarah Jones also had Green winning, but their scores (98-93 and 96-93) were booed.

"Philly, they told me, was the greatest place to fight," said Zavala's 34-year-old trainer Freddie Roach, his long red hair tied in a ponytail. "Great traditions, knowledgeable fight crowd. It's a knowledgeable fight crowd all right, but what about those judges. What fight were they looking at?"

Everyone in the Blue Horizon must have sweated off 10 pounds. Green got $10,000, Zavala $7,500, but the fight took its toll. Zavala lost four of his next seven and retired in 1997. On July 4, 1998, his car spun off a California highway at 3 am. When he crossed the highway to get help, he was hit by a truck going 80 miles an hour. He left behind a wife and three kids.

Green was positioned for a world title fight and I didn't want to take any chances. He sat out a year until he challenged Alejandro Gonzalez, of Mexico, for the WBC featherweight belt at Foxwoods. It was his only fight outside Philadelphia or Atlantic City.

Gonzalez, 21, was 36-2, 26 K0s. He had won the title earlier in 1995 by knocking out previously unbeaten (41-0, 29 K0s) Kevin Kelley, of New York. Gonzalez was the best 126-pounder in the world and Green was worn down. Gonzalez won in nine rounds. The

$30,000 purse was Green's biggest. He lost his next two and retired nine months later. He was 30 years old.

Chapter Forty-Six

A Decade of Sellouts

Thomas Tate probes for openings against Joseph Kiwanuka. (Peltz collection)

There were 219 boxing cards in the Philadelphia area in the 1970s, 200 in the 1980s. It dropped to 167 in the 1990s, 112 at the Blue Horizon. Small cards popped up at the National Guard Armory in Northeast Philadelphia, the Felton Supper Club off Roosevelt Boulevard and the James Shuler Memorial Gym in West Philadelphia. We did a black-tie event at the Bellevue-Stratford Hotel downtown. I also worked with Art Pelullo, making matches for his company, Banner Promotions.

There were cards in bigger venues. Meldrick Taylor's 1992 win over Glenwood Brown, paired with WBA/WBC/IBF lightweight champion Pernell Whitaker's 10-round non-title shutout of Harold Brazier, which I co-promoted with Dan Duva, sold all 3,200 seats at Pennsylvania Hall. The live gate was $135,840. HBO paid $2,650,000 and there was money from overseas TV.

Don King brought Mike Tyson to the 18,000-seat Spectrum on three weeks' notice late in 1995. Tickets were $500, $400, $300, $200 and $25, too high for Philadelphia, especially nine days before Christmas. Fox televised the card and fewer than 5,000 paid to see the ex-heavyweight champ's third-round knockout over 25-to-1 underdog Buster Mathis, Jr. It was Tyson's second fight since being released from jail for rape.

North Philly's Bernard Hopkins won the IBF middleweight title in 1996 in Landover, Maryland, and later unified the title. He might have drawn but made only one of his 20 defenses here, in 2003, when he chased inept No. 1 challenger Morrade Hakkar, of France, around the ring, stopping him in eight rounds. Heavyweights David Tua and Hasim Rahman met in the co-feature but, again, the crowd was under 5,000.

At the Blue Horizon, every card sold out. Fighters from out of town—some out of the country—could develop a following there.

Alfred Kotey was from Ghana, where he had knocked out his first seven opponents before flying to England and winning the British Empire Flyweight title. British, Empire and European titles had lost importance due to the glut of alphabet belts. Kotey had not boxed in 12 months when he re-located to Silver Springs, Maryland, where he resumed his career. He was 23.

Between July, 1991, and November, 1992, Kotey boxed for me nine times. He won the first eight, six at the Blue Horizon, two at Harrah's Marina. When he looked listless losing a 10-round split decision to Mexico's Julio Borboa at the Blue Horizon, I asked his management to take a step back with a lesser-paying fight. They balked and we split.

Borboa won the IBF super flyweight title six months later in Mexico and Kotey won the WBO bantamweight title 20 months later in London. Never judge a fighter after a single loss or a single win. My bad! Two future champs fought for me and I let them both go.

Joseph Kiwanuka, originally from Uganda, was living in Las Vegas when he came to the Blue Horizon in 1996 and beat Rodney Toney, Segundo Mercado, Antoine Byrd and Thomas Reid. He had lost once in 28 fights and had scored 19 knockouts. He was the NABF champ at 168 pounds and many, myself included, felt he was a future world champion.

Thomas Tate, of Houston, had scored a 12-round decision over Kiwanuka in 1995 in Auburn Hills, Michigan, so I re-matched them in 1997 and Tate won by knockout in the 11th round of an even fight (95-95 twice, 96-94 Tate). The loss to Tate ended Kiwanuka's hopes of an IBF title fight with Charles Brewer and sent him into a tailspin. He lost seven of his next nine fights and retired in 2004.

I could have found someone easier than Tate and milked Kiwanuka along to a title fight, but I enjoyed promoting fights more than promoting fighters. If that cost me over the years, I have no regrets. If I was interested in promoting fighters, I would have been a manager. Nigel Collins once wrote that, as a promoter, I was "a lighthouse in the fog." It was one of the nicest things ever written about me. Those who said I was more of a fan's promoter than a fighter's promoter did not understand I took that as a compliment.

I never had contracts with Kotey or Kiwanuka. Some promoters insisted on options in the event the "opponent" won. This was good for the promoter but not for the sport. It tied fighters to a handful of promoters who monopolized TV dates. It cut into the earnings of the opponent's promoter and relegated that promoter to second-class status. I had a relationship with USA because I made good fights, not because I had great fighters under contract.

Future undisputed light-heavyweight champion Antonio Tarver stopped Benito Fernandez, of Spartanburg, South Carolina, on the Kiwanuka-Tate card. It was one of five K0s Tarver scored on North Broad Street. Brad Jacobs had asked me to work with Tarver and I did, but Tarver and I parted ways late in 1998, another brilliant move on my part. Six years later he knocked out Roy Jones to win the WBA/WBC light-heavyweight titles.

After Kiwanuka, Tate defeated Anwar Oshana and Demetrius Davis at the Blue Horizon, and Merqui Sosa in Las Vegas to earn a shot at Sven Ottke's IBF super middleweight title. Tate was the No. 1 challenger but he didn't want to pay Bob Spagnola the 10 percent he had been giving him as his agent. He was wrong. Spagnola had brought Tate to me. Tate and I argued but he wouldn't budge.

Spagnola and I had much in common. We got hooked on boxing early and trusted people. He had managed or worked with some talented boxers besides Tate: Calvin Grove; Orlando Canizales; Gaby Canizales; Joe Mesi; Ike Ibeabuchi; Frank Tate; Reggie Johnson. He had contracts with some, handshakes with others. Some were loyal, some were not. Like they say, verbal contracts aren't worth the paper they're written on.

Including step-aside money to let Ottke defend against Gabriel Hernandez in May, Tate got $97,000 for his title challenge on September 4, 1999, in Magdeburg, Germany. Spagnola got nothing.

Italian referee Raffaele Argiolas stopped the Ottke-Tate fight 25 seconds into the 11th round, ruling that an accidental head butt in the ninth had opened a cut over Ottke's left eye. Tate, insisting a punch caused the cut, began to celebrate.

Television replays showed the cut had been opened by Tate's right hand, but we were in Germany. The referee conferred with the German boxing officials and they went to the scorecards. Ottke led 96-94, 97-93, 97-93 and kept his title. Had Argiolas ruled the cut had come from a punch, I'm sure Ottke would have finished and won by decision anyway. I sent Spagnola $4,500, 10 percent of my end of the promotion.

For most of the 1990s, I was busy with super middleweights—Kiwanuka, Tate, Tony Thornton, Charles Brewer (whom I will discuss later) and Bryant Brannon.

Brannon was from Trenton. He turned pro at 25 in 1992 after serving five years of a 15-year sentence at Rahway State (New Jersey) Prison for strong-arm robbery. When he knocked out

Demetrius Davis in four rounds in 1994, I thought he was on his way, but he never lived up to expectations.

He won the NABF title at 168 pounds on a technical decision over Frank Rhodes. An accidental head butt had opened a cut over Brannon's left eye in the first round and the fight was stopped after four with Brannon ahead on points. He also earned a 12-round decision over future WBC champion Eric Lucas, of Canada.

Brannon became No. 1 in the IBF when he was 16-0, 10 K0s, and he got $250,000 to fight Roy Jones, Jr., on October 4, 1996, at the Theatre inside Madison Square Garden. Las Vegas casinos refused to take bets due to Jones' skill and Brannon's lack of quality opposition. They were not wrong.

"Brannon deserves a profile-in-courage award just for showing up," said Fred Levin, Jones' attorney and advisor. HBO thought so little of Brannon that they hosted a question-and-answer session with Jones while he sat on a stool in the middle of the ring at the start of the telecast.

Steve Farhood, editor of *The Ring* magazine; Tony Paige, president of the Boxing Writers Association of America, and Ron Borges, columnist for the *Boston Globe*, asked questions as did fans. Some criticized the opposition—past and present—but Jones claimed every fighter presented problems. Less than 90 minutes later, he solved Brannon's, knocking him down once in the first round and twice in the second before referee Ron Lipton stopped it.

I had interests in other divisions, too. Two weeks earlier, my heavyweight, Darroll Wilson, of Atlantic City, who had surprisingly knocked out Shannon Briggs in March, was knocked out in one round by David Tua in Miami, also on HBO.

Wilson was hot and cold. Nine months later, he boxed Courage Tshabalala in a rare heavyweight main event at the Blue Horizon.

Tshabalala was from South Africa and managed by Lou Duva. He was 20-1, 17 K0s, and his record looked legit when he knocked Wilson down in the first round. Late in the third Wilson went down again and it didn't look like he'd get up. Referee Rudy Battle did a modern-day *Long Count* and Wilson made it back to his corner.

Duva ripped into Battle but the fight continued and Wilson stopped Tshabalala in the next round.

"The guy wasn't up in time," Duva told Kevin Tatum, of the *Inquirer*. "When he fell backwards the referee should have stopped the fight. (The ref) almost helped him back to his corner." Future WBO junior middleweight champion Bronco McKart out-pointed Glenwood Brown in the co-feature and Omar Sheika boxed a four-rounder. The place was sold out despite the June heat and the Philadelphia Flyers hosting the Detroit Red Wings at the Spectrum in the Stanley Cup playoffs.

Cruiserweight Nate "Mister" Miller was kicked out of Germantown High School in 1981. I was the class clown and I always wanted attention," Miller said. "I got kicked out for pushing around a teacher and poking him in the head."

Miller was 18 when he was sent to Daniel Boone, "a school for bad boys," he called it, in the Northern Liberties section of Philadelphia. "I was bad," Miller said, "and my parents couldn't say much because I was in and out of foster care since I was 4. I went to Daniel Boone in 11th grade and I was there for two years."

Miller hung out at the Happy Hollow gym in Germantown, where Stan Williams trained fighters. "Nate used to come in and watch other guys train," Williams said. "Then one day some kids ran in and said I should start training Nate because he had just knocked somebody out on the basketball court. That's how we got started."

After 30 amateur fights, Miller turned pro in 1986, winning his first 13, 11 by knockout. We took him to Bordeaux, France, in 1988 where Prince Charles Williams defended his IBF light-heavyweight title against Rufino Angulo. Miller went as Prince Charles' sparring partner and lost an eight-round decision to Boubakar Sanogo, of the Ivory Coast.

Besides loading up on French pastry, which made him sluggish in a fight he should have won, Miller was up to his class-clown tricks. At dinner, he put a rubber mouse on the waitress' shoulder with the expected results. He also put one in Linda's empty wine glass which had been covered with a linen napkin.

Four months later, Miller K0d Bert Cooper to win the NABF cruiserweight title, which he successfully defended against Andre McCall and Tyrone Booze. He was 18-1 and No. 1 by the IBF, No. 3 by the WBA and WBC.

In his third defense, at Harrah's Marina, he lost the title to former three-time world heavyweight kickboxing champion James Warring, of Miami. In the final seconds of the first round, after Miller motioned to referee Joe Cortez about a head butt, Warring landed a right hand and Miller went down on his face. He got to his feet at nine, wobbled back to his corner, managed to last 12 rounds, but lost by scores of 114-113, 116-114, and 116-112.

Gary Hegyi, who had managed Earl Hargrove, worked with Miller, and kept me involved, but after the Warring fight his agreement ran out and so did Miller.

When Miller out-pointed Dwight Qawi in 1992 at the Blue Horizon, it was two cruiserweight champions passing in the night—future and past. Qawi then quit for five years, returning in mid-1997. He won fights at venues like the Boys and Girls Club in Paterson, New Jersey, and at the Trop in Atlantic City, but left for good at 45 after Tony LaRosa out-pointed him in 1998 at the Ramada Inn in Rosemont, Illinois. Not a glorious exit for the future Hall-of-Famer.

Miller went to Don King and won the IBF title in 1995 in London when he K0d Orlin Norris in eight rounds. After four successful defenses, he lost to Frenchman Fabrice Tiozzo in 1997 in Las Vegas. Miller dropped four of his next five and retired in 2001.

"Don King treated us with respect," Miller said. "He even gave me some money to help me finish paying for my house."

Miller carries around his championship belt "to inspire the youth" and his answering service says: "This is Nate 'Mister' Miller, cruiserweight champ of the universe." He drove a dump truck for the Philadelphia Housing Authority and retired with a good pension.

"I play keyboard, harmonica, saxophone, flute and trumpet," he said. "I play guitar, electric guitar, acoustic guitar, bass guitar, electric violin and regular violin. I cannot read music but I could open a show for someone. I live right across the street from the Happy Hollow gym. I did a remarkable job. I had fun. I loved it and I loved the people I met. I loved every aspect of boxing."

Chapter Forty-Seven

The Hatchet

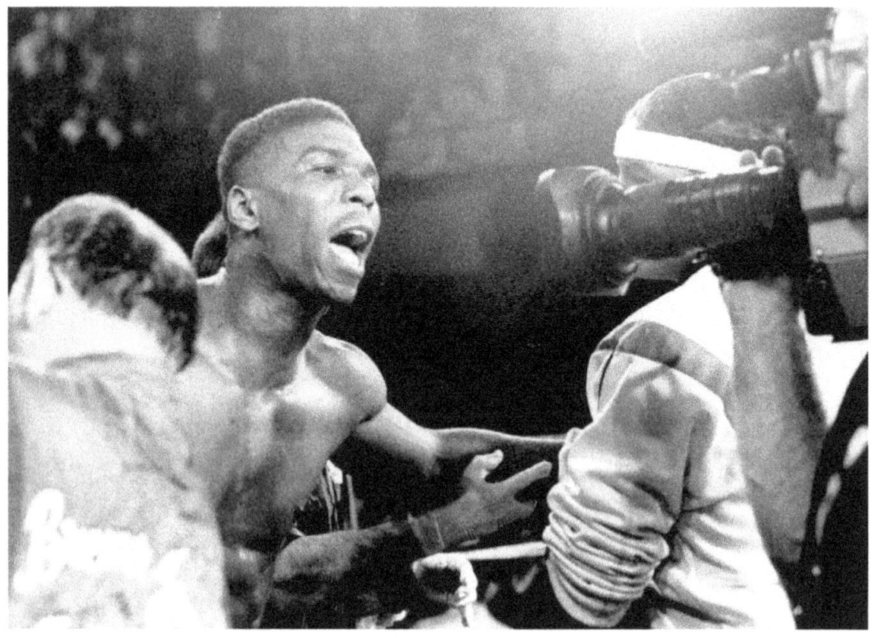

Charles Brewer is animated after blitzing Mario Munoz. (Peltz collection)

Charles "The Hatchet" Brewer was one of the most entertaining fighters of his time—1989 to 2005. Thirty-three of his 51 bouts ended early, 28 for him, five against. He lost five split decisions. It was a struggle to get him on HBO or Showtime, the two highest-paying media outlets. Duller, tamer "name fighters" got priority. Brewer won the IBF super middleweight title and made three successful defenses. Had HBO or Showtime been more astute, he never would have gone overseas to get hosed.

I signed Brewer's stablemate, Hammer Jones, who made his debut in 1989 at the Blue Horizon. Jones was 17-0, 15 K0s, before junior middleweight Eric Holland outpointed him over eight rounds in 1992. Jones was diagnosed with myasthenia gravis, a neuromuscular disorder which affected his vision. He lost again to Holland, retired, and became a policeman.

Brewer was always in the gym, but I had been so focused on Jones I never paid attention.

I put Brewer in his pro debut in the summer of 1989 at the Blue Horizon. Junior middleweight Jorge Maysonet had knocked out Donald Gwinn in one round in the semifinal and Brewer's "swing fight" with Jerome Johnson, of Baltimore, got on USA before the main event. Brewer K0d Johnson in two. Ron Katz, one of Bob Arum's matchmakers, was watching at home and Boogaloo Watts and Augie Scimeca, Brewer's managers, were headed to Top Rank.

Within two years Brewer was 14-0, 8 K0s, and Katz said, "I finally stole a good fighter from you."

In his 15th fight, Brewer boxed lefty Robert Thomas, in an all-Philly match at Harrah's Marina. Thomas had won only 10 of 54 fights and had been stopped six times. What should have been an easy fight for Brewer became a six-round split-decision loss. When Thomas beat him again four months later at the National Guard Armory in Northeast Philadelphia, Top Rank released him.

"It was a wakeup call," Brewer said. "Boogaloo was my father figure in boxing and he had been telling me how promoters can be with you one minute and the next minute they can be against you."

Scimeca wanted me to sign Brewer.

"Bobby (Watts) didn't trust you," Scimeca said. "He blamed you for his career never going where he thought it should go. I told him that he got as far as he did because of you. I also told him that this was business and that you were the best guy to take Brewer to the top. I guess I was right because Bobby finally came around and thanked me."

Brewer boxed Willie Harris on June 25, 1992, at the Blue Horizon. Harris was from Eagleville, 25 miles from Philly, and was 22-1, 18 K0s. Brewer stopped him in under two minutes, the first of eight consecutive knockout wins. After he K0d unbeaten Mario Munoz, of Denver, in one round late in 1993 at the Blue Horizon, Brewer was No. 6 among IBF middleweights.

When Tyrone Trice pulled out of a February 1, 1994, fight with Brewer, Jackie Kallen, who'd been in boxing since the late 1970s, handling publicity and marketing for Thomas Hearns, offered me Lonny Beasley, from Detroit like Trice. Beasley was 20-1-1 but only had six knockouts. I didn't think anyone without power could hang with Brewer.

"We found out that Trice had pulled out…five days ahead of time," Kallen said. "Lonny was really a junior middleweight and people were saying, 'Are you crazy, you're sacrificing your fighter,' but Lonny was coming off a good win over Emmett Linton and he was full of confidence. Lonny knew that Brewer was bigger, but also slower.

"It never bothered me going into someone's hometown. I did it with James Toney when we substituted against Michael Nunn (in Davenport, Iowa) and won the (middleweight) title. I took crazy risks with my fighters. Today, no one would do that."

A snowstorm the day of the fight didn't bother another big Blue Horizon crowd. Brewer was pumping hard jabs and moving forward, but two minutes into the first round, Beasley threw a right uppercut and all the hard work getting Brewer into the Top 10 vanished. Beasley's punch split Brewer's gloves on its way to his chin and he went over backwards as if someone had bent his body at the waist. He got up, limped to the ropes, and referee Rudy Battle stopped it at 2:32.

"Beasley threw the perfect punch at the perfect time," Brewer said. "I kept getting hit with that punch in the gym. Augie had told me to fight more on the angle but I didn't listen. When I got hit by Beasley, I tore three ligaments in my left ankle."

In Beasley's dressing room, I joked that I hated him. "That's okay," he said, "just pay me."

Kallen told me she felt badly, knowing the work I had put into Brewer. "Boxing was like that back then," she said. "It was one happy family. Those things don't happen today. I'm constantly in touch with Lonny." Beasley has a job at PVC Chemicals in Detroit where he works purifying water for railroad cars.

Brewer lost three out of four fights in 1994, two by knockout.

"That year, 1994, was what it was," Brewer said. "I had reached the Top 10. I knew me better than anyone. I knew how committed I was to the sport and I was not a know-it-all kind of guy. People were telling me to get a new trainer. When I was winning nobody said anything about my trainer."

Scimeca asked me not to give up. He said Brewer still had the desire. I wanted to walk away but Scimeca persisted.

"You (Russell) had years of experience and, I am sure, had seen worse nights than the ones I had in 1994," Brewer said. "We just waited for an answer from you to see how things were gonna be."

Brewer was back in the summer of 1995—more comfortable at super middleweight—and scored two quick knockouts in Blue Horizon semifinals. Frank Rhodes, of Louisville, the USBA champion at 168 pounds, was 22-3-3, 12 K0s, and he agreed to defend against Brewer on March 12, 1996. Rhodes was managed by Buddy Ryan, who'd coached the Philadelphia Eagles from 1986 to 1990.

"That may have intimidated someone else but that motivated me," Brewer said. "Buddy Ryan wasn't gonna be the guy inside the ring. I picked up on everything Rhodes had done. I executed all those things in training. I was well prepared and I was very confident.

"Once I got in the ring and felt he had no punch…that was great. I always tried to spar guys who were bigger than me so I learned how to deal with the weight and the strength. When I got in there and he was shooting his best shots and I thought, 'Brother, you gotta come better than this.' From one to 12 I just continued to go forward."

That 12-round victory was, in my opinion, the most dominating performance against a quality opponent by any fighter in the history of the Blue Horizon. Scores were 120-109 and 120-108 twice.

Brewer worked an eight-hour day. After graduating from the Computer Learning Center in 1993, he'd become a data analyst for Pep Boys. He left Pep Boys in 1996 and became a technical consultant for Bristol Myers Squibb, AT&T, JP Morgan Chase and Aramark. He got his Network Administrative Diploma from Chubb Institute in Cherry Hill, New Jersey. Not exactly what you would expect from a professional boxer.

The win over Rhodes got Brewer in the IBF Top 10 at 168, and two fights later he became No. 1 contender for Roy Jones' world title. When Jones moved up to light-heavyweight, Brewer knocked out Gary Ballard, of South Africa, for the vacant title, on June 21, 1997. Don King gave me $150,000, and $120,000 of it went to Brewer. Showtime televised the fight from the Sun Dome at the University of South Florida in Tampa.

"Charles Brewer came back from the brink of oblivion," I told Bernard Fernandez, of the *Daily News*. "To me, he was a champion even before he did what he did (Saturday)."

Six months later, Brewer became the only man to defend a world title at the Blue Horizon, outpointing Joey DeGrandis, of Boston, over 12 rounds on USA. Four months after that, he got $210,000—his biggest purse—and survived two third-round knockdowns to stop lefty British challenger Herol Graham in the 10th on the Lennox Lewis-Shannon Briggs WBC heavyweight championship card at Atlantic City Convention Hall.

"Graham caught me with a straight left hand and I went down and tore two ligaments in my right ankle," Brewer said. "I had to go from the third round on against this unorthodox southpaw without being able to put any weight on my right foot. My ankle was throbbing and I thought it was going to burst open. I was ready to call it quits. The pain was building but so was my anger. No one in Graham's corner noticed I was dragging my right foot. I saw the opportunity to land a right hook from the orthodox stance and I hit him on the button in the 10th round and I stopped him.

Scores were split after nine rounds: 86-86, 85-84 Graham, 86-84 Brewer.

Another lefty, Antoine Byrd, of Pomona, California, was No. 1 for Brewer's title but I couldn't sell it to an American network. Cedric Kushner brokered a two-fight deal for Brewer to fight Byrd in August in Germany with the winner to box Sven Ottke there. Brewer K0d Byrd in three rounds in Leipzig.

Ottke was next. He had represented Germany in the 1988, 1992 and 1996 Olympics, never reaching the semifinals. He was 31 years old, 12-0 as a pro with one knockout. It looked safe. I had the choice of a European referee, two American judges and one European judge, or an American referee, two European judges, and one American judge. I chose the latter, thinking that a European referee would inhibit Brewer's body attack.

Brewer-Ottke was in Dusseldorf, known as the Paris of Germany for its fashion industry and art scene. Ottke fought like an amateur, jumping in and out, throwing pitty-pat punches which excited the crowd, though most missed or landed on Brewer's gloves. I thought Brewer was comfortably ahead going into the 12th round but we were in Germany.

Looking at the video years later, it confirmed my memory that Brewer showed no sense of urgency in the final three minutes, doing little more than jabbing. Ottke did his thing—in and out—bringing cheers.

George Hill, of Pennsylvania, scored 117-111 for Brewer. Manfred Kuechler, of Germany, had 116-112 for Ottke. Luca Montella, of Italy, the "neutral" judge, had 115-113 for Ottke. Hill was so upset he ran to me and asked how this could have happened. It took time to convince Brewer to attend the post-fight press conference, where one European writer captured it. He said Brewer had kept it "close enough for them to steal it."

"I take *some* responsibility," Brewer told me, "but I feel my team let me down. Ottke may have been known in Germany, but they put him in the ratings just to get him a shot at my title. The contract should have included a rematch in a venue of my choosing. Of all my people, the one who should have looked out for me should have been you."

Brewer couldn't accept that a rematch had no value in the United States. He won three fights against second-rate opposition. Ottke made six defenses, all in Germany, site of 33 of his 34 pro fights, the other having been in Austria in his seventh pro fight.

The rematch, on September 2, 2000, was in Magdeburg, a manufacturing center founded in 805 by Charlemagne and bombed by the Allies during World War II. Judge Shafeeq Rashada, of New Jersey, scored 116-113 for Brewer. Artur Ellensohn, of Germany, had 116-112 for Ottke, and the "neutral" judge, Manuel Maritxalar, of Spain, 116-111 for Ottke.

Two nights earlier, at a pre-fight dinner, I had seen Maritxalar, seated at the promoter's table, downing liquor shots the way college kids do at fraternity parties, laughing and joking while others cheered him on. I wondered how the NFL would react had owner Jerry Jones partied with the referees and umpires prior to a Dallas Cowboys football game.

Eight months and one fight later, Brewer got a Showtime slot against Antwun Echols. Echols was from Davenport, Iowa, and was 24-4-1, 23 K0s. He had twice lost to Bernard Hopkins for the IBF middleweight title, once by decision, once by knockout. Brewer versus Echols had *Fight of the Year* written all over it but we were second fiddle on a card showcasing young talent signed by Main

Events—Vivian Harris, Jeff Lacy, Juan Diaz, Malik Scott, Rocky Juarez, Francisco Bojado—all in six- and four-round fights.

Brewer-Echols was at the Mohegan Sun casino in Uncasville, Connecticut. Brewer knocked Echols down three times in the second round and referee Michael Ortega could have stopped it even though the three-knockdown rule had been waived. When Echols survived, I told Linda he would knock Brewer out. I figured Brewer had lost control and he would wildly attack Echols and get nailed.

Echols hurt Brewer with a right 20 seconds into the third round. Ortega gave Brewer a standing eight count even though Echols was thrown to the canvas when Ortega pulled him off Brewer. Brewer got extra time to recover but went after Echols again and got hit with nine unanswered shots. Ortega stopped it at 1:21.

"My corner should have calmed me down after the second round," Brewer said. "I expected them to see me going outside myself. They should have told me to calm my ass down and go back to the basics. I wanted to kill that guy. That's how I felt. They needed to be my eyes outside my eyes. But I think losing to Echols gave (Joe) Calzaghe the confidence to fight me."

Brewer won the NABF belt five months later against Fernando Zuniga, of Ecuador, at the First Union Center in Philadelphia, and then flew to Cardiff, Wales, to challenge Calzaghe for the WBO world title. Showtime was there and it was a brawl.

Calzaghe was 32-0, 27 KOs. Brewer was 37-8, 28 KOs, but the fight went 12 rounds. Brewer had his best moments late in the seventh when he backed Calzaghe up with several good shots. It was a terrific fight, but unanimous for Calzaghe (117-112, 118-111, 119-109). People who had questioned Brewer's chin were shocked he stayed on his feet. I thought Calzaghe was the first man Brewer had fought who was decisively better. Brewer agreed.

Ron Katz, then working for Sugar Ray Leonard Boxing, Inc., offered us Scott Pemberton four months later on ESPN from Foxwoods. I wasn't high on Pemberton, who was 24-2-1, 21 KOs, against limited opposition, even though he would be fighting at home. But it was too soon after Calzaghe.

Brewer had Pemberton down in round two but was hurt in the third and fourth and cut over the left eye. After another bad round, Linda worried that Brewer was getting hurt, so I told Scimeca to watch him. Then Brewer nailed Pemberton with a right to the head, left to the body and three more left hooks. After one standing-eight count, referee Steve Smoger stopped it at 2:03 with Pemberton down on his knees, his head on the canvas.

Our contract had run out six months earlier but I wasn't concerned. We were a team. But two fights after Pemberton, Scimeca told me Brewer had signed with Lou DiBella, who had left his position as Senior Vice President of HBO Sports in 1999 to promote. I was stunned, hurt, and furious. I couldn't believe it. Brewer was the one who said Boogaloo had told him: "Promoters can be with you one minute and the next minute they can be against you."

We were No. 1 in the WBO, waiting for a date for the world title challenge. "I wanted $20,000 to sign a new contract with you," Brewer later told me, but we had never discussed that. And he hadn't asked Watts or Scimeca for money when their contract ran out?

I had signed him after Top Rank released him. I had not given up after he lost three of four in 1994. Linda reminded me that all fighters are the same—which I always had told her—but they were not all the same. Not Bennie Briscoe, Marvin Johnson, Jeff Chandler, Tony Thornton or others. Times were changing but change is not always for the better.

British promoter Mickey Duff once said, "If you want loyalty, get a dog," but I never bought into that. I was more in line with Marty Feldman: "There is no such thing as 99 percent loyal. You're either 100 percent or you're nothing."

Scimeca was against the move, but Brewer said, "The train is leaving the station. If you're with me, hop on." I took my anger out on DiBella, but it should have been on Brewer. DiBella hadn't pursued Brewer—Brewer had pursued him.

"I don't think I did anything wrong," DiBella said. "Brewer told me he was a free agent and I think Augie wanted to stay clear of Brewer signing with someone like Don King so he pushed me to sign him. In hindsight, I would have passed. I had left HBO and I had not been a promoter long enough to experience that kind of disloyalty."

Brewer got no money to sign with DiBella. They did one fight together. Thirteen months after his last fight for me, Brewer was stopped in the ninth round in Germany by Mario Veit for the WBO interim title. I watched at home on my computer. DiBella and

Brewer parted. Five months later, Brewer was K0d by Lolengo Mock in Denmark and retired.

Time heals! You can forgive but you can never forget. Charles Brewer, Jr., turned pro for me on a 2020 card at Parx Casino in Bensalem. His dad trains him and also helps to manage his wife Sophie's *Jazzy Shears Hair Studio* in North Philly.

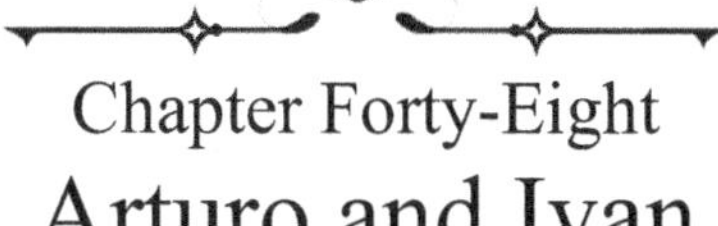

Chapter Forty-Eight

Arturo and Ivan

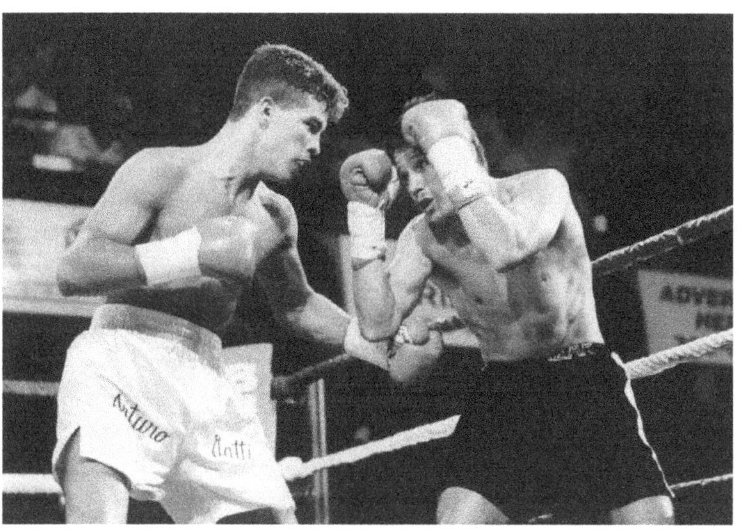

Arturo Gatti attacks Ricardo Salazar's body. (Peltz collection)

I signed Dynamite Douglas' son, Buster, to a promotional contract in 1983. He was 15-1-1, 12 KOs, but looked ordinary our first time together, winning a majority 10-round decision over Dave Johnson. It was Johnson's 10th straight loss on his way to a 13-16 record. Three months later, Douglas scored a first-round knockout over Eugene Cato, who was in the middle of a 3-5 career. Later that year, Douglas led Mike "The Giant" White (winless in his previous four) by 8-0, 7-0-1, 7-1 after eight rounds. In the ninth, he collapsed along the ropes and was counted out. When he came to my hotel room at the Sands to get his $3,000 purse, his dad reminded me that I owed them $2,500 for extending the contract for a second year. I countered that the contract stipulated I could cancel after any one loss—and I did just that. Dynamite started at me for a few seconds, then turned and left with his son, the future heavyweight champion of the world. So if a fighter is looking to sign with a *promoter who has a keen eye for talent, don't call J Russell Peltz. Sometimes, however, you get lucky.*

Joe Gatti, a middleweight from Jersey City, was managed by two ticket brokers, Pat Lynch and Richie Seibert. They had used my New Jersey promoter's license for a 1990 card at the Quality Inn in Newark. After Joe knocked out iron-chinned Eric Holland, of Philadelphia, I signed him. Joe won his next four fights, but Lynch and Seibert thought I was more interested in making competitive fights than I was in protecting Joe. Why would they think such a thing?

Joe's younger brother, Arturo, was born in Italy and moved to Canada where he became a member of the Canadian National amateur team. When Arturo turned pro later as a junior lightweight in 1991, Lynch and Seibert took him to Dan Duva and Main Events.

After Arturo had a couple fights, Duva called: "I have Arturo Gatti and you have Joe Gatti. Why don't we go partners? You give me 50 percent of Joe Gatti and I'll give you 50 percent of Arturo Gatti." That phone call was our contract. Duva was smart, tough, and a man of his word. I had 50 percent of Arturo Gatti's promotional contract from 1991 until 1998. Whenever he boxed, Main Events sent me a check for half the profit. Joe had a decent career, but Arturo's soared.

Dan passed away at 44 from a brain tumor in 1996 and younger brother Dino took over. We readjusted the percentages in 1998 to 65-35 in Dino's favor, and it stayed that way. When Dan's widow, Kathy, took over Main Events in the summer of 1999, she honored my verbal agreement until 2002. After Arturo K0d Terron Millett that year, I didn't want to put up money—for my share—to re-sign Arturo. I missed out on his paydays with Micky Ward and Floyd Mayweather, but I have no complaints.

Arturo was to fight November 14, 1992, at the Playboy Club in McAfee, New Jersey. Instead, he boxed for me three days later. He was 20 and his record was 6-0, 5 K0s. Philly's King Solomon, 27, was 6-1-3, 1 K0. He knocked Gatti down in the first round and won by split decision after six (58-55, 56-57, 59-55).

"Richie (Seibert) was *out* after the Solomon fight," Lynch said. "We wanted Arturo to fight on the same card as Joe but Richie said he had made a commitment to you to fight at the Blue Horizon and told us Arturo would get exposure on USA Network, so we went along and Arturo got beat. Arturo and Richie never got along and when our contract was up, Arturo wouldn't sign a new one if Richie was involved."

After Solomon, whenever it was my turn to use Arturo, Main Events instead gave me Ivan Robinson, their local lightweight prospect. But Main Events was fine when Arturo defended his USBA title for me in 1994 against Ricardo Salazar at the Blue Horizon and again in 1995 against Barrington Francis at Caesars, Atlantic City. He won both by knockout.

Gatti was known as "the human highlight reel," often coming from the brink of disaster to win. One fight you rarely hear about was the 10-rounder I made with him against Li'l Joe Hutchinson, of Indianapolis, on September 8, 2000, at the Molson Center in Montreal. Hutchinson, a southpaw, was 18-0-2, 8 KOs, but few gave him a chance against Gatti, then 32-4, 27 KOs.

Canadian middleweight rivals Stephane Ouelett and Davey Hilton were in the co-feature. Hilton was in the middle of a divorce from Gatti's sister, Anne-Marie, and there was no love lost between the soon-to-be former brothers-in-law. Gatti didn't even want to be in the same room with Hilton and it made for great pre-fight publicity. Gatti was in between his two world championship reigns (IBF junior lightweight 1995-98; WBC junior welterweight 2004-05) and 18,150 filled the Molson Centre.

Hutchinson was better than advertised, despite giving up five pounds (141.25 to 146.75).

"The main event had a little bit of everything—mostly blood emanating from Gatti's left eye," Herb Zurkowsky wrote in *The Montreal Gazette*. "He fought that way from the second round on, and ringside physician Pierre Meunier came dangerously close to stopping the fight at that point. By the fourth round Gatti had blood streaming from both eyes. The last time a boxer was cut so severely, his name was Rocky Balboa. Indeed, were it anyone but Gatti, the star attraction, it's unlikely the fight would have continued."

I was the on-site coordinator for ESPN2, wearing the headset to communicate with the TV truck. I planted myself at ringside in a baseball catcher's crouch, next to Mario Latraverse, chief inspector for the boxing commission, and pleaded with him not to stop the fight because we needed "air time." Talk about a conflict of interest. I was involved in Gatti's career and working for ESPN2 at the same time. Hardly anyone outside of Main Events knew.

While I was doing my best to keep the fight alive, Gatti was deducted one point for a low blow in the fourth round and Hutchinson a point for a head butt in the eighth. Gatti scored a knockdown in the sixth round, but Hutchinson got up and gave as well as he got. It went 10 rounds and Gatti won 98-93, 98-92 and 100-92 even though he had lost one point for low blows. *The Gazette* had it 96-92.

Whether or not my ringside pleas had anything to do with the fight going on I cannot say, but I certainly did not hurt Gatti's cause. His $250,000 may have been the most paid to that time for a fighter on ESPN2 in a non-world championship fight.

Seven months later, Gatti fought Oscar De La Hoya in Las Vegas in what was supposed to be his "going away present" from HBO. He was stopped in five rounds, took a year off and returned to beat Millett and have a trilogy with Micky Ward, win the WBC junior lightweight title, and become *The Franchise* for boxing in Atlantic City. Gatti's final record was 40-9, 31 K0s, but the excitement of his fights was more important than his statistics. His death from hanging in 2009 in Brazil at age 37 remains a mystery. His wife, Amanda Rodrigues, was cleared. Brazilian authorities ruled it a suicide and closed the case in 2011.

Gatti was involved in *The Ring* magazine *Fight of the Year* four times—against Gabriel Ruelas in 1997, against Ward in their first fight in 2002 and their third fight 2003. The fourth was against Ivan Robinson.

Robinson grew up in North Philly and graduated from Simon Gratz High School in 1989. He started boxing when he was 9 and was a two-time national amateur champion. "I followed that kid all around when he was an amateur," said Eddie Woods, who had 14 pro fights as a welterweight from 1958 to 1961. "His dad told me they were going big-time but I told him I could handle it."

Woods was secretary-treasurer and business agent for Teamsters Local 107 in Philadelphia. His partner, Kathy Nicolosi, owned Mother's Bakery, which made cheesecakes and other desserts from old family recipes, in Burlington, New Jersey.

Madison Square Garden boxing was Robinson's first promoter. Carl Moretti, its matchmaker from 1986 to 1993, was close with Robinson and took him to Main Events when MSG became Garden State Boxing and joined forces with Duva. "Carl Moretti always had my back," Robinson said. "He guided my career."

Robinson boxed six times for me at the Blue Horizon in the mid-1990s, including his 1995 fight with Jimmy Deoria, of Phoenixville, which he won with an assist from USA Network. Deoria, a member of the Schuylkill Township Police Department, was 20-4, 8 K0s, but had lost his last two to Angel Manfredy and Charles Murray. Few gave him a shot against Robinson, then 18-0, 8 K0s, and ranked No. 5 in the world by the IBF.

Deoria was scoring with body shots when he suffered a deep gash over his right eye in the fifth round. Referee Rudy Battle stopped the fight but there was confusion about what had caused the cut.

A head butt would have given Deoria the victory since he led on two of the three scorecards. Brad Jacobs, who was in charge of buying the fights at USA and coordinating the telecast from ringside, asked commissioners Greg Sirb and George Bochetto to look at TV replays. When they did, they ruled the cut had come from a punch. Robinson was awarded the knockout victory.

"When did they go to instant replays? asked John Mulvenna, Deoria's trainer. "After the fight I complained to Sirb that we had to go to the scorecards because that cut was opened by a butt. Rudy Battle told me it was a butt. Then I was told they had gone to the replays and they didn't see a butt. Hey, a cut like that isn't opened by a punch. I mean, Jimmy's eye was just laid open."

I agreed with Mulvenna. "How can you go to instant TV replay when it's not in the rule book?" I asked Sirb. "I can do anything I want to get it right," he said. I could not disagree.

Sirb knew boxing and he knew the rules. If a fighter was on a 30-day suspension, he would not let him fight on the 29th day—unlike a few commissions. He'd been a two-time All-American wrestler (118 pounds) at Edinboro (PA) College and, after getting his Masters in

Public Administration from Penn State, became Executive Director of the Pennsylvania State Athletic Commission in 1989.

He remains the longest-serving, full-time executive director in the country and is a founding member of the Association of Boxing Commissions (ABC), which formulated rules for governing boxing and implemented Federal ID cards to prohibit fighters from boxing under assumed names in different states. We had our run-ins over the years but that doesn't change my opinion of him.

Victory could have turned Deoria's career around. The loss took the air out of him. He lost his next two fights and retired in 1996 at 20-7, 8 K0s. He still works as a police officer in Phoenixville.

Eighteen months after beating Deoria, Robinson (23-0, 10 K0s) challenged Phillip Holiday (29-0, 16 K0s), of South Africa, for Holiday's IBF world lightweight title at the Mohegan Sun casino in Uncasville, Connecticut. Robinson lost a 12-round decision by scores of 116-112, 117-111, 118-110.

"I was young (25) and married and my wife was pregnant and she and my Dad didn't get along," Robinson said. "I got in between them and I fired my Dad from my corner. I went into camp with Butch (Odell Cathay) as my head trainer but Main Events thought Tommy Brooks should be the head trainer. Brooks was the hottest thing at the time because he had worked with Junior Jones, who had just upset Marco Antonio Barrera. They said they were bringing Brooks in as head trainer. I didn't speak up.

"Butch stayed in the background. I thought Tommy gave me all kinds of bad instructions in the corner so I fought what was good for me. Eddie (Woods) was a great manager but when it came to family issues, Eddie didn't do it. If my dad had stayed in my corner, I wouldn't have had some of the losses I had."

After the, fight, Kathy Nicolosi left boxing. "Kathy loved boxing and she loved to get into the ring during the introductions." Woods said. "We were together five years. She had been paying most of the expenses and I hadn't made a dime at that point. Neither had she."

Six months later, Robinson was stopped in three rounds by Israel "Pito" Cardona, of Hartford, Connecticut, at the Wildwood (New Jersey) Convention Center.

"I was fat and out of shape and I had to lose 10 pounds two days before the fight," he said, "but losing to Cardona helped me because they thought I was through." Two wins later, Robinson fought Gatti in a HBO-televised fight from Atlantic City. Gatti had relinquished his IBF junior lightweight title and moved up to lightweight, but had lost on cuts in January of 1998 to Manfredy. Robinson was supposed to be a tuneup.

"We were offered $40,000 but I got it up to $51,000," Woods said. "I told Ivan we were gonna take the fight because I knew he could beat Gatti and then we could make big money in a rematch and get back to where he had been."

At the press conference, Robinson said Gatti was "a good fighter and a good puncher and the fight was gonna be a brawl." Gatti was not so diplomatic. "Gatti made a comment that 'you don't bring knives to a gun fight' and I didn't understand what he said," Robinson said. "Butch explained to me that Gatti meant that I couldn't punch. And then, the morning of the fight, Gatti told me he was gonna knock me out and I said, 'no problem.'

"We had been in camp together a few times but we never had sparred. I had a great team. I brought in Bouie Fisher to work with Butch and I had Leon Tabbs, who was my cut man and also a good trainer himself. I got great sparring and I had a good conditioning coach and Eddie took me out for running and to breakfast and dinner. On the way to the ring that night I decided I was gonna fight, not box. I don't know if he did it on purpose but I felt Gatti had disrespected me. Gatti was gonna have to kill me."

Not only was it *The Ring* magazine's *Fight of the Year* but also the *Upset of the Year*. Robinson threw four-, five- and six-punch combinations. It was a war and Robinson won a 10-round split decision (96-94, 93-96, 98-93).

"After I beat Gatti the first time, my wife and I had planned to go on a delayed honeymoon to Jamaica," Robinson said. "HBO pressured me for the rematch. They offered $200,000 and that wasn't nearly enough money. Jim Lampley started calling me and so did Larry Merchant but I told Eddie I wasn't fighting Gatti for $200,000 even though we really didn't have any other big offers at the time."

Woods got Robinson $410,000.

He still planned to go on his honeymoon, "but they offered us training expense money if I canceled the trip so I stayed home and went into training," Robinson said. The second fight, less than four months after the first, saw Robinson earn a 10-round unanimous decision (95-94 twice and 97-72) at the Trump Taj Mahal.

Robinson's career should have blossomed, but four months later he lost a lopsided 10-round decision to Manfredy, which began a slide in which he lost 10 of his last 17 fights. He quit midway through 1997 at 32-12-2, 12 K0s. Gatti's career lasted a decade longer and was more lucrative, but Robinson isn't bitter.

"I wished I could have made that kind of money," he said, "but it just wasn't in the cards."

After boxing, Robinson worked in different drug rehabilitation centers and he also worked with mentally disabled people. He trained young fighters but he was not a slave to boxing.

"The fighters today are nothing like when I was coming up and nothing like when you (Russell) were coming up," he said. "You definitely gotta be real, a hard worker and look forward to what you are doing. It's not a four- or five-hour job. Boxing takes years of sacrifice and a lot of these guys today don't have it.

"It's kind of hard being a manager today. I'm not one of those hungry, greedy managers. I've been in the game and I know the game. I help the kids. I talk to them and I tell them the right things to do. If they're not moving along, I tell them to leave it alone and do something else."

Chapter Forty-Nine

USA Closes Shop

USA Network terminated its Tuesday Night Fights series in the summer of 1998. It was a major blow to boxing and to promoters trying to establish or maintain a foothold in the sport. Other television outlets tried to fill the void, but none with the quality or consistency of the USA series. It had been one of the longest continually running boxing programs on television since its

debut in 1982. Unlike ESPN, which had dealt exclusively with Bob Arum's Top Rank, Inc., from 1980 to 1996, USA was not a closed shop. It dealt with promoters around the country.

Promoters like me, Art Pelullo, Mike Acri, Bill Kozerski, Murad Muhammad, Ron Weathers, Rock Newman, Houston Boxing Association, Rick Parker, Dan Goossen, Square Ring, Main Events and Cedric Kushner had benefitted from USA. Top Rank got an occasional slot. It was smart to spread the wealth.

While it had telecast fights from the casino capitals of Las Vegas and Atlantic City, USA also traveled to Galveston, Texas; Steubenville, Ohio; Cherokee, North Carolina; Erie, Pennsylvania; Fort Bragg, North Carolina; Bismarck, North Dakota; Long Beach, California; Flint, Michigan; Bay St. Louis, Mississippi, and Washington, DC. Fights were held in arenas, National Guard armories, hotel ballrooms and one on the deck of an aircraft carrier. The Blue Horizon was a regular stop. USA went twice to England, once to Mexico.

Appearances by George Foreman, Larry Holmes, Hector Camacho and Roberto Duran (in his 100th fight), who were trying to prolong their careers and catapult themselves into major events, were showcased. So were future champions like Riddick Bowe, Bernard Hopkins, Lennox Lewis, Arturo Gatti, Oscar De La Hoya and Roy Jones, Jr. World championship fights were rare but ratings were solid.

"USA pulled the plug because people who watched boxing on USA on Tuesday nights did not watch anything else on the network," said Brad Jacobs, its program consultant, "and the people who watched everything else on the network were not necessarily a boxing demographic."

The finale, on August 25, 1998, featured two USA staples: Butterbean and the Blue Horizon. Arizona senator John McCain joined Pennsylvania governor Tom Ridge at ringside with Greg Sirb. It was a celebration and a wake.

Georgia-born Eric Esch was a five-time World Toughman Heavyweight Champion. He was nicknamed "Butterbean" after he went on a diet of chicken and butterbeans to meet the 400-pound Toughman limit. He was 5-foot-11 and his trunks resembled the American flag. He went from being a cartoon character to a cult hero. Though I was *old school*, I couldn't help but like him. He gave me a ceramic statue of himself for my memorabilia collection.

Butterbean was known as the *King of the 4 Rounders*. He turned pro in 1994 and by the time he got to the Blue Horizon, he was 39-1-1, 32 K0s, against so-so opposition. No one complained. Tim Pollard, of Louisville, Kentucky, never had a chance. Except for a quick loss to a 54-year-old Ron Lyle, Pollard's 6-4-2 record had been against foes on the same level as Bean's. It was over in 97 seconds. The crowd loved it.

At the end of the night, fans looking for autographs surrounded Bean on the steps leading from the Blue Horizon to North Broad Street. It was the end of our own *Era of Good Feelings.*

Nine months earlier, Bill Cayton had approached me about becoming the matchmaker for another television network. But let me back up.

Cayton and Jacobs ran Big Fights, Inc., which owned the world's largest collection of boxing films. They also had managed Cyclone Hart, Edwin Rosario, Wilfred Benitez and Mike Tyson. Jacobs passed away in 1988 but Cayton moved on with the business and managed Tommy Morrison, Vinny Pazienza and Omar Sheika.

In the late 1970s, while still at the Spectrum, I had signed a deal with Big Fights to distribute videos of my fights worldwide. The beauty was that every fight was equal. A Jeff Chandler video was worth as much as a Jack Dempsey film. A Bennie Briscoe fight was equal to a Joe Louis. If Australia purchased a package of 10 fights for $100,000 and a Marvin Hagler fight from the Spectrum was included, I would get a check for $10,000.

I got one check.

Jim Barniak, former sports columnist for the *Bulletin*, was sports director of PRISM, which had televised many of the Spectrum cards in the 1970s and my Atlantic City cards in the 1980s. When PRISM moved its offices out of the Spectrum, Barniak wanted to get rid of its three-quarter inch videotapes. I bought the boxing collection for $750 and the worldwide rights in perpetuity, and added them to the Big Fights package.

In the spring of 1998, Cayton sold his fight film library to ESPN. Newspaper reports put the sale as high as $100 million, but the actual figure was closer to $70 million. How much was stock and how much was cash never was divulged. My contribution to Cayton's 3,000 or 4,000 films was somewhere around three percent. Cayton, who wanted control of a new *Friday Night Fights* series on ESPN 2, insisted they hire me as matchmaker.

Cayton had ESPN over a barrel. Big Fights, Inc. had licensed its films to Classic Sports Network for a limited amount of time. When ESPN purchased Classic Sports Network they needed those fights since boxing got better ratings than videos of old baseball, football or basketball games. ESPN was worried that Cayton would sell outright to Fox or Madison Square Garden Network, so it kept raising its offer.

It also agreed to pay Cayton $1,000,000 a year for 10 years as CEO of *Friday Night Fights* and another $12,000 a month to cover his office expenses in New York. Whether or not the salary and office expenses were included in the $70 million is uncertain.

I thought my role, choosing which fights to televise, was a reward for years of promoting competitive fights. My contract also gave me the ability to promote six cards a year on ESPN2, which raised conflict-of-interest charges from other promoters. Cayton was managing Pazienza and Sheika and that also raised eyebrows. Several websites took shots. It didn't bother me because I was going to do what was best for ESPN. Not everyone bought into that.

After the USA finale on August 25, ESPN2's *Friday Night Fights* began October 2 at the Blue Horizon. Thomas Tate outpointed Demetrius Davis, of Washington, DC, in an NABF super middleweight title defense. ESPN2 also piped in the telecast of Andrew Golota's 10-round decision over Tim Witherspoon from Wroclaw, Poland. It was a mediocre show.

Switching from Tuesday to Friday nights caught our fans off guard, but two months later we sold out when Richard DeJesus, of Wilmington, Delaware, upset former IBF bantamweight champion Orlando Canizales by majority decision over 10 rounds. Canizales stopped DeJesus in their 1999 rematch and retired later that year after losing on points to David Toledo, both at the Blue Horizon.

I tried to avoid the minor alphabet groups and I tried to keep women's boxing off the air. I love women's basketball, women's soccer, women's volleyball, women's softball. I love Christy Martin, Jacqui Frazier, Laila Ali, Lucia Rijker and Heather Hardy, but I don't like seeing women getting hit. Sue me!

Bob Papa remained the blow-by-blow announcer on ESPN 2. Teddy Atlas traded in his job as a trainer and replaced Al Bernstein as ringside analyst. That was the start of my friendship with Atlas, one of the most "real" people I've ever known. He attacked the boxing establishment, vehemently criticized bad decisions and dared to go where other analysts feared to tread. Fans crowded around him in every city we visited, asking for autographs and talking boxing.

Bernstein did not suffer. He blossomed at Showtime and was inducted into the International Boxing Hall of Fame in 2012. Atlas got there in 2019.

I wanted to do fights away from casinos. We did the second card with Don Elbaum and Joe DeGuardia at the Capitol Theatre in Port Chester, New York. Light-heavyweight David Telesco beat Frank Tate.

As a young fan, I had read in *The Ring* magazine about the big crowds in Canada, so when Don Majeski asked about boxing at the Molson Centre in Montreal, I was delighted. The 18,000-seat building sold out November 27, 1998, when Davey Hilton, trailing on points, knocked out Stephane Ouellet with 18 seconds left in the 12th round to win the Canadian middleweight title. It was a great night for boxing. Anthony Giordano, ESPN's on-site director, joked that "even a blind squirrel can find an acorn in a snowstorm," referring to my success at landing that fight in that atmosphere.

We did a card with promoter Tony Trudnich at the Orleans casino, off the Las Vegas strip, early in 1999. Thomas Tate stopped Merqui Sosa in the 10th round of their 12-round NABF title fight, an ESPN classic.

One week after Tate-Sosa, I matched two more super middleweights, Sheika and Anwar Oshana. Fred Berns promoted the card in Carmichael's Restaurant in Chicago. Future IBF lightweight champ Paul Spadafora beat Rocky Martinez in the semifinal.

Sheika was born in Paterson, New Jersey, of Palestinian descent. Oshana was born in Syria and living in Chicago.

Flags of both Middle East nations filled the catering hall at Carmichael's. Contingents representing Palestine and Syria sang and swayed to their music. Though the countries were friendly, pride took over. The place was electric, the atmosphere surreal. The dressing room was a loft over a storage area and all 14 fighters shared it.

When Fredda Berns told me she had sold all 800 tickets, I begged her to sell standing room to create an even greater atmosphere.

"The tickets were $75," Fred Berns said. "My daughter Francie, who was 25, started scalping them for $200 apiece. I taught her well." Sheika stopped Oshana in three rounds. Despite a brief post-fight melee in the ring caused by an Oshana fanatic, this was what I wanted for ESPN. I was tired of antiseptic casinos. I wanted old-school, blue-collar boxing. I wanted to take boxing back to the real fans.

Al Valenti did a card in the summer of 1999 with junior welterweight Micky Ward, of Lowell, Massachusetts. Valenti's grandfather, Rip Valenti, had been around since the 1930s. He was the financial backer for promoter Sam Silverman and had been involved with Marvin Hagler. Silverman and Rip both made it to the International Boxing Hall of Fame.

I had co-promoted two cards with Al and trainer George Cruz in 1997. ESPN2, an afterthought in those days, televised both from the San Juan Center, a gym in Hartford. Our headliner, featherweight Angel Vazquez, looked like the real thing until some people got in his ear and he sued me to break our promotional contract. We went to court, and, thanks to my attorney, Alan Epstein, the judge ruled in our favor and they bought me out. I walked away and Vazquez' career stalled.

Valenti's 1999 card was at the Casino Ballroom on the Boardwalk in Hampton Beach, New Hampshire, which he'd dubbed the "Redneck Riviera." You could fit 1,536 in the Ballroom—built in 1899—where entertainers from Bing Crosby and Buddy Rich to Led Zeppelin and Whoopie Goldberg had performed. Ward stopped Philly's Jermal Corbin in five rounds to rejuvenate his career. Two years later, almost to the day, Ward's classic win there over Emanuel Augustus was voted *Fight of the Year* by *The Ring* magazine. Valenti promoted seven cards in Hampton Beach, all on ESPN2.

Some promoters complained. One claimed I was "taking food off his table" by not awarding him dates. A couple websites accused me of taking money under the table to use certain fighters, but when the whispers, innuendos and accusations went unproven, retractions were printed in agate typeface.

By the end of that first season at ESPN2, the people who'd hired me had moved to ABC. Those left in charge cut my salary in half to $1,000 a week and relegated me to overseeing the cards instead of choosing them. Bob Yalen, who'd been Director of Programming, took over. I stayed because it was my best option, but it became a hollow, frustrating job. I made some fights, but not many.

In 2002, shortly before the statute of limitations expired, I sued Cayton for my share of his film sale to ESPN. George Bochetto, former Pennsylvania boxing commissioner, was my attorney. Our discovery uncovered several sales of films worldwide that had included some of my fights, but I only had been paid that once. Cayton died late in 2003 and Bochetto tied up his estate.

Cayton should have made a deal with me when he sold to ESPN. He could have asked if I wanted my films taken out of the sale or a price to include them. I have no idea why he didn't but I would have settled for a fraction of what I eventually got.

Late in the summer of 2003, Yalen told me that unless I dropped the lawsuit against Cayton, ESPN would not let me promote any fights on the network because Cayton had sued ESPN after I sued him. I reminded Yalen I had a contract guaranteeing me so many fights a year. That was the end of the conversation and the beginning of the end of my time at ESPN. I was gone within a year but that was as much my choice as theirs.

Working with ESPN was one of the most disappointing experiences of my half century in boxing. We settled my lawsuit with Cayton's son, Brian. I don't know if the money came from Cayton's estate or from ESPN or both. I gave some to my two sons, Matthew and Daniel, and Linda and I bought a winter home in Florida.

Chapter Fifty

Give My Regards to Broad Street

The smiling face of Kassim Ouma hid a tortured childhood. (Ray Bailey photo)

There were nine cards in Philadelphia in 1999, matching the lows from 1964 and 1966. The next decade would have 221, an increase of 54. Bernard Hopkins carried the flag for the city. He unified most of the middleweight title (IBF, WBC, WBA), by knocking out Felix Trinidad in Madison Square Garden in 2001, and three years later K0d Oscar De La Hoya in Las Vegas to add the WBO version.

ESPN2 had replaced USA as the television home of the Blue Horizon, but Friday night did not have the same feel as Tuesday night and out-of-town fighters dominated the main events. The big fights of the 1970s in Philly and the all-Philly Blue Horizon showdowns of the 1980s and early 90s were history. Missing from North Broad Street were the locals: Ivan Robinson, Anthony Boyle, Tim Witherspoon, Rodney Moore, Frankie Mitchell, Tony Thornton, Tony Green. Not that their replacements were shabby.

Lightweight Billy "The Kid" Irwin became a regular. Irwin was from the Canadian side of Niagara Falls and was 23-2, 13 K0s, in the fall of 1998, when he debuted here. He was stone-faced, slow-moving, heavy-handed—a favorite with the Philly crowd. He had a powerful left hook and mixed his shots to the body and head.

Booking agent Rick Glaser asked me to use him and we agreed that if Irwin made it big, we would be partners. Glaser was from Buffalo, New York, and he had signed Irwin to a two-year promotional agreement despite not holding a promoter's license in New York or Pennsylvania.

I paid Glaser a booking fee when Irwin boxed at the Blue Horizon and Glaser booked him in Canada when there was nothing in Philly. It did not start well. Gerald Gray's slick style was all wrong for Irwin, and the New Yorker won an eight-round split decision on the non-televised portion of the first *Friday Night Fights* card late in 1998.

Glaser asked if we should give up on Irwin, but I gave him another shot, this time against Chucky Tschorniawsky, a popular Polish lightweight from Philadelphia. Chucky T was 15-1-1, 8 K0s. It figured to be a competitive fight between two tough White kids. It wasn't. Referee Joe O'Neill gave Chucky T standing eight-counts in the second and seventh rounds before pulling Irwin off him 23 seconds into the eighth. It would be the first of seven consecutive knockout wins for Irwin at the Blue Horizon, all televised by ESPN2.

Flying back to Niagara Falls was expensive on Saturdays. It was cheaper to pay for an extra hotel room night and have Billy and his trainer, Pat Kelly, fly home Sunday. Linda and I took them out to dinner Saturday nights at Italian restaurants in South Philly. We became close.

The air time on ESPN2, which included a devastating one-punch, left-hook knockout of contender John Lark, helped Irwin secure an IBF title fight with Paul Spadafora on December 16, 2000, in Pittsburgh.

Mike Acri, who promoted Spadafora, warned me that "Glaser is looking to screw you" on the title fight. I had sent a letter for Glaser to sign to ensure we were 50-50, but he never did. He said "all partnerships are not 50-50." Yeah, okay!

"Russell sent a contract to Rick for 50 percent and Rick said no," Irwin told Dan Dakin, of *The Review*, a Niagara Falls newspaper, in October, 2000. "I tried to tell Rick to make it a partnership but it didn't work. I was kind of the middle man. I had 10 or 11 fights under Rick and seven of them were at the Blue Horizon promoted by Russell. He was the one who put me on television. He got me the exposure and that's a big thing."

Glaser got a lawyer to handle the case in New York. I didn't want the hassle and expense. My mistake! The situation dragged on until 2004 when I paid Glaser $8,760, which was more than I netted from Irwin's title fight. After losing on points to Spadafora, Irwin boxed for me once more at the Blue Horizon. He lost to Dorin Spivey and we parted ways.

"He (Glaser) sued me," Irwin recalled. "We went to court. I lost. Then he said forget about it if you re-sign, which I did. I had a few wins, got the (Juan) Diaz fight (for the WBA title), got the flu the week of the fight. And it is what it is." Irwin was stopped in nine rounds by Diaz and retired in 2005.

The relationship between me and the latest owners of the Blue Horizon was deteriorating. Vernoca Michael and Carol Ray were part of a group that purchased the Bluc Horizon from Ross Collette in 1994. We never hit it off. I had a verbal agreement with Collette that no other promoter could run a show within two weeks of mine—on either side—but that was disregarded. The women also wanted to be part of the negotiations with USA and ESPN2, but I had concrete deals with both networks. I should have sat down and explained things but I got my back up and there was friction.

For goodwill, I bought a television for their concession stand—income from food and beverage sales was theirs—and USA and ESPN2 sent a "live feed" (cable) so customers in line would not miss the action. But the ESPN2 technical crew complained about locals who dealt illegal drugs on Carlisle Street behind the Blue Horizon where the TV truck parked on fight nights. One night Maureen Sacks asked, "What are we doing here?" My only answer was financial. So we left.

My last card there was September 21, 2001, 10 days after 9/11. It was another sellout. We draped an American flag over the West balcony and positioned another one on the stage. Several fighters wore red, white and blue trunks. When junior welterweight Miguel Figueroa walked to the ring, his entourage followed with a boom box, blasting Ray Charles' version of *America the Beautiful*. Local R&B recording artist Bunny Sigler sang *God Bless America* from the ring. Chants of "USA, USA, USA" reverberated throughout the building.

Tickets were $45 for ringside and the lower balcony, $40 for the upper balcony. Junior middleweight Nick Acevedo, of New York, won a 10-round split decision over Carlos Bojorquez, of Mira Loma, California, in the main event. "I only live seven blocks from the World Trade Center," Acevedo told Bernard Fernandez, of the *Daily News*, "and a friend of mine lost his cousin in the attack. Winning this fight meant a lot to me."

Our profit was $18,437.66. Two months later we went to the Park Hyatt at the Bellevue in Center City for a black-tie affair. All tickets were $100, which included two drinks and hors d'oeuvres, but less than 400 paid to see Julian Wheeler, of Virginia Beach, outpoint Efren Hinojosa, of Lakeside, California, over 12 rounds for the USBA lightweight title. Even with $65,000 from ESPN, we lost $3,071.08.

Leaving the Blue Horizon was not my smartest business move. We went from a packed house on a patriotic night to a tomb, and from paying $4,400 rent to $24,439.01 for rent, food and drinks. I thought we would get at least 500 customers and the additional 100 would have brought an extra $10,000 to put us over the top. But it's not always about the money.

The following February we went back downtown to the University of the Arts on South Broad Street. The building had been home to the YMHA (Young Men's Hebrew Association). The auditorium sat 1,072 and there was a balcony on three sides, similar to the Blue Horizon, though not as steep and not as cozy, but perfect for Center City where customers could have dinner, then go to the fights.

We sold 1,109 tickets ($50,041.75 gate) and junior middleweight Kassim Ouma, of Uganda, out-pointed Michael Lerma, of Waco, Texas, over 10 rounds, in a battle of action southpaws. We made a few dollars even though ESPN2 had cut the rights fee to $52,500. The bills were high so we went on the road and took Ouma with us.

I had spotted Ouma in Mississippi. Sal Musumeci, a retired New York City fireman who had made his fortune building hotels, promoted an outdoor card at the Grand Casino in Gulfport in the summer of 2001. Ouma dissected former world-title challenger Tony Marshall like we did frogs in 10th grade biology. He took Marshall apart with punches from every angle. Scores were 100-90, 99-91, 97-93, reminding me of how Bobby Chacon had taken down Augie Pantellas in 1978 at the Spectrum.

I went to Ouma's dressing room and he thanked me for the opportunity to fight on ESPN. He was a fun-loving 22-year-old with a smile that could warm the coldest heart. I wanted to sign him.

Three months later, Ouma outpointed former WBO champion Verno Phillips at the Dakota Magic Casino in Hankinson, North Dakota, a town with a population of just over 1,000, an hour south of Fargo. Sugar Ray Leonard, whose new company promoted the fight, wanted him, too.

Steve Shepherd, a five-time world kickboxing champion, had a piece of Ouma's managerial contract. He wanted to go with Sugar Ray, but was overruled by Jim Rowan, the majority owner.

Rowan was from Philly. His mother, Rena, had co-founded, with Sidney Kimmel, *Jones New York*, the women's clothing store chain. She was a philanthropist and later married singer Vic Damone. "We heard you were cheap, but honest," Rowan said. Shepherd was out shortly afterward.

The seventh of 13 children, Ouma was 5 when the Ugandan rebel army abducted him. He did not see his family for three years, and, until he was 17, he was in the National Resistance Army. When he was 7, he was ordered to shoot a fellow child soldier who had lost some ammunition. The alternative was to be shot himself.

Ouma joined the Ugandan amateur boxing team and, in 1998, came to the U.S. for an international boxing tournament. He never returned home. Uganda considered him a deserter and soldiers beat his father to death.

Dino Duva also was trying to sign Ouma. I could have gone it alone, but I agreed to a partnership because I had benefitted from my involvement with Arturo Gatti when Dino and his brother, Dan, had been in charge at Main Events. Main Events had done the bulk of the work with Gatti and I did the same with Ouma.

Beginning with a fourth-round knockout over Pedro Ortega on December 13, 2001—one day after his 23d birthday—Ouma won seven straight, the biggest over Angel Hernandez, of Chicago, and J.C. Candelo, of Colombia. Three were in Connecticut, two in Delaware, one in Mississippi, one in Philadelphia. All were televised by ESPN2. By 2003, Tom Moran, an independent TV producer from Philadelphia, who had been involved with Tim Witherspoon's post-championship career, joined Rowan as co-manager.

When a training injury forced Ouma out of a rematch with Phillips for the vacant IBF world title in the spring of 2004, Philips won the belt by beating Carlos Bojorquez—another Ouma victim—on June 5, 2004. Four months later in Las Vegas, Ouma beat Phillips for the title.

At the time, Ouma owned the record for most punches thrown and most punches landed by any junior middleweight in a single fight, according to Compubox, which counts punches at ringside for television. At the end of his first title defense early in 2005, a masterful 12-round decision over Kofi Jantuah in Atlantic City, HBO analyst Larry Merchant hailed Ouma as "one of the new faces in boxing, replacing some of the old faces that are fading away."

The new face quickly faded. As good as Ouma looked against Jantuah, that's how bad he looked losing the title that summer to Roman Karmazin in Las Vegas.

"The night before he won the world title against Verno Phillips, Kassim and I had a wonderful African dinner with friends of his, a couple from Kenya who lived in Vegas and were prominent leaders in the African community," Moran said. "It was nice, quiet and relaxing for Kassim.

"Since we were back in Vegas for the Karmazin fight, Kassim asked if we could go there again for a barbecue the night before the fight. We had a dozen of our close friends and he invited them. Then a whole bunch of Ugandan fans followed us from the casino lobby, and Kassim invited them along. I should have said no but I didn't pay attention. At this couple's house, it became a big party and a major mistake. Kassim's head was never in the fight."

Dino and I had split before the Karmazin fight. Without telling him, I had signed over three options to his former company, Main Events, which had control of the Jantuah card since Arturo Gatti was in the main event against Jesse James Leija. Dino felt I had done this to hurt him, but it was the only way to have gotten Ouma HBO exposure. We settled out of court. I should have told Dino what I was doing even though he never would have agreed.

I got a new partner, Richard Schaefer, CEO of Golden Boy Promotions. The loss to Karmazin was our first fight together and it was a disaster. Kassim got knocked down early and lost a unanimous 12-round decision. Golden Boy and I had paid him a bonus to re-sign. That, plus the settlement with Dino, put me in a financial hole it would take more than two years to climb out of.

After Karmazin, Kassim won four in a row, the hardest a 12-round split decision over Marco Antonio Rubio on May 6, 2006, in Las Vegas. After Rubio dropped Ouma in the first round, Merchant remarked that Golden Boy and I had given Ouma a $400,000 bonus and "so far he hasn't been a very good investment." When Ouma took over late in the fight, Merchant said, "He (Ouma) may yet earn that $400,000 bonus." Scores were 117-110 and 116-111 for Ouma, and a preposterous 114-113 for Rubio from Dalby Shirley, who had a history of odd scorecards in Nevada.

Ronnie Shields had replaced ex-junior welterweight champ Johnny Bumphus as trainer, but left after the Rubio fight in a dispute with management over money. Had Shields stayed, I believe Ouma would have remained elite. The bigger problem, according to Moran, was that Shields trained his fighters in Houston and there would be no one to look after Ouma once he left the gym. Countryman Fred Muteweta took over and Ouma trained in Florida.

"Kassim had demons from his childhood and he was always vulnerable to PTSD issues we can never imagine," Moran said. "Training camp and discipline clashed with his head so we needed positive outlets—bowling, playing pool, 4 or 5 a.m. training sessions—anything to keep him active. Otherwise, Kassim would find outlets—drinking, smoking weed, gambling—all of which were serious problems. We took him to AA sessions, NA sessions and tried to get him help. Houston was the worst because there was a large Ugandan population that he could party and hang out with."

A lopsided win over Sechew Powell (20-0, 12 K0s) in August in Madison Square Garden landed Ouma a world middleweight title fight with Jermain Taylor in Little Rock, Arkansas, Taylor's backyard. HBO would televise. Ouma was 25-2-1 and he got $500,000 for the fight which Lou DiBella promoted. He was too small at 160. Scores were 115-113, 117-111, 118-110, all for Taylor.

Ouma lost four of his next five and we split. Sadly, at 42, and living in Munich, Germany, he still fights. Early in 2021, he lost an eight-round decision in Belgium to Tony Browne, of Dublin, Ireland. It was Browne's third pro fight after a so-so amateur career. The loss, his 13th in his last 17 fights, dropped Ouma's record to 29-15-1.

"On a trip back to Africa, Kassim wrongly overstayed his Refugee Travel Document," Moran said. "That had entitled him to re-entry into the U.S. Because of his police record, he was barred from renewing the Refugee Travel Document overseas....In effect, he'd barred himself."

Chapter Fifty-One

New Alhambra

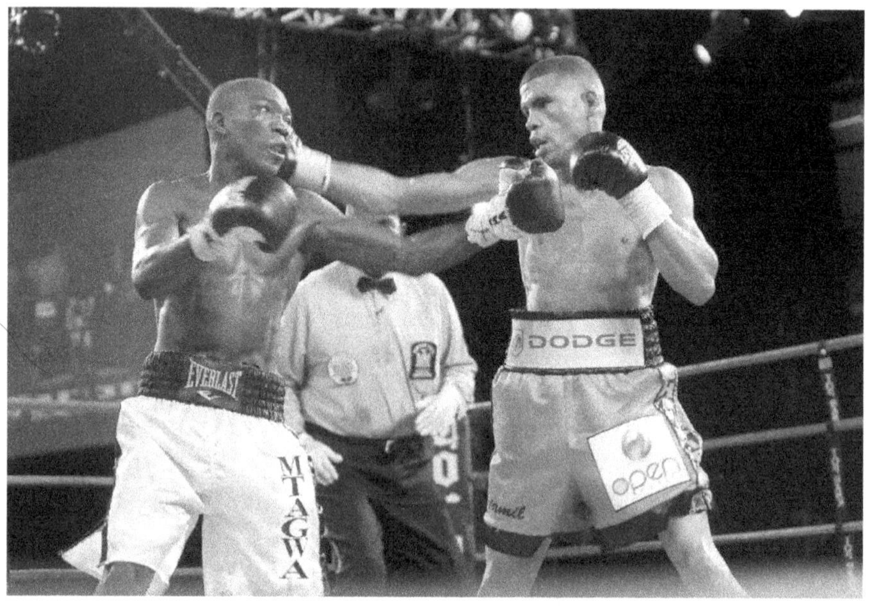

Rogers Mtagwa trades with Juan Manuel Lopez in 2009. (Ray Bailey photo)

Hall-of-Fame promoter Don Elbaum, of Erie, had staged one card at South Philly's Viking Hall in 1993. Diane Fischer followed with three in 2000. Fischer, an Atlantic City hair stylist who been drawn to boxing watching Friday Night Fights on television with her dad in the early 1960s, had begun promoting in 1997 at the Tropicana Hotel Casino where she owned the DeeMar salon. Fischer quit Philly for Kahunaville, a dining/entertainment complex on the Wilmington, Delaware, waterfront, where entertainers from Bob Dylan to Hall and Oates had performed. She was tough enough to survive in boxing's macho world. One night at Kahunaville, when we were talking business, she sat on my lap and said, "I always kiss my men before they screw me." Fischer became the most successful small-club female promoter in the country, running cards in Delaware, New Jersey, Pennsylvania and Virginia.

Don Chargin, one of boxing's greatest promoters and matchmakers, along with his wife Lorraine, were among my best friends—in or out of business. He was the original "boy promoter," his first card coming in 1951 when he was 23. We had met in 1972 in the middle of his 20-year run (1964-1984) as matchmaker at the Olympic Auditorium in Los Angeles.

Chargin had a contract for dates with Telefutura, a Spanish language television network owned by Univision. He wanted to do a card with me at the Blue Horizon. I couldn't say no.

Vernoca Michael had been promoting there after I'd left, her best pupil being heavyweight Eddie Chambers, who fought there 18 times between 2002 and 2006, eventually losing to Waldimir Klitschko for the world title. We made peace and Chargin and I ran a card January 30, 2004. Junior welterweight Miguel Figueroa, of Camden, lost a 10-round decision to Rogelio Castaneda, of Sacramento, in front of 1,352 ($63,165). Telefutura paid $35,000. I made $3,483.47.

I could never recreate the atmosphere of the Blue. Viking Hall, the renovated warehouse at Swanson and Ritner, was my best bet, so the 1,100-seat building became home in 2004. Joe Hand had turned me on to it and we became partners. I dubbed it the New Alhambra in honor of the original Alhambra, the former movie theatre at 12th and Morris where Jimmy Riggio had promoted from 1959 to 1962. Joey Giardello, Eddie Perkins, George Benton and Kitten Hayward had boxed there.

Omar Sheika, fighting as a light-heavyweight, knocked out E.T. Whitaker, of Warren, Ohio, in two rounds on May 14, 2004. All seats were $50 but only 632 came. The gate was $28,050 and we lost $24,932.05.

Six weeks later junior welterweight Mike Stewart was in the main event against Carlos Antonio Escobar, but before the show started, the electrical system shut down and the lights went out. In the box office, someone had placed a blanket over the transformer, which overheated and blew out all the circuit-breakers.

Linda grabbed me from behind and said, "Do you really need this aggravation?" One week earlier, she had been with me in Canastota, New York, for my induction into the International Boxing Hall of Fame. Now I was in a converted warehouse in South Philly, trying to run a club show, with no electricity.

Roger Artigiani, who'd recently taken over the building, found the main circuit-breaker panel in the rear of the building and got the system working. Too bad! Only 659 showed up. The gate was $28,730, and we lost $23,934.39.

"It was close to 100 degrees outside and I thought you wanted to kill me," Artigiani reminded me years later.

Welcome back to South Philly!

Hand and I promoted 21 cards at the New Alhambra through the end of 2008. Six made money—those that were televised through partnerships with Chargin, Golden Boy and Top Rank, and one we did one on our own with ESPN2.

Chargin delivered the TV money. We added the gate receipts and went 50-50. Golden Boy and Top Rank kept their TV money, paid for the main event and a few prelims. We kept the gate, paid the other prelims and everything else. Both scenarios worked.

Featherweight Rogers Mtagwa boxed at the New Alhambra six times. He was 20 when he arrived from Tanzania, the best of four African fighters who migrated to Philly between 2000 and 2002. Elvin Thompson, a preacher at the Grace Tabernacle Church at 52nd and Greenway in Southwest Philly, trained them.

"I've been a preacher all my life," Thompson said, "and Joe Brown was a member of my congregation. He had lived in Africa and he began sending fighters to me. Our church had been sending money to Africa to help underprivileged children. Joe was an old man with money and he came with them and turned the cellar in his home at 19th and Reed in South Philly into a place for them to live. He put in a shower, kitchen and a TV and they began to train with me at the Marian Anderson Rec Center in South Philly. Joe got them jobs at places like 7-Eleven."

Mtagwa came with 10 wins in 12 fights and the African Boxing Union super bantamweight championship. I booked him first at Poor Henry's Brewpub on American Street in Northern Liberties. Henry Ortlieb, a fifth generation of the Ortlieb's Beer founder, wanted boxing on the second floor of his warehouse. I labeled it the Big O Center. Anthony Boyle promoted and I made the matches. Mtagwa was down in the first and lost an eight-round decision to Debind Thapa, a lefty from Nepal then living in Atlantic City. How's that for international flavor?

"I can't remember how much money I lost," Boyle said, "but it definitely was more than $1,000. After that I got involved with the Pennsylvania Golden Gloves for the next 10 or 12 years. That was a better look for me."

Mtagwa struggled early, going 4-5-2. Nine of his opponents had winning records. One of his draws, a 10-rounder with New England favorite Edwin Santana at the Casino Ballroom in Hampton Beach, New Hampshire, came in a fight he took on 24 hours' notice when Santana's foe pulled out.

After losing an eight-round split decision to Jose Reyes on a show promoted by ex-pro Damon Feldman—one of Marty's sons—in 2002 at the Spectrum, Mtagwa cried in the dressing room. He asked Joe Parella, his cut man, for help. Parella, who worked for the City of Philadelphia in Licenses and Inspections, had been in boxing since the early 1990s, and briefly had managed light-heavyweight Eric Harding.

"Rogers was frustrated," Parella said, "but I didn't want to get between him and Elvin. When I went to the gym and he asked me again, I bought Elvin out for $5,500 and I put Monte Carter in as trainer. After Monte passed away I got Tommy Barnes, but later I replaced him with Boogaloo (Bobby Watts)."

Mtagwa became boxing's Silky Sullivan, the American thoroughbred race horse known for his come-from-behind style. Two 10th-round knockdowns earned him a split decision over Mexico's Fernando Trejo in 2005 at the New Alhambra. Four months later he rallied to knock out Joe Morales, of San Antonio, in the 10th to win the vacant USBA featherweight title in New Haven, Connecticut. He was 4-3-1 after that, but cracked the world rankings on November 7, 2008, when he K0d Tomas Villa, of Midland,

Texas, in the 10th at the Casino del Sol in Tucson. Chargin promoted the Telefutura card.

"It was one of the best local fights in memory," Steve Rivera wrote in the *Tucson Citizen*. "Both fighters came in saying that neither would back down and they lived up to that."

Villa led after eight rounds and knocked Mtagwa flat on his back with a right hand in the last minute of the ninth. After he got up, I waited for referee Rocky Burke to stop it, but Mtagwa made it to the bell.

"Mtagwa didn't know where he was," Parella said. "I told him I was gonna stop the fight if he didn't start throwing punches. He still spoke hardly any English. I let it go because I had seen him nail Villa with a right hand in the last 30 seconds, but I told the referee to stop it if Mtagwa went down or got caught on the ropes. I told him 'don't even count' if that happens. I wasn't gonna let him get hurt."

When Mtagwa dropped Villa with a right hand 10 seconds into the last round, I thought it would be remembered as a great fight. When Mtagwa dropped him a second time, I was trying to figure out how a 10-7 round would affect the scorecards. Everyone was standing. It was like watching two kids fighting on a street corner. When Villa went down a third time, Burke waved it off at 1:20. Mtagwa showed no emotion. His face was swollen and he had no idea where he was. Ring announcer Lupe Contreras asked the crowd for "one more round of applause for both fighters for giving us the *Fight of the Year*."

Mtagwa got $50,000 to box southpaw Juan Manuel Lopez, of Puerto Rico, for the WBO world super bantamweight title, on October 10, 2009, in the (now named) WaMu Theatre at Madison Square Garden. Lopez was 26-0, 24 K0s, hailed as boxing's next superstar. Mtagwa was 26-12-2, 18 K0s. He had boxed one No Contest and had been stopped twice. The media was focused on Lopez next facing Yuriorkis Gamboa, Cuba's WBA featherweight champion, who would K0 Whyber Garcia, of Panama, in four rounds in the semifinal.

Lopez-Mtagwa was a battle of the haves and have nots. Lopez entered the ring with his colorfully embroidered robe and trunks covered with sponsorship patches. Mtagwa came in with the standard Everlast white robe and white trunks with black trim. The WaMu was filled with Puerto Rican fans. Mtagwa's supporters—

besides his corner—were me, Linda, my younger son Daniel and his fiancé, Lauren Rosenfield.

Lopez was a classy boxer-puncher who had been perfectly managed and promoted. Due to Mtagwa's punishing schedule, Showtime commentator Steve Farhood said: "He must have been managed by the Marquis de Sade."

Lopez won the early rounds but rarely had a moment's rest. Mtagwa went down from what looked like a slip in the fifth round, but he came alive in the seventh. He punched after the bell several times, but referee Eddie Cotton never deducted a point. Mtagwa almost ended it in the last 10 seconds of the 11th when he landed four power shots. The ropes and bell saved Lopez, who wobbled to his corner.

Brad Goodman, Top Rank matchmaker, said, "No way Lopez can survive." By the start of the 12th round, I was on my knees at ringside. Everyone else was standing.

Thirty-year-old Rogers Mtagwa was on the verge of a world title. He had been in the United States nine years. He lived in rooming houses. He couldn't read, write, or drive a car and he couldn't pass an eye exam because he didn't understand the alphabet.

"*I* passed those eye exams," said Parella, who coached Mtagwa through them. "One doctor told me I should teach him the alphabet. Yeah, okay! When I bought his contract he didn't have a belt to hold up his pants and they were two sizes too big. I got him a job with a roofer and he was making $100 a day under the table. He also worked at a car wash for $25 a day, plus tips. I took him to Forman Mills to buy him some clothes. I did the best I could and I always paid him his purse by check."

The 12th round had to be the longest three minutes of Lopez' life! Mtagwa chased him, falling over himself trying to end it, almost flying through the ropes at one point. Mtagwa was "throwing punches from New Jersey," said Showtime analyst Al Bernstein, who called it one of the five greatest fights he had seen live. "The Marquess of Queensberry rules are dead tonight."

Cotton could have stopped it as Lopez staggered backwards on several occasions, sometimes after getting hit, sometimes not. Mtagwa was overanxious and out of gas. The scores for Lopez were 116-111, 114-113 and 115-111. They should have fought again, but Bob Arum announced in the ring, "There will be no rematch."

Neither fighter recovered. Lopez went 9-6-1 after beating Mtagwa and lost his title less than two years later. Mtagwa fought Gamboa three months later for the WBA featherweight title in the same ring. We had to beg HBO for the opportunity, despite how well he had performed against Lopez.

Goodman and Bruce Trampler had predicted Mtagwa-Lopez to be a war, but Goodman said, "Mtagwa won't get out of the second round against Gamboa," even though HBO announcer Bob Papa said to analyst Max Kellerman, "When you fight this guy (Mtagwa), it's like undergoing a root canal." Unfortunately for Mtagwa, he was Dustin Hoffman to Gamboa's Laurence Olivier in *Marathon Man.* Gamboa knocked him down three times and stopped him at 2:35 of the second.

Mtagwa didn't fight for over 18 months. Oswaldo Kuchle's company, *Promociones del Pueblo*, got him a win in Acapulco to set up a title fight five weeks later with WBC featherweight champion Jhonny Gonzalez in El Paso. Gonzalez K0d Mtagwa in two.

He came back in 2014, but lost two fights and retired. The last Parella heard, Mtagwa was working at a car wash on Torresdale Avenue.

Chapter Fifty-Two

A Tale of Two Mikes

Mike Jones lands inside against Lenin Arroyo at Bally's. (Mike Baluk photo)

A couple of guys named Mike—Stewart and Jones—were a big part of my business in the early years of the 21st century. Stewart was an outgoing, gregarious, fun-loving kid. "You gotta get up, get out and give 100 percent every day," he said. "Not just one day, every day. I got that from my grandmother. She was a descendant of John Brown from Harper's Ferry in the Civil War." Jones was an introvert. His ability and power should have made him a world champion, but he lacked Stewart's drive. Had I been able to meld them, I would have had a superstar.

Dover Downs is a hotel, casino and racetrack complex in Delaware. The harness track and the Dover International Speedway for NASCAR opened in 1969, the casino in 2002. Diane Fischer promoted one card inside the racetrack clubhouse in 2001. A year later, Ed Sutor, president and CEO of Dover Downs, made the new 1,800-seat Rollins Center available for boxing. I promoted three cards there with ESPN2. Stewart, of New Castle, boxed on all three. He was the Michael Jordan of Dover Downs.

Stewart was an overachiever. He turned pro in 1996 and had boxed at the Blue Horizon, mostly for the DePasquale Brothers, at Kahunaville in Delaware for Fischer, and in Mississippi for Murad Muhammad. He and Dave Tiberi were the two most popular fighters from Delaware since 1940s' welterweight Al Tribuani, who beat "Bummy" Davis and Lew Jenkins and lost an unpopular decision to Henry Armstrong.

Not a great boxer and not a great puncher, Stewart was tough and determined. He was managed by Keith Stoffer, a high school social studies teacher and all-state basketball player at Newcomerstown (Ohio) High School, where Ohio State football coach Woody Hayes had played.

Dorin Spivey, of Portsmouth, Virginia, handed Stewart his first loss in 31 fights, a 10-round split decision Feb. 15, 2002, at the Arts Palace. Three months later, on the Rollins Center's first card, Stewart got his career back on track—figuratively and literally—outpointing John Bailey, of Portsmouth, West Virginia, over 10 rounds. Kassim Ouma vs. Jason Papillion, of Broussard, Louisiana, was the main event, but Stewart brought the crowd. Three fights later, he K0d Chucky T in seven rounds to win the vacant USBA junior welterweight title before another packed house.

Stewart moved into the IBF Top 10 by beating veterans Terron Millett and Ivan Robinson. Millet, of St. Louis, had been IBF champion at 140 pounds, but he was one day short of 35 when Stewart stopped him in 2003 at the Tropicana in Atlantic City.

"Terron agreed to the fight but told me he was a little heavy," said Kurt Emhoff, a New York attorney managing Millett. "I didn't know until I got to Atlantic City that he had been about 40 to 50 pounds overweight six weeks earlier and had been in a car accident. The weight cut was extremely difficult for him. I noticed he was slurring a bit and that scared the hell out of me.

“I remember talking to you (Russell) the day of the weigh-in about how I wasn't comfortable with him fighting in this condition. I knew he needed the money. I didn't take a dime from this fight and I was going to give him a chance to rehydrate and recover. I told you if he looked sluggish in the ring and was in trouble I was going to stop it immediately.

“Terron got wobbled in the first round but fought back. The second was pretty even. But he got dropped in the third. I immediately jumped up on the ring apron, as did his father and trainer, Marvin ‘Coots’ Millett. Referee Randy Neumann's back was to us. Neumann asked Terron if he was all right. He said, ‘I'm OK, but I don't think my dad thinks I'm OK.’ Neumann turned around and saw us on the apron and waved it off. That was Terron’s last fight.”

Two fights later, Stewart beat 32-year-old Robinson, who didn’t come out for the ninth round at the Spectrum. I had gone back to Broad and Pattison because ex-pro Damon Feldman had some success there a year earlier when Chucky T beat Robinson. It was my second card there since leaving in 1980, but the crowd, on Veterans Day, was only 2,131, the gate $94,395. Even with $8,270 in sponsorships, I lost $13,791.42.

Nevertheless, mission accomplished. Stewart landed a $68,000 payday—I got $17,000 on top of that—against former WBA champion Sharmba Mitchell on April 3, 2004. Showtime televised the 12-round eliminator from the 21,000-seat Manchester Arena in Manchester, England, because Ricky Hatton, England’s most popular fighter, was in the main event against Dennis Holbaek Pederson, of Denmark. Mitchell, a southpaw from Washington, DC, was 53-3, 28 K0s. He knocked Stewart down three times and won easily.

After Stewart K0’d Juan Carlos Escobar, of Mexico, at the New Alhambra, Sampson Lewkowicz, working for promoter Frank Warren, gave us $125,000 to fight Hatton, also in Manchester. Stewart got $100,000 but Hatton stopped him in five rounds.

Stewart won 12 of his last 19 and retired in 2012. He missed a chance to fight Arturo Gatti in 2007 for $400,000 when he lost a majority decision to Enrique Colin, of Mexico, at the New Alhambra.

"I didn't have the same drive late in my career," Stewart said. "I was working a full-time job as a union laborer, roofer and contractor. I went a lot further than anyone thought I could, especially coming from a state with no real boxing history."

North Philly's Jones was a 6-foot welterweight with power in both hands. Late in 2005, in a four-round prelim underneath Miguel Figueroa's 10-round decision over crosstown rival Jose Medina at the New Alhambra, the 22-year-old Jones turned pro. Jason Thompson had lost in the finals of the New York Golden Gloves but had won his pro debut. When Jones stopped him in two, it resonated. Jones boxed five times in 11 months at the New Alhambra and no one got past the second round.

Alfred "Doc" Nowicki, who was in the automobile refinishing business, managed Jones. Doc got into boxing in the mid-1990s with Figueroa. When we met, he said, "I'll be unlike any manager you've ever worked with." That was no lie.

"When we signed Mike, we really wanted (welterweight) Kaseem Wilson," Doc said. "Kaseem was left-handed, taller, and could box. Then we saw Mike's power, and Kaseem had a hard time getting to the gym and staying out of trouble. One time he got arrested the night of the weigh-in and I had to get him out to make the fight. Mike pretty much listened to (trainer) Vaughn Jackson, not to me or my partner, Jimmy Williams."

Doc was *too* good. Some of his fighters lived in a house he owned in Frankford. He'd give them money for food and clothes. I told him to slow down, but he couldn't help himself.

Jones got experience out of town. He scored knockouts in Spokane, Washington, on an Art Pelullo card at the Northern Quest Casino; in Las Vegas on a Golden Boy card the night before the Floyd Mayweather-Oscar De La Hoya fight at the MGM, and in Niagara Falls on a show I did with Al Valenti at the Seneca Niagara Casino.

His "coming out" party was November 9, 2007, when he stopped former world-title challenger Israel "Pito" Cardona in three rounds at the New Alhambra. Cardona (36-7, 28 K0s) was three fights from the end of his career and the loss to Jones was one of two times he was K0d.

When Jones reached 16-0, 14 K0s, after a one-punch knockout over Luciano Perez in Reading, I went back to the Blue Horizon on March 6, 2009. Vernoca Michael's promotions never equaled our success. With one story in the *Daily News* and nothing in the *Inquirer*, we sold out.

Vernoca wouldn't let us sell standing room even though I offered her 20 percent of the extra income. She said she was concerned about the Fire Marshall, but an extra 200 people at $40 apiece would have added $8,000. Her end would have been $1,600 and we never had a problem with the Fire Marshall in all the years I had been there.

It was one of those nights when each of the seven fights was solid. Super middleweight Dennis Hasson outpointed future cruiserweight contender Garrett Wilson in an all-Philly six-rounder and local bantamweight Teon Kennedy got off the floor to decision Andre Wilson, of St. Louis, in eight.

It didn't matter that Jones' opponent, 35-year-old Dairo Esalas, of Colombia, was 31-15, a late replacement for Larry Mosley, of Las Vegas. People wanted to see Jones. Esalas never had a chance, but he threw bombs. The last of three knockdowns came when Jones hurt him with a left hook to the body, and, as Esalas was going down, drilled him with a left hook to the chin. Referee Gary Rosato stopped it at 1:56.

During the card, the State Athletic Commission's Greg Sirb got up from his seat at the ring, called to me, raised his arms to shoulder height, spread his palms up, and spanned the crowd as if to say, "You still have the touch." Steve Weisfeld, one of the ringside judges whom I'd met at the Palestra when he was going to Penn, later said, "If I were to bring someone to a fight for their first time, this would have been the one."

I have a photo of Jones, in the center of the ring, arms raised to the cheering crowd. That was the pinnacle of his career. He never again displayed such ferocity. And it was the last great night of boxing at the Blue Horizon.

Tickets were $60 and $45. The gate was $72,140. Even with $8,000 in sponsorship money, Joe Hand and I split only $2,295.34, but I didn't care. Jones was going to be world champion.

Jones' next five fights were in Atlantic City, but he didn't fight to win—he fought not to lose. The combined record of his opponents—Lenin Arroyo, Raul Pinzon, Henry Bruseles, Hector Munoz, Irving Garcia—was 99-21-6, but none will make it to the Hall of Fame. After he stopped Garcia in the main event of a Showbox card at Boardwalk Hall in the summer of 2010, Jones was ranked by all four sanctioning bodies.

Promoter Lou DiBella had partnered with me on the card. I couldn't get Jones back on ShoBox on my own, so when Top Rank later called about a co-promotional deal, which included a slot on the Manny Pacquiao-Antonio Margarito pay-per-view card in October from Cowboys Stadium in Arlington, Texas, I accepted.

Halfway through the second round, Jones hurt Mexican contender Jesus Soto-Karass with a right to the body, drove him across the ring and unloaded power punches for one minute. Some landed, most missed. Soto-Karass survived and had Jones backing up by the end of the round.

"There was more action in that one round than in the whole 12 rounds of the previous fight," HBO analyst Emannuel Steward said, referring to Guillermo Rigondeaux' dreadful 12-round win over Ricardo Cordoba in their super bantamweight contest.

Jones had punched himself out, and even though he came back to win the 9th and 10th rounds, most people favored Soto-Karass. On my way to the dressing room I heard the majority decision for Jones (94-94, 95-94, 97-93), so I went to Soto-Karass' trainer, Joe Goossen, and asked for a rematch. Here I was, the promoter of the winning fighter, asking the trainer of the losing fighter for another chance. HBO aired Jones' clear 12-round victory over Soto-Karass three months later in Las Vegas.

But on the flight home from the first Soto-Karass fight, Jones had read that one of the undercard fighters had been paid more than his $30,000. That began an *Era of Bad Feelings*. He didn't accept that he had been moved to the semifinal only because the Kelly Pavlik-Brian Vera middleweight fight had fallen out and Top Rank didn't want a potentially boring Rigondeaux fight leading into the main event.

"At first, things went really good, all wins and mostly knockouts," Nowicki said. "Then came the first Soto-Karass fight and Mike learned you cannot knock everyone out. After that fight, while training at the Joe Hand gym, people got into his head and that's when we lost control. It seemed like Mike didn't want anything to do with us except pay for everything, which we did. Two cars, a house for him and his family to live in and money from time to time to pay for things like his cell phone and his cell phone bill. We still had our contract and the deal with you and Top Rank, and Top Rank was paying us directly after his fights even though Mike wanted us gone."

Jones' wallet had a better year in 2011 than he had in the ring. He got $90,000 for the Soto-Karass rematch but remained tentative as the fights got bigger. After he was paid $25,000 for a two-round wipeout of overmatched Raul Munoz at what was now the Asylum Arena (formerly New Alhambra), he got $130,000 to fight Sebastian Lujan, of Argentina, at Madison Square Garden. Before Miguel Cotto stopped Margarito in the main event, Jones boxed safely to a 12-round decision, 118-110 and 119-109 twice.

"Mike Jones fought on two of the biggest stages possible—Cowboys Stadium and Madison Square Garden—and he failed to make an impression either time," said Top Rank matchmaker Bruce Trampler.

The IBF ordered Jones and Randall Bailey, of Miami, to fight for the welterweight title vacated by Andre Berto. Neither HBO nor Showtime were interested, so Top Rank added it to the HBO pay-per-view telecast of Manny Pacquiao's first fight with Tim Bradley for Pacquiao's WBO welterweight title on June 9, 2012, at the MGM in Las Vegas.

Jones was upset with his $125,000 purse: "I'm 26-0 in the ring and 0-26 at the negotiating table." He couldn't accept that his transformation from slugger to safety-first boxer had dulled his appeal.

Bailey was 42-7, 37 K0s, but he was three months shy of his 38th birthday and 12 years removed from his time as WBO junior welterweight champion.

"I don't think too much of him (Bailey)," Jones told Matt Breen, of the *Philadelphia Inquirer*. "He has a strong right hand and that's about all I've seen."

Trainer Vaughn Jackson agreed: "He's an old man. About three years and he should be able to get a free bus ride because he's a senior citizen. He might as well give us the title and make it easy for himself so we don't have to take it. I don't even know why he's still boxing. Bailey has one shot. He has to try to hit the lottery."

And Bailey did. Jones led 99-91, 98-92 and 97-93 after 10 boring rounds. The only reason it was that close was because late in the 10th Bailey knocked him down. Jones was winning the 11th when Bailey countered a slow jab with a right uppercut and Jones went out at 2:52.

I had left my seat midway through the fight, disgusted at the lack of action. I watched the rest on a TV monitor in the dressing room, telling myself we would have to go overseas to defend the title since no U.S. network would be interested. Bailey took care of that.

On the way back to our hotel room, Linda and I stopped by the MGM Sports Book where I collected $2,000 for betting $500 on Bailey, a 4-1 underdog. It was a tradition from my days with Bennie Briscoe. I'd bet against my fighter, hoping to lose the bet and win the fight.

John DiSanto wrote it best on his *Philly Boxing History* website: "Jones lost this fight trying to be safe when he should have been fighting. Trying to be perfect rarely leads to perfection. There was a major disconnect to the plan that Team Jones carried out against Bailey. It seems they attempted to mathematically lock down the decision before trying to make something happen. After nine rounds of coasting, Jones began fighting with some urgency in the 10th, as if it was finally time to go for a KO. But over the first nine rounds, Jones did nothing to set Bailey up for the knockout. He did not back Bailey up, wear him down, work the body, or tax his old legs.

"By coming out more aggressively in round 10, against a big puncher who is hopelessly behind on the cards, Jones played into Bailey's hands, making the KO inevitable. It would be easy to wish that Jones had milked the last three rounds, and come home a champion, but that would have been no way to win a title. The idea that he might have been crowned champion with such a tepid performance is hard to take. It was a passionless attempt that was not of championship caliber."

Jones did not fight for two years. His contract with Nowicki expired. He hired a lawyer and demanded twice the $10,000 I offered. But he finally agreed and returned August 13, 2014 at Bally's. He knocked down Jaime Herrera, of Chicago, in the second round with a sweeping left hook. Referee Earl Brown could have waved it off when Herrera got up and fell back into the ropes, but the bell ended the round and Jones' career.

Herrera was down again in the third, but got up, staggered Jones late in the round and took control. Jones did not answer the bell for the eighth round. He led 66-65 on all three scorecards. When I drove him to the airport the next day, he did not remember knocking Herrera down the second time. He never boxed again.

"When he fought Herrera, he never said a word to us," Nowicki said years later. "Wow! To sum it up, for all that was done for Mike, he could have been the most ungrateful person I ever knew."

Chapter Fifty-Three

Nightmare Revisited

Francisco Rodriguez awaits Teon Kennedy in 2009. (John DiSanto photo)

Philadelphia hosted between 21 and 26 cards annually from 2003 through 2007. Those numbers dropped to between 4 and 19 for the next 13 years. When S&S Family Partnership, which owned the New Alhambra, raised the rent in 2008, I left. Joe Hand moved his gym from the rear of the building to 5th and Spring Garden. Greg Robinson, who had promoted sporadically around the city, promised lease-holder Roger Artigiani he would keep the New Alhambra busy, but left after five cards. He and Vernoca Michael were the busiest in the first decade of the 21st century. Ex-pro Damon Feldman ran a dozen shows at various venues. P.J. Augustine, who dubbed himself the "Black Moses," ran a handful of cards at the Adams Mark hotel on City Line Avenue, then left boxing.

The success of my return to the Blue Horizon in 2009 with Mike Jones was impossible to duplicate. Two months later, only 880 paid $46,110 for Rogers Mtagwa's 10-round decision over Mexico's Ricardo Medina. I lost $3,483.47 and still owed one more card.

Teon Kennedy, two-time Pennsylvania Golden Gloves titlist and 2004 National Golden Gloves flyweight champion, headlined November 20 against Francisco Rodriguez. Kennedy was 23, unbeaten in 14 pro fights with one draw. Rodriguez, of Guadalajara, Mexico, was living in Chicago. He had won five Chicago Golden Gloves titles, the 2001 National Golden Gloves championship, and had defeated Kennedy in the amateurs. He was 25 and his record was 14-2, 8 K0s. He had been stopped once.

The USBA sanctioned the match for its vacant super bantamweight title. It was Rodriguez' first fight outside Illinois and, after visiting the Rocky statue at the Art Museum, looked forward to telling his friends.

Late in the first round, referee Benjy Esteves gave Rodriguez an eight-count after Kennedy staggered him with a left hook and a right hand. "(Rodriguez) reached for the ropes, touched them and fell forward," Esteves told Bernard Fernandez, of the *Daily News*. "Technically, it was a knockdown." Standing eight-counts had been eliminated in Pennsylvania and some claimed Rodriguez had not touched the ropes. Kennedy said he would have knocked out Rodriguez had Esteves not intervened.

Rodriguez fought back, working Kennedy's body, and Fernandez wrote it was "one humdinger of a boxing match." By the end of the eighth, Rodriguez had erased most of Kennedy's lead, but a bad ninth round left him behind 86-84, 86-83, and 87-83. When Kennedy hurt him again in the 10th, Esteves waved it off at 1:52.

I went to Kennedy's dressing room. He came back alone with the championship belt around his waist, the happiest kid on the block. I headed back to the ring, but Commissioner Greg Sirb had canceled the walkout bout because Rodriguez had been taken to the hospital.

After being led back to this corner, "his (Rodriguez') body went limp and his breathing became labored," Fernandez wrote. "Ring physicians and EMS personnel frantically administered to him before he was removed from the ring on a stretcher and transported to Hahnemann University Hospital, where he underwent emergency surgery to relieve pressure for a brain bleed."

Maureen Sacks and I went to the hospital, but were not permitted to see Rodriguez. We gave his brother the purse and our sincerest prayers. Rodriguez died 48 hours later, leaving behind his wife, Sonia, and 5-month-old daughter, Ginette.

Some fans said had Esteves not given Rodriguez the eight-count in the first round Kennedy would have finished him without further damage. Pure speculation! If I never had made the match, Rodriguez also would have lived. It was a fight between two talented, well-conditioned athletes, who had passed the required pre-fight medicals.

"I probably made a mistake in that first round," an emotional Esteves said when I spoke to him for this book. "At first I thought Rodriguez had touched the ropes, but even if he had, the ropes did not keep him from going down. I should not have given him a count because the standing eight-count was not in the rules. After Teon had a big ninth round, I went to Rodriguez' corner before the 10th and I told his father and (trainer) George Hernandez that I was going to stop it the next time the kid got hurt.

"After the fight, I called (referee) Joe Cortez, who was my mentor. He said it would be okay to go to the hospital. He suggested I trust my conscience and go with my heart and he didn't see anything wrong in doing so. When I got there, I told them I was a family member and they let me in, but Rodriguez was in surgery at the time. It's about 78 miles from Philly to my home in Sayreville, New Jersey, and I cried all the way."

Kennedy's trainer, ex-pro Wade Hinnant, cannot forget: "After the fight was stopped, I remember walking over to Rodriguez' corner to offer some words of encouragement. Francisco had his head down while he sat on his stool and never looked up at me. As I walked away I turned around and, at that very moment, Francisco slumped to the canvas. His corner and ringside doctors came to his aide and I got right down to my knees in our corner and said a prayer for him. I knew that young man was in trouble.

"Later that night, as always, we did our celebratory ritual of a late-night meal and drinks. During this time we had gotten word that Francisco was in a coma from bleeding on the brain. That kind of news definitely changed the mood. This was a Friday night.

"We decided to go to the hospital to show support for him and his family. That was Sunday afternoon. His young wife was there with their daughter, his father, brothers and an uncle. We hugged and prayed with them. His mom was there but I never saw her because she was so distraught she had to be hospitalized. Five hours after we left the hospital, Francisco was taken off life support. I went down to my basement, opened up a bottle of liquor, got drunk and cried like a baby for hours."

I refused to answer phone calls from the *Inquirer*, which had not covered the fight. It hadn't thought the fight was important before, but jumped on the tragedy to sell papers. Rodriguez' was the first ring fatality in Pennsylvania in 31 years. I had promoted the previous one—March 21, 1978—when Jody White died after being stopped by Curtis Parker in the same building.

Rodriguez' death was where one story ended and five others began. Sonia Rodriquez designated her husband's organ for recovery and transplant, which gave renewed life to Ashley Owens (both lungs); Alexis Sloan (heart); Meghan Kingsley (liver); Vicky Davis (kidney and pancreas), and a relative, Ramon Tejeda (kidney). Sadly, Ashley and Alexis have since passed away.

Kennedy went 3-1-1 in his next five fights and challenged for the WBA bantamweight title, but was knocked down five times and stopped in the fifth round by Guillermo Rigondeaux on the same Las Vegas card when Mike Jones lost to Randall Bailey. He returned one year after the Rigondeaux fight, won twice at Bally's Atlantic City, but developed cataracts, suffered a detached retina, and retired in 2013 at 19-2-2, 7 K0s. He was 27. Now known as Zachariah Kennedy, he owns a cleaning business in Philly.

On June 4, 2010, the Blue Horizon passed away. The *Daily News* mentioned, among other causes of death, operating without the proper licenses for food and beverage sales, and unpaid taxes.

Rodney Rice, who managed and trained cruiserweight contender Garrett Wilson, worked for the Philadelphia Department of Public Health, Office of Food Protection: "While reviewing establishments that had not been inspected in over a year, I came across the Blue Horizon. Further investigation revealed several issues which prompted the collaboration between the Health Department and L&I (licenses and inspections). On the night of the final inspection (June 4), it was by chance there was a boxing show in progress. We allowed the show to continue, but without food and beverage service."

At last report, the Blue Horizon was being turned into a 13-story apartment tower while mainting the façade of the fight arena.

Five months later, the Spectrum was demolished. The 21,000-seat Wells Fargo Center—which has undergone several name changes since opening in 1996—became the major sports and entertainment venue in Philadelphia. It stands on the site of where once stood JFK Stadium (previously named Municipal Stadium and Sesquicentennial Stadium).

There was a more upsetting death in 2010. Bennie Briscoe, 67, passed away December 28. I was in Florida and received the news from Karen James, who had lived with Bennie since 1978 after his divorce from Rita Ann McNeil.

Shortly after being inducted into the Pennsylvania Boxing Hall of Fame in 2007, Bennie had fallen in his bedroom and struck his head against one of those cast-iron radiators that look like metal accordions. His health had deteriorated and he passed away in hospice care at Temple University Hospital. Eddie Mustafa Muhammad flew in from Las Vegas for the funeral. Several local contemporaries of Bennie were there, but the only active Philly fighter present was heavyweight Chazz Witherspoon.

Years later, I asked Karen if Bennie really loved me. "More than you could ever know," she said.

My biggest regret is that in 2004 when I was inducted into the International Boxing Hall of Fame, I didn't take Bennie and Karen. I never would have made it without him and he would have had fun. He would have been one of the most beloved celebrities there, especially since he rarely went out in public. He would have stood out with his shaven head and had a chance to be Bennie Briscoe again.

Had I never hooked up with Bennie Briscoe, the title of this book would be *50 Weeks in Boxing*. I couldn't have made it without him.

Boxing historian John DiSanto inaugurated the Briscoe Awards in 2008. I had taken DiSanto to Bennie's home and Bennie signed an agreement allowing DiSanto to use his name. Those 15-inch bronze statues are held in high esteem.

"My mission was to seek new ways to honor the great participants from Philly boxing history," DiSanto wrote on his website, *Philly Boxing History.com*, "and creating an award seemed like a natural step. After briefly considering many of Philadelphia's greats, I came back to my original plan of making Bennie Briscoe the subject matter of the award. The reason was simple. Briscoe perfectly represents boxing in Philadelphia. We all love Rocky, but it is Bennie Briscoe that embodies so much of what Philly boxing is really all about. It was always clear that Bennie was the "One" and that the award just had to be *The Briscoe*."

Chapter Fifty-Four

Bally's and Bethlehem

Ref Steve Smoger ends Ronald Cruz-Hector Munoz fight. (Kate Warburton photo)

Two Jersey boys and one Jersey girl played key roles in my business in the 21st century. Ken Condon was from Orange. He had become Atlantic City's first casino host in 1978 at Resorts International. From then until his retirement in 2007 as president at Bally's, Condon was involved in nearly every important boxing match in Atlantic City. By 2009, he was Boxing and Entertainment Consultant for all Harrah's properties, which included Bally's and Caesars. Bob DeSalvio was born in Ridgewood and grew up in Glen Rock. He started in gaming in 1976 and was at the Sands Atlantic City during my years there in the 1980s. We later did business when he was at Foxwoods, but by 2009 he had become president of the Sands in Bethlehem. Kathy Duva was from Dover. She hired me in 2007 to make matches at Main Events.

From 2009 through 2014, I promoted 21 times in Atlantic City, all with Condon—19 at Bally's, one at Caesars, one at Boardwalk Hall. Bally's bought 500 of the 1,427 available tickets for each card in their Ballroom/Events Center, comped us with rooms and meals, set up the night of the fight, and did marketing. We sold the rest of the seats, usually filling the room. Headliners included Mike Jones, Teon Kennedy, Gabriel Rosado, Jason Sosa and Garrett Wilson. Sosa was the only one to win a world title. The others had chances.

Wilson was nicknamed the "Ultimate Warrior" because he fought everyone, everywhere, and at any time. He had been a restroom attendant at Cebu, a restaurant/nightclub at 2nd and Chestnut. A pair of one-punch, 12th-round knockouts of Chuck Mussachio and Andres Taylor earned him an IBF cruiserweight eliminator early in 2013.

Manager/trainer Rodney Rice claimed I should have gotten Wilson more money for the eliminator, and a string of nasty emails between us—from him in Romania, where Wilson lost to Alexander Alekseev, and me in Atlantic City—ended that relationship. I watched the fight on a computer in my hotel room at Bally's where I had a fight scheduled the next evening. Sometimes it's not worth fighting back. Wilson was 13-5-1 when we split, 5-12 after.

A new group, *GoFightLive.TV,* televised most of my Bally's shows on an internet stream. They paid between $75 and $200 per, depending on how many people bought the stream. Our bottom line showed profits from $7,000 to $25,000. Some of the *GoFight* cards did better than the ones we did with Top Rank on *Teleftura* because the boxers cost less and we had no partners.

The last time I promoted at Bally's was August 23, 2014, the night Chicago's Jaime Herrera ended Mike Jones' career, getting up from two knockdowns to stop him after seven. The ballroom was full, but after a dispute with the box office over the ticket sales report, I never went back.

Welterweight Ronald Cruz was 5-0 the first time he boxed for me at Bally's in 2009. He was born in Manati, Puerto Rico, but moved to Bethlehem when he was 10. "My mom had friends there and they told us it would be a good place to live," Cruz said. "When I was a kid, my favorite sports were baseball and boxing. I was a big fan of Tito Trinidad and I watched the *Rocky* movies."

By the time he fought Jeremy Bryan late in 2010 at Bally's on a card promoted by John Lynch's Pound For Pound Promotions, Cruz was 9-0. Bryan, from Paterson, New Jersey, was 14-1. After Cruz dropped him three times and won by knockout in six rounds, I saw he was special.

"I felt so hungry for the Bryan fight," Cruz said. "I was the underdog and everyone had him winning. I saw so many videos. I pictured the fight in my mind even before it even happened. I saw myself breaking him down to the body and that's how I did it. I was in such good shape I could have fought all night."

Cruz' manager, Jimmy Deoria, told me a casino was opening in Bethlehem.

"We had a press conference in Bethlehem before one of Ronald's fights in Atlantic City in 2010 and Bob DeSalvio showed up," Deoria said. "He was new in town and I assume he wanted to get to know as many people as possible. We spoke for a few minutes and he told me when the Sands could accommodate boxing, he would be interested in having Ronald there. He said he knew you from Atlantic City."

Cruz was 12-0 by the summer of 2011 when DeSalvio and I got together for a card in a temporary tent on the Sands' parking lot. He agreed to the same deal I had at Bally's. The Sands bought 500 tickets and we sold all but four of the remaining 798. We would have sold more but since you had to walk through the casino to get to the tent, no one under 21 could come. Still, the gate was $70,355.50 and Cruz knocked out Doel Carrasquillo, of nearby Reading, in the sixth round of the eight-round main event. *GoFightLive.tv* aired the fights.

Kathy Duva signed a one-year deal with NBC Sports Network (NBCSN) for a series of cards in 2012 on the East Coast. It was the best thing to happen to boxing in years because it provided overlooked fighters television exposure, even if it was a one-promoter deal.

NBCSN paid a six-figure rights fee and Kathy and I put the opener at the Asylum Arena (formerly New Alhambra) on January 21. Philly's Bryant Jennings outpointed DC's Maurice Byarm over 10 rounds in a battle of young heavyweights. Junior middleweight Gabriel Rosado stole the show, blasting out Mexican contender Jesus Soto-Karass in five. NBCSN executives loved Rosado so Kathy secured an extra date for him on June 1 in the Sands' newly opened Event Center.

Rosado stopped Sechew Powell, of Brooklyn, in nine rounds in the main event, and Cruz won his 16th straight, outpointing Prenice Brewer, of Cleveland, over 12 in the semifinal. It was the first of eight times Cruz would fight inside the Event Center. An SRO crowd of 1,819 paid $125, $75 and $50. The gate was $125,075. Cruz was as important to boxing at the Sands as Mike Stewart had been to Dover Downs. His fans had traveled to watch him at Bally's and now enjoyed him at home.

"Main Events came close to going under in 2008," Duva said. "Then Tomasz Adamek threw us a lifeline by defeating Steve Cunningham (IBF cruiserweight title). I had no US TV deal for Tomasz, but he was so popular in his home country and he sold so well at the gate in Newark that we were able to maintain a series with the rights to his fights in Poland. We limped along until Tomasz lost to Vitali Klitschko (WBC heavyweight title) in September, 2011.

"When we met with NBC during the third quarter of 2011, we sold them on the idea that we could replicate our success with Tomasz by working with other international fighters and use the foreign revenue to expand our budgets. They loved our idea of focusing on the future of the heavyweight division by building young contenders.

"Our plan worked well for two years and NBC was happy. Fighters like Tyson Fury and Joseph Parker—both future heavyweight champions—made their US debuts on the series. We turned Bryant Jennings into a legit heavyweight contender. Guys like Rosado became popular. We delivered names like Zab Judah, Adamek and Cunningham on the back ends of their careers. We delivered a Top 10 pound-for-pound fighter in Sergey Kovalev, who proved we could turn Russians into big stars in the US. Kovalev dominated the light-heavyweight division. NBC wanted us to showcase the PPV fighters of the future. Sergey and Fury got there."

Rosado returned to the Sands on September 21, stopping contender Charles Whittaker, of Miami, in 10 rounds. The crowd was slightly down—1,532 paid $111,810—due to Friday night high school football. Cruz lost a 10-round split decision (96-94 and 94-96 twice) to Antwone Smith, of Miami, in the co-feature.

Smith was 21-4-1, 12 KOs, but had lost three of his last six. It was scheduled for 12 rounds for a minor title at 147, but Smith had not been 147 for any of his previous four fights and had been as heavy as 154. He weighed 150 for Cruz and, to save the fight, we cut it to 10 rounds and Smith paid a fine.

"I had sweated to get down to 147 myself," Cruz said. "By the weigh-in, I didn't feel good. I was dry. Jimmy (Deoria) didn't want me to fight because of the weight. Smith beat me with his jab. It was constant and that was something I should have done more of myself. I was ranked by that time and it was a big setback. Then I had problems with my eye."

When he was 13, Cruz was shot in his right eye with a BB gun.

"I guess that started the problems with my retina," he said. "I had surgery after I lost to Smith but I think it made my eye even worse even though the doctor said I was okay to fight again. My vision went from 20/20 to real bad. The surgery messed up my vision. I cheated to get through the eye tests. I would peek with the other eye. I was fine with glasses, but not without them."

Nine months after Smith, Cruz lost to Ray Narh, an awkward fighter from Ghana, who was 25-2 going in, but had not boxed in two years. Cruz won his next three, but lost his last three, including decisions to ex-world champ Kermit Cintron and future world champ Errol Spence. He was 20-5 when he retired late in 2014, losing five of his last eight fights.

"My career was one great roller coaster ride," Cruz said. "It was exciting and I had some big adrenalin rushes. The experience of just being a boxer helps in life. I am much stronger mentally from being a boxer. You go through so many ups and downs. You learn how to push your body so intensely that you become stronger mentally. I'll always miss it but I'm over it now. At first I was going through depression. I should have taken a longer break after my eye surgery.

I appreciate every single person who helped me in my career—my team, the fans, everyone who was part of my team I appreciate them."

By the time Cruz' career was winding down in 2014, DeSalvio had left to pursue ventures elsewhere. Boxing at the Sands would not be the same without him or Cruz, who worked part-time there in security and drove trucks for a living.

Chapter Fifty-Five

BHOP

Bernard Hopkins and his Executioner bodyguards in 1993. (Peltz collection)

A supernatural work ethic, the will to win, and a chip on his shoulder—real or imaginary—enabled Bernard Hopkins to become a boxing great. I did not always agree with the stances he took or the things he did, but he treated me with respect, perhaps because he enjoyed talking to Linda and figured, "How bad can he be? She married him." He was a gentleman and never failed to ask about her. I cannot say that about many fighters. Hopkins climbed the boxing ladder, not only in the ring but also in the boardroom.

Born in 1965 in a North Philadelphia housing project, Hopkins began mugging people as a teenager, graduated into armed street fights and, at 17, was sentenced to 18 years for nine felonies. He continued his amateur boxing career (95-4) at Holmesburg Prison and, later, Graterford Prison. After his release in 1988, he turned pro in Atlantic City. He lost his first fight and did not box again for 16 months. He returned early in 1990 and his only loss from then until 2005 (48 fights) was to Roy Jones, Jr., a setback he would avenge.

Hopkins had eight of his first 20 fights in Philly. I wanted to sign him in the early 1990s, but his management said my offer was too low to discuss.

"They told me you said I was just an ordinary fighter," Hopkins said. "That made me even more determined to become a great fighter, just to show how wrong you were." I don't recall saying that. When I pressed Hopkins, he said, "Rob Murray (co-manager) said that to keep us apart."

He boxed for me twice, once on a 1993 show I promoted with Butch Lewis. By that time he had signed with Lewis, who had done a brilliant job with Michael Spinks, the first light-heavyweight champion to win the heavyweight title.

Lewis, once a used-car salesman in Philadelphia, had gotten into boxing after befriending Muhammad Ali. He later helped Bob Arum sign the Spinks brothers following their gold medal-winning performances at the 1976 Olympics.

Hopkins' 12-round decision loss to Jones came in 1993 for the vacant IBF middleweight title in Washington, DC.

"I (later) had found out there was $700,000 available for my end when I fought Roy Jones, and $700,000 for Jones," Hopkins said, "but my purse was only $250,000. "My management got $120,000 in training expenses which I knew nothing about and I can only guess where the rest of the money went.

"When I questioned Butch, he gave me that old, 'C'mon Ex (for his Executioner nickname), that's crazy.' But I kept digging and I got the actual paperwork—the contracts with HBO—which televised the fight. I felt betrayed. These were the people who sold me on how we should stick together because we looked the same. It was supposed to be us against the world. We went to court.

"I didn't want to be a statistic of the past. All promoters are not bad and all fighters are not angels. When I found out Butch and my managers were not honest with me, it threatened my career."

Lewis had a clause in their promotional contract calling for a three-year extension if Hopkins won "a title" and he wanted to invoke it after the Mercado fight. But Lewis did not specify "world title" and, late in 1992, when Hopkins knocked out Wayne Powell in one round in Atlantic City, he'd won the USBA title. The judge ruled that the USBA belt was, in fact, "a title," and since three years had elapsed since had Hopkins won it, the contract had expired.

That experience soured Hopkins on promoters. "Most of them I didn't like," he said, "because they were self-serving." Besides Lewis, he also worked with Bob Arum, Dan Goossen, Lou DiBella, Don King and Golden Boy. "I did get along with Golden Boy," he added.

Jones moved up to super middleweight in 1994. The next year, Hopkins knocked out Segundo Mercado, of Ecuador, for the vacant IBF middleweight belt in Landover, Maryland.

Hopkins had never been a typical street-corner guy like many Philly fighters. He moved to Delaware in the early 1990s—on the advice of middleweight Dave Tiberi—because of the tax advantages. It also "was a good place to raise my family," he said.

He eventually became undisputed world middleweight champion during a time when it was next to impossible to get the alphabets to agree on anything. Hopkins also won pieces of the world light-heavyweight title. He boxed 19 times in Atlantic City. Half his fights were in casinos or in arenas sponsored by casinos, either in Atlantic City or Las Vegas.

Hopkins' biggest win was September 29, 2001, the night he knocked out unbeaten Felix Trinidad in Madison Square Garden to unify three of the four middleweight belts. The fight had been postponed two weeks due to 9/11 and the atmosphere was patriotic.

In newspaper polls, I was one of the few who picked Hopkins to win, not because he was a great boxer—he was not—not because he was a great puncher—he was not. But there was something inside Hopkins which would not let him lose such a marquee fight. He trained like a middleweight Rocky Marciano. He examined every ounce of food that went into his body. His mind was the key.

Would "old school" guys like Carmen Basilio or Joey Giardello be thrown off stride if Hopkins said, "I would never lose to a White boy," which is what he said prior to fighting Joe Calzaghe? Would Archie Moore or Ezzard Charles lose focus because of Hopkins' pre-fight tactics, the way Trinidad and his crew did when Hopkins threw down the Puerto Rican flag during a pre-fight press conference? Would Hopkins have felt confident enough to do pushups in the ring between rounds were he fighting Harold Johnson or Gene Fullmer, the way he did them when he boxed Jean Pascal the second time. You tell me!

I look at Hopkins as someone who was ripped from the 1940s and inserted into the 21st century and brought with him the mindset boxers had when they fought for survival. He used those thought processes against what boxing had to offer in the 21st century. To me, that is what set him apart.

When he ended his career in 2016, he was 51 years old. Incredible! He was 55-8-2, 32 K0s. He became a minority shareholder in Golden Boy Promotions, learning what it's like to be on the other side, and he was voted into the Hall of Fame in 2020. I doubt we'll see another like him.

Chapter Fifty-Six

Indian Summer

Chino Rivas hugs Jason Sosa after upset win in Beijing. (Sumio Yamada photo)

In the middle of my disappointment with 21st century boxing, there were bright spots. For a while, Camden's Jason Sosa was the brightest. A junior lightweight, Sosa turned pro in 2009 after three amateur fights. He had played linebacker in high school even though he was 5-foot-7 and weighed less than most wide receivers. About boxing, he said: "Russell, I was born for this."

Sosa was 3-0-1 when he boxed Tre'sean Wiggins in 2010 at Bally's. Doc Nowicki managed Sosa and Miguel Corcino. When Corcino, Wiggins' original opponent, injured his left ankle the week of the fight, Martin Diaz, who trained both, asked Doc to replace him with Sosa. Sosa had been sparring Corcino, but was not in shape. Wiggins, a lefty, was 142.5 pounds at the weigh-in. Sosa was 138.5, 10 pounds over his best weight. Wiggins knocked him down three times in the first round and it was over at 2:02.

Sosa disappeared. His contract with Nowicki ran out and he didn't re-sign. He returned one year later and had two wins and two draws, and then went with Raul "Chino" Rivas as his trainer/manager.

Brittany Ann Michele Rogers (BAM), a 23-year-old senior at Temple University, had come to work with me and Maureen Sacks in April, 2011. Rogers' dad, Mike, had boxed as an amateur and BAM trained in local gyms. She was aware of the young talent coming out of the amateurs. Greg Robinson was promoting a card at the National Guard Armory and BAM suggested we go see Anthony Burgin, a 20-year-old lightweight turning pro.

After Burgin scored a first-round knockout, BAM introduced me to Rivas. He agreed for me to promote Burgin, but only if I signed Sosa, who K0d Clinton Douglas that night. I didn't want Sosa, even though he had boxed for me three weeks prior. But I had no choice. Rivas reminded me of Marty Feldman. They were built the same and both knew how to make friends and "take over" any room they entered. They also were excellent trainers.

Rivas was 10 when his father, an auto mechanic, was shot and killed outside their Paterson, New Jersey, apartment by a friend who needed his car fixed sooner rather than later.

"That's why I'm so close with my fighters, because I had to raise myself," Rivas said. "My mom had it rough after the murder and she had five kids to raise. We moved to Puerto Rico and then back to New York. I'd work each summer at Red Apple market in Manhattan, bagging groceries, to help out."

Oscar Suarez, Rivas' older cousin, who had trained world champions Acelino Freitas and Naseem Hamed, interested him in boxing. After one pro fight in 1997, Rivas was jailed for selling cocaine. He got out in 2001 and began training fighters with Suarez. "Oscar told me I had good eyes," Rivas said.

Burgin's career never reached the heights—he was 10-4 when he retired in 2017—but Sosa's took off. The win over Douglas was the first of 13 consecutive knockouts. As with Mike Jones and Kassim Ouma, I couldn't get Sosa TV exposure on my own. The perfect place would have been ShoBox, the little brother of Showtime, which featured young prospects. Midway through 2014, when Sosa was in the middle of his K0 streak and on the edge of the Top 10, I offered them a fight between him and Edner Cherry, a world-rated junior lightweight from Wauchula, Florida. ShoBox was not interested.

The highlight of Sosa's streak was his KO of southpaw Michael Brooks, of Long Island, in nine rounds on April 12, 2014, at Bally's Atlantic City. Sosa got $7,000, Brooks $7,750. There was no television but I made $23,899.66 based on ticket sales. It was more profitable than going to my 50th high school reunion the same night.

After the Brooks fight, Mark Cipparone, who was in the automobile collision business in Pennsylvania and New Jersey, purchased Sosa's managerial contract from Rivas. Cipparone, who managed flyweight Miguel Cartagena, junior lightweight Tevin Farmer, junior welterweight Raymond Serrano and heavyweight Joey Dawejko, put Sosa on a weekly salary. Cipparone and I put up money for a fight in Catano, Puerto Rico, where Sosa blew out hapless Juan Cruz in two rounds, but Cipparone and Rivas never hit it off.

Cipparone felt, as manager and financier, he should have final say on which fights to accept. Rivas felt, as trainer, he knew which fights were better for Sosa. When an opportunity came for Sosa to pick up some money and experience in training camp with prospect Gary Russell, Cipparone liked it, Rivas did not.

"When Sosa did not stand up and disagree with Chino, that was a 'no go' for me," Cipparone said. "I realized that Sosa was never going to accept anything from me but my money, so I decided to cut my losses. Make no mistake, there were losses." Cipparone gave Sosa back his contract.

We got an offer from Top Rank to put Sosa in a six-round fight in the fall of 2014 in Puerto Rico. It was a good way to get Sosa's career to the next level by showcasing him, and it worked. Top Rank promoted Sosa's next three fights, all without a promotional agreement—and all knockout wins—two in Puerto Rico, one in The Theatre in Madison Square Garden.

Carl Moretti, now Vice President of Boxing Operations at Top Rank after stints with Main Events and Lou DiBella, had an option to put Sosa under a promotional contract with me. Sosa signed the co-promotional agreement in September, 2015, and the next month I matched him with Jorge Pazos, of Mexico, at the 2300 Arena, the latest name for the New Alhambra. Sosa won by K0 in four rounds, but that fight, combined with the one the previous year there—when Sosa K0d Bergman Aguilar, of Nicaragua—wiped out the money I had made at Bally's with Sosa-Brooks. Sosa had not caught on in Philly, neither Pazos nor Aguilar was known, and we drew half-a-house each time.

Nicholas Walters, of Jamaica, the WBA featherweight champion, was moving up to junior lightweight, so HBO agreed to televise Walters-Sosa as co-feature to a heavyweight contest between Bryant Jennings and Luis Ortiz on a Golden Boy card.

Walters was 26-0, 21 K0s, and under contract to Top Rank. Sosa got $80,000 for the fight—by far his biggest purse—at the Turning Stone Casino in Verona, New York. He also got a draw few thought he deserved. Scores were 96-94 Sosa and 95-95 twice.

I sat ringside with Moretti. After the second round, he asked if I knew who the officials were. I had no clue. Sometimes you're the windshield, sometimes you're the bug. This night, Sosa was the windshield.

After the Walters fight, Top Rank had nothing for Sosa, and I didn't want to put him in an eight-round fight for his minimum, which was $6,000. He was world-ranked. So we waited.

Sampson Lewkowicz, a Uruguayan-American boxing promoter credited for discovering Manny Pacquiao and Sergio Martinez, called. I had known Lewkowicz for years, but the only business we had done was in 2004 when he put together the Mike Stewart-Ricky Hatton fight in England. Lewkowicz offered us WBA junior lightweight champion Javier Fortuna, of the Dominican Republic. The purse was $50,000. Rivas thought Sosa could win so we accepted. Brad Goodman, who started at Top Rank in 1983, was the only person outside our camp who gave Sosa a shot.

Fortuna, 27, a lefty, was 29-0-1, 21 K0s. Sosa, 28, was 18-1-4, 15 K0s. The fight was June 24, 2016, in the 18,000-seat National Indoor Stadium in Beijing. Fortuna led early and knocked Sosa down in the fifth round, but as the fight went into the eighth and ninth, Fortuna got braver. I told Linda that Fortuna, by becoming more aggressive and crowding Sosa, was giving Sosa a puncher's chance—his only chance.

In June, 2012, Mike Jones was so far ahead of Randall Bailey after nine rounds of their IBF welterweight title fight that the only way he could lose was by getting knocked out. Which he did, getting knocked down in the 10th round and out in the 11th. Four years later to the month, Sosa was so far behind he needed a knockout to win. Midway through round 10, Sosa knocked Fortuna down and finished him in the 11th with a left-right-left combination. Fortuna got up, but referee Raul Caiz, Jr. waved it off after 45 seconds. Fortuna was ahead 94-93, 95-92, 96-91.

Linda jumped out of her seat screaming and crying, something I never had seen. Sosa was a fighter you could fall in love with and that had happened for Linda and me. He was like a little kid with a soft, high voice that made you want to hug him. He wasn't a great boxer but he had power in both hands and he'd come from nowhere to win a world title.

Our hotel was across the street from the stadium. We had a wonderful walk back. Linda was tired and went to our room. Sosa, Chino and assistant trainers Nick Rosario and Rasheem Jefferson went upstairs to call home. I went to a dimly lit ultra-modern neon bar just off the lobby. Only one of perhaps 20 booths was occupied. I sat at the empty bar, thinking about the people in Philly who were just waking up—due to the time difference—to read the results on the internet.

If the Bennie Briscoe-Tony Mundine fight in 1974 in Paris is my No. 1 boxing highlight, Sosa-Fortuna is 1A. To have played a part in Sosa's trip from three amateur fights to a world championship was especially satisfying, coming so late in my career. Even when I later found out that it was for the WBA's "regular" title and not their "super" title, it wouldn't have changed how I felt at that moment. No drug on the market—legal or otherwise—nor any type of alcohol could give me the high I got that night, alone at that bar, drinking two beers. I felt like Buster Douglas must have, the night he beat

Mike Tyson, with odds 42-1 against. I knew the time would quickly pass so I made sure to enjoy every second of my private celebration.

Five months later, Lewkowicz got Sosa $100,000 for a 12-round points victory in a title defense against Steve Smith, in Monte Carlo, the first of Lewkowicz' three options.

Vasyl Lomachenko, whom Bob Arum was calling the greatest fighter since Ali, was the WBO junior lightweight champion and an HBO favorite. We couldn't get Sosa our own TV date in the US and the point of fighting is to make money and Lomachenko brought the most. Top Rank offered Sosa $350,000, more than triple Sosa's highest career purse.

But we owed Lewkowicz two fights.

Harrison Whitman, Top Rank's in-house attorney, asked if Lewkowicz had informed me in writing of his decision to exercise the remaining options. Since he had not, Whitman said Lewkowicz was "out." But I remembered 1980, when Muhammad Ali Professional Sports (MAPS) had failed to notify us in writing it was exercising its options after Jeff Chandler had won the WBA bantamweight title. I had told Chandler's managers, Willie O'Neill and K.O. Becky, we were free agents, and they told me they weren't going to screw the promoter who had delivered the title fight. Now 37 years later, I honored their teaching.

Whitman and Moretti were furious. They said I had agreed to the terms and threatened to sue me. I had told them Lewkowicz would have to be satisfied financially. I couldn't tell Lewkowicz that Sosa was free because he hadn't sent me a piece of paper.

After the all-capped emails and verbal threats ceased, Top Rank agreed to pay Lewkowicz $25,000. I paid him $20,000 from the $100,000 I received as co-promoter. I also paid Doc Nowicki 20 percent of my fee and Joe Hand five percent. Doc, who'd been cut out of Sosa's career when Jason did not re-sign with him in 2011, had done so many nice things for me over the years that I wanted to include him. Hand had been my partner on financially draining shows Sosa had headlined at the 2300 Arena.

The fight was April 8, 2017, at the MGM National Harbor casino in Oxon Hill, Maryland. It was competitive for three rounds, but Lomachenko dominated after that and Chino stopped it in the corner before the 10th. Scores were 89-82 twice and 90-81. Sosa broke down crying in the dressing room but I got a laugh out of him when I said the only difference was the 400 amateur fights Lomachenko had.

Unfortunately, Sosa made poor financial decisions, including investing in a hookah bar in Isla Verde, Puerto Rico. I had been nagging him since the Walters fight to watch *Broke*, ESPN's *30 for 30* special about athletes who had squandered their money. Promoters and managers always get blamed when fighters go broke so I kept telling him, "Watch the show!" He never did.

When he boxed ex-WBA/IBF featherweight champion Yuriorkis Gamboa, at the Madison Square Garden Theatre seven months after Lomachenko, he spent most of training camp shedding excess weight. He paid a small fine for being less than one pound over, but he knocked Gamboa down in the seventh round and picked up another point in the 10th when Gamboa was penalized for holding. Still, the scores went to Gamboa, 94-94, 95-93, 96-92.

There was an outcry from the press and the fans. HBO's ringside judge Harold Lederman had it 97-91 for Sosa. I didn't complain. People would have reminded me of the draw Sosa got with Walters in 2015. That night, Lederman had it 99-91 for Walters.

Sosa returned the following summer for the first of three wins which put him in line to challenge Miguel Berchelt, of Mexico, for the WBC junior lightweight title on November 2, 2019, in Carson, California. Rivas was so confident Sosa would win he convinced me to bet the fight. I lost. We lost. After a good first round, Sosa was dropped in the second and fourth and Rivas threw in the towel at 2:56.

I stayed in touch with Sosa. On June 14, 2020, I texted: "Get in the gym fatso. Stay safe." He responded: "Hahaha, I'm going now...been on my diet but really excited to get back. I took the break I needed...feels like I got an extra round in. Let's do it again, Russ. Let's be champs again. Thank you and you, too, stay safe my *Viejo*." He always called me *El Viejo*, the old man.

Sometime in September, Sosa posted on Instagram that he was broke and his phone had been cut off. In follow-ups on Twitter, he posted: "Sad world wc livc in. They took 60% out of all my fights. I'm just looking at this numbers. I was too focus in training while they was taking 60%. God Bless you all. I knew they was taking this but all I wanted is to be a world champion. I did that. I'm from the hood, wasn't educated in the world of boxing. It's ok 30% trainer

30% co-promotion, but it's ok, I'm educate myself now. I'm not going to say I didn't see this numbers i did I signed this papers, but because they made it seemed I had no chance to make it to the top I get it not mad just upset I forgive everyone that took advantage."

Since Sosa's phone was off, I contacted him through Facebook: "I have no idea who is talking to you but before you go public with comments about who cheated you, you should produce the proof…You should be ashamed of yourself for making those accusations."

All the joy of winning the title in Beijing was drained out of me, along with the heart-warming scene of Sosa crying on Rivas' shoulder when he was honored at Camden's City Hall.

It was not the first time this happened in boxing but I never thought it would happen with Sosa. Top Rank released him after the Berchelt fight and I was not sure if that affected me since I was part of the co-promotional agreement, but I released him after meeting with his new manager in October, 2020.

The only thing I can say to Sosa is that *the ride with you was worth the fall, my friend.*

Chapter Fifty-Seven

The Future Is Here

Fred Jenkins, Jr., nails Isaiah Wise at the 2300 Arena. (Darryl Cobb, Jr. photo)

New venues and new promoters sprang up around Philly in the second decade of the 21st century, but the 2300 Arena remained the go-to place. Cut man Joey Intrieri (Joey Eye) became the first promoter at a Pennsylvania casino with cards at Harrah's Chester in 2011. Marshall Kauffman, an ex-manager/trainer from Reading, followed at Harrah's and the Valley Forge Casino, 25 miles outside Philly. Kauffman also promoted at 2300 and the SugarHouse Casino, which opened in 2010 on Columbus Boulevard. Manny Rivera was at the National Guard Armory, SugarHouse, Sheet Metal Workers Local 19 Union hall and The Filmore, all on or around Columbus Boulevard. Rivera also ran at the refurbished Metropolitan Opera House on North Broad Street.

Andre Kut, of North Jersey, ran a few cards at the 2300, then known as the South Philly Arena or the Asylum Arena.

Two female Temple grads joined me. Brittany Rogers (BAM) promoted twice, once at the Armory, once at the Newtown Athletic Club. When she began working full time with Joe Hand in 2017, they promoted at the Parx Casino in Bensalem Township, 20 miles northeast of the 2300 Arena. I made the matches. Michelle Rosado (aka Raging Babe), who grew up a boxing fan in Bristol, Pennsylvania, began working with me and BAM in 2014, then got her own license in 2018 and promoted successfully..

But the numbers didn't lie. From 2010 through 2019, the Philadelphia area hosted 146 fight cards—33 in the suburbs—the fewest since they began keeping records.

Sixty miles east, things were worse. Atlantic City's boom years had been the 1980s, when it hosted 841 boxing cards. Between 2010 and 2019 there were 103.

By the end of the 20th century, as I've said, boxing had 17 weight classes with as many as four champions in each. Casinos and networks wanted championship fights, but the term became meaningless. Plus, casino gambling's spread throughout the country had diminished Atlantic City's allure. In 2019, it hosted only five fight cards, the fourth time in six years it didn't reach double figures. Philadelphia had 15 in 2019.

New Jersey required additional pre-fight medical exams. Referees, judges, deputies, doctors, etc., were more expensive than in Pennsylvania, but the main reason for the decline was lack of casino interest. The days of big site fees, complimentary hotel rooms and free meals were gone.

Larry Hazzard, who'd replaced Bob Lee in 1986 as head of New Jersey's Athletic Control Board, did his best to keep Atlantic City competitive. Hazzard was different than most boxing commissioners, who are politically appointed, often with no boxing background.

A three-time New Jersey golden gloves champion, Hazzard had a Bachelor of Science degree in Physical Education and Health from

Montclair State. He was a principal in the Newark school system, and, at the same time, refereed many of the biggest fights in the world. He had been a no-nonsense referee and he was a no-nonsense commissioner. He dressed and acted like a drill sergeant. Everything from head-to-toe was perfect and in place. He was tough and by the book but he knew boxing, which put him above most of his peers.

Hazzard ran the New Jersey commission until 2007, then returned in 2014. By the time of his second term, he had to deal with a new generation of promoters, managers, trainers and fighters who were more interested in padding records and winning bogus titles than in learning their craft. No one accepted what manager Lou Duva said—and I believed: "Fighters get better by fighting better fighters." The new group was all about the "W." But network execs wanted fighters with the best records, not necessarily the best fighters.

In Philly, no one understood that success depended on local matchups. "Why should I knock off another Philly guy," was the tired line. Some accused me of wanting Philly vs. Philly to save on travel, hotel and meals.

No one had paid attention when, in the summer of 2010, we had an SRO crowd in my return to the 2300 Arena by matching junior middleweights Derrick Ennis and Gabriel Rosado, both from Philly, in a USBA title fight. Ennis, the winner by majority decision, lost three of his next five and retired in 2014, while Rosado, the loser, went on to six-figure purses and two title shots.

Rosado, then trained by old-schooler Billy Briscoe (no relation to Bennie), was the perfect embodiment of my kind of fighter. He'd fight anyone, anywhere, and at any time. Just pay him!

Five years later in the same ring in front of another packed house, heavyweight Joey Dawejko lost on points to Amir Mansour in another all-local matchup, but Dawejko still enjoys a lucratiive career. Case closed!

The second decade of the 21st century also ushered in "paid fights." A manager would bankroll an entire bout—paying both boxers, travel, hotel, meals, medicals—to "bring his own opponent" and get a win for his fighter. The promoter got a free fight and also a "slot fee" from the manager, often between $400 and $600 per fight. This practice, which had been common in states like North Carolina, spread up the East Coast and around the country. I rarely did that and never more than one per card. I couldn't charge people $100, $75, $50 or even $25 to watch that garbage.

Kathy Duva lost her NBC Sports Network series—and I lost with her. We had delivered solid cards, like one in 2014 at Temple University's Liacouras Center where former IBF cruiserweight champion Steve Cunningham got up from two fifth-round knockdowns to outpoint Mansour in what became a contender for *Fight of the Year*. It was another all-local war.

"That main event produced some of the best sports TV I have ever witnessed," Duva said. "By the time the TV crew followed Mansour back to the locker room and taped that amazing video of him in tears, pleading for people to give money to the Cunninghams to help them with their daughter's upcoming heart transplant, I thought we had cemented our prospects for a new deal. That show not only did well live, but it topped those live numbers each time they reran it.

"(But) Al Haymon had made a deal with NBC months earlier. One of the terms was that NBC couldn't tell anyone, but I got someone at NBC to tell me a partial truth. They said there was no money for a series beginning in 2015. When I asked if they were talking to someone else, he responded that NBC would not pay a rights fee to any promoter other than Main Events for a series. That statement is still true today."

Haymon, a Harvard grad, had left music promotion for boxing in 2000. His first star was Vernon Forrest, who won world titles at welterweight (IBF/WBC) and junior middleweight (WBC). Haymon took control of Floyd Mayweather's career after 2006, arranging for Mayweather, the best fighter of his era, to buy back his promotional contract from Top Rank—the company that had developed him.

When Waddell and Reed—a Kansas-based asset management and financial planning company—invested upwards of $500 million with Haymon in 2014, instead of networks paying promoters to televise their shows, he paid networks to televise his.

"Haymon bought the time from NBC," Duva said. "The network decided boxing had some life based upon our success. Haymon pledged to pay six- and seven-figure purses for all of the fights, in addition to paying for production and $20 million for the time. It was an offer that NBC couldn't refuse."

Similar Haymon *time-buy* deals followed with Spike-TV, CBS, Bounce-TV and ESPN. Haymon's company, Premier Boxing Champions, also closed exclusive deals with Fox and Fox Sports 1. He continued his relationship with Showtime, which paid him. British promoter Mickey Duff once said Don King didn't want to be the *best* promoter in boxing, he wanted to be the *only* promoter in boxing. Haymon appeared to want the same.

Haymon paid fighters purses not reflected in television ratings or ticket sales. It was great for some fighters, not for the business. The matches that could have been made with that kind of money boggles my mind. By 2020, Haymon's exclusive deals with NBC, ESPN, Spike and Bounce-TV were over, but televised boxing still was controlled by a handful of promoters: Bob Arum with ESPN; Haymon with Fox and Showtime, Eddie Hearn—and, to a lesser extent, Oscar de la Hoya—with DAZN, a European-based streaming service which did well in some countries but struggled here. HBO was out of the boxing business.

An independent promoter like Duva or me could not get consistent television exposure without turning over half of his—or her—promotional contract to a promoter who had exclusive television agreements, written or oral.

It had been fun with Duva and her all-female staff. I had been the token male, working with Jolene Mizzone, a legit badass, whose eye for spotting and developing talent turned her into one of the country's best matchmakers. Being a woman, she struggled to get the kudos she deserved.

Philly boxing soldiered on. Once or twice a year Top Rank worked with me and Raging Babe on cards featuring local fighters it had signed, like super middleweight Jesse Hart or heavyweight Bryant Jennings, either at the 2300 Arena or the Liacouras Center. We partnered with Eddie Hearn and DAZN at the Liacouras, too. Philly's WBA junior lightweight champion Tevin Farmer was in the main event, Gabe Rosado in the co-feature, plus an all-local lightweight fight between Avery Sparrow and ex-world title challenger Hank Lundy, but we sold less than 4,500 tickets. Farmer, who once had been 7-4-1, won his 21st straight that night, but most of them had been far from Philly.

Haymon worked with Kauffman at Liacouras with West Philly's Julian Williams defending his WBA/IBF junior middleweight titles—which he lost—but again less than 4,500 paid. It was Williams' first local appearance in over than eight years, proving again a fighter cannot build a following in his hometown if he never fights there.

In 1978, there were boxing writers at each of four local dailies: *Inquirer, Bulletin, Daily News* and *Journal*. When football, baseball, basketball or hockey fans read the sports section, they would come across a boxing story. Now, the *Bulletin* and *Journal* were long gone. With the decline of newspapers and sparse coverage in the remaining few, boxing fans went to boxing websites. Football, baseball, basketball and hockey fans went to their own websites, eliminating the crossover when newspapers were in vogue.

Former *Daily News* boxing writer Bernard Fernandez: "When I got the boxing beat in 1987, the health of the newspaper industry was much stronger than it is now. Philadelphia had a deserved reputation as a great boxing city. We covered all the major fights. I went to Tokyo for Tyson-Douglas, to the United Kingdom several times, and I spent more time in Las Vegas than Wayne Newton.

"Over time, the travel budget was tightened and so was the news hole. That didn't affect the Eagles, Phillies, 76ers and Flyers, or Villanova when the school became a contender for NCAA championships. Where once the executive sports editor asked me where I needed to go and the request was routinely approved, I had to submit a list of fights I thought we should cover. Instead of getting approval (to travel) for five fights, it became approval for four, then three, then two. Since we did not have a Sunday edition, I would not go to Saturday fights.

"I felt like I was no longer as active a participant in my sport. It eats away at your sense of pride and satisfaction in doing your job at the level you believed it required. I stuck with it for a couple of years, but when the next round of buyouts was offered, I decided it would be best for me to step away. I wish I could have turned the *Daily News* boxing beat over to a younger version of myself to carry on the rich tradition crafted by fight people like Larry Merchant, Stan Hochman, Tom Cushman, Jack McKinney and others, but it's impossible to pass the baton if the relay race has been called off."

Fernandez left on April Fools' Day, 2012.

There is no sadder story than the fates of the suburban kids who made the 69th Street Forum a hot fight club in the late 1970s.

Richie Bennett (Darby), who beat Bennie Briscoe there in 1980, was not the only one to succumb to drugs. Kenny Carpenter (Upper Darby), who turned pro in 1978, died from drugs in 1984. He was 14-9-1, 11 K0s, and had boxed at the Spectrum, Convention Hall, several Atlantic City casinos and had a slot on the Jeff Chandler-Jorge Lujan championship card in 1981 at the Franklin Plaza Hotel.

Then there were Mic, Pic and Vic, whose families had moved to Folsom, in Ridley Township, from West and Southwest Philly, because they sought a better environment.

Micky Diflo beat the trend. He quit boxing in 1978 after 13 pro fights (10-2-1, 8 K0s). "It was the times and the geography," he said. "Addiction was rampant. Boxing helped me stay clean for a time. I'd be clean for four weeks before a fight, then three, then two. Finally, I hoped I could just go into the ring without being high.

"It always started with booze, then topped it off with something crazy like angel dust. I quit boxing at 23 because I had double vision—since corrected by two surgeries—and I was taking too many shots. I got clean at 28 and became a certified addiction counselor for 15 years. I went to Delaware Community College and began taking acting classes."

Diflo became a comedian and an actor and moved to New York in 2001. He got married at 48 and he's been clean for 37 years.

Mike Picciotti boxed from 1976 to 1986 and was unbeaten in 12 fights at the Forum, including a third-round knockout over fellow-unbeaten Joe Tiberi, of Wilmington, in 1978. He was on the verge of an NBC-TV fight after knocking out former world-title challenger Pablo Baez late in 1985 at the Sands, but a shocking K0 loss in his next fight to Juan Alonso Villa ended that dream.

Picciotti retired after losing his next fight to Englishman Kirkland Laing. He was 28 and finished at 31-4-3, 16 KOs. He had issues with alcohol and has undergone a liver transplant and a triple bypass.

I went to a memorial service for Victor Carmen Pappa in 2016. He was 59. Pappa won 20 of 23 fights from 1976 until 1982, and returned 11 years later to win two more. He was 7-0 at the Forum. One of his losses was by eight-round decision to future WBC junior welterweight champ Johnny Bumphus. He worked as a brick mason during his fighting days, and kept that job for 40 years until he passed away.

"Victor always looked out for his three sisters," said Louise Pappa Mizzola, one of them. "He took it hard when (sister) Candida died that same year. He got involved with the wrong crowd, did heroin, and he left behind two sisters, two daughters and a grandson."

Epilogue

Lou Scheinfeld with me after I signed the Spectrum S in 2019. (Peltz collection)

It's been difficult for me to adjust to 21st-century boxing. It's not only the multiple champions in multiple weight classes. Fighters lose titles by being overweight, pay minimal fines and receive mild suspensions from toothless commissions. When I think of what Jake LaMotta had to do to get his 1949 shot at Marcel Cerdan's middleweight title—"throw" a fight to Billy Fox to satisfy the mob—and I see how nonchalantly today's fighters give up their titles on the scales, the lack of respect for the belts sickens me, however cheaply they come. Do we really need YouTube stars—or 50-year-old ex-pros in exhibitions—to draw crowds? I get more satisfaction working with lunch-pail fighters trying to turn their careers around, than with prima donnas scoffing at seven-figure paydays.

Michelle Rosado gave me a wonderful sendoff October 4, 2019, when she promoted *Blood, Sweat and 50 Years* at the 2300 Arena, a tribute to my half century in boxing. Rosado's staff—Emily Pandelakis and Mike Williams—wrote stories and produced video highlights of my career. We showed the best that night.

In the weeks leading up, I was honored with a Resolution from Philadelphia City Council for my 50 years. I signed—in my office—the nearly six-foot tall, 70-pound Spectrum S, which had been removed from the building before it was demolished and won at auction by Andrew Kay for about $300. He keeps it at home when he is not transporting it to have it signed by athletes, music stars and execs, who worked or performed at Broad and Pattison.

The nine-fight card that evening consisted of a six-round main event and matches between earnest, striving fighters who deserved to have their own careers, rather than being served up as bullseyes for Olympic medalists and unbeaten prospects. Perhaps as many as half a dozen people in the crowd had attended my first card, including ringside judge George Hill, who had boxed for me that first night in 1969. Sadly, Hill died in a fire in his West Philly home 17 months later.

Blood Sweat and 50 Years was the last card in Philadelphia in which I played a major role. What remains of my career will be as a consultant.

When I was 22, money didn't enter into my decision to become a promoter. I just wanted to be in boxing. You spend most of your waking hours at your job, I told myself, so you had better find one you enjoy. Writing this book has been a pleasure. Reading newspaper accounts and watching videos of fights I promoted, or was involved in, and speaking with people with whom my career put me in contact, brought me satisfaction and occupied my time during the Covid-19 pandemic.

There are few real promoters and few real managers today. Many promoters sign fighters to promotional contracts but never promote them. They place them on cards promoted by others and take a percentage without ever having done much work. Others run shows in which most, if not all, of the fights are financed by the managers of the fighters, either with cash or ticket guarantees. I am now a licensed manager, but promoters today are the real managers. They promote fighters, not fights.

Instead of a *Manager of the Year* award, the Boxing Writers Association of America should have a *Promoter of the Year* award instead. Once a manager signs his fighter with a promoter, he becomes little more than a financier and baby-sitter. The promoter selects the opponent, the venue and the date, leaving the manager to say yes or no. Many promoters are boxing lifers, many managers are not. And as I mentioned before, some fighters, after they make it big, start calling the shots. The managers become their business agents. Where have you gone, Gil Clancy?

I made life-long friends through boxing—some long gone, others still here—but the list would be too long and I'd forget someone. I *will* mention Don and Lorraine Chargin, since no one was closer. They were my mentors late in life. Before she passed away in 2010, Lorraine insisted I give the acceptance speech for her if she were ever to get into the International Boxing Hall of Fame, something I was honored to do in June, 2018. Don passed away three months later, just as my plane landed in Los Angeles on my way to see him at the West Coast Boxing Hall of Fame banquet. I miss them terribly.

Small-club promoters like Jimmy Burchfield in New England, Fred Berns in Indiana, Bobby Hitz in Chicago, Tutico Zabala in Florida, Les Bonano in New Orleans, Roy Englebecht in California—these men are the real Hall-of-Famers. They stock the cupboards before the big-time TV promoters move in, take over and toss them a few dollars for their hard work.

I did business with icons—Clancy, Chargin, Joe Gramby, Angelo and Chris Dundee, Bob Arum, Eddie Futch, Teddy Brenner, Tito Lectoure, Don King, and Rafael Mendoza, the Mexican Godfather, who, during his 2015 Hall-of-Fame induction speech, said he never had a contract with any of his fighters. Then, pointing to his wife in the audience, he said, "That's the only person I've ever had a contract with." These people knew the business inside out. They were men of their word, and they showed respect to a young kid trying to get established.

I worked under several commissioners in Pennsylvania—Frank Wildman, Zach Clayton, Jimmy Binns, Howard McCall, George Bochetto, Rudy Battle and Greg Sirb.

No promoter in recent years has worked as hard as Michelle Rosado. I wish she had been around earlier, perhaps when Brittany

Rogers came to work with me in 2011. Maureen Sacks was as valuable as anyone for her quiet efficiency in handling tickets, finances and customer complaints—a major contributor to my success from 1986 through 2014—and Pat Doris before her. They had the energy and dedication most young men lack.

I won't tell you the good old days always were wonderful. A rival promoter might staple his posters over mine on abandoned store fronts and light poles, or send letters to newspapers criticizing my matches. Twice, fighters who weighed in the day of the fight didn't show up that night. One left the Blue Horizon—and never returned—after learning he was in the walkout bout. Two were arrested the day of the weigh-in.

More recently, one refused to leave his corner after being introduced in the ring when he realized he was fighting the son of ex-heavyweight champion Hasim Rahman. One was locked up the day before his fight in California after being surrounded by four police cars and a helicopter.

I got an attack of guilt writing this book, so in July, 2021, I sent a cashiers check for $1,000 to Thomas Hearns to somewhat compensate for the money I had stiffed him out of in 1979.

More than 30 years after I did, Floyd Mayweather and Canelo Alvarez declared boxing needed one champion in each division. And that remains boxing's biggest problem. Not the UFC, not the MMA, not YouTubers, not names from the past on a seniors tour. Boxing didn't need those groups to bring it down—it did it to itself with greed. Having four or more world champions in each weight class—plus interim champions, super champions, franchise champions, regional champions, lineal champions, silver champions, regular champions—is a farce.

It's no longer can I beat him. It's now how much money can I get to fight him? Sports should be about trying to beat the best, not how much money can I grab. It should be about development through competition. I've never seen Roger Federer refuse to play Rafael Nadal at Roland Garros because of money. Perhaps one day boxing will get itself together, because when it's done right, it's as good as it gets.

Some say I'm too critical, but boxing has problems which need to be fixed. Dan Rafael, the most prolific boxing writer of the last 20 years, calls me "Grumpy" and it's a nickname I wear with pride. I get it! No one who makes a living from boxing wants to hear anything negative. Some simply can't handle the truth. Do you really think Teddy Atlas lost his gig as the analyst for ESPN's boxing telecasts because he couldn't tell a jab from a hook?

In the meantime, rather than watch a fighter from Texas fight one from Florida in a casino ballroom in Michigan for an interim title, I will turn on my television, insert a disc, and watch Carlos Monzon and Bennie Briscoe go 15 rounds for the world middleweight title in front of 17,000 in Luna Park. I will again enjoy Matthew Saad Muhammad against Marvin Johnson from the Spectrum.

Sure, I could have signed Marvin Hagler, and held on to Buster Douglas and Antonio Tarver, but then I wouldn't be writing about my 50 years in boxing because I would have retired long ago and traveled the world watching fights. I also could have sat front row at Ali-Frazier I near Frank Sinatra, Aretha Franklin and Diana Ross, but missing out makes it—maybe—a better story.

Who could imagine that Don Dunphy, whom I worshiped while listening to on TV when I was a teenager, would be behind the microphone in 1980 the night Jeff Chandler won the WBA bantamweight title in Miami? Or calling one of my fights in Atlantic City in 1984?

I have attended funerals for men who boxed for me and those who worked with me. I have stayed in touch with others, lost contact with a few. Some have thanked me for what I did for them, others blamed me. I never was the most well-known promoter in boxing, but I may have been the richest. Not in terms of finances—not by a long shot—but in terms of the richest at heart. I fell in love with boxing when I was 12, saw my first live fight at 14, decided to make it my life, and never looked back. I had a dream and I lived it. How many of us can say that? If today was 1969, I'd do it all over again.

And here's one reason why….

Osnel Charles is an Atlantic City boxer who works as a chef at the Cedar Food Market. He was 9-1 when I signed him in 2011, but won only four of his next 24 fights. Our contract ran out years ago, but he won't leave me. He calls me the "world's greatest promoter" and I call him "my favorite Haitian lightweight." He made me—along with his manager, Arnold Robbins—Best Man at his wedding to Catherine Reynolds in 2018.

As an official member of the wedding party, I rented a three-piece cream-colored suit—with tan shoes—and walked down the aisle with Tameka, one of Charles' four sisters, to *Why I Love You*, by MAJOR. Linda and I were the only two White people out of 500 at the reception. We had a wonderful time and I enjoyed watching Linda do the *Soul City Walk* with Hassan Hameed-El, who manages and trains fighters when he is not cutting and styling hair at Hassan's Hair Hut in Vineland, New Jersey.

Osnel Charles won't win a world title, but he won my heart with that honor. Money can't buy that.

Author's Notes

IBF junior middleweight champion Buster Drayton. (Peltz collection)

There were other chamionship-caliber Philly fighters. Some boxed for me, some did not. Here are several who challenged for, or won, world titles.

Buster Drayton, a junior middleweight, boxed from 1978 to 1995, but just four of his 56 fights were in Philadelphia. He had 21 in Atlantic City, 12 outside the United States. By 1984, he was 16-8-1, but won 16 of his next 17 and the IBF title, outpointing Carlos Santos over 15 rounds in 1986 in East Rutherford, New Jersey. Drayton defended twice in France, but lost the title in 1987 in Montreal to Matthew Hilton, who lost it to Robert Hines the next year. Drayton boxed until he was 43 and finished at 40-15-1, 29 K0s.

Lightweight **Freddie Pendleton** boxed from 1981 to 2001, four times in Philly. He was 12-12-1 when he K0d Darryl Martin for the Pennsylvania junior welterweight title in 1985 in Harrisburg. Pendleton went 12-3-3 before losing to Pernell Whitaker for the WBC/IBF lightweight titles in 1990. When Whitaker vacated, Pendleton won the IBF belt in 1993 with a 12-round decision over Tracy Spann. Then living in Florida, Pendleton lost in his second defense a year later to Rafael Ruelas. He was 38 when he retired after Ricky Hatton K0d him in two rounds. He was 47-26-5, 35 K0s.

Tyrone Crawley never boxed for me, but said he was inspired watching my cards at the Spectrum in the 1970s. He won the All-Army championship while stationed at Fort Bragg, North Carolina, and Fort Lee, Virginia. Discharged in 1979, he turned pro in 1982, and won 20 of 22 fights, three in Philly. He beat champs Gene Hatcher and Choo Choo Brown, but retired at 29 in 1988, two years after being stopped in 13 rounds by Livingstone Bramble for the IBF lightweight title. Crawley became a police officer and retired after 28 years. "Boxing is a rough game," he said, "and it never was my main priority. There is life after boxing and most fighters don't prepare for it. I did." Crawley died from cancer in 2021. He was 61.

Featherweight **Benny Amparo** had 39 amateur fights in the Dominican Republic before moving to the United States in 1987, first to New York, then to New Jersey. He boxed from 1989 to 1994. His seventh-round knockout of crosstown rival Tommy Barnes in 1992 is a Blue Horizon classic. Two years later he was unlucky to get only a 12-round draw with Francisco Segura for the USBA featherweight title, also at the Blue Horizon. Amparo was 12-2-5, 5 K0s, when his career ended after IBF champ Tom Johnson K0d him in the 12th in 1994 in Alantic City. "I had a short but exciting career," he said. "I met Nelson Mandela in South Africa. I quit boxing when I was 26, in my prime. Too much politics! My brain is not like most fighters today. My mentality is pretty good."

Heavyweight **David Bey**, a Philadelphian who never boxed here, was 14-0 when he was K0d in 10 rounds by Larry Holmes for the IBF title in 1985. He lost 10 of his next 15 and retired in 1994. Bey was killed in 2017 when he was struck by a steel sheet pile while working construction on the Camden waterfront. He was 60.

John David Jackson was born in Denver, but boxed out of Philly from 1984 to 1999. He won both the WBO junior middleweight and WBA middleweight titles. His first 16 fights were in Pennsylvania or New Jersey, but few after that. He boxed for me three times, once at the Blue Horizon, stopping Sidney Outlaw in 1987 in an all-southpaw battle for the Pennsylvania junior middleweight title. He was 36-4, 20 K0s, and became a world-class trainer.

David Reid won Olympic gold at light middleweight in 1996 in Atlanta with a one-punch, last-round knockout. Despite developing ptosis—a drooping or falling of the upper eyelid—he won the WBA junior middleweight title in his 12th pro fight, but lost it in his 15th when Hall-of-Famer Felix Trinidad got off the floor to drop him four times and win on points. Reid boxed once in Philly, stopping ex-welterweight champ Simon Brown in 1998 at the Liacouras Center. He was 17-2, 7 K0s, when he retired in 2001.

Zahir Raheem, also a member of the 1996 USA Olympic team, boxed as a pro from 1996 to 2014. He upset Hall-of-Famer Erik Morales in Los Angeles in 2005, earning him a WBO lightweight title fight seven months later, which he lost by 12-round split decision to Brazil's Acelino Freitas. Raheem was 37 when he retired. His 35-3 record included 21 K0s. He boxed once in Philadelphia—for me and Anthony Boyle—at the Big O Center.

Lajuan Simon, Eric Hunter and **Yusaf Mack** all came up short in title fights. Simon (25-3-2, 12 K0s) was stopped in one round by Gennadiy Golovkin for the WBA middleweight title in 2011. Hunter

(22-4, 11 K0s) lost a 12-round decision to Lee Selby for the IBF featherweight belt in 2016. Mack (31-8-2, 17 K0s) had two shots. He was stopped in eight rounds by Tavoris Cloud in 2011 for the IBF light-heavyweight title and in three by Carl Froch in 2012 for the IBF super middleweight belt. The trio had 97 fights between them, but only Hunter boxed for me—twice.

Danny Garcia won world titles at junior welterweight (WBC/WBA) and welterweight (WBC) in the second decade of the 21st century and didn't duck anyone. Four of his first 39 fights (36-3) were at home, three at the 2300 Arena, one at the Liacouras Center. Eight were at the Barclays Center in Brooklyn. Garcia told me he would never fight another Philly fighter, but I didn't hold it against him. He is still active, as is **Stephen Fulton,** who won the WBO super bantamweight title while I was writing this book. As of 2021, Fulton was unbeaten in 19 fights with eight K0s.

Though I'm not a fan of women's boxing, I love **Jacqui Frazier Lyde**, daughter of Hall-of-Famer Joe. Nicknamed "Sister Smoke," she lost only to Laila Ali in 15 fights. They boxed during the 2001 Hall-of-Fame weekend in a tent at Canastota, New York. Laila won by majority decision after eight rounds. It was billed as Ali-Frazier IV. At 39, Jacqui was 16 years older. She became a lawyer and serves as municipal court judge in Philadelphia. Her husband, Pete, was our personal security guard at the Blue Horizon in the 1990s. He made sure no one got in through the exit doors.

Acknowledgements

Maureen Sacks in the Blue Horizon box office. (Hinda Schuman photo)

It's difficult to know where to start but it's gotta be with Bob Levin, a transplanted Philadelphian who grew up a fight fan before relocating to Berkley, California, in 1968. Bob had represented injured workers in industrial accident claims for half a century. He contacted me in the summer of 2020, looking to purchase Philly fight posters for his home gym. The more we corresponded, the more we learned about each other. He had written some books, the first of which he sent me—*Cheesesteak*—was about growing up in West Philly in the 1950s. I sent him a chapter from my book, and the next thing I knew, he had agreed to help me with it. His guidance was invaluable.

I knew Jill Porter from journalism school and the *Temple News.* I spent weekends during the summer of 1966 sleeping in a basement apartment in Atlantic City she rented with my first wife. I rarely saw her after graduation, even when she became the city-side columnist for the *Daily News* from 1979 through 2009. She contacted me in 2017 after reading my Facebook post about my son, Matthew, who had passed away. The only fight she ever attended was my 50th anniversary celebration in 2019 at the 2300 Arena. She is the greatest proofreader—not of this time, not of that time, but of *all time*.

Experienced authors like Tom Hauser, Gabe Oppenheim and Mark Kram, Jr., offered advice. Bill Dettloff said I'd wake up one day and ask myself, "Who in the world is going to read this?" He told me to ignore those thoughts. Nigel Collins told me to disregard all advice. "It's your book!" he said. "Write it the way you want to." Ex-*Daily News* boxing writer Bernard Fernandez did some editing and put me in touch with the company that published this book.

Boxing historians Henry Hascup, Mike Silver and Chuck Hasson helped set the facts straight. Frank Lotierzo, who breaks down fights—past and present—as well as anyone, assisted with recollections of Joe Frazier's gym and fighters he saw while training there from 1977 to 1982. Former *Atlantic City Press* reporter Dave Weinberg kept me informed on stats from the seashore town.

John DiSanto, who has picked up the torch from me and Chuck Hasson to keep the stories of Philly boxing alive on his *PhillyBoxingHistory.com* website, assisted with choosing photographs, scanning them, sizing them and putting the manuscript together. Writer George Hanson, Jr., guided me through some sensitive descriptions dealing with race.

Teddy Atlas recalled stories of Catskill Mountain training camps and Rick Farris came through with anecdotes from the Olympic Auditorium in Los Angeles.

I appreciate the use of photos and drawings from Mike Feldman, El Grafico, Sumio Yamada, Hinda Schuman, John DiSanto, Eugene Mopsik, Ray Bailey, Charles Baltimore, Chris Farina, Tom Casino, Arnold Weiss, Pete Goldfield, Bill Lichtenberg, Kate Warburton, Mary Anne Seymour and Susan Seymour.

Also Darryl Cobb, Jr., whose photo of Isaiah Wise and Fred Jenkins, Jr., in *The Future Is Here* chapter, was voted by the Boxing Writers Association of America as *First Place Action Photo* for 2017. Al Valenti spent more than two months getting permission from the *Worcester Telegram and Gazette* so that I could use the photo of Kevin Howard knocking down Sugar Ray Leonard.

Independent videographers who helped chronicle my career were invaluable: Abe Fox; Richie Powers; Joe Mellek; Bryanna Carzo, and Rachael Rose. Carzo and Rose doubled as program sellers. One night I told Carzo that she couldn't punch out until she sold out, so she offered her phone number to anyone who bought a program. It did the trick and she got to watch the main event.

I cannot omit my nieces, Liz and Rachel, who held up round cards during the early years, along with my nephew, Steven.

EM Hughes and her staff at New Book Authors Publishing in Madison, Wisconsin, guided me through the publishing process. She tolerated my constant emails and questions.

A big shoutout goes to Maureen Sacks, my right hand for more than 30 years. She was the glue that kept the business together.

My wife, Linda, raised our family while I was on the road with fighters for many years. She has made me a better person, but she had to share me with this book for 18 months. She also did a final proofreading.

Thanks to all the promoters, managers, trainers and arena landlords I reconnected with for this book, and to my favorite ring announcer, Ed Derian…Derian. Finally, thanks to all the fighters I knew and dealt with for half a century. They are my heroes.

Index

A

B

C

D

E

F

G

H

I

J

K

L

M

N

O

P

Q

R

S

T

V

W

Y

Z

About the Author

J Russell Peltz fell in love with boxing when he was 12, saw his first live fight at 14, and was hooked for life. He was named *Outstanding Male Journalism Graduate, Temple University, 1968*, but after a short career on the sports copy desk of the *Evening and Sunday Bulletin* in Philadelphia, he became a boxing promoter when he couldn't land the boxing *beat* at the newspaper. In his more-than-half century in boxing, Peltz has promoted fights at every major venue in Philadelphia as well as most of the casinos in Atlantic City. His fights have been televised by ABC, CBS, NBC, HBO, Showtime, ESPN, USA and SportsChannel. He has promoted or co-promoted more than 30 world championship fights and his business has taken him around the world, from Beijing to Buenos Aires and from Paris to Tokyo. Peltz was inducted into the International Boxing Hall of Fame in 2004, the Temple University School of Communications and Theatre Hall of Fame in 2010, and the Philadelphia Sports Hall of Fame in 2020.

CPSIA information can be obtained
at www.ICGtesting.com
Printed in the USA
BVHW032336150122
626373BV00001B/20

9 781737 569619